The History of St. Dogmaels Abbey

Together With Her Cells, Pill, Caldey And Glascareg, And The Mother Abbey Of Tiron

Emily M. Pritchard

Alpha Editions

This edition published in 2020

ISBN: 9789354186516 (Hardback)
ISBN: 9789354185427 (Paperback)

Design and Setting By
Alpha Editions
www.alphaedis.com
email - alphaedis@gmail.com

LIST OF CHAPTERS.

CHAPTER		PAGE
I	ORIGIN	11
II	AN ALMOST BLOODLESS CONQUEST	22
III	THE MOTHER ABBEY	30
IV	GIFTS FLOW IN	40
V	THE MARTINS	56
VI	LITTLE IRELAND IN WALES	62
VII	GERALD THE WELSHMAN	66
VIII	SILENT GROWTH	79
IX	PALMY DAYS	88
X	THE DISSOLUTION	93
XI	THE OLD ORDER CHANGETH	113
XII	THE ABBEY'S RICHEST DAUGHTER	124
XIII	HER DECLINE AND FALL	139
XIV	ERIN'S TRIBUTE	159
XV	GEVA'S GIFT	168
XVI	QUEEN ELIZABETH	173
XVII	A LITTLE RIFT WITHIN THE LUTE	187
XVIII	RELICS	199
XIX	SIDELIGHTS	213
XX	"FISHERIES AND FISHINGS"	221

LIST OF ILLUSTRATIONS.

			PAGE
I	ST. DOGMAELS AND THE TEIFY ESTUARY	*Frontispiece*	
II	THE CHAPEL OF ST. DOGMAELS ABBEY	TO FACE	11
III	ST. BRYNACH'S CROSS, NEVERN CHURCHYARD	,,	12
IV	NEAR COMBMARTIN, ON THE COAST OF NORTH DEVON	,,	22
V	ANCIENT CHURCH OF THE ABBEY OF TIRON	,,	30
VI	ANCIENT COLLEGE OF THE ABBEY OF TIRON	,,	31
VII	ST. ANNE'S POND, TIRON ABBEY	,,	33
VIII	SALMON FISHING FROM CORACLES ON THE RIVER TEIFY	,,	47
IX	VIGNETTE OF ANCIENT GATEWAY WITH BALL FLOWER MOULDING, ST. DOGMAELS ABBEY	... ...	55
X	TEIFY FISHERMEN CARRYING THEIR CORACLES	TO FACE	56
XI	INTERIOR OF THE ANCIENT CHURCH OF THE ABBEY OF TIRON ...	,,	62
XII	WEST END OF THE CHAPEL, ST. DOGMAELS ABBEY	,,	66
XIII	ANCIENT CHURCH AND COLLEGE OF THE ABBEY OF TIRON ...	,,	79
XIV	VIGNETTE OF SHAFT OF FAN TRACERY, ST. DOGMAELS ABBEY		92
XV	SEAL OF ST. DOGMAELS ABBEY		93
XVI	ACT OF SUPREMACY	TO FACE	93
XVII	CALDEY ISLAND, FROM TENBY CASTLE	,,	103
XVIII	WEST END OF CHAPEL OF ST. DOGMAELS ABBEY AND EAST END OF PREVIOUS CHURCH	,,	113
XIX	A CATCH OF SALMON, ST. DOGMAELS	,,	124
XX	THE RUINS OF PILL PRIORY	,,	139
XXI	SEAL OF PILL PRIORY	... ...	141
XXII	ST. DOGMAELS FROM THE NETPOOL, CARDIGAN	TO FACE	161
XXIII	TOWER OF OLD PRIORY CHURCH, CALDEY	... ...	169
XXIV	ENTRANCE TO OLD HARBOUR AND RIVER GWAYNE, FISHGUARD	TO FACE	187
XXV	UPPER AND LOWER TOWN OF FISHGUARD	,,	188
XXVI	A SALMON FISHING FLEET, ST. DOGMAELS	,,	198
XXVII	SALMON FISHING; DRAWING IN THE SEINE ON THE POPPITT SANDS	,,	221
XXVIII	BLAEU'S MAP OF PEMBROKESHIRE	*the end*	

INTRODUCTION.

ANY friends and strangers, both in St. Dogmaels and in North and South Wales, since the publication of "Cardigan Priory in the Olden Days," have expressed the wish that I would write a similar book on St. Dogmaels Abbey. The following is the result. I could have wished that I had found, for a certainty, Martin of the Towers' original domicile; but, as in the case of the most brilliant of his successors, little is left but their works to testify of them, Martin's and Robert's names being remembered by their buildings and grants, George Owen by his pen.

The map here reproduced is one of Blaeu's, of Amsterdam. On the authority of Dr. Leendeuly, of Amsterdam, obtained for me by the kindness of Mr. Gudendag, of the same city, these maps of the Welsh counties were published in the 1648 edition of Blaeu's Atlas. "Blaeu was not only," he writes, "an excellent cartograph, but also a good merchant. Long before the Atlas was accomplished he sold the single maps, or a collection of the maps of one country. . . . . But he did more. In order to please the buyers, or to allure them, he added to some maps their arms, etc. . . . . He did not send an artist to Wales, but copied it from an older description of Wales that he possessed. . . . In the complete work also that was finished at the end of 1647, England and Wales find their place in the latter part." It may be noted that this map of Pembrokeshire is one of these special maps, made "long before" to please some patron, by the number of coats of arms thereon engraved, among which those of Strongbow (Earl de Clare), William Marshall and William Herbert are specially interesting to Pembrokeshire folk. The Arms of Edward, Prince of Wales, doubtless belong to the Black Prince, who was at Cardigan for some weeks; but the most remarkable is that of Anne Boleyn—why her arms should figure on this map is strange, and stamps the date of the original map, from which this was copied, as about 1534, the date of the signing of the Acknowledgment of the King's Supremacy, when Anne Boleyn was still in full favour.

What collection of maps Blaeu used, from which to copy, is unknown, his maps being far more accurate than those now existing of that period. He may have bought some that had never been published.

From the prominence given to William Herbert, by his coat of arms being twice inscribed on the map, one would infer that it was ordered by some member of that family.

One of this series of Welsh maps is dedicated to Charles, Prince of Wales. If the Charles, who was afterwards Charles I., then they must have been engraved by Blaeu before 1625; if his son Charles, born 1630, it is remarkable that they should have been dedicated to a lad, and also at a time when his father was already a prisoner in the hands of the Parliamentary party.

EMILY M. PRITCHARD,
The Priory,
Cardigan.

July 12th, 1907.

Drawn by J. Randall.

The Chapel of St. Dogmaels Abbey.

CHAPTER I.

ST. DOGMAEL.

ORIGIN.

BOUT fifteen hundred and fifty years ago the first Dogmael of whom any account is found was the son of Cunedda[1] Wledig, (Wledig meaning Emperor or Overlord) who settled in Dogfeiliog or Denbighshire. His grand-nephew, Dogmael the Saint, after whom the ancient borough of St. Dogmaels was named, was the son of Ithael, the son of Ceredig,[2] who conquered what is now called Cardiganshire, and gave his name to the County. Ceredig married Meleri or Eleri, daughter of Brychan Brycheiniog (Brychan, Prince of Brecon). Cunedda's mother was Gwawl,[3] daughter of Coel Godebog, according to the British Chronicle 72nd King of Britain, founder of, and namegiver to, the persent town of Colchester, and the hero of the old English song "Good King Cole was a jolly old Soul." King Cole, or Coel Godebog, had a second daughter, Helen, born about the year 250, the wife of Constantius, and mother of the Emperor Constantine the Great, who was saluted as Emperor by the Roman Army in 306. On his succession as Emperor he caused his mother to be proclaimed Augusta (Empress) and medals were struck in her honour and inscribed "Flavia Julia Helena." At the age of nearly 80, in 326, the Empress Helena visited the Holy Land. She succeeded in discovering what was attributed to be the Holy Sepulchre, and, after digging to a great depth, discovered three crosses, which are claimed to have been those on which Christ and the two thieves were crucified.

The date usually assigned to Cunedda is 350 A.D., but, if Helen was born in 250, it would more probably be earlier, unless it is to be understood that he

---

[1] Cunedda Wledig lived in Strathclyde. He is stated to have had seventeen sons, many of whom ruled in Wales.   [2] Son of Cunedda Wledig.   [3] The radiant one.

died in 350. Thus it may be safely concluded that St. Dogmael lived between 450 and 500 A.D., the date usually assigned to him, probably as the date of his death, being 500 A.D. If Helen at the age of 80 was able to undertake the arduous task of travelling to Jerusalem, no easy matter in those days for an elderly woman, possibly they were longer lived then, as they seemed to have been in Cemaes during the Tudor period, William Owen, Lord of Kemes, dying in 1574 at the age of 105, his father and grandfather living to still more advanced ages.

This second Dogmael, the Saint as he will be hereinafter called, lived on the left bank of the river Teify, in Pembrokeshire, and being of a religious disposition, he founded a religious house. There seems to be no reason to doubt that the site of this religious house was in the field now called " Yr hên Monachlog " (the old monastery), which, besides being well known by this name, is also so marked in the larger edition of the map of the Ordnance Survey, and is about a mile from the present ruins of St. Dogmael's Abbey.

Try and picture this old home about 650 ft. above the level of the sea. On a clear day looking north and seeing the range of the North Wales mountains, and the coastline northwards; first Cardigan Island, then Lochtyn, New Quay, Aberystwyth, the saddle back beyond Harlech, Snowdon, Moel Hebog, and yr Eifl. At times so clear that one can see the houses in Portmadoc, and Criccieth; then to the north-west the rounded hill behind Nevern, in Carnarvonshire, and on to Bardsey Island, where about a hundred years later Dubricius, Bishop of Llandaff, died at what seems to us the almost incredible age of 130. Would not such a glorious view help somewhat to make up for the renouncing of a worldly life? But that is not all. At sunset turn your eyes slightly to the north of west, and you will see the Irish Coast and the undulations of the Wexford Hills. To the south-west you will also see the ever-varying billows of the Atlantic Ocean, and feel the sea-breezes from across those miles of ocean fanning your fevered brow, when wearied with the work of life. To the south and south-east, a nearer but hardly less pleasing view, commencing on the west with Dinas and Strumble Heads, the two points of Fishguard Bay, the name Dinas showing that it had once been occupied by the Danes; then " Carn Engli," the beginning of the Precelly Range, on the west, where St. Brynach, the tutor of Brychan, Prince of Brecon, lived for a while, and where the Angels are credited with having conversed with him, hence the name " Angels' Cairn,"[1] followed by the whole Precelly range, with its

---

[1] Tops of mountains are often called "Carn" (cairn) in Wales, from the cairns found on them being built over ancient graves.

St Brynach's Cross, Nevern Churchyard

various points, the highest now called Preceley Top, but four hundred years ago called "Pen Cerwyn," because it was at the head of Cwm Cerwyn (the Stags' Valley), Moel Tregarn, with its ancient encampment with double fortifications enclosing three large cairns, and Frenny[1] fawr (the great highland) standing boldly forth, a landmark for many miles inland, having three large tumuli on its top. Inland the view is ever varied, but misses the grandeur of the north, west, and south. Here St. Dogmael settled; at first he called his place a hermitage, but many flocking to join him, it became a religious house,[2] and it was probably here that Robert Fitzmartin brought his first thirteen monks from Tiron, in 1113, as will be seen further on, calling it the "Priory de Guales"; before he built the Abbey of St. Dogmaels, Cathmais, in 1118, when he incorporated the old Priory de Guales, or the old religious house of St. Dogmael with the Abbey, keeping up the name of the first founder, St. Dogmael.

St. Dogmael was evidently a hardy, as well as a cleanly man, for one reads of one of the rules he made being that his monks, or "holy hermits," as they are called in the original Latin, were to bathe daily in the waters of the river Teify, both in the icy water in the winter, as well as the rest of the year. Dogmael was later canonized as a Saint, his festival being on June 14th. So far no record has been found of his death. In Brittany he is known as St. Toêl, possibly he may have visited his great-aunt, St. Nennoc, who founded the Abbey of Sainte Croix Quimperle, and not far from which there still exists a chapel dedicated to St. Non,[3] the mother of St. David.

In R. P. Michaelis' "Alfordi Annales Ecclesiastici et civiles Britanorum Saxorum, Anglorum," 1668, he is found ranked amongst the saints of Britain, and "who in our martyrology is described as celebrated for his holy life and miracles," he lived about "A.D. 500," Festival, June 14.

Before proceeding further it would be well to analyse the name "Dogmael."[4] It is a sort of hybrid name due to the Roman influence then extending over Britain, and that part of it that is now called Wales. The first syllable, Dog, is derived from the Latin "Doctus" (learned), which word we find surviving in the present degenerate Welsh language, under the form of

---

[1] "Frenny," the name the people call it, I judge to be more correct than the "Brenhin fawr" of the maps, "fawr" being the feminine form of "mawr" (great) and "frenny" is feminine, whilst "Brenhin" (a king), is not.

[2] Not the same building, but the same establishment, owing to the Saxons destroying it 300 years later, and again 100 years later it was pillaged by the Danes.   [3] His great aunt.

[4] Also written "Dogfael," "Dogvael," "Degwel," "Tegwel," and "Dogmell," and in Brittany "Toêl."

" doeth " (wise, sage), " doethor " (doctor), and other similar words, and " mael "
(work or metal), hence the name Dogmael is equivalent to learned in works or
metals, or, as we should say at the present day, a clever or master artificer. In
conjunction with this let us take the noted Ogham stone, with its inscription
clear even to the present day, in both Ogham character and in Latin, which now
rests against a wall of the old Abbey. In its earliest days it probably stood
in the burial ground of the old religious house founded by St. Dogmael at
" Yr hên Monachlog." The inscription on this stone in Latin is: —

[1]Sagrani fili Cunotami,

or in Ogham, Sagramni Maqi Cunatami, Maqi being the Irish form of the
Welsh mab (son).

Now let us find out the meaning of this name Sagranus. The Welsh form
of Sagranus is Saeran, and means, according to Pugh, a wright, an artificer,
therefore the names Dogmael and Sagranus are synonymous, and probably
belonged to the same person. But whether this Sagranus stone is the tombstone
of the Saint or of his great-uncle, Dogmael, the son of Cunedda, cannot be
certainly ascertained.

In old days grandsons were often spoken and written of as sons; perhaps
great-grandsons may have been similarly written of, especially where the
names were the same. Or, when Dogmael the great-uncle grew old, he may
have left Denbighshire, where he had settled, and have entered his grand-
nephew's religious house, in order to spend his last days in quiet, leaving
Denbighshire to be ruled by one of his sons, for we read that Dogmael ap
Cunedda Wledig was married, and that Meurig ap Elaeth, last Prince of
Dogfeiliog (now Denbighshire), was descended from him.

There are some who think that Sagranus is one and the same with " Sir
Sagramore " (see Vivien, " Idylls of the King," Tennyson), but taking into
consideration that the inscription is in Ogham character, as well as the meaning
of the name Saeran, the stone must be far older than the time of Arthur. If it
refers to Cunedda's *son*, then it probably dates from about 375-425 A.D. But
if it referred to Cunedda's great-grandson, it would very probably date from
about 500, and would, in this latter case, be the gravestone of the founder of
the first religious house. The following is the description of the famous
Ogham stone, the tombstone of Sagranus, Saeran or Dogmael, and its history,
as far as known. The stone is a long narrow slab of porphyritic greenstone,
such as is found on the ridge of the Preceley Hills. It is about 7 feet high,

---

[1] Sagranus, son of Cunedda.

average thickness of about 7 inches. This peculiar kind of igneous rock does not decompose readily; its greenish base, and the dull white crystals with which it is filled, resist the effects of weather and of vegetation to a remarkable degree, and the fourteen to fifteen hundred years that have passed since it was first inscribed have left but few traces of weather wear on the stone. Stones of this kind are prized all over Pembrokeshire, as, from their peculiar form and hardness, they are very useful as gate posts. The present stone shows, by two holes drilled into its surface, that it has also been used at some time for a similar purpose. " This stone, however, has been used not only as a gate post, but as a bridge by generations now dead and gone, for it was used over a brook, not far from its present resting-place, and had acquired a sort of super-natural reputation when thus used, the people near by firmly believing that at the witching hour of midnight a white lady constantly crossed over it, and no man or woman touched it willingly after dark, and it was this very tradition, added to its peculiar form, that probably led to its ultimate rescue." The Rev. H. J. Vincent, Vicar of St. Dogmael's over fifty years ago, found the stone covered with a thick coat of whitewash, in a wall adjoining his house. When this wall was taken down, the stone fell and was broken in two; it was, however, mended, and conveyed to the spot where it now rests, against the Abbey wall.

The inscription had been previously known, for that exact observer, Edward Lhwyd, had drawn the lettered surface most carefully, though his sketch was not known to exist till 1859, when it was found by Mr. J. O. Westwood at Oxford.

With regard to the meaning of the Welsh word " SAER " already given, one finds, in the Archæologia Cambrensis, Vol. II., third series, p. 245, corroborative evidence : —

Now "Saeran" signifies an artisan par excellence, and I believe it to be synonymous with "Dogvael." The prior element of the name, that is "*Doc,*" appears derived from the Latin "doctus," which became in Welsh first "doct," and later "doeth" (*learned or wise*), but "*mael*" brings the matter almost to a certainty, for "*Dogvael*" (*learned in the arts*) is really identical with "*Saeran.*" The Abbey of St. Dogmaels derives its origin from another Dogvael, the son of Ithel ab Ceredig ab Cunedda, consequently the grandnephew of Dogfael ab Cunedda.

(Robert Williams, M.A., Rhydycroesau, Oswestry).

Not far from this " Hên Mynachlog " is a place called Caerau, which at first sight one would think was an ancient encampment; here, again, let us take the early meaning of the word " caer," which now means walls or mounds for defence, or a fortress (Pugh), but in *old* days meant simply a house and

" caerau," the plural form, houses. This meaning of the word caer is retained to this day in Brittany.

The following extract from the " Archæologia Cambrensis," written by the late Mr. Vincent, the antiquarian Vicar of St. Dogmaels, who lived at the time the following occurrence took place, and who therefore describes it with the pen of an intelligent eye-witness, gives a good account of Caerau, which might have belonged to the ancient Monastery of St. Dogmaels. It stands on high ground overlooking the sea, hence, as anyone may imagine, the air is of the purest and most bracing. The extract in the " Archæologia Cambrensis " for October, 1864, p. 302, is as follows, and is an account of " Caerau " in St. Dogmaels, by the late Rev. Henry Vincent, of St. Dogmaels Vicarage :—

My attention has lately been called to " Caerau " (an earthwork, in a field called " Parc y gaer " on the farm of Penallt Ceibwr, on the brow of a hill overlooking Moylegrove) by a stone coffin enclosure found in the space between the second and third lines of fortification on the east, in what appears to have been an old cemetery extending to the east, north, and south of the earthwork ; which seems to give further proof that the defences were intended against attacks from the sea. In this place several graves have been found during the last seventy years. In one was a hammer and a cutlass ; in another the figure " T " grooved in the mould, and filled up with scoriæ of the smithy ; in another a fragment of bone ; . . . . and in all five pebbles of pure quartz, taken evidently from the sea-shore, of the size of a small apple. These graves seem to have been all of the same type, from the materials scattered around the field, consisting of fragments of slate, white pebbles, etc. In ploughing the field last spring, something white was turned up by the plough, which the ploughman mistook for a piece of lime ; but the lad who drove the plough took it up, and found it to be a human tooth. This led to further examination, and about fourteen inches below the surface they came to a coarse stone coffin of the rudest formation, consisting of five untrimmed slate stones about an inch thick in the middle, and tapering to a thin jagged edge ; one at the head, two on each side, both of which had two small grey rubble stones at the foot, probably to make out the length. It had neither lid, bottom, nor footstone, and gives one the idea of a warrior buried hastily on the battlefield ; but this could hardly have been the case, for the place was evidently a cemetery. This stone inclosure, now covered in, is of the following dimensions : length, six feet seven inches ; width at the widest part, one foot eleven inches ; width at the head and foot, eleven inches ; depth, eleven inches ; lying from north-west to south-east, and probably intended to face east. How singular that, after the lapse of so many ages, ... this coffin, rudely, flimsily and hastily got up from materials found at or near the spot, should still remain. It probably owes its preservation to its insignificance and the isolation of its resting-place. The only thing indicating anything like care was the fine yellow mould with which the coffin was filled, which differed widely from the coarse, stony earth by which it was surrounded. At the head was found a small portion of the skull, which turned to dust the moment it was touched, fifteen small pieces of calcined bone, and eight human teeth (six molars and two canines) in a state of more or less perfection. One of the canine teeth, now in my possession, is covered with enamel, and bears no symptoms of decay except in the root. A medical gentleman thinks that the teeth belonged to a young man about thirty years of age. There were also found there a piece of crystal and five white pebbles, like those already described . . . . The owner of the jaw and teeth might have been a monk, for tradition says that there was once here a monastic establishment ; and it is not impossible but that it might be the Religious House of Llandudoch, destroyed by the Danes A.D. 987. In speaking of the monks of Caerau, Fenton describes them as having been located at Monachlog, which is a mistake ; for Monachlog is a cot situated in the grounds of Pantirion, ... overlooking the Tivy ; and the names "Pantirion" (valley of God's Acre) and "Llan yr Arglwydd," on "Esgyrn" (bones) land, as well as several monastic remains discovered near the said cot, seem to indicate that there must have once have been a religious cell near the spot ; but this could not have been Caerau. We read nothing of the kings of Caerau, or warriors of Caerau, or knights of Caerau, but we have of the monks of Caerau. A monk could fight well at a pinch, and in troublous times a monk not unfrequently exchanged the cowl for the helmet, and his religious vestments for armour of proof. Could the cutlass found in the grave referred to have belonged to a monk? But surely a [1] fortress could scarcely have been a suitable abode for a company of non-combatants. If the field of Caerau was the site of the Religious House referred to as destroyed by the Danes in the tenth century, could not the monks have subsequently fortified the place against the incursions of the enemy? Tradition says that there is a subterranean passage from Caerau to Castell Iôn (the lord's castle) ; perhaps another religious fortress at Pantsaeson (valley of the Saxons) . . . . so that when the occupiers were driven out of it they might descend to Castell Iôn at the foot of the hill and attack the enemy in the rear. If the monks of Caerau were Benedictines they verified the old Latin distich :

> " Bernardus valles, colles Benedictus amabat ;
> Oppida Franciscus, magnas Ignatius urbes" ;

for they were perched on the brow of a high hill. Martin, as well as his monks, was a reformed Benedictine (a Bernardite) ; and in bringing (if he did so) the monks of Caerau into his new establishment, he lowered them as to place, if he did not reform them ; at any rate they must have found a great change of climate in the winter. There are two cottages on the south side of the earthwork, called Caerau and Penallt Esgob (the top of the bishop's hill), which shows that Caerau had something ecclesiastical about it. Near these cottages on the south-east was, within the memory of men now living, a wall of very superior masonry about thirty feet long and nine feet high, which might have been a part of the monastery of Caerau.

Caerau is situated in the hamlet of Pantygroes (the valley of the cross). Where the cross was it is hard to say, unless it was at the cross-road hard by called "Bwlch Pant y Groes" (Bwlch=gap), where a lady in white was formerly seen at the witching hour of midnight . . . . There must have been, however, a cross somewhere, Croes

---

[1] Mr. Vincent here takes the modern meaning of "Caer," not the ancient houses, which is singularly applicable, the ancient Benedictine Monasteries ofttimes containing many houses.

2

Bigog, where funerals coming from that part of the parish used formerly to stop, because, according to tradition, there the Abbey first came to view[1]—a more probable reason for this custom is that it was once the site of a wayside cross—it being a hamlet of the Abbey.

THE TRADITIONS OF CAERAU.

In the road near Caerau, and opposite the second embankment (Caerau consists of three concentric, circular embankments within and above each other at intervals of about twenty yards ; with an elevation in the second of two feet, and in the third, or innermost, of four feet). There are some men living who remember these embankments much higher than they are at present ; particularly the innermost agger, which on the seaward side was about ten feet, is a hollow which rings when any wheeled vehicle goes over it. About eighty years ago two men had the curiosity to dig there, and they solemnly declared that they came to the frame of a doorway ; but when they went to dinner, the rain descended, accompanied by thunder and lighting, and on their return the whole was closed, as they supposed by supernatural agency. A little above the place where they had been digging they affirmed that there had been no rain.

At Castell Iôn some stairs were seen, supposed to lead to some passage. A farmer's wife about ninety years since, having risen very early one morning, was thus accosted by a woman bearing the semblance of a gipsy : "Would you like to take your rest of a morning instead of leaving your bed so early?" "Yes," was the reply. "Then," said the woman, "if you dig in a certain spot in the subterranean passage between Caerau and Castell Iôn, you will find what will make you the richest lady in the land."

About sixty years ago a respectable man declared that he was cutting a hedge between Trefâs and Pant y Groes when a grey-headed old man came to him and told him that there was an underground way from Caerau to Pentre-Evan ; and that if he excavated a certain place he would find two hundred "murk" (? marks).

A woman once appeared to a ploughboy and told him that there were ten murk under the threshold of Caerau Bach. When the cottage, which had been probably built on the site of the outpost referred to, was taken down, a number of people assembled to search for the marks, but none were found.

Tradition gives Castell Iôn a different derivation to the one given by me. It is said to have been the abode of one IÔAN ; but whether he was saint or sinner is not known. On one occasion it is said that, when pursued by the enemy, he crossed the stream, and left the impression of the hoof of his charger on the stone, which has something like the mark of a horse's shoe upon it.

Probably these traditions might be the ingenious produce of a tump hard by, called "Cnwc y Celwydd" (the tump of lies), where men and women were formerly in the habit of assembling on the Lord's Day in large masses, to disport themselves by inventing and telling the most lying and wonderful tales that their imagination

---

[1] On the road from Hendre to the Abbey a cross used to stand at a place where the first glimpse of the Abbey was seen.

could devise. Though this practice has been happily discontinued, and people now betake themselves to their respective places of worship, yet it is feared that falsehood has not yet left the neighbourhood; indeed, it would have been well for this village if the "father of lies" had left it, and travelled so far to the extremity of the parish as Cnwc y Celwydd (it is as well that Mr. Vincent has passed beyond the reach of the inhabitants of St. Dogmaels, for one knows not what would happen were it otherwise). But alas, such is the case.

The old chronicler of Caerau, who used to say that he had been baptized by a vicar of St. Dogmaels (dead since 1768), and who had spent almost all his lifetime on the farm of Penrallt Ceibwr, was alive a few months ago. He told me that the whole neighbourhood was considered "fou." That men were led astray there all night, not knowing whither they went until cock-crowing, when they discovered that they were not far from home (hence the white gate-posts). A man carrying a bundle of hoop-rods, in one of these midnight wanderings, dropped them one by one to ascertain the extent of his journey; and when he went after them in the morning, he found he had travelled an incredible number of miles. A St. Dogmaels fisherman having been to a wedding at Moilgrove, lost his bearings on his way home at night, and was for some hours not able to find his course, until at last he fortunately discovered the north pole (? the polar star), by which he sailed homewards . . . . This, however, cannot be said of them all; for an old clerical friend of mine of sober habits, had once the honour of joining in this magic dance for the great part of a night. All the land round Caerau was once unclosed, which may account, in some measure, for these vagaries. When a man in the dark loses every idea of the *terminus a quo*, he is not likely to arrive speedily at the *terminus ad quem*. A person in this parish told me that he one night heard groaning in the field where the lady used to appear, which frightened him so much that he was ill for several days. Could the groans have been caused by the disappearance of the lady, who, I believe, has not been seen for many years?

. . . . About a mile to the right of Caerau is Hendre, where there was once a fine mansion belonging to the Lloyds, who were descendants of Gwynfardd and Cwhelyn, who might have founded (or benefitted) the monastery of Caerau: for they were the *reguli* of the district and had been great benefactors to the church, particularly Arcol Llaw Hir . . . . "To William Lloyd, one of the family" (the Lloyds of Hendre) writes Fenton "there was an indulgence granted by Pope Eugenius,[1] A.D. 1442, 14th November, at the city of Florence, to have '*altare portabile ad missas et alia divina officia etiam ante diem et in locis interdictis celebranda.*'" John Lloyd of Hendre was Sheriff of Pembrokeshire in 1623.

A part of the old house, and what was probably an oratory attached thereto have been converted into a cowhouse. The keystone of the arch of the doorway of the dwelling house is thus inscribed, T.LL.ESQ.1744.C.W. The supposed oratory has no entrance from without. The door on the north-west, leading to it from the dwelling house, is not dissimilar to the door of what used to be called the Refectory

---

[1] A copy of this Bull was years ago in the possession of a former tenant of Hendre; his widow has, however, been unable to find it.

in the Abbey of St. Dogmaels.   On the south-west once stood an image, which was taken down when an opening was made in the wall at a place where the said image had long stood.   It was exhibited at the Cardigan Archæological Meeting in 1859, and is now at Clynfiew, the seat of Major Lewis, the proprietor of Hendre . . . . In the east was a small window, the size of which may now be traced.   It was probably a doublet, its breadth being much greater than its length.   The walls of this building are very strong, and partly built of sea-pebbles embedded in very hard mortar.   It is 19 feet long (the choir), 15 feet 7 inches wide, 9 feet high; and whatever it may have been, it certainly has the appearance of having once been devoted to religious worship.[1]   To the left is Pant y Groes (in the parish of Moylgrove)—so called from having been once the site of the cross, now at Treprisk, an illustration of which appeared in the Archæologia Cambrensis some time ago.   A little further on is Tregamon, on the brook Conan, the birthplace of Maud (Matilda) Peveril, wife of Robert Fitzmartin, who, in the language of the charter, "with the approbation, or rather by the exhortation of my wife Matilda," largely endowed the Abbey of St. Dogmaels.   A little beyond Tregaman is TREICERT [now Trecart] and Trewrdan, so-called from their owners, Ricart and Jordan, signers of two of the grants in the Barony of Cemaes, sons of Lucas de Hoda, a favourite of Martin's.

With regard to Hendre (the old chapel), which formerly belonged to the Abbey of St. Dogmaels, the walls and roof are in almost perfect preservation. It was formerly cruciform in shape, but has now lost its north transept.   The nave, choir, and south transepts are intact; there is a room over the south transept which in all probability was a priest's chamber, as it is about two miles from the Abbey.   The chancel arch still exists, and the remains of one old window in the choir to the east.   It is at present used as a cow-house.   It is capable of holding about a hundred people, so that the population of Hendre[2] (the old village) must in those days have been far in excess of what it is now.   It adjoins the farmhouse of Hendre.   The Mr. T. Lloyd,[3] 1744, afterwards of Cwm Gloyne, whose initials are inscribed on what is really half a holy water stoup built into the wall, acquired leave to turn this old chapel into a dwelling-house, after which its nave was turned into a cow-house, and the choir into a stable.

During the existence of the Abbey funerals from Hendre were apparently

---

[1] Mr. Vincent here evidently describes only the chancel.   The whole chapel at Hendre is far longer, also what he describes as a "keystone" is half a holy water stoup.

[2] "Hendref" in older MSS.

[3] The founder of the family of Lloyds of Hendre is given by Lewis Dŵn as Fylip Lloyd of Hendref; later Ieuan Lloyd of Hendref, gentleman, married, in 1613, Mari, daughter of George Owen, Lord of Cemaes; this Ieuan was Sheriff for Pembrokeshire in 1623.   These Lloyds of Hendre were descended from Gwynfardd and Cwhelyn, reguli of Dyfed (Pembrokeshire) before the conquest by Martin of the Towers.   Gwynfardd lived at Castle Nevern, where Martin and his son and grandson afterwards lived.

held at the Abbey, as one sees from the descriptions given of the resting of funerals at the cross where they first came in sight of the Abbey on their way there from Hendre. Two hundred and eight years after the dissolution the chapel was converted into a house. The valley beneath where this cross formerly stood is still called Pant y Groes (the Valley of the Cross).

CHAPTER II.

AN ALMOST BLOODLESS CONQUEST.

THE history of St. Dogmaels, as we have seen, is very frag-
mentary up to the time of the Conquest of England and
part of Wales by the Normans, a period of such varied
happenings to the Welsh and English, the treatment the
inhabitants received depending so much on the individual characters of the
knights, under William the Conqueror's banner, to whom he apportioned the
subjecting of the different parts of Britain. Cardiganshire he, or rather his
son, gave to his cousin, Gilbert de Clare, whilst Cemaes he apportioned to a
knight, Martin, of the Towers, in 1087, who had come over in his train, as is
seen by three of the Battle Abbey Rolls, though his name is not found inscribed
in the roll of those who set sail from Dives,[1] near Caen, in Normandy, with
William the Conqueror. Still, he is in three lists of those who fought with
William at the Battle of Hastings, so it may have been that he sailed from a
different port. Martin had subdued part of Devonshire, where he first settled,
and where one of his sons succeeded him after his death. He has left his name
there in Combmartin. After living for some years in Devonshire, William
granted to him, in addition, a portion of Pembrokeshire if he could subdue it.

Martin of the Towers was so-called from the three towers blazoned on his
shield and banner, and not because he came from Tours, in Touraine, or
any other Tours in France, no town in France bearing crests anterior to
1200 A.D., the only place in France where one finds that he is known being
Tiron, now called Thiron-Gardais, in Eure et Loir, on the south-east borders
of Normandy. Taking this into consideration with the fact that he is always

---

[1] At Dives there is a column set up to commemorate the sailing of William, Duke of Normandy,
for England. The hotel there is also called "Guillaume le Conquerant," and there is a list of the
knights who sailed with William, in the Church Porch.

Drawn by Wm Zwuevells

Near Combmartin on the Coast of N Devon.

called a Norman knight, and that he came over with William the Norman, and that his son Robert, on founding the Abbey of St. Dogmaels, went over to this same Abbey of Tiron for the second time to bring back monks[1] and an abbot, what more likely than that Martin himself came from the neighbourhood of Tiron.[2] Also that George Owen, Lord of Cemaes, in his search as to his ancestor Martin, who he was and from whence he came, might after all have found this out, and it might have been no slip of his pen when he described him as Martinus Tironensis, or Martin of Tiron, and also so frequently called him Martin of the Towers or Martin Towres. Many things point to his coming from Tiron, and his being described as from Tours, Touraine, is simply through "tours" being the French for towers. Through this also, in the Middle Ages, he was confounded with the noted Bishop of Tours (Touraine), afterwards canonized as St. Martin of Tours, who lived from 316 to 400 A.D.

Even the present Church of Combmartin, in Devonshire, is dedicated to Saint Martin, and has a window to the Saint, thus showing that even there they imagined the name Martin came from the Saint, and not from the Norman knight. Happily, it is proved, both by the Domesday Book and by many other sources, that the Norman knight, Martin, lived there (in Devon) and many of his descendants after him, even after the family had become extinct in the male line in Cemaes.[3]

Accordingly, Martin set sail with a small following, and landed in Fishguard Bay, to which landing one will revert after giving extracts from Westcote and Risdon relative to Martin. Westcote writes :—

"Le Sire Martin de Turon, was a man of much worth, and assistance to William Duke of Normandy, when he conquered this land, of whom he had this (Combe Martin), and other great possessions given him."

Risdon also mentions "Martin of Turon" among "men of renown, in military employments, and in Council, that came over with William the Conqueror, and seated themselves in this shire (Devon) some of whose posterity yet remain."

It would be well to consider the derivation of the name of this province Martin conquered, namely, Cemaes, before proceeding further.

In the earliest grant referring to it, it is written Cathmais, and is evidently derived from the Welsh "cath" (Latin caedes), signifying slaughter, and the

---

[1] Called also "monachi de thuron," p. 443 George Owen's "Pembrokeshire," also p. 430.

[2] The late Duchess of Cleveland, in the Battle Abbey Roll, states that he came from Tours, four miles from Bayeux, though this is erroneous, as also does Risdon. Mons. Etienne Dupont has not yet reached his name in his work on the companions of William the Conqueror.

[3] Written also "Caithmais," "Cathmaes," "Cemmais," "Kemes," "Kemmes," "Kames," "Cames," "Kemeys," "Camoys," etc.

Welsh "mais," maes, a field. Therefore, the name Cemaes, as it is now spelt, means the Field of Slaughter. This is undoubtedly the real old name for the Barony, and is also, and in this no doubt all will agree, a most appropriate name, for it must often have been a field of slaughter.

In Roman times it is known that there was fighting here from various relics of that time found in the neighbourhood, notably the gravestone of a retired Roman *lieutenant* (not a soldier), removed some years back to Nevern Church-yard from the higher lands of Cathmais. Also the great number of Latin roots in the Welsh language, the Latin names of the days of the week adopted by the Welsh tends to show that Wales was more thoroughly occupied by the Romans than it is believed to have been at the present day.

In 860, according to the "Brut Ieuan Brechfa," the Saxons destroyed all the monasteries in Pembrokeshire, and tradition tells how they fought the Welsh at Pantsaeson (the Valley of the Saxons), which is close to Yr hên Monachlog.

Later the Danes harried the coasts and banks of the river Teify, climbing the hills from the Teify, and pillaging around in 987,[1] it being specially recorded in the annales that they devastated St. Dogmaels. Then comes the battle in which Rhys ap Tewdwr, then living at St. Dogmaels, is suddenly attacked by the four Welsh princes, and defeats them, it is stated, with "great slaughter."

In this one notices the lack of cohesion in the Welsh character, which exists to the present day. They are not *truly patriotic*, the love of country, though one would think, if one listened to them, they were brimful of it, does not exist in them; if truly patriotic they would all unite when common danger, or a common foe faced them, or for the common good in improving their country or their towns; but all through their history it is the same, jealousy and treachery soon show forth, and they will not unite for the common good in anything, either in things pertaining to peace, or in things pertaining to war. They have ofttimes had the finest of leaders arise, but in every case they have failed, and still fail, from lack of cohesion, treachery, and petty jealousies—this has been, and still is, their undoing.

It was this that rendered the conquest of Cemaes, about 1087, so easy to Martin of the Towers.[2] Each village met him separately, and, after the first slight resistance at Fishguard, meekly surrendered, till, going north-east, he reached Eglwyswrw, where the only fight occurred,[3] and there being but a

---

[1] *See* "Annales Cambriæ."

[2] Called also, "Martinus Tironensis," "Martinus Turonensis," "Martin de Tours," "Martin de Turribus," and "Martinus de Turonibus."

[3] After the very slight attack with stones at Fishguard.

handful of Welsh, he easily defeated them; continuing his course to the Teify, all the villages including St. Dogmaels, surrendering. Most fortunately for them Martin was a thoroughly good man, and what was rare in those days, both humane and just. Instead of burning their houses, and putting the men to death, he built himself a castle at Nevern,[1] and there issued leases of their farms to the inhabitants, allowing them to remain in the homes of their ancestors. A few of the farms he kept and gave to his followers. The names of two of these followers, or rather of the sons of his favourite knight, de Hoda, are still retained in the names of farms, Trecart and Trereicert, that is, the Home of Risiart, and Trewrdan, the Home of Jordan, which are on the high lands not far from Crugiau Cemaes. Also Martin's great-great-great-granddaughter, Ales, or Nesta, married Richard de Hoda, the grandson of this young Norman knight, and through her the Barony of Cemaes descended to their son, Philip, who in his turn married Nesta, great-great-great-granddaughter of Rhys ap Gryffydd, Prince of South Wales.

Martin, having now peacefully settled in the castle he had built at Nevern, his family lived there for three generations, till his grandson, William, built Newport Castle in the thirteenth century, and went to live there. It is very difficult to trace this castle. There is a place marked Castell Nevern in the ordnance maps, which on first reconnoitring one would immediately think was the site of Martin's old castle, being almost surrounded by a deep moat, and having an inner mound, but when reaching the top of this mound one finds traces of a circular wall of unmortared slate-stone, hardly larger in circumference than a large-sized well, and on probing the outside banks of this site, one finds no trace of masonry.

Martin and his descendants for three generations would certainly not have lived in an earthwork, but would in all probability have built a strong Norman castle, especially as he had many followers, who would all have helped in the work. There is one point in its favour, namely, the Welsh having no respect for the religion of their ancestors, despoiled the old druidical circles, and at Pentre Evan have not only taken away the stones from the double circle[2] that once surrounded the cromlechs, but have also taken away the stones of two out of the three cromlechs that formerly stood there, and have used them for gate-posts, how much more likely then would it be for them to take the old stone from this deserted castle for building their cottages and farmsteads, instead of having the

---

[1] On the site of the Welsh castle formerly inhabited by Gwynfardd the Regulus.

[2] The late Mr. Bowen, of Llwyngwair, assured me that he knew there had been a large double ring of stones with three cromlechs, of which only the centre one remained.

trouble of quarrying stone for the same, so this is probably the site of Martin's old castle, and the rubble of the old walls has simply become overgrown with grass. The moat still has water, and must have been a work of much labour.

At Nevern Castle there also remains a large round tump which certainly resembles the remains of an ancient Welsh castle, which were simply "rounde turrets without any courtledge," and of which no other traces remained in George Owen's time save "highe and rounde toompes of earth." Around this is grassland, with a double row of grass-covered earth banks on three sides, suggestive of former buildings, surrounded again by a deep moat, and having apparently a high watch tower. This would rather lead one to believe that Martin built his Castle of Nevern on the site of an ancient British castle. That there are so few traces of stonework is not surprising, as Nevern Castle was abandoned in the thirteenth century, whilst of Henllys, abandoned only in the eighteenth century, not a stone remains.

According to Geraldus Cambrensis, "the ancient and chief castle which the princes of Wales possessed in this part of the country (Pem.) was Castrum de Lanhever," that is the Castle of Nevern, "where still remain the ruins of a very strong hold, surrounded on three sides by a very deep moat, evidently cut out at a vast expenditure of labour, which even to this day contains water." In one of the old documents relating to Martin can be seen how immediately after his conquest of Cemaes he set to work to build the Castle of Nevern, and the Martins are described as of Nevern Castle, when his grandson, William, married Angharad, daughter of Rhys ap Gryffydd, Lord of Cardigan, the building of Newport Castle being ascribed to him after his marriage in the thirteenth century.

Mr. Laws, in page 97 of his "Little England beyond Wales," writes concerning the conquest of Cemaes by—

One Martin de Turribus which is translated as "of Tours," though perhaps "of the Towers" would be the better rendering. [as it most undoubtedly is.] Martin was a man of might, and had been rewarded with broad lands in Somerset and Devon for valiant deeds done in England. He landed at Abergwayn, or Fishguard, with a considerable following, where according to local tradition he docked his little fleet, but the natives in the night rolled great rocks down on them and so damaged the vessels, that next day, having repaired them as well as he could, the Norman leader sailed on to Newport, where the harbour is on the flat, and safe from projectiles from above . . . . pitched his camp at Cronllwyn, a hill on the banks of the Gwayn, about two miles from the shore and well adapted for his purpose, as its base was protected by a morass, whilst its summit commands an extensive view over the surrounding country. The Norman force remained in camp for some days unassailed by the

Welsh. Martin then moved towards the hills, where the enemy was reported to be massing.   He came up with the natives at Morvill, and repulsed them in a sharp skirmish.   Martin then followed the Welsh across Precelly.   On the further side the men of Meline, Nantgwyn and Eglwyswrw came out to meet him ; but what could these poor villagers do against Norman veterans.   Seized by a sudden panic they laid down their arms without striking a blow.   This surrender concluded the war, and the hundred of Cemaes yielded without further bloodshed, becoming a March with Martin and his successors as lord Marchers.   He took up his quarters at Nevern, where he appropriated the stronghold previously occupied by Cuhelyn, a regulus of Dyved.   This was subsequently strengthened by successive members of Martin's family, though as will be seen they (afterwards) made Newport the capital of their barony.

Martin, approaching the last years of his life, turned his thoughts to religion, and decided to build an abbey at St. Dogmaels. He began to make plans for the same, but the hand of death prevented him from accomplishing this desire of his heart. His death is noted by some writers as occurring in 1089.

Martin changed the name of the cantref of Kemes into the Barony of Kemes; but left the ancient boundaries practically intact, "obtayninge of the kinges of England, upon his holding the same of them in capite to be by them erected onto a barony, and to have place in parliam[t] of England, by the name of Lords of Kemes," he also divided the Barony into diverse knights' fees, and each knight's fee into ploughlands, and these into oxlands. He also changed their order of conveyance of land, to be after the use of the common laws of England, namely, by " fines and feoffementes, liverye and seisin, which was not used by the Welshmen, nor permitted by the laws of Howel dha, by which laws the then Princes of Wales governed their countreys."

" He also encorporated, and erected townes, and made thereof boroughes, and appointed officers as Portrives and other officers (catchpolle or petty officer of justice such as a sheriff's officer or bum-bailiff) to governe the same, and made free burgesses, and gave them great liberties after the maner of England, never used or hard of among the Ancient Britaines."

Soon after this, Robert, the eldest son of Martin, who had succeeded him as Baron of Cemaes, married Matilda, daughter of William Peverel of Trecamon.[1] Moylgrove was a part of her marriage dowry. Evidently Robert and his wife were both of one mind as regards the building of the Abbey, also Robert may have looked on it as a trust imposed on him by his father, which it was his duty to carry out, for he set to work and caused the Abbey to be built, some writers say from plans of his father's, anyway, he and he only had

---

[1] Now Tregammon.

to do with the building of this Abbey, on the site of the present ruins, in the Village (formerly Borough) of St. Dogmaels, within a short distance of the river Teify. When the Abbey was finished in 1118, he arranged with the abbot, William, of Tiron, to let him have an abbot and thirteen more monks for his new Abbey. This Abbey of St. Dogmaels was the first dependent Abbey belonging to the Abbey of Tiron, out of several that were founded. Robert richly endowed it, giving certain lands in St. Dogmaels to it for ever, and other rights of chapelries, and fees in different parts of the barony, also other lands in Devonshire; namely—

1st. The old Church and Priory of St. Dogmaels, with their adjacent lands, as well as the new Abbey and its adjacent lands.

2nd. A large tract of land in the neighbourhood, bounded by the Breuan (Broyan), the Teify estuary, and other limits, and among them a stream that bounded Llanbloden.

3rd. Lands in the Precelly range, lying in the fork between the stream called Combkaro,[1] (now Cwm Carw or Cwm Cerwyn, by both of which names it is still known, and has been for many hundred years), and the Cledi; this grant also appears to include Mynachlog Ddu, alias Nigra Grangia.

4th. Caldey Island, given by his mother, Geva, and Moylgrove, by his wife, Matilda.

5th. The Manor of Rattery, near Totnes, South Devon, and at Cocklington, near Torquay, South Devon, he gave the "Church and two farthings of land to the Abbey of Cemois," for one reads that Robert Fitzmartin also granted to St. Dogmaels other lands, some at Cocklington, near Torquay, as appears from the following passage of Risdon's "Survey of Devonshire," p. 147, written before 1630, wherein is noted—

"Cocklington was bestowed on William Fallaise, one of the Conqueror's followers, and not long after it became the land of Robert Fitz Martin, lord of Camois, who gave it to his younger son, excepting the church and two farthings of land, which he

---

[1] Cwm Carw, or Cwm Cerwyn, is interesting as being mentioned in the Mabinogion, in Olwen and Kilkwch, when King Arthur, overlord of Britain, rides through Cwm Cerwyn with many of his followers to hunt the "Trwch Trwyth," supposed to have been some horrible monster. It was also known by both names in the days of George Owen, Lord of Cemaes (1552–1613), for in one of his smaller MSS. he writes of it, noting the enormous number of Irish settlers in the villages north of the Preselies, so that in some villages every third house was inhabited by Irish, in others every fifth— he also notes the valley called in Welsh Cwm Cerwyn (a cauldron) or Cwm Carw (a stag), adding that either name would be applicable, as there were plenty of stags in the valley, and also plenty of cauldrons, since nearly all the Irish have stills for whiskey.

gave to the Abbey of Camois with other lands. In the time of Henry the first the posterity of this Robert Martin took the surname of Cockington.

"There was a great controversy between Sir Robert and the Abbot of Camois about the tenure and service of the two farthings of land, which was appeased by Bartholomew, Bishop of Exeter (1161–1181)."

Concerning Rattry, a parish about four miles from Totnes, in Devon (the Ratreu of the grant), it belonged, under William the Conqueror, to William Fallaise, but was sold by him to Robert Fitzmartin, in the time of Henry I, who was also Lord of Dartington and Kemes. Robert Fitzmartin also bought Cockington from William of Fallaise, and gave it to his younger son, except the church and two farthings of land, which he gave to the Abbots of St. Dogmaels.

CHAPTER III.

THE MOTHER ABBEY.

BEFORE proceeding further with St. Dogmaels, it would be well to know something of Tiron,[1] now called Thiron-Gardais, near Nogent-le-Rotrou, in Eure-et-Loir, France, close to the south-east border of Normandy. The founder of this Abbey, Bernard, leaving a wealthy Abbey, for the sake of poverty, and a desire to lead a life of hard work and holiness, started in what was then a barren waste, but is now a fertile land. Thiron is sometimes called Thiron au Perche, the department of Eure-et-Loir being composed of two small provinces, called " Beance " and " Perche." Chartres is the chief town in the province of " Beance," a flat country having no rivers, whilst Thiron-Gardais is in " Perche," a land of charming hills, of verdant fields, and numerous rivulets.

Nogent-le-Rotrou, close to Thiron, is the chief town in this province of Perche, and contains now about 9,000 inhabitants.[2]

The old Monastery of Tiron has ceased to exist since the French Revolution, but the ancient abbey church still remains, and is used as the parish church of Thiron-Gardais; also a few other buildings of the old monastery[3] remain, used now for other purposes.

The photograph representing the parish church shows the ancient Church of Tiron; it is in the pure Renaissance style, the old Gothic choir having fallen in 1830, the arch was walled up, having three windows left in it. This new work is plainly visible in the photograph.

---

[1] Tiron is the old French name, Thiron, or Thiron Gardais, or Thiron au Perche, the modern French name, and Tyron the Latin.

[2] Letter from the Rev. C. Claireaux, of Nogent-le-Rotrou, Eure-et-Loir, France.

[3] Not of *St. Bernard's* Monastery ; but built later, probably by John of Chartres.

Ancient Church of the Abbey of Tiron

Ancient College of the Abbey of Tiron.
Eure et Loir, France

The other buildings show what is left of the college of the Abbey, and the pond, which might have been their old fishpond.

Bernard, by the hard labour of himself and his companions, changed this desolate spot to a "fertile land." Bernard, "a noted admirer of poverty, leaving a most opulent monastery, retired with a few followers to a wooded and sequestered place," and there, "as his light could not be hidden under a bushel," vast numbers flocking to him, he founded a monastery, A.D. 1109, more celebrated then for the piety and number of the monks than for the splendour and extent of its riches.[1]

Robert Fitzmartin is described as a most noble man of holy life, who, the first time that he returned to Tiron, took back with him to St. Dogmaels, in 1113, thirteen monks. This was probably for the priory of St. Dogmaels, which was known in France as the "Priory de Galles."[2] On the occasion of his second visit to Tiron, 1118, he took back with him thirteen more monks, and also an abbot,[3] Fulchardus. This second visit of Robert Fitzmartin to Tiron would be in 1118, as we see later in the Cartulary of Tiron that the Priory of Guales was raised into an abbey in 1118; also Robert's grants to the abbey were therefore made in, or before, 1118, though confirmed by Henry I in 1119.

The Abbey of Tiron seems to have been held in high esteem in Great Britain, for not only did Robert Fitzmartin often go there, but also Henry I of England and his son, William, as well as bestowing gifts on the Abbey, as did also Henry Earl of Warwick, and David King of Scotland, together with his son, afterwards Malcolm III. The two latter also founded abbeys in Scotland under the Abbey of Tiron. David journeyed to Tiron expressly to see and honour the holy St. Bernard, but arrived too late, the founder having died,[4] so that he was only able to pay his devotions at his grave.

Bernard was apparently succeeded by William as abbot, and in 1120, by the inscription round the coat of arms of Geoffrey le Gros, in the old Abbey Church of Tiron, Geoffrey le Gros was then abbot; later he was Bernard's historian.

Bernard was born at Ponticum, close to the town of Abbeville, of honest and pious parents. He studied diligently, and after he had become proficient in religion and literature, he joined the monks of St. Cyprian under the Abbot, Raymond II (seventeenth abbot since its foundation), a man of great erudition

---

[1] William of Malmesbury. [2] Or Guales. [3] "Cartulaire de la Ste. Trinité de Tiron."
[4] According to the Patrologie Migne, Vol. CLXXII, St. Bernard died April 7th, 1117. According to the Cartulary of Tiron, he died April 25th, 1117. His fête used to be kept April 14th, but is now kept on April 19th.

and eloquence, and gifted with high powers of administration. From this monastery, Bernard, having profited greatly by the example and learning of Raymond, was translated to Savigny as Prior. Bernard, however, indignantly condemned both the wealth and luxury of these two abbeys, and though he governed the Abbey of Savigny with wisdom and regularity, he determined, after seeing a vision one night in the oratory at Savigny, to take the vows of poverty, and, quitting the rule of the wealthy Monastery of Savigny, to go out into the wildest part of the province and found a hermitage.

This he did; but so many flocked to him that he finally founded the Monastery of Tiron, where they lived for a time in great poverty, Bernard becoming its first abbot.

The earliest spelling of this mother abbey of St. Dogmaels Abbey was " Tiron,"[1] though in later years an " h " was added, making it the Thiron of the present day.

The life of the founder, now always called St. Bernard of Tiron, is still extant, and has lately been reprinted in the " Patrologie Migne," Vol. CLXXII. It was written by Geoffrey le Gros, Abbot of Tiron, who lived at the same time as St. Bernard, and was one of his most faithful disciples. He was a monk, and later Chancellor and Prior of the Abbey of Tiron, a contemporary and also a companion of St. Bernard, and in 1120 was made Abbot of Tiron. After the death of St. Bernard, yielding to the request of the Bishop of Chartres, Geoffrey wrote what he had witnessed in the life of St. Bernard for the edification of his *confrères* to come. Mons. Lucien Merlet, Archivist of Eure-et-Loir, states that he has read and re-read this work, and accords to him (Geoffrey le Gros) full and entire confidence. Geoffrey writes: " It is not the recalling to you of the many and great miracles by which we would make you admire our father, Bernard, but rather by telling you that he was gentle and humble of heart."

Geoffrey accompanied St. Bernard when he left the Forest of Savigny, near Fougeres, which had been given to Bernard by Raoul, Count of Fougeres, and where his companions had built a dwelling-place, and where they had spent many years, living by the work of their hands. Later, Bernard resolved to seek further for greater solitude, and charged four of his monks to find some vast desert, where they could raise large buildings to give shelter to all pilgrims who might come there. They were unable to find this desert, but one of them, having a vision, saw in his sleep a young man of resplendent beauty, clothed in white, who, placing his hand on his head, said to him, " Arise at

---

[1] *See* introduction to the " Cartulary of Tiron."

St. Anne's Pool. Torran Abbey.

once; go to Rotrou, Count of Perche; he will give you what you desire." On his relating this vision to his companions they laughed at him, and returning to Bernard, related their non-success; but later recalling the dream of their *confrère*, they determined to visit Count Rotrou. On seeing him he granted their request. Possessing a property called Arcisses, about a mile from his Castle of Nogent, he conducted two of Bernard's disciples there, and promised to give this domain in perpetuity to St. Bernard and his companions. It was a fertile land, surrounded on all sides by forests, abundantly watered by springs and brooks, which kept the meadows always green. The soil was perfectly suited to the culture of the vine, and would also furnish them with all they needed; already the Count's predecessors had built there an oratory, had made a fishpond, planted orchards, and had, in fact, done all that was useful and agreeable for life. They were delighted with it, and returned to fetch Bernard; but by the time Bernard arrived Rotrou had changed his mind, and, withdrawing his promise with regard to Arcisses, giving them instead a place named Tiron.

This changing of his mind is ascribed to the influence of his mother, Beatrice, who, hearing of what he had done, came to him in a greatly disturbed state of mind, begging her son on no account to allow Bernard and his monks to settle so close to the castle, and by her prayers and entreaties persuaded him to retract his promised gift, and to offer them instead a tract of more sterile land further from the castle. The reason for this is supposed to have been that she favoured the monks of Cluny, who, in later years, succeeded Bernard's followers at Tiron. Bernard was in no wise troubled by this *contretemps* : he accepted the newly-offered land, and sending his two disciples to Tiron, who, after examining it returned, reporting that it lacked everything needful to life; but during the night Bernard saw, in a vision, a lamp glowing in the middle of the sky and shedding its rays on all the surrounding places. This vision determined him to accept the Count's offer. To his brethren he said, " Here is the place really suited to us, it is indeed the solitude we have so long sought." On reaching Tiron with Bernard, the brothers, after giving thanks to God, tied Poitevin (the donkey that had carried Bernard) to a tree, placed their light baggage on the ground, and quickly constructed a simple cell, and a few days later Bernard gathering his followers together, brought them to Tiron. At Easter, in the year 1109, Bernard celebrated the first mass in a wooden sanctuary, which he found on the place given him by the Count. Bernard worked with his followers, helping them to build their dwellings, at the same time instructing them in the doctrine of the Lord. Their necessities became dire, as owing to the superabundance of rain, they were unable to sow their seed; but William, Count of Nevers, had pity on them, and sent them a large golden vase, so that they were enabled to buy the necessities of life.

They now worked night and day building their cloisters; they wore a monk's habit; but it was different to that of other orders, being made of sheep's-skin, owing to their great poverty. Meanwhile, rich and poor flocked to hear Bernard. The monks of Cluny, becoming jealous of Bernard's popularity, disturbed them in their possession of Tiron; Bernard then went to the Bishop of Chartres, and begged him to give him a small portion of land of which he was lord, whereon to build a monastery. The Bishop and Chapter of Chartres accordingly gave him the straggling Village of Gardais, on the river Thironne, the confirmation of this gift being dated February 3rd, 1114, and is the veritable charter of the foundation of the Abbey of Tiron. Adela, fourth daughter of William the Conqueror, came to Bernard after this and offered a more fertile land, but he gratefully refused the offer. Bernard's reputation for holiness increased from day to day, and spread far and wide, even to England and Scotland, one of his most fervent admirers being Henry I, King of England, and Duke of Normandy, who sent to him begging him to settle in Normandy. Henry's affection for the Abbey lasted even after Bernard's death; besides giving them a yearly revenue of fifteen marks, he also sent the monks each year fifty or sixty marks, and also built a magnificent dormitory for the Abbey. Louis le Gros, King of France, also held Bernard in high esteem, so much so that he wished Bernard to baptise both his sons, Philippe and Louis. There were many other benefactors to the Abbey besides these two kings, notably William Duke of Acquitaine, Foulques Count of Angou, then King of Jerusalem, Robert of Caen, Count of Gloucester[1], Henry Earl of Warwick, Guy the Younger, Count of Rochfort, William II, Count of Nevers[2], Robert, son of Martin, Lord of Cemaes, and many others. Thus is seen that the reputation for sanctity of the blessed founder of Tiron, and the piety and devotion of his followers, drew to the new monastery the most generous gifts, so that even in the same century in which it was founded, it is seen by the Cartulary of the Abbey, that it already owned eleven abbeys (four of which were in Britain), more than a hundred priories, also owned the supremacy of the Abbey of Tiron, and were designated as of the Order of Tiron.

Each year there was a general chapter at Tiron, where delegates from all

---

[1] Natural son of Henry I of England, died about 1138.

[2] The Abbey of Tiron was not ungrateful to its benefactors, for when William, Count of Nevers, was taken prisoner by Thibaut IV, Count of Blois, Bernard went to Blois with Robert of Arbrissel to crave his liberty.

the abbeys and priories dependent on the mother house met, and the Abbot of Tiron, surrounded by "eleven other crossed and mitred abbots," sat in judgment on all delinquents, named or dismissed abbots and priors, and regulated the administration of their properties, etc. Such rapid and great prosperity led to abuses. The abbots succeeding Bernard, who, according to Mons. Lucien Merlet, died on April 25th, 1116 or 1117, more probably the later year, lost the humility and modesty of their saintly founder, their power blinded them, and they vied with the highest prelates in their magnificence and state. Towards the end of the thirteenth century, the Canons of the Chapter of Chartres bitterly upbraided John of Chartres, then Abbot of Tiron, because he would not appear in public without being surrounded by a host of sergeants carrying silver maces before him. An ancient miniature, preserved in the Abbey of Tiron, represented this John of Chartres in the Church of "Notre Dame de Chartres," preceded by six seculaires walking, with raised wands of office, and followed by four clerks.

The monks no longer inhabited the modest cells of their founder; but the most sumptuous of palaces. John of Chartres rebuilt the monastery, and for the expenses of this and his gorgeous train, it was necessary to raise more money, which he did in ways more or less admissible. The authors of "Gallia Christiana" have portrayed the state of luxury and license of the Abbey after the rule of John of Chartres. Indeed, in the time of Giraldus (1188) the monks of St. Dogmaels are described in his works as already living in wickedness and luxury.

Towards the end of the English wars in France, the English seized all Normandy, Beance, and Perche, etc. The revenues of the Abbey of Tiron were seized, the monks dispersed, the priories destroyed, and on June 13th, 1428 (not 1450, as given in the "Gallia Christiana"), the Earl of Salisbury, on his way to Orleans, passed by Thiron and partly burnt down the Abbey of Tiron. Their revenues being reduced by one-half, and no gifts coming in, as in the twelfth century, and not being able to procure money for the restoration of their ruined abbey,[1] they decided to do it themselves, and of their own private authority, taking their first Charter, they skilfully introduced clauses to their profit, giving them enormous privileges, and made themselves suzeraine lords of the domaine, overthrowing the feudal rights of the reigning lords, especially of the Chapter of Chartres, which was the richest landlord in the country, and the original giver of the land on which the Abbey of Tiron was built. The Chapter refused to acknowledge this usurpation of the Abbot of Tiron; finally the dispute came before Parliament, and was the occasion of a long and interesting trial,

---

[1] In 1505, Louis de Crevant was Abbot of Tiron.

wherein the monks most skilfully defended the falsified charter of their foundation. On the 3rd October, 1556, Parliament condemned the monks of Tiron as usurpers, and confirmed this sentence on the 22nd March, 1558; but did not condemn them as forgers, so that the monks still hoped to win and proclaimed themselves as victims to the power of their adversaries.

On the 19th March, 1562, three thousand German mercenaries, on their way to rejoin the Prince de Condé, passing the Monastery of Tiron, killed three of the monks, pillaged their sacred vessels, turned the church into a stable, broke the crucifix and the figures of the Trinity on the super altar, completely smashed the altars of St. Martin and St. Eloi, fired many times at the windows of the choir, broke into the Treasury, appropriating all their treasures and relics, among them a chasuble, mitre, and cross belonging to the Abbot Bernard, their founder; the whole estimated as worth over three thousand pounds sterling, besides five hundred crowns worth of linen, cloth of gold, etc. All the furniture of the house, provisions, wheat, rye, oats, barley, twenty-five puncheons of wine, forty puncheons of cider, also became the prey of the troopers; also all the bullocks, cows, calves, horses, and poultry in the stables and farm buildings were killed or led off, only the animals in the wood escaping.

Eight " lits garnis " (elaborate beds and hangings), a very large quantity of linen, and vessels of pewter, were also carried away. The pillage lasted three days, and what the troopers could not carry away they damaged.

The abbot of that time, Hippolyte d'Este, Cardinal of Ferrara, tried by wise rules to bring order out of this disorder; but in the year 1563 he resigned in favour of Charles de Ronsard; this abbot (1563-1575) and René de Laubier, his successor (1575-1578) carefully governed the Abbey; but after their rule discipline was again relaxed, the monks thinking only of their own comfort. In 1627, insubordination existing in the Abbey, the monks of St. Maur replaced those of the order of Tiron. Louis XIV gave his protection to Tiron, under the rule of St. Maur, and also permitted the monks to take the title of Royal Military School, for their college; they also took in invalid soldiers in return for the King's protection. The Abbey of Tiron ceased to exist in 1792. The first Church of Tiron was commenced about the year 1115; it was cruciform in shape. The old choir fell down February 10th, 1817, and what now remains is the later church of the Monastery of Tiron; it was twenty-five yards long, and was partly rebuilt by Lionel Grimault, abbot from 1454 to 1498, the high altar was dedicated to the Trinity, the old choir was in the Gothic style. The coat of arms of Bernard were in this chancel, having a scroll with Bernardus, 1109; also Geoffrey le Gros' " Abb. Monast. de Tironio, 1120," with his coat of arms is there, which proves by the date that St. Dogmaels was founded before that date, as all three confirmations were during the rule of Abbot William.

The fête of St. Bernard of Tiron is still celebrated in the diocese where he lived; until lately it was also celebrated in the diocese of Chartres on the 14th of April, but Pope Leo XIII changed the date of St. Bernard's Fête to April 19th, owing to the 14th of April being also the Fête of St. Justin, the apologist. The following prayer is taken from the Office of St. Bernard : —

· Grant, we beseech thee, oh our God, that we may be uplifted through the intercessions of the blessed Abbot Bernard, that through him, by whom thou hast granted thy servants evidence of the perfection of the gospel, thou mayst mete out to us help to everlasting salvation. Through God the Father, etc.[1]

In the Cartulary of the Abbey of Tiron, Vol. I, p. 41, are the confirmation of the grants made by Robert Fitzmartin to the Abbey of Cathmais (St. Dogmaels), *circa* 1119, by Henry I, King of England. The first confirmation is signed by Prince William, son of Henry I, who was drowned, together with his sister,[2] on his voyage back from France to England, by the capsizing of the vessel, almost within sight of his father, who was in another vessel leading the way, on November 25th, 1120; his name also appears in the third confirmation. All these confirmations must have been after Robert Fitzmartin's second visit to Tiron,[3] the third containing a mention of the "Abbot then for the first time elected" at the request of Robert Fitzmartin, to the Lord Abbot William, and all the Convent of Tiron, that an Abbot should be appointed to the Priory of . St. Dogmaels. After the appointment of an Abbot, the Priory de Guales naturally was incorporated in the new abbey, built and endowed by Robert. This grant also contains rules for the seemly behaviour of the new abbot, and also for the fitting reception to be accorded to the Lord Abbot of Tiron, on the occasion of his visits to St. Dogmaels Abbey.

The formula or nomination of abbots dependent on the Monastery of Tiron, though of a later date, namely, during the abbacy of the lordly John II of Chartres, about 1277, follows well here, as it comes from the Cartulary of Tiron.

In the Cartulary, fº ii Vº, under the name of John II of Chartres, who was Abbot of Tiron, from 1277 to 1297, is the formula for the nomination of Abbots dependent on the Monastery. "Brother John, by divine permission, lowly Abbot of

Tiron, and the whole convent of the same place, to their beloved sons in Christ to the prior and convent of (such and such a) Monastery greeting and sincere love in God, whereas you by your letters patent announce to us the resignation (or decease) of brother (so-and-so), formerly Abbot of your Monastery, and you have in consequence entreated us to appoint for you a day on which in our Monastery of Tiron provision should be made in the customary way for a pastor for your widowed Monastery, we readily assenting to your request have decided to assign (such and such) a day on which you are to appear at Tiron in the Chapter and at the hour of the Chapter by deputies fixed and appointed and sufficiently instructed, who are to have from you the mandate and the power, viz., to ask for and receive in your stead, and in your name, the one whom we in our Monastery of Tiron in the customary way shall have thought fit to elect. Nevertheless we intimate to you that whether you will send on the appointed day or not we shall proceed to the election of an Abbot of (such and such a) Monastery as we ought. to proceed by right and in accordance with approved custom."

In Vol. II, p. 60, CCXCI, of the Cartulary of Tiron, there is a confirmation by Pope Eugene III of the possessions of the Abbey of Tiron to William, Abbot of Tiron, and amongst them is mentioned the Church of St. Mary of Cathmais (St. Dogmaels), with all its appurtenances, dated 1147, 30 May. Given at Paris.

Also Vol. II, p. 98, CCCXXVI, dated 1175-1176, is a confirmation of Pope Alexander II to Stephen, Abbot of Tiron.

And, again, p. 103, CCCXXVIII, dated August 23rd, 1179, there is a confirmation by Pope Alexander II of the possessions and the privileges of the Abbey of Tiron to William, Abbot of Tiron, and first among these possessions is "the Monastery of Chamais" (Cemaes St. Dogmaels). There is also another bull of Pope Alexander II to the same effect.

Also Vol. I, p. 201, CLXXXII, dated 1232-3, March 16th, one finds a confirmation by Pope Innocent II to William, Abbot of Tiron, of the possessions of the Abbey as follows:—" In the kingdom of England Diocese of St. David's the church of St. Mary's of Cathmais (St. Dogmaels) with all its appurtenances. Given at Valence."

Vol. II, p. 264, one finds the Abbey of Cathmais Cemaes (St. Dogmaels) was founded in 1118, in the County of Pembroke, in the diocese of St. David's (England). It was formerly a priory under the name of the Priory de Guales.

Vol. II, p. 235, in a list of abbeys and priories belonging to the Abbey of Tiron, the Abbey of the Blessed Mary of Cathmais (St. Dogmaels), and again in the same list, on p. 236, Abbey of St. Dogmaels, in the English diocese of St. David's, Wales, dated 1516.

We also find under the heading of St. David's, Cathmais (Santa Maria de) in the County of Pembroke. First a priory under the name of the Priory de Guales, raised to an Abbey in 1118, the grant of Robert, son of Martin, confirmed by Henry I, King of England, etc.

This proves that St. Dogmaels owned allegiance to Tiron till 1516, so that it is safe to believe she remained with her cells under Tiron to the dissolution.

CHAPTER IV.

GIFTS FLOW IN.

TO return to St. Dogmaels Abbey, after giving this brief account of the Mother Abbey of Tiron, and the grants made to it by its founder, Robert Fitzmartin, Lord of Cemaes, eldest son of Martin of the Towers, and of Geva, his wife, together with the confirmation of those grants. The original grants of Robert and his father were in all probability destroyed at the dissolution of the monasteries; but fortunately Henry I and succeeding Kings of England had a custom of incorporating previous grants in their confirmations, having their predecessors' grants and confirmations placed before them, and causing them to be copied in full, re-confirming them, and sealing them with their seals, at the same time stating that the original documents, or parchments, lay before them, and having their seals witnessed.

In this way a record happily remains of one of the grants of Robert FitzMartin, and a confirmation by him of his parent's gifts to the Monastery, also the confirmation of the grants by Henry I.

In the first document yet found, which unfortunately bears no date, but which is certainly not later than 1113, Robert confirms the bestowal by his parents of lands in Devonshire as follows : —

Robert son of Martin to all the sons of holy church, and all your men. French English and Welsh. Let all men know that I grant to the church of St. Mary of Cemaes [that is St. Dogmaels] the church of Tregent, the church of Wadtre and the chapel of Cockington with land and other priviledges. This I have done for the good of the souls of my parents, who have in former times made these gifts. I confirm these same by my charter Farewell.

In this confirmation, of the previous charter of Martin, by Robert Fitzmartin, there is one point that should not be lost sight of, which is, that his parents had given these three churches and chapel to St. Dogmaels, and he emphasizes this when he adds, "This I have done for the good of my parents' souls, who in times past made these gifts." He never adds his own soul, thereby inferring that the gifts were none of his, but were his parents' gifts solely, and merely confirmed by him.

Tregent cannot now be identified with certainty, unless it should be the East Brent of to-day. This parish adjoins Rattery, mentioned in later charters as Rattre; neither can Wadtre be identified unless it should be Rattre. These places, however, with the exception of Rattre, passed away from the possession of the Abbey at quite an early date, for in the Taxatio of Pope Nicholas, 1291, the Chapel of Cockington belonged to Tor Abbey, and East Brent to Buckfastleigh Abbey. The next charters after this are a confirmation by Henry I reciting the gifts of Robert Fitzmartin, and the charters taken from the Cartulary of Tiron; in reviewing these it may be taken as an established fact that the Abbey was endowed and established in 1118, but that the Priory de Guales was an earlier incorporation of the old Religious House of St. Dogmaels, with the addition of the thirteen monks brought over by Robert from Tiron in 1113, and the endowment of this priory by Robert's parents, with the revenues derived from the three churches and chapel, and land in Devonshire, between 1089 and 1113.

There seems no possibility of fixing the exact date of this endowment; if Martin died in 1089, it might have been a death-bed grant of his, or Martin may have endowed the old religious house of St. Dogmael, to which Robert later brought the first thirteen monks.

The first visit of Robert to Tiron is mentioned in the Cartulary of that Abbey as taking place in 1113; a corroboration of this visit is found in the Preface to the "Calendar of Documents,"[1] France, of which the following is a translation :—

At the same time a certain Robert of most noble birth approached a holy man[2] beyond the seas and taking with him thirteen of his disciples passed through Norman and English territories and reaching the furthest limits of the land of Wales on the coast of the Irish Sea close to the river Teify he established first indeed a cell but afterwards with an equal number of Monks together with an Abbot at their request as we have mentioned he established a Monastery fitted with all appurtenances.

One very important point in the confirmation of the first grant (No. 25) relating to St. Dogmaels is that Prince William Henry's son " doth also make

---

[1] By J. H. Round, p. xxxv.   [2] Doubtless this holy man was St. Bernard, Abbot of Tiron.

this grant." Now, William was shipwrecked crossing from France to England, and drowned, together with his sister, November 25th, 1120,[1] therefore it proves conclusively that the confirmation of these grants by Henry I were anterior to that date. The Cartulary fixes the foundation of the Abbey as taking place in 1118, and Henry's confirmation of Robert's grants as being in 1119. The charter No. 31 of the Cartulary, which was posterior in date to No. 25, inasmuch as it is evidently later than the election of the Abbot Fulchardus to St. Dogmaels, refers to the "future election of abbots for that same place of Cemaes," and already shows how soon after Bernard's death they had departed from his rule of poverty and humility, and were striving after dignity and state; for in this charter it is particularly specified that the chief seats in the choir, chapter, and refectory are to be reserved for the Abbot of Tiron when he visits St. Dogmaels, and also that the Abbot of St. Dogmaels shall himself prepare a reception for him worthy of his dignity. This charter also mentions Prince William, so that it is earlier in date than November, 1120.

XXV.

Cartulary of the Abbey of the Holy Trinity of Tiron Vol. I. p. 41. Confimation to the Abbey of Cathmais (St. Dogmaels) of the grants made by Robert Fitzmartin. (Circa 1119).

Henry King of England to the Abbot and all the convent of Tiron greeting.

I grant to God and to the blessed Mary and to the Abbey of Cemaes the lands and all things which Robert Fitzmartin has given or will hereafter give to the aforesaid Abbey. And let the same Abbey be free and undisturbed as I have allowed if to be free and undisturbed as long as it has been a religious house.

Witness—William de Albineio a Briton at St. Walburga.

And know ye that my son William[2] doth also make this grant. Witness—Other[3] son of a count.

XXVI.

Confirmation of the grants made by Robert Fitzmartin in Wales.

Grant of the King of England concerning Wales (c. 1119). Henry King of England to the archbishops and bishops and all the barons and to his subjects throughout all England and especially to those who dwell in wales greeting.

I grant to God and the Monks of Tiron for my souls sake and that of my wife and of my offspring as well as of my father and my mother and my ancestors that

---

[1] Also Abbot Geoffrey succeeded Abbot William in 1120.

[2] Prince William, son of Henry I, was shipwrecked whilst crossing from France to England, November 25th, 1120.

[3] Other, son of a Count, was tutor to Prince William.

gift and alms for a perpetual possession which Robert Fitzmartin for his soul's sake granted of his right to the same Monks in Wales.

Witnesses—Ranulf chancellor and Geoffrey son of Paganus and William Puerello-Cloure and Hugh de Montfort[1] and William de Rollo.[2] At Moritonium.

XXXI.

Confirmation of the Abbey of Cathmais (St. Dogmaels). Concerning Cathmais (c. 1120).

Since of necessity all things temporal soon pass into oblivion it has pleased us to make known to all present as well as future that the Monastery of Wales in the Bishopric of St. David's in the district of Cemaes near the ancient religious house of St. Dogmaels not far from the channel of the river Teivy formerly established in honour of Mary the Mother of God is a religious house of the Monks of the Holy Saviour of Tiron many brethren abiding there under their prior but because Robert Fitzmartin who at that time under Henry most good King of England held dominion over that land for the honour and glory of the holy church made a request of the Lord Abbot William and all the Convent of Tiron that an Abbot should be appointed in the priory of the aforesaid place God willing his request was granted. The King himself moreover and his son William and the aforesaid Robert granted that the same Abbey of St. Mary's of Cemaes should at all times be free in such a way that nothing could be established in it by any secular power viz. neither by the King himself nor by his princes nor by his or their successors. The King himself also granted and William his son and the aforesaid Robert and the Abbot then for the first time elected in the aforesaid place of Wales and his Monks that every future election of Abbots for that same place of Cemaes and for all places adjoining that same place if perchance they too should establish Abbeys should by right forever be in the province and the power of the Lord Abbot of Tiron and of the whole Convent as witness William de Albignero and Other[3] son of a count at St. Walburga. If indeed any Abbot whatsoever of the oft-mentioned place of St. Mary's of Cemaes or of other places subject to the same governs himself and his men otherwise than he ought to in an unseemly or irreligious manner—which God forbid—or departs from our rule of humility or our other religious observances by the rod and power of the pastoral rule of the church of Tiron he must be removed and another who is worthy must be set in his stead. Heed must be taken however how some in one way or another even while making grants blinded by greedy desire run the risk of the charge of simony whoever does so let him as is right be anathema from Christ. Next to the bond of love and the unity of the brotherhood, which neither space nor distance of time ought to separate provision is made that when any one of the Abbots of the above-mentioned church of

---

[1] Hugh de Montfort belonged to the family of Montfort sur Risle.

[2] William de Roullours (Rollo) was father of Richard, celebrated for his agricultural achievements in the Lordship of Bourne and Deeping, co. Lincoln, where he drained the vast marshes of Deeping, and succeeded so well that he formed a wealthy parish.

[3] Other, the son of a count, was according to Orderic, tutor to Prince William.

the Blessed Mary of Cemaes has been chosen and appointed by the Lord Abbot and the whole Convent of Tiron then to the mother church of God the Saviour at Tiron in the presence of the Abbot who is at that time its head and of the whole Convent of Tiron to the same church of Tiron and to its rulers he the newly elected Abbot and his Monks who are at that time present shall in the presence of God promise obedience and due subjection. Moreover when the Lord Abbot of Tiron comes to the oft-mentioned place of St. Mary's of Cemaes or to any place soever subject to it as is fitting let him be received with due honour and let the Abbot himself of that place prepare a reception for him worthy of his dignity forsooth in the choir in the chapter and in the refectory and everywhere let the reverence due to a father be shown him as saith the Apostle " Honour to whom honour is due " and likewise " excelling one another in honour." Whatever temporal things are lacking to our monastery let them be sought for from others. And of spiritual benefits as well for the living as for their own brethren let charity shine forth according as the difference is great. Further it is decreed and settled by the Lord Abbot William and all the congregation of Tiron that the Abbots subject to the church of Tiron who are and will be in regions beyond the seas shall always every third year for the sake of strengthening and confirming our religion and of visiting the brethren assemble at the Convent of Tiron at the feast of holy Pentecost. And if any of the brethren disobediently fails to fulfil these conditions he must by no means be admitted any where else as associate without letters of recommendation. Let this likewise be known to the sons of holy church that the church of Tiron has this privilege from the holy and apostolic church of Rome that whoever wishes in any matter and for whatever cause to injure it is excommunicated by the Pope himself the pastor and ruler of all blessed Christendom who in especial instead of the apostles has received the power of binding and loosening in the blessed church to those however who support and increase that same patrimony of Christ blessing and peace from the Lord Jesus Christ who though he was rich for us became poor that he might enrich us through his poverty and might heal us through his infirmity. These things indeed were done in the year of the incarnation of the Lord 1120 in the reign of Louis King of France and of Henry King of England.

PREFACE TO CAL. OF FRANCE.

J. H. ROUND.

The three Charters [from the Cartulary of Tiron] relating to St. Dogmaels are not only new but are all earlier than the Charter given in the Monasticon, as the history of its foundation is admittedly obscure, they are valuable especially for the light they throw on the conversion of a Priory into this Abbey, which had been, we find, effected before the King's return to England at the close of 1120. It should be noted that one of the King's Charters is separately confirmed by his son, whose act is witnessed by Other " Fitz Count," who perished with him in the White Ship— his tutor. The Monasticon Charter cannot be earlier than 1121, being witnessed by Queen Adeleya, but as it was granted when the first Abbot was blessed by the Bishop of St. Davids, it not improbably belongs to the King's visit to Wales in that year,[1] in which case we could say that he was in the Pembroke district, September 11, 11..

It has been suggested that the original founder of the Abbey's Welsh house, was the father of Robert Fitzmartin. Of this father nothing is really known. The Editor would suggest that his name was not "Martin de Tours," as is always stated, but that we may detect him in "Martinus de Wales," the first witness to the foundation Charter of Totnes Priory.[2] This would carry back to a very early date his settlement in Wales. But the narrative quoted above is conclusive as to Robert's claims.

The charter of 18 Edward III has been selected for the confirmation of Henry I charter, and the recital of Robert Fitzmartin's gifts, wherein he mentions the monastery established by him " in my land of Guales " and the ancient Church of St. Dogmaels. The boundaries are also given of the land granted by Robert to the Abbey. It is bounded by the river Teify, and the sea on the north, north-east, and west. On the east by the stream called the Bryan, which river in old maps is represented under the name of Braian, and as flowing into the river Teify near the " Forest " quarries, and from that river stretching south of certain farms belonging to Martin's followers, namely, Robert of Languedoc, Roger of Mathone, to the boundaries of Hugo, surnamed Gualensis, and as far as the river, which divides his land from Llanbloden Manor. Also in the Presely Mountains, from the land of Hubert de Vaux to Cwm Carw (or Cerwyn) and from thence to the source of the river Cleddau.

Also his mother, Geva, granted to the monastery the Island of Caldey, which had been given to Robert by Henry I, who in his turn had granted it to his mother, whereon had stood an ancient religious house. This Island of Caldey was granted with all rights of fishing, milling, wood, and of the chase. Also in England Robert granted Rattre, in Devonshire, with all its appurtenances. Possibly this Rattre is the same as the Wadtre of the former grant.

This confirmation also states that William Lord Abbot of Tiron came to St. Dogmaels for the installation of Fulchardus, as Abbot; Bernard Bishop of St. David's was also present, and both, amongst others, signed the original charter. This confirmation of Edward III was in its turn signed, amongst others, by Gilbert de Clare, who had married one of Edward III's daughters, and the Bishop of St. David's, in 1290.

Moylgrove, so named from Matilda's (Welsh Mallt) Grove, belonged to the Abbey at the dissolution, and, with Llantood, still belongs to St. Dogmaels. It is stated to have been part of the dowry of Matilda, the daughter of William Peverel, and wife of Robert Fitzmartin, and was so-called by the Normans

---

[1] Sym Dun II, 263, 4.   [2] 3/MS. 5446, f. 269.

because it was Matilda's favourite place for walking. It was given to the Monastery by her; it may have been in a later grant than the one of 1118, now lost, as it is mentioned in subsequent deeds.

By Matilda urging Robert to make gifts to the Abbey, it is natural to believe that she also made some gift, as her mother-in-law, Geva, had done.

Moylgrove will be heard of again in a later chapter[1] under its Welsh name of Trewyddal, the Irish hamlet, or village, in the argument as to the meaning of " Guales." The grove at Moylgrove, or Trewyddal, was stated to have been two hundred acres in extent.

CHARTER R (76) 18 Edw. 3[2] m. 13, No. 47.

In the name of the holy and indivisable Trinity I Henry King of England and Duke of Normandy for the redemption of my soul and souls of my predecessors have granted to the Monks of Tiron my wife Adelaide also concurring whatever grants Robert son of Martin has given or shall give to the same Monks to be an undisturbed possession for ever as is written below in the parchment now before me.

I Robert son of Martin thinking of reward in heaven with the consent or rather at the suggestion of my wife Matilda for the glory of Holy Church in my land of Guales commiserating the poverty of the Monks of Tiron established a Monastery in honour of the Holy Mother of God the ever Virgin Mary for the religious brethren there abiding I have obtained an Abbot from the Lord Abbot William and all the convent of Tiron with God's help at length after many entreaties desiring to meet their needs as far as the extent of my resources allowed Henry the illustrious King of England urging and likewise confirming what grants I have made and shall make to the Abbot and his Monks and their successors to be an undisturbed possession forever I have effected that in the same Abbey nothing can be set up by any secular power contrary to canonical authority viz. neither by the King himself nor by any prince of his soever nor by any of their successors I have given to them the ancient church of St. Dogmael with possession of the land adjacent to the same church whose name is Landodog in the Province of Cemaes by the bank of the river Teify. I have also given them all the land situated on the confines of the same aforesaid church and place which at that time I used to hold under my sway whose boundaries are as follows. From a certain river whose name is Braian[3] which in those parts divides between [4] Emlyn and Cemaes as it descends to the next river the Teify and thence as the same river flows into the nearest sea. Likewise the land from the same aforesaid river towards the south as far as the land of Robert of Languedoch and thence along the land of Roger of Mathone towards the west until one reaches the land of William son of Roger and thence as far as the boundaries of Hugo with the surname[5] Gualensis

---

[1] Chapter VI.

[2] I have also a copy of Edward I and Edward II Charters. They are identically the same.

[3] The Braian falls into the Teify west of Cilgerran Church. Does it take its name from the de Brians?

[4] The old hundred of Emlyn is now half in Carmarthenshire, half in Pembrokeshire, the Pembrokeshire half being now called the hundred of Cilgerran.

[5] A division of Pembroke called Guales in the "Mabinogion," Galles in the "Cartularie de Tiron," and Walenses in G. Owen's "Pembrokeshire."

Salmon fishing from Coracles on the River Teify.

(The salmon net is between each pair of Coracles)

viz. as far as the river which divides his land and Lanbloden manor which belongs to them. All that land accordingly which lies within these boundaries as well cleared as covert with the trees belongs to the Monks. I have also given them one of my knights by name Alen with his land which also lies within the aforesaid boundaries and also in the mountain districts the district named Breselech[1] from the land of Hubert de Vaux as far as the source of a certain brook which is called Comb. Karo[2] and thence until it flows into a river whose name is Cledi[3] and thence towards the source of the same Cledi until it reaches a fair-sized brook which descends from the summit of the mountain on the right and thence along the summit of the same mountain as it extends lengthwise until one again reaches the land of Hubert de Vaux I to the aforesaid Monastery have granted. Whosoever indeed of my men for the remission of his sins shall have made grants of their land to the same Monastery—those grants I altogether allow. Likewise to the same Monks my mother has granted the island of Pyr which is now called by another name Caldey which granted to me by my lord the King I had granted to my mother and this grant I willingly confirm. I have granted them also in addition that wherever in my own woods my swine are fed their swine may also pasture and that they may take without let or hindrance from thence for themselves whatever timber they may wish for building purposes. I have likewise given them the fishery of St. Dogmaels and have granted them all the waters as far as their land extends to use for milling or seine-fishing or any other fisheries or for whatever other purpose they can practise or devise. I have also given them of all the stags or hinds taken in my chase all the skins except those which belong to the hunters. And in England I have given them a certain manor named Ratreu[4] with all its appurtenancies. Accordingly although I may have made these grants at different times nevertheless at the ordination of the Abbot this donation was solemnly made on the day when the first Abbot of the same place Fulchardus by name was enthroned in his seat by the lord Bernard Bishop of the Church of St. Davids with the consent of the same Bishop whatever of my tithes I had given to the same Abbot as well of produce as of animals whether of sheep or of foals or of calves or of any cattle soever of which a tithe ought to be rendered of wool of cheese and butter in Guales. These were accordingly given on the 10th of September in the presence as witnesses of the same of Bishop Bernard and William lord Abbot of Tiron and also Richard son of G(osner?) and Humphrey son of Gosmer[5] and Stephen Dapifer the King's Steward of Richard Alfred de Bennevilla[6] the same attesting this Charter.

SEAL   SEAL

of   of

HENRY + King.   ADELAIDE + Queen.

of   of   of

+

Seal + ROBERT.   Seal + Bishop BERNARD.   Seal + MATHILDA.   Seal + RICHARD

+   son of G.

+ of STEPHEN + of ALFRED + of HUMPHREY.

---

[1] Presely.   [2] Cwm Carw.   [3] Cleddau.   [4] Rattre, Devon.

[3] See G. Owen's "Pembrokeshire," p. 363, Godfrey.   [6] ? Alfred of Bayvil.

We accordingly ratifying the aforesaid donations and grants on behalf of ourselves and our heirs as far as in us lies allow and confirming them as duly witnessed in the aforesaid Charter. As witnesses whereof the venerable fathers R. Bath and Wells A. Durham J. Winchester and Thomas Bishop of St. Davids. Edmund our brother. William de Valence our uncle. Gilbert de Clare Earl of Gloucester and Hertford. John de Warrener Earl of Surrey. Humphrey de Bohm Earl of Hereford and Essex. Peter de Champnent. Richard de Wood and others. Given under our hand at Westminster the 16th day of June [1290].

The further ratification of this grant by Kings Richard II Henry IV and Henry V as follows.

And we the gifts grants and confirmations aforesaid being ratified the same for us and our heirs as far as in us lies to our beloved in Christ the Abbot and Convent of St. Dogmaels the Monks of Tiron and their successors have granted and confirmed as the aforesaid Charters reasonably witness as they and their predecessors the aforesaid lands and tenements have hitherto held and the liberties aforesaid have reasonably used and enjoyed. These being witnesses the venerable fathers W Archbishop of York primate of England our Treasurer J bp of Winchester our Chancellor W bp of Norwich John of Eltham Earl of Cornwall our beloved brother John de Warrenne Earl of Surrey Thomas Wake Ralph de Nevill Steward of our Household and others. Given by our hand at Langele the 3rd Feb. the 5th year of our reign. And we the gifts grants and confirmations aforesaid and all and singular in the Charter aforesaid contained being ratified the same for us and our heirs as far as in us lies we have accepted and approved and to our beloved in Christ the now Abbot and Convent of the place aforesaid have granted and confirmed as the Charter aforesaid reasonably witnesses and as they and their predecessors the lands and tenements aforesaid have hitherto held and the liberties aforesaid have been wont to use and enjoy. In witness whereof these our letters patent we have caused to be made. Witness myself at Westminster the[1] 2nd June the 20th year of our reign. And we the gifts grants and confirmations aforesaid and all other and singular in these aforesaid Charters contained being ratified the same for us and our heirs as far as in us lies we accept approve and to our beloved in Christ the now Abbot and Convent of aforesaid place we grant and confirm as the letters aforesaid reasonably witness and as they and their predecessors hitherto had and held and the liberties aforesaid have been wont to use and enjoy. In witness whereof these our letters patent we have caused to be made. Witness myself at Westminster the [2] 1st July the 7th year of our reign. And we the gifts grants and confirmations aforesaid and all and singular in the Charters and letters aforesaid contained being ratified the same for us and our heirs as far as in us lies we accept approve and to our beloved in Christ the now Abbot and Convent of the place aforesaid and their successors by tenor of these presents we have granted and confirmed as the Charters and letters aforesaid reasonably witness and as they and their predecessors the lands and tenements aforesaid have hitherto had and held and the liberties aforesaid have been wont to use and enjoy. In witness whereof we have caused to be made these our letters patent. Witness

---

[1] 20 R. 2.   [2] 7 H. 4.

myself at Westminster the 2nd April[1] the fourth year of our reign. And we the letters aforesaid of such liberties and customs not revoking by the advice and consent of the lords spiritual and temporal in our Parliament held at Westminster the 1st year of our reign accept approve ratify and to the now Abbot and Convent of aforesaid place and his successors confirm as the letters aforesaid reasonably witness and as the said Abbot and Convent the liberties and customs aforesaid ought to use and enjoy and as they and their predecessors the aforesaid liberties and customs have always hitherto been wont to use and enjoy. In witness etc. Humphrey Duke of Gloucester Keeper of England at Westminster the 6th day of July.

By the King himself and Council in Parliament.

In a confirmation of a grant by Richard II of a grant made by Nicholas, son of Martin, Richard states that he had viewed the original confirmatory charter of Nicholas Fitzmartin, wherein William, son and heir of Jordan de Cantington (near Eglwyswrw), granted the land of Fishguard to the Abbey of St. Dogmaels; this land remained in the possession of the Abbey to the end, and afterwards passed with St. Dogmaels into the hands of Mr. Bradshaw.

In this grant the land given lay on both sides of the river Gwaine, and also extended to the sea.

Nicholas herein speaks well of the hospitality and manner of life led by the monks at that time, and also comments on their *poverty*; so that in all probability this grant was made shortly after the pillaging of the Abbey by the Irish under the four Welsh princes in 1138, of which we read in the "Annales Cambriae," when Anaraud, Cadell, Owain, and Cadwaladr, with fifteen ships full of men (most probably Irish) came to Aberteivi (Cardigan) at Martinmas, 1138, and made great slaughter all the way (up the river). These people also pillaged the town and Church of Llandudoch (which is St. Dogmaels), and carried off exceeding great booty to their ships.

Naturally, after this, for a time at least, the monks would be poor.

It is clearly indicated that this grant of William de Cantington, grandson of Lucas de Hoda,[2] was made during the life of Robert Martin, inasmuch as both Robert and William Martin are among the witnesses. This would prove that this Nicholas whose confirmation Richard had before him was Robert's brother and Martin's son, and not "the Nicholas, Lord of Cemaes, and son of Martin" as he styles himself, though sixth in descent from Martin. This Nicholas Martin of the grant does not claim to be Lord of Cemaes.

Moreover, immediately after 1138 the monks were undoubtedly poor, having just been pillaged by the Irish, whereas in the time of Nicholas, Lord of Cemaes, the Monastery was nearing the zenith of its prosperity.

---

[1] 4. H. 5.   [2] One of Martin's followers.

4

Jordan, the first de Cantington, was one of Lucas de Hoda's sons, so would certainly be a contemporary of Robert, and Jordan's son, William, would certainly be living at the same time as Robert Martin and his son William. Also Philip de Stackpool, another of the witnesses, was a contemporary of Robert and William Martin, so that the date of this charter may certainly be fixed as soon after 1138. In 1188 we know the Monastery had again become prosperous.

According to Fenton, Fishguard was settled by some of Martin's followers under Jordan, son of Lucas de Hoda, who later on lived near Eglwyswrw. It is clear that he possessed Fishguard, for his son, William, granted land on both sides the river Gwayne[1] to the Abbey of St. Dogmaels.

The names of Jordan and his brother Richard are still preserved in the names of farms in North Pembrokeshire, as Tre Wrdan (Jordan's home) Tre Wrdan Uchaf, Tre Wrdan Isaf (upper and lower homes of Jordan), Rhos Wrdan (Jordan's Moor), all adjoining. The next farm to Rhos Wrdan is Trereikart (Richard's home), whilst another farm bears the name of Tre[rei]cart. Both they and their sons were naturally followers of the Martins, as their father had been, and Jordan and Richard, or their descendants, signed several of the charters of the Martins, copies of which are printed in the Baronia de Kemes, though most of these charters refer to the Barony and not to the Abbey.

In the Charter Roll No. 3 is an Inspeximus (" we have viewed.")
CHARTER R. (76) 18 Edw. III No. 3.

On behalf of the Abbot and Monks of St. Dogmaels of Cemaes.*
The King to the Archbishops greeting we have examined the confirmatory Charter which Robert son of Martin made to the Monastery (margin and the Abbot and Monks of the same place) of St. Mary and St. Dogmaels in Cemaes . . . .* with donation and grant of the land of Fishguard in these words. To all of the church of St. Mat(thew ?)'s to whom the present writing may come. Nicholas son of Martin sends greeting in the Lord . . . .* Jordan son and heir of the Lord William of Cantington which he made to the Monastery of St. Mary and St. Dogmael in Cemaes and to the Abbot and to the Monks of the same place granted above . . . . in these words. Let all present and future know that I William of Cantington son and heir of Jordan of Cantington etc.

Leaf Charter R. 76. 18 Edw. I. No. 47 missing.
PATENT ROLL (346) 20 Ric. 2 p. 3. m. 12. (1396-7).

We have viewed the confirmatory charter which Nicholas son of Martin made to the monastery of St. Mary and St. Dogmael in Cemaes and to the abbot and monks

---

[1] The Welsh name is Abergwayne.
* All to be seen (well written) in Pat. R. 20, R. 3, p. 3, m. 12, 346.

of the same place concerning the gift and grant of the land of Fishguard in these words. To all the sons of holy church to whom the present writing comes Nicholas son of Martin sends greeting in the Lord. The charter of William of Cantiton[1] son and heir of Jordan of Cantiton which he made to the monastery of St. Mary and St. Dogmael in Cemaes and to the Abbot and Monks of the same place concerning the gift and grant of the land of Fishguard we have viewed in these words. Let all present and future know that I William of Cantiton son and heir of Jordan of Cantington on behalf of myself and my heirs have given granted and by this my present charter confirmed for God's sake and for the sake of my soul and of the souls of my predecessors and successors as a free and perpetual alms to God and to the monastery of St. Mary and St. Dogmael in Cemaes and to the monks serving God and St. Mary and St. Dogmael in that place forever all my land of Fishguard on both sides of the river Gwain with all its appurtenances and with all my rights which I hold or shall hold in the aforesaid land of Fishguard to have and to hold forever all the said land with all its appurtenances to God and to the monastery of St. Mary and St. Dogmael in Cemaes and to the monks who forever there serve God and the Blessed Mary and St. Dogmael as a pure and perpetual gift in woods and plains in roads and paths in meadows and pastures in land arable and not arable in waters mills fisheries fishponds in common of pasture in harbours in the sea with all liberties and free customs of the said land within and without forever actually or possibly appertaining to it so that the said land or other land can be given or held better and more freely and more fully as a pure and free and perpetual gift. And I the said William and my heirs will warrantise all the said land of Fishguard in Cemaes with all its appurtenances in the aforesaid form to God and to the monks of the said monastery who there serve St. Mary and St. Dogmael against all mortal men forever. And that my gift grant and confirmation and warrantisation of my present charter may remain forever firm and valid I strengthen the present charter with the impress of my seal. As witnesses whereof the lord William of Bolevill then seneschal of Pembroke Tankard of the Household then sheriff Robert of Crippinges then constable lords David de Barry David de Wydeurze Philip (?) of Stakepol John of Castlemartin John de Buffeto Knights Roger de Mortimer Gilbert de Roche William de Canvill William son of Maurice Walter Malensant Herbert St. Leger John de Castro and others.

These accordingly having been carefully inspected and (solemnly and piously considered) I Nicholas son of Martin having heed to the honourable manner of life and hospitality of the aforesaid monks and no less to the *poverty* of the said monastery for the sake of my soul and of my predecessors and successors all things which by the aforesaid William of Cantington have been conferred upon the aforesaid monks and their successors and upon the aforesaid monastery in lands and liberties which I and my heirs can rightly give and confirm I grant and by my present charter confirm and will to be held forever firm valid and undisturbed and to be preserved without any gainsaying or diminution on any pretext or annoyance firmly and faithfully by me and all my heirs and assigns. And so that none of my heirs or assigns may go counter to this my grant and confirmation or in any thing contradict

[1] This was a manor in Eglwyswrw belonging to the Cantingtons, Jordan being a son of Lucas de Hoda.

it I have strengthened the present charter with the impress of my seal. In witness whereof Lords Stephen of Edesworth then seneschal of Pembroke *William Martin* Guy de Brian Robert de Vaur William de Kannvill *John of Castlemartin Robert Martin* Gilbert de Roche Knights John of Sherburn then Sheriff of Pembroke Roger de Mortimer *Robert Martin of Cemaes* Eynon son of William Llewelyn Goch then constable of Kemmeys and others.

We accordingly ratifying and approving the aforesaid gift grant and confirmation on behalf of ourselves and our heirs as far as in us lies grant and confirm them in so far as the aforesaid charter reasonably testifieth. In witness whereof the venerable father R. of Bath and Wells Bishop our Chancellor William de Valence our uncle Henry de Lacy Earl of Lincoln Humphrey de Bohun Earl of Hereford and Essex Robert de Tybbot Walter Beauchamp Richard de Wood and others. Given under our hand at King's Clifton[1] on the sixth day of November in the eighteenth year of our reign. We accordingly etc. Given under our hand at Langley on the third day of February in the fifth year of our reign. We accordingly etc. As witness the King at Westminster on the second day of June.

In return for 50 shillings paid into the Kings Treasury.

Pat. 14 Edw. 2 pt. 1 m. 13.   Printed Col. page 513.

It is not surprising that the monks complained, as they did, of great poverty, in the ancient petitions, and begged the king to permit that Elena Brazon, of Cardigan, may be allowed to help them to the extent of eleven shillings, referring to their having been pillaged of late, as seen in the following:—

ANCIENT PETITIONS.
No. 6880.

To our Lord the King and his Council the Abbot and Convent of St. Dogmaels in Wales shew that as they have been often pillaged of late and are living in great poverty through the war which has been in their country they pray the King for love of God and for the soul of the Queen that they may have help from a lady who wishes to advance them by a rent of eleven shillings in the town of Cardigan if the goodwill of the King will allow it which they pray the King that he will allow and confirm the deed of the lady if it pleases him.

Elena Brazon who was the wife of Henry Brazon.

Following on this, in the Harleian MSS., is the confirmation by Bishop Bernard, of St. David's, who died 1147, of the grant of Lisprant, by Hugh de Fossar, to the Abbey of St. Dogmaels, with the exception of half the mill, the mill dwelling-house, and a bovate of land. However, a century and a-half later we find the Manor of Lisprant was given to Llawhaden. This deed was witnessed by Hubert Abbot of St. Dogmaels, possibly successor to Fulchardus,

[1] Chepstow.

and what is singular, by three Canons of St. David's, all rejoicing in the name of John, one being dignified as Master John, the second having nothing but John by which to know him, the third was more fortunate, being known as John of Osterlof.

In 9 Edward I we find the king writing to Bourgo de Neville regarding the Manor of St. Dogmaels, about the possession of which there was evidently some dispute.

HARLEIAN MSS. 1249, f. 109 b.

Bernard by the grace of God Bishop of St. David's to all his faithful parishioners cleric as well as lay present and future the spirit of truth is not extinguished but of its own grace it grows through all things more abundantly let all of you know and understand that we in common council and with the assent of our church and of our faithful ones at the request also and with the consent of Hugh de Forsar have granted and given to the church of St. Mary's of the abbey of Cemaes and the brethren who there serve and will serve the Lord all the land Lispranst with the church saving however all episcopal custom to be held by right in perpetual alms for the soul of Henry the King and Matilda the Queen and their sons and all our ancestors and for our soul in that full liberty with which St. David holds his other lands with the exception of half the emoluments of the mill if they shall use the same and half the fish there caught the dwelling-place also connected with the mill being retained for us together with an ox-plough of land to remain in the common service of the mill if indeed it can be done let the brethren have the lordship of the mill quit all the rest of the emoluments to be reserved for us. Besides we have provided that it ought to be set down to pure charity that between us and Hugo it was so arranged that he appointed none except our church to be the heirs of his land which inheritance we assign to the aforesaid church and the profits of the same to be held uninterruptedly and the contents of this page we fortify and strengthen with the authority also of God and of our church. To all moreover who confirm and support this our gift we wish all happiness and grace but all who contradict or in anyway gainsay let their souls be driven to destruction by the scourge of eternal damnation. As witness Jordan Archdeacon and Master John and John together with John of Osterlof canons Augustine prior Walter chaplain and the laymen Jordan the steward Stephen the steward Abbot Hubert Edgar Hubert nephew of the bishop and many others besides.

ORIGINALIA. 9 Edw. I, m. 10.

The King to his beloved and faithful Burgo de Neville his Justicia in West Wales greeting. Concerning the agreement and will of our beloved and faithful Robert del Val we command you that the manor of St. Dogmaels with its appurtenances which recently at our command you took into our power and to which the aforesaid Robert says that he has a right you are to deliver to Master Thomas Beke to hold at our will so that of the revenues thence arising he is to render us account whenever we wish to have it. You are to deliver also to the same Thomas the other lands and tenements which likewise at our command you took into our power in the

manors of Loghaden[1] and Landfey[2] on the occasion of the death lately of the Bishop
of St. David's to hold at our will. So that of the revenues thence arising he is
to render us account in the manner aforesaid at our command As witness whereof
the King at Westminster the 6 day of June [1281].

ORIGINALIA. 9 Ed. I, m. 13.

It is commanded Bogo de Knovill the King's Justice in West Wales that he shall
deliver to Master Thomas Bek the manor of St. Dogmaels with appurtenances
and other lands of Loghaeden and Landsey by reason of the death of the Bp. of
St. Davids.

Dugdale commences by calling St. Dogmaels a priory in the County of
Pembroke, a cell of the Monastery of Tiron; but continues by calling it an
abbey of the order of *St. Martin of Tours*, declared to be of the order of St.
Benedict. Speed falls into the same error, both evidently confounding the
knight and the saint. Dugdale also adds that—

"Flood, precentor of the church of St. Davids told him, that Martin of the
Towers, the first among the Normans who acquired Cemaes by war, and who founded
the Monastery, and was buried in the middle of the choir," together, as we find
elsewhere, with his wife and son Robert.

Leland is equally erroneous in his statements.

John Stevens, who compiled the "History of Abbeys and Monasteries, etc.,"
in 1733, is correct, he evidently having taken the trouble to read the charters,
whereas it is simply impossible that Dugdale could have read the charter he
gives of Henry I, for if he had, he would not have made so many gross
mistakes. Stephens adds that in Royal Charters the monks of Tiron were
always called "The Black Monks of Tiron." On p. 257 of the Appendix in his
second volume, is the following quotation, under the heading of—

"MONASTERIES OF THE ORDER OF TIRON."
ST. DOGMAELS.

Monastery of the Order of Tiron in Pembrokeshire.

"This Monastery is to be found in the Monasticon, Vol. I, p. 454, and in the
English abridgment, p. 55 ; but the little there said of it is confused and erroneous.
In the head or title it is called a cell of Tyron, which it was not properly, but an Abbey
of that congregation or Order. In the next lines it is called an Abbey of St. Martin of
Tours, wherein is a visible error, for having said it was of Tiron, it could not be
of Tours. Leland there quoted is no more to be regarded, where he says this
Monastery was founded by Martin of Tours, whereas the founder was his son Robert."

---

[1] Llawhaden. [2] Lamfrey.

Here Stephens continues to point out that the charter Dugdale gives of Henry I "plainly shows all these mistakes," and that it could not be called a "cell of Tiron," for cells never had abbots, but were only governed by priors. "Besides the monastery is there thrown among the Benedictines, whereas in reality it was of a distinct congregation, or order, the Rule of St. Benedict being indeed the ground of their profession, but having many other observances added to it."

Rymer relates that William Abbot of Tiron was present at the instalment of the first Abbot of St. Dogmaels, but is in error as to date, making it about 1126, and also states that Bernard Bishop of St. David's was present, "who seems to have been of the same order."

Tanner ascribes the commencement of the Monastery to Martin of Tours, and that it was endowed and made an Abbey by his son; it was dedicated to St. Mary, and had a yearly income of 96*l. os. 2d.* gross, and 87*l. 8s. 8d.* net. Leland also erroneously calls St. Dogmael "a priory of Bonhommes."

ANCIENT GATEWAY, ST. DOGMAELS ABBEY.

Photographed by Bishop Mitchinson, Master of Pembroke College, Oxford.

CHAPTER V.

THE MARTINS.

IN the Duchess of Cleveland's Battle Abbey Roll, Martin, or, as his name is spelt in Norman, Marteine, is mentioned, both in Holinshed's Roll, and Duchesne's Roll, as among the knights, who came over with William the Conqueror, and was consequently with him at the Battle of Hastings.

He is also mentioned in Leland's Roll as Martine, though oddly enough he is not mentioned in the list, which is still in existence at Dives, near Caen, in Normandy, and it is from Dives that William the Conqueror is known to have sailed. The Duchess of Cleveland, in the Battle Abbey Roll, calls Martin "Sire de Tour, four miles from Bayeux," in Normandy, and states that "he came over with William of Normandy, in 1066, and conquered the territory of Kemeys, in Pembrokeshire. It was erected into a Palatine Barony, which he governed as Lord Marcher. . . . He was a great benefactor to religious houses, and began the foundation of a Benedictine Abbey[1] at St. Dogmaels, annexing it as a cell to the Monastery of Tirone, in France. The endowment was given by his son, Robert Fitzmartin,[2] whose charter is witnessed by Henry I, who afterwards granted a further confirmation charter. In the next generation William Fitzmartin (Robert's son) married a Welsh princess, the daughter of Rhys ap Gryffydd . . . . from whom he received great injury, for by force of arms he took from him his strong castle of Llanhever (Castell Nevern), in Kemeys Land, contrary to his oath and solemn promise of peace and friendship." William's grandson married Maud, daughter of Guy de Brian[3] and Eva, his wife, daughter of Henry de Tracy, Baron of Barnstaple. William Martin acquired, through her, the honour of Barnstaple and numerous estates in

---

[1] Should be Priory.   [2] Who also built the Abbey.
[3] There were six Guy de Brians in succession.

Teify Fishermen carrying their Coracles.

Devonshire; he also owned a great deal of property in Devonshire, both what had belonged originally to his great-great-grandfather, Martin, from the time of the Conquest, and the lands that had once belonged to William of Fallaise. This William Martin (fifth in descent from Martin) had three sons, Nicholas (Lord of Cemaes), who left an only daughter, Colinetus, and Robert; Colinetus thus became heir to Nicholas, and was father of Sir William, who succeeded to the Barony of Cemaes. He was engaged in the Scottish wars and "constantly summoned to every Parliament as 'Baron of Kemeys' from 17 Edward I to 16 Edward II, in which year he died." His son died the following year without issue, when Cemaes passed through Joan Martin to the Audleys. One of Martin's descendants, in the younger branch, lived, in Queen Mary's time, to be nearly one hundred, and was noted for his charity.

In Chapter II, on the conquest of Cemaes by the Normans, one sees something of the character of Martin, and in Chapter IV how his son, Robert, is described as a man of most noble birth and evidently pious. Let us now consider some of the many acts of Robert, and it will be seen at the same time that he was a man of note and substance both in France and various parts of England, as well as Wales, and also the esteem in which he was held by the number of charters he witnessed in various parts of England.

With regard to the Martins there are several small things that tend to demonstrate their *Norman* origin. Not only is it seen how they are connected with Tiron; but they also contributed largely to the Abbey of Savigny, the Abbey which St. Bernard left when he founded his Abbey of Tiron. In the Cartulary of the Abbey of Savigny is a charter of Robert Fitzmartin, and Matilda, his wife, daughter of William Peverel, granting to the Abbey at Savigny the land of Venions, which had belonged to William Peverel; this land, according to the Cartulary, was granted by Robert and Matilda before 1121.

CARTULARY OF SAVIGNY

In the Archives of La Manche, at St. Lo, France.

Folio 6. Ante 1121.

Charter of Robert son of Martin and Matilda Peverel his wife notifying that they have given to the Abbey of Holy Trinity Savigny the land of William Peverel at Venions as it was held by himself and have placed that gift on the altar for the love of God and the redemption of their souls and those of their relatives.

About ten years later there is a charter of Henry I, King of England, in the "Calendar of Documents," France, about 1130, addressed to the Archbishop of Rouen, etc., confirming this grant of Robert and Matilda of the land of Vengions to Savigny. This Venions, or, as it is called in modern times,

Vengeons, through the "i" of Venions mutating into "g" and making Vengions, whilst in the seventeenth century the "i" changed into "e," hence the present form, Vengeons,[1] is about ten miles distant from Savigny.

CALENDAR OF DOCUMENTS PRESERVED IN FRANCE,
From Documents formerly of the Abbey of Savigny, p. 290.   Circa 1130.

Charter of Henry I addressed to the Archbp. of Rouen and all his officers in Normandy. He grants to the Abbey of the Holy Trinity, Savigny, the gift of the land at Vengeons, which Robert, son of Martin, and Matildis his wife, have given by consent of Count Stephen of Mortain, of whose fee is that land, and of Earl Richard of Chester, of whom *Robert and his wife* held it etc.

Together with the following and fuller confirmation of Henry II : —

P. 299.   A.D. 1157.   Charter of Hen. II granting to the Abbey of Savigny among other things, the land of Veniuns with the mill, multure etc. given by Robert, son of Martin, and Matilda, his wife, by permission of Richard, Earl of Chester, and Stephen, Count of Mortain.

Again, there is a later charter of Richard I, 1198, confirming to the Abbey of Savigny all its possessions in Normandy, including the gifts of Robert Fitzmartin and his wife, Matilda, of the land of Wenion (Vengions, Veniuns, Venions) with the mill, etc., and all its other appurtenances, as follows : —

Charter of Richard I confirming to the Abbey of Savigny all its possessions in Normandy including the gift by Robert son of Martin and Matilda his wife, with consent of Richard Earl of Chester and Stephen Count of Mortain of the land of Wenions with the mill and the multure of the mill and its other appurtenances and taking the Abbey under his protection for the remission of his sins and the redemption of his soul.

The following being witnesses thereof : —Saverinus, Bishop of Bath, Robert Leicester, Baldwin Count of Albimare, William, son of Ralph Seneschal of Normandy, Robert Marmion, Seberius of Quineaco, Geraint, son of Gerald, Thomas Basset, Allen Basset, William of Stannus, Master Roslyn, Joel, the Chaplain, Baldwin, the Chaplain, and many others. Given by the hand of Eustach Bishop of Ely at my Court, the 31st day of July, in the ninth year of our reign, at my house at Caen[2] (1198).

In Symon of Durham's "History of the Acts of Kings of England," p. 236, is the following : —"In the year 1113 the monks of Tiron came to England. . . . . Now the first place that the monks of Tiron came to in Great Britain was St. Dogmaels," as already given in the Cartulary of Tiron; also St.

[1] Mons. Etienne Dupont, Judge of the Civil Court, St. Malo.
[2] Taken from the Cartulary of Savigny, f. 145.

Dogmaels was their first priory, and, later, their first abbey, followed by the founding of several other abbeys by their order both in England and Scotland.

Thus 1113 is confirmed as the date of Robert Fitzmartin's first journey to Tiron to bring over thirteen monks to the Priory de Guales, to which priory, lands, and churches in Devonshire had been given by Martin before he died.

This journey of Robert's, in 1113, was followed by another in 1118, when he again went to Tiron, bringing back with him thirteen more monks, and an abbot for his newly-founded Abbey of St. Dogmaels, with which was incorporated the Priory de Guales.

In Helyot's "Histoire des Ordres Monastiques," Vol. IV, p. 573, Congregation of Tiron, is the following mention of Robert Fitzmartin :—

"There were also an endless number of princes who came to see Bernard in his solitude, and not only made him big presents, but even built monasteries both during his life, and after his death, which they put under the Abbey of Tiron ; like William, Duke of Acquitaine ; Foulkes, Count of Anjou, who was later King of Jerusalem ; Guy, the young Count of Rochfort ; Robert Martin, etc. . . . . This Robert, whom we believe to be the same as the one we are just about to mention, and to whom the King of England had given lands in his kingdom, took over there thirteen monks from Tiron, for whom he caused to be built the Abbey of Cemaes, in the diocese of St. Davids. This was before 1116, in which year Bernard died."

In the Montacute Charters, 1119-1129, there is a charter of Robert, son of Martin, who grants his Manor of Taunton to the Church of St. Peter of Montacute, at Carswell, for the souls of Hugh Earl of Chester and his wife, etc. ; and for the souls of his father, Martin, and his mother, Geva.[1] This is a very important charter, as though Robert's mother has often been mentioned, this is the only charter so far known wherein her name is given.

Martin came over in 1066, so that in all probability he married in Britain, perhaps at Taunton, the only place in connection with which her name is mentioned. In 1087 he came to Wales, so that it is possible that he might have married in Wales, as, presuming that he married about 1089, Robert, his eldest son, would probably have been twenty-three in 1113, the first we hear of him, and quite old enough to have journeyed to Tiron, or to have built the Abbey in 1118.

This grant was also signed by four of the Peverels, the last of the four being Matilda, afterwards his wife.

In 1141, in "Geoffrey de Mandeville," p. 94, Robert Fitzmartin witnesses a charter of the Empress Matilda to Geoffrey de Magneville.

---

[1] Geva is an uncommon name—what was her nationality ? Was the name derived from [G]Eva, Ginivra, Genefer, or what?

Again his name occurs in the Pipe Roll, 31 Henry I, in connection with Dorset, wherein Robert Fitzmartin is excused his Danegeld xvjs.

Also Robert witnessed two other charters of the Empress Matilda, both of them at Oxford.[1]

The Charter of Baldwin de Riverius, Earl of Exeter, who granted to the Monastery of James, the Apostle, near Exeter, the Church of Tiverton, with tithes, etc., 1141-1155, also contains among the witnesses the name of Robert Fitzmartin, so that he was evidently well-known in England, Wales, and Normandy. One of his sons, in 1166, held five knights' fees of the Abbot of Glastonbury.

MONTACUTE CHARTER.

Published by the Somersetshire Record Society, 1119–29.

Charter of Robert son of Martin, who grants his Manor of Taunton to the Church of St. Peter of Montacute at Carswell for the souls of Hugh Earl of Chester and his wife, for the Welfare of Ranulph Earl of Chester, etc., and for the souls of his father Martin and his mother Geva . . . . [among the witnesses] Richard Peverel Hugh Peverel Ralph Peverel Matilda Peverel.

From Matilda signing herself " Peverel " it is evident that Robert had not yet married, therefore this grant must have been earlier than 1118, as in Robert's grant to St. Dogmaels, that same year, he names Matilda therein, his wife.

In a MS. at SS. Sergius and Bacchus, Angier, there is a grant of Judhell, or Joel, to the Priory of Totnes, a cell of the Great Benedictine Abbey of SS. Sergius and Bacchus, wherein Joel desires that his sword might be hung over the altar in the Priory Church of Totnes. The first witness among others is Martin of Wales, etc., " all men of good memory."

It has been already shown in one of the grants in a previous chapter that Robert had a brother, Nicholas; also another, Robert Martin, is mentioned in the same grant, who would be either Robert's son or nephew; this grant is also signed by John of Castle Martin, but whether this is a brother, son, or nephew of Martin's, so far has not been ascertained. David, Bishop of St. David's in 1328, was a descendant of Robert Martin's.

Further researches in the Domesday Book reveal that Martin held lands both in Buckinghamshire and in Lincolnshire.[2] In the former county, under the heading " The Lands of Martin," it is stated that—

Martin held lands in Urchetone [Wroughton], in the Hundred of Sigelai, five and a-half hides of land for one manor. The land is five carucates. Under his sway

---

[1] Journal Bristol Archæological Association xxxj, pp. 391 and 395.
[2] This dates from before 1086, so that Martin held these lands before coming to Wales.

is one and a-half, carucates and possibly another half. Six villeins, with three bordars[1] have three ploughs there is meadow land two carucates, there are four slaves. In all the total value was one hundred shillings, in the time of King Edward[2] six pounds. Azor, the son of Totus, a theign of King Edward, held this manor, another theign, his man, held one hide and might sell it.

In Lincoln, under the heading of "The Lands of Martin," it appears that—

In Glentworth, Gamel hath six bovats of land subject of taxation. The land for ten oxen. Martin hath there four sokemen and one villain with five oxen to the carucate, and thirty acres of meadow land. In the time of King Edward it was valued at eight shillings, now ten shillings.

In Helmswell, Sperrus hath ten bovats of land subject to taxation. The land for thirteen oxen. Martin hath there one carucate and one sokeman with two oxen on this land, and four villains and four bordars with one plough. In the time of King Edward valued at eleven shillings, now twenty shillings.

In Hagetom, Sweyne hath three bovats of land, and four-fifths of a bovate subject to taxation. The land is four bovates, Martin has here two villains having three oxen to the carucate, and ten acres of meadow land. Value time of King Edward, and now, five shillings.

In Owstrop, Godrie hath six bovats of land subject to taxation. The land for five Oxen. "Ber in Greuebi." [?] There are two villians and eight acres of meadow land, and at least one acre of wood. In the time of King Edward valued at ten shillings, now at eight shillings.

This appears to be all the land held by Martin in these two counties.

It seems to be certain that this must have been the same Martin, inasmuch as only one Martin is mentioned among the followers of William the Conqueror, though there was also the name Martinvast, yet all the brothers, of that name, kept the name in full.

Mons. Etienne Dupont, Judge of the Civil Court, and President of the Historical and Archæological Society of St. Malo, who is now writing a book on "Les Compagnons de Guillaume le Conquérant," has also made researches as to the place from which Martin originally came. He writes that he can affirm that Martin did not come from Tour, near Bayeux, nor from Tours, Ille et Loir.

If Robert had come from Tour, near Bayeux, his name would certainly have been in the Dives Roll, as this Tour and Dives are both in the same department. Mons. Dupont also thinks it will be necessary to search for Martin in the direction of Poitou.

---

[1] A superior villain owning a cottage.   [2] King Edward the Confessor.

CHAPTER VI.

LITTLE IRELAND IN WALES.

REGARDING the name given by either Martin, or Robert Fitzmartin, to the Priory at St. Dogmaels, before it was promoted to be an Abbey, namely, the "Prieuré de Galles," in the Diocese of St. David's, in Cemaes, it seems ridiculous to translate this as the "Priory of Wales," knowing that both Cardigan Priory, and the Priory of Llanbadarn fawr were founded in 1109 by a Norman knight, Gilbert de Clare, son of Gislebert de Crispin, son of Godfrid or Goisfred Conte d'Eu and de Brionne, a natural son of Richard the Elder, Duke of Normandy, who was thus a second cousin of William the Conqueror. This Gislebert, the father, and Martin came over at the same time, and were both held in high esteem by the Conqueror; they were therefore naturally well acquainted, as well as their lands being only separated by the rivers Teify and Brian. Thus it was quite impossible that Robert Fitzmartin should not know of these two earlier priories. Moreover, this Prieuré de Galles is designated as being in the Diocese of St. David's, and in Cemaes. On p. 264, Vol. II, of the Cartulary of Tiron, is found "Cemeae, Cathmeae, Chatmeae, Abbaye érigée en 1118, dans le comté de Pembrock au diocese de Saint-David's (Angleterre); auparavant (that is before 1118) prieuré sous le nom de Prieuré de Galles," and on p. 277, under "Galae," is again found, "prieuré dans le diocese de Saint-David's en Angleterre, érigé en Abbaye en 1118 sous le nom de Cameae." Galles is also written in Latin in other parts of the Cartulary as "*Gallis.*" Referring to the "Mabinogion," in "Branwen, daughter of Lyr (King Lear), it is stated that after the death of Branwen, in Anglesea, her companions "went forth to *Guales*, in Penfro (Pembrokeshire), and they found a fair and regal spot overlooking the ocean." Later, George Owen, in his "History of Pembrokeshire," p. 503,

Interior of the Ancient Church of the Abbey of Iron

under No. VI, Kemes Tracts, entitled, " Baroniae de Kemes Brevis Descriptio," writes : —

3[1] Carucates terre extra feoda pre- dicta videlicet 32[1]	*Wallensium* [*? Guales*]	Morva 8 Kilgwin Vechan 4 Penkelly 1 Coedy Winoke 2	[in Nevern Parish over- looking the Sea.] 15[1] [in Nevern Parish now called Coed Wynog.]

Here again appears the same word, but apparently applied to a very small part of Cemaes, not more than fifteen or thirty-two carucates of land, a carucate in the time of George Owen measuring sixty-four acres, hence the fifteen carucates of land were only equivalent to nine hundred and sixty acres, or, if thirty-two carucates is correct, they were equivalent to 2,048 acres; this did not include all the land belonging to the Prieuré de Galles.

Thus it is evident the " Wallensium " of the sixteenth century, the " Galles, Gallis, Galae " of 1118 and earlier, of the Cartulary of Tiron, and the " Guales " of the " Mabinogion," all refer to a certain region in Pembrokeshire overlooking the sea, and certainly the mention in the Cartulary indicates a larger extent of country than that mentioned by George Owen.

The most probable derivation of these names is from the Teutonic word " Walisc " or " Waelisc," in Anglo-Saxon, " Wealh " meaning " foreigner," which meaning is also found in the names " Gaul," " Gallia," " Wallachia," " Walloons," " Galatia," in "Wälschland," the old German name, and " Wallach," as the Germans called the Romans, and in " Wales " and " Welsh," as this part of Britain and its inhabitants were called by the Anglo-Saxons, and are still so-called by the English of to-day. Though the name is not in the so-called Welsh language, nor do the people so call themselves in their own language; 'for " Wales " is, and ever has been, " Cymry " (hence the Latin " Cambria "), and " Welsh " is " Cymraeg."

Roman remains in this region have already been noticed, also the Roman language must have been well understood here, as all the old inscribed stones found have Latin inscriptions. The Irish have also been already noted in Cemaes. A strong point in favour of the settlement of Irish in this neighbour-hood is that the Ogham inscriptions on these same stones are in Irish, thus indicating that the two languages then spoken in Cemaes were Latin and Irish, not Latin and Welsh. Also there are several place names around, wherein the Celtic word Gwyddel (Irish) still lingers, for example, " Trewyddel,"[2] the Welsh name for " Moylgrove," meaning the Irish village.

---

[1] Apparently 17 carucates of land have been omitted.
[2] Though some authorities derive this from Gwŷdd, a shrub, which seems to be far-fetched.

It is futile to trust the "Mabinogion" unsupported as evidence, for though some of the stories refer to events in the fourth and sixth centuries, and even earlier, still the earliest copy of it extant only dates back to the twelfth century, and in it traces are found both of Norman modes of thought, and customs. Before 1118 this Priory at St. Dogmaels was called the Prieuré de Galles, in Cathmais, but neither Norman, nor English, was at that time spoken in any part of Pembrokeshire, beyond the few Norman followers of the Martins, so that no one then living in Pembrokeshire could have picked out this portion of Cemaes and called it Guales or Galles, meaning foreigners, more especially as Martin's followers were settled in different parts of Cemaes, among the Welsh. Consequently the prevailing language was Cymraeg (Welsh), and is it likely that these Welsh people would call any part of Pembrokeshire "Galles," meaning by that term "Welsh" or foreigners, evidently we must look further for the meaning of this name—"Guales," "Galles," "Gallis," "Galae." The cognate term was well known to the Romans as meaning strangers or foreigners; they were called Wallachs or foreigners by the Teutons, and the Welsh, learning from the Romans this name for foreigner, applied it to the Irish settled in this part of Cemaes, calling this portion of the cantref Guales, or Galles, and later Wallensium. Taking into connection with this, the Irish inscriptions on the Ogham stones, the traces of Irish in so many place-names, the legends as to Irish settlers, the raids from Ireland mentioned in the "Annales Cambriae," Cunedda Wledig sending some of his sons from Strathclyde to help to drive out the Irish it would certainly indicate that this northern portion of Cemaes had been settled by Irish, and was called Guales or Galles by the surrounding Welsh.

Guales might easily be a corruption of Gwyddel[1] (pronounced Gwy*thel*), the *dd* in Gwyddel disappearing, Gwy-el would remain, not unlike Gual, as Goi*dh*el also changes later into Gael by the elimination of the *dh*, and Ca*th*mais into Camais, Cemaes by the similar disappearance of the *th*.

Another very important point is that in the Erse language the word for Irish is Gaedeilg, Gaedeilge, equivalent again to Goidhel, Gael, Gaules, Galles.

Referring again to the "Mabinogion," in Killwch and Olwen, the west coast of Pembrokeshire was in those days subject to invasion from the Gwyddel Fichti,[2] and George Owen, a thousand years later, picks out Penkelly, in Wallensium, as well as Cwm Carw, as being particularly Irish, every third cottage, in some of the villages, being inhabited by Irish.

---

[1] Meaning Irish.
[2] Meaning the Painted Irish, or Irish Picts.

Still one thing more may be noted on the subject to forestall criticism; in part of George Owen's "History of Pembrokeshire," published by Fenton, in 1796, in the Cambrian Register, George Owen writes of the upper part of Pembrokeshire, Northern Cemaes, as the "Welshery"; this is due to Welsh being spoken in these parts in the sixteenth century, whilst in South Pembrokeshire Welsh is hardly ever heard. Still, this would in no way affect the derivation of the ancient name Guales or Galles.

In connection with this subject, the old legend still rife among the elders of the parish may be noted, namely, that an Irish Princess was buried in the Abbey grounds in a golden coffin, with steps leading down to her grave, but that anyone descending these steps was struck with death in punishment for prying, or intent to thieve. This legend is only useful inasmuch as it refers to the Irish or foreigners, "Wallenses" or "Guales," in St. Dogmaels. Later on[1] these steps will be again referred to, whither they led, and the reason of their being filled in.

---

[1] In Chapter XIX.

CHAPTER VII.

GERALD, THE WELSHMAN.

NEXT in succession comes the visit of Archbishop Baldwin, of Canterbury, and Giraldus Cambrensis, to St. Dogmaels Abbey in 1188. The Archbishop, accompanied by Gerald, was touring throughout Wales preaching the Cross, and endeavouring to enlist as many as he could to follow his standard and go with him to fight the third Crusade.

Gerald, being a Welshman, was chosen by him as his chief companion. His real name was Gerald de Barri, he was born about 1147 at Manorbier Castle, Pembrokeshire, and was the youngest son of a Norman knight, William de Barri, who, according to Gerald, took his name from Barry Island, and his second wife, Angharad, daughter of Gerald of Windsor, Castellan of Pembroke, by the notorious Nesta, daughter of Rhys ap Tewdwr, who lived at St. Dogmaels. Baldwin, speaking of Gerald's oratory, ofttimes during his progress, confessed "that he never before on one day was witness to so much shedding of tears"; this was during and after Gerald's discourse at Haverford.

Gerald writes: "We slept that night in the Monastery of St. Dogmaels, where, as well as on the next day at Aberteify, we were handsomely entertained by Prince Rhys." The next day after being entertained at the Abbey they proceeded towards Cardigan, and on the Pembrokeshire side of the river, in St. Dogmaels parish, near the end of the old bridge, Archbishop Baldwin and Gerald, who mentions that "he uttered persuasive words of the Lord," preached to the people, whom Prince Rhys had collected together.

Among the crowd were Rhys, a kinsman of Gerald, with his two sons, Malgwyn and Gryffydd. Baldwin knew no Welsh, so that few could understand him. Gerald also addressed the people in Latin, not being sufficiently fluent in Welsh to preach in that language; yet such was the magic of his voice

West End of the Chapel. St Reynolds Abbey.

that even though the people could not understand what he said, they were carried away by his enthusiasm, and he persuaded many to take the Cross. At the conclusion of his sermon a certain jester, John Spang, who was accustomed to amuse Prince Rhys and his Court by his feigned foolishness and biting railery, said to his master, "You owe a great debt to your kinsman, the Archdeacon, Oh! Rhys, who has sent a hundred or so of your men to serve the Lord, for if he had only spoken in the Welsh tongue I do not think that one of the whole multitude would have remained to you."

The following is Gerald's own account from his "De Rebus a se Gestis," and two anecdotes that he relates relative to the taking of the Cross, one of which related to a certain man having taken the Cross, although—

The only son, and the sole comfort of his aged mother, who steadfastly gazing on him, as if inspired by the Deity, uttered these words : "O most beloved Lord Christ, I return thee hearty thanks for having conferred on me the blessing of bringing forth a son, whom thou mayst think worthy of thy service." Another woman of Aberteivi, of a different way of thinking, held her husband fast by his cloak and girdle, and publicly, and audaciously prevented him from going to the Archbishop to take the cross ; but three nights afterwards she heard a voice in her sleep, saying, "Thou hast taken away my servant from me, therefore what thou most lovest shall be taken away from thee." On her relating her vision to her husband, they were struck with mutual terror and amazement, and on falling asleep again, she unhappily overlaid her little boy, whom with more affection than prudence, she had taken to bed with her : the husband relating to the bishop of the diocese both the vision and its fatal prediction, took the cross, which his wife, with her own hands, sewed on her husband's arm.

Near the head of the bridge where the sermons were delivered, the people immediately marked out the site for a chapel on a verdant plain, as a memorial of so great an event ; intending that the altar should be placed on the spot where the Archbishop stood while addressing the multitude, and it is well known that many miracles (the enumeration of which would be too tedious to relate), were performed on the crowds of sick people who resorted hither from different parts of the country.

On the Pembrokeshire side of the river Teify, near the end of the old bridge, which in those days crossed from the present Gloucester Row to where the railway station now stands, there is a place still called Parc y Capel, or the Chapel field, this Chapel stood where the engine-house now stands. It was circular, being called Capel Sidan (meaning, in old Welsh, circular or round).

Gerald gives the story of a youth devoured by toads; this is reputed to have occurred at a house named Trellyffant (Toad's House), a farm which lies next to Rhos Wrdan, on the south-west. The story is still repeated by old people who have never heard of Gerald. At this house there was a carved

Italian mantlepiece, with a large toad carved in green veined marble over the centre of the fireplace. This carved toad was treasured for many generations; but was afterwards cut out. Eventually it came into the possession of its present owner, who lives at Haverfordwest. The toad is life-size. We give the story and another in Gerald's words : —[1]

Two circumstances occurred in the territory of Cemaes, one in our own time, the other a little before, which I think not right to pass over in silence. In our time a youth of this country during a severe illness suffered such a violent persecution from toads, as if the reptiles of the whole territory had flocked together by agreement; and though they were killed without number by his friends, they still came together in crowds from all parts, like hydra heads. At last his friends were wearied to such an extent that he was hoisted up into a somewhat lofty tree stripped of its foliage, but even there he was not safe from his enemies, for they climbed up eagerly in great numbers, attacked and devoured him. The youth's name was Seisylt Esceif or Seisylt longshanks.

It is also recorded, in like manner, that by the secret but never unjust judgment of God, another man suffered a like persecution from great rats. Also in the same barony, during the time of Henry the first, a certain wealthy landed proprietor, having a house at the northern extremity of the Presely Range, for three successive nights was warned by dreams that if he put his hand under a stone hanging over a bubbling spring near by, called St. Bernard's Well, he would there find a golden torques, accordingly he went the third day, but received instead a deadly wound from a viper.

This last reads rather like a story with a moral.

Soon after this occurred the long dispute regarding the election of a bishop to the see of St. David's. Three candidates were elected; firstly, Gerald, who undoubtedly would have made an excellent bishop; secondly, his kinsman, Walter, Abbot of St. Dogmaels, who, unfortunately for him, could neither read nor write, neither was he a wise governor of his Abbey; the election of such an ignorant man as abbot shows more than anything else how the Monastery had degenerated within seventy years of its foundation; thirdly, the Abbot of Whitland.

Gerald had the keenest desire to be Bishop of St. David's; he had refused the offer of other bishoprics, among them Bangor, hoping to be elected to this see. One of his uncles had been the previous bishop, and when he became old and feeble Gerald had virtually ruled the diocese for him, and it was during this time that Walter, Abbot of St. Dogmaels, and Reginald Ffolliat had despoiled the diocese, and been compelled by Gerald to refund their spoils; but

---

[1] Translated from the Roll edition of Gerald's works.

both the King and the Archbishop of Canterbury feared that he would become too powerful, and would probably refuse to acknowledge the supremacy of Canterbury. In the end both he and his illiterate kinsman, the Abbot of St. Dogmaels, were passed over.

In his "De Invectionibus," Lib. I, Gerald waxes wrath over the Abbot of St. Dogmaels being a candidate, describing him as absolutely illerate and ignorant; in one place he writes of him, "the poor Abbot of St. Dogmaels was an illiterate monk, who could not read his Psalter," and who, Gerald writes, was instigated by the King, and the Archbishop of Canterbury, to contend for the see against him.

The history of this dispute regarding the Abbot of St. Dogmaels, the only one of the three with whom this history is concerned, will be better learned from Gerald's own letters, taken from his "De Invectionibus." Many noted people from different parts of England were concerned in this dispute, among others the Bishops of Worcester and Ely; the Bishop, the Precentor, and Master J., Canon of Hereford; the Dean of London; the Archdeacon of Buckingham; the Archbishop of Canterbury; the Abbot of Worcester, and the Prior of Wenloc, etc.

"De Invectionibus," Book I : —

And the Archbishop in order that he might gain his point procured that the illiterate and in short ignorant Abbot of St. Dogmaels of our country and a kinsman of mine by autocratic violence should be elected. And hearing that I was returning with a severe mandate associating himself with two false English brethren he inquired of them if by any art or ingenuity they could detach the Chapter from me to which they answered that if he could bring it about that the Abbot of the Cistercian order to wit of Whitland who was a son of our church and who had canonical sons and brethren cousins and very many relations in it although the Abbot of St. Dogmaels may have been elected all of them could support him against the Archdeacon. Hearing which the Archbishop summoned to him by letter the Abbot of Whitland firmly promising him that if he could detach the Chapter from me he would confer our See on him notwithstanding the election made of the Abbot of St. Dogmaels which had been cancelled by the lord Pope. And the said Abbot (of Whitland) otherwise a man of great religion although he was then engaged in the remote parts of Ireland on the duties of a visitation enjoined on him allured by the hope of preferment he flew across the Irish Sea into Wales, on the wings of ambition so that on the feast of the Assumption of the Blessed Mary passing through the gate of his Abbey when scarcely dawn before the hour of mass he did not think fit to hear mass or to celebrate or to salute his brethren. Being received with joy and honour by the

---

[1] King John wrote, April 10th, 1202 : " We have not assented to the election of Giraldus to the See of St. Davids ; but to that of the Abbot of St. Dogmaels."

Archbishop at Worcester and forthwith having come to a mutual agreement he was sent by him back to St. Davids and immediately calling together the brethren and reading the letters of the Archbishop and the Justiciar secretly and with closed doors and he was elected with trembling and in subdued voices.   Now it is worthy of note that he inveighs against either abbot concerning his mode of action of whom the first was his kinsman and the other his friend neither have kept their oaths made.   Then he returns to the Archbishop.

Now forthwith when he elected the first Abbot[1] he appointed as of his following our false brother Foliot and binding him to himself more firmly by an oath made him as it were a messenger between them a runner and courier between England and Wales and a carrier of news and letters between Canterbury and St. Davids.   But afterwards he caused another Abbot to be elected and was not ashamed to bind the said Foliot also to him by an oath so that Foliot should support the one openly and the other secretly fulfilling contradictory offices strictly keeping his vow to both his loyalty however being well rewarded as was fitting by both the Abbots and the Archbishop. Who then was the author of this double perjury? God forbid it were the Archbishop! The oaths however he took to each of the two for different purposes. The same person was also the author of a third perjury who so often sent the prior Foliot with letters of the King the Archbishop and Justiciar to oppress the liberties of the church of St. Davids to which he had canonically sworn obedience and sent the same also to Rome for a similar purpose that he might work against the liberties of the church of St. Davids. Together with Andrew [in short he once more enumerates four offences of these persons against himself.]

Cap. VIII.

Of intestine discords of the persecutors among themselves.

[Giraldus here commemorates no facts but is speaking ironically against the Abbot of St. Dogmaels he thus begins.] While the peoples are crying and shouting the Abbot of St. Dogmaels is alone conspicuous by his learning and discretion and so being called to that dignity by a holy man did not realise his impending fall. You shall hear what has been written veiledly and mockingly to him on this subject.

Cap. IX.

The Archdeacon to the Abbot Walter.

You have three great enemies in three degrees positive comparative and superlative namely position comparison and exaggeration. If you ask who they are? The horned one who wears the pallium[2] the sheepish one who wears a cowl[3] the wolf-whelp.[4] The horned one he bears a horn beware of him and the cloaked one for he cloaks deceit. Beware of the cowled one for he sighs pants desires and canvasses would that they were far from thy presence. In all the strivings to this end I contend through all right and wrong that he will overthrow you and cast you

---

[1] Walter of St. Dogmaels.

[2] *i.e.*, the pallium, or mantle, sent to an Archbishop or Bishop on consecration by the Pope. It refers to the Archbishop of Canterbury.   [3] The Abbot of Whitland.   [4] Reginald Ffolliot.

out.   And the sheeplike one because according to the gospel.   "Beware of those who come to you in sheep's clothing but inwardly are ravening wolves."   And beware of the whelp who bearing the fraudulent business of both with frequent passings to and fro that he may deceive you and then overthrow you with vulpine duplicity runs to and fro.

Pope Innocent I later writes from the Lateran, on the 8th May, in the third year of his Pontificate, to the Abbots of Whitlands, St. Dogmaels, and Strata Florida, concerning the canonization of the Venerable Caradoc, and enquiring as to his life whilst he lived—

"And concerning the miracles which were wrought after his death by the right hand of the Lord news of which have reached the hearing of the Apostolic See. Wherefore lately we were recently entreated that he whom God had exalted in heaven we should have a care to glorify on earth by inserting him in the 'Calendar of the Saints'" but not wishing to act hastily in this matter he continues "we have thought fit to commit the inquisition of the same to you charging you by Apostolic writing that you diligently enquire as to what had been the former life of the said man what kind of death and what miracles followed him.   What you shall find out on these matters you shall faithfully intimate to us in your letters" . . . . Taking due precaution that you so aim at simply enquiring the truth that no fraud or falsity may be mixed with it.

Now these letters, by the ill-will of two of the abbots, namely, Peter of Whitland and Walter of St. Dogmaels, were maliciously suppressed, the two abbots thinking thereby to spite Gerald, who was very keen on the matter, having begged the Pope to canonize Caradoc.

On the 23rd of August, the following year, Innocent writes to the Abbot of St. Dogmaels from Signia, charging him that he had appointed Gerald "keeper of the Church of St. David's as well as of the houses and the lands belonging to the bishopric and all the proceeds thereof," and that the Abbot Walter "should resign without diminution to Gerald, nor should he impeach him in the keepership of the Church of St. David's," and charging the Bishop of St. David's, the Precentor, and Master J., Canon of Hereford, that "they compel you to this."

This is followed by another letter from Innocent, written three days later from the same place, but addressed to the Bishop of Ely, the Dean of London, and the Archdeacon of Buckingham on the spoliation of Gerald, and the illiteracy of the Abbot of St. Dogmaels, wherein he relates "how it had been signified to him how Gerald, whom he had made keeper of the Bishopric of St. David's," had "by violence been spoiled by the Abbot of St. Dogmaels and Reginald Foliot; and that the said Foliot has committed sacriledge in the said spoliation

and has incurred the sentence of excommunication." However, Foliot again took
the vows of allegiance to the Church, was forgiven, and soon after was made
Prior of Llanthony; and charging them to "compel these robbers to render
Gerald his due," also charging them to enquire as to "the learning and fitness"
of the Abbot of St. Dogmaels to be elected to the see of St. David's, as it was
reported to him that he was "almost wholly unlearned."

Again, three days later, Innocent writes to the same three stating that
Gerald had brought his witnesses before the appointed auditors, and when he
demanded that their evidence should be published, the Abbot of St. Dogmaels
"prayed for delay in order to produce witnesses," and after some reference
to Gerald's claim to the bishopric, and commands that Gerald "shall plead
his cause in person at Rome, but the Archbishop of Canterbury by proxy."

In the fourth book, of this same work of Gerald, is seen how the Abbot
of St. Dogmaels was at length elected, as Gerald writes :—" Whereupon, as
they say, having understood at length by the letters of the Archbishop, and
the letters of the Justiciar, that the king consented to the Abbot of St. Dogmaels,
they elected him to the pastorate" (St. David's). Nearly two years later
Innocent again writes about this same Abbot of St. Dogmaels to the Bishops
of Ely and Worcester from Florence, on the 24th of May, as follows :—" The
cause which is pending between our beloved sons, the Abbot of St. Dogmaels
and G, Archdeacon of Brecon, each of whom asserts himself to have been
elected to the Bishopric of St. David's," and after examining in "our con-
sistory" the evidence given "before delegated judges," the Cardinals say that
the process of election was irregular.

In another letter to the Abbot of St. Dogmaels ordering him to make
restitution to Gerald of his spoliations, the Pope orders that he should submit
to a test regarding his learning, and Reginald Foliot was commanded to set
out the case of the Abbot of St. Dogmaels, for he acted as the Abbot's proxy,
and here Gerald waxes caustic at Foliot's expense, owing to his mistaking the
date of the Abbot's election, writing, "it behoves liars to have good memories
lest perchance they forget the lie in which they have been instructed."

But in spite of all, and Gerald's previous election to the Bishopric, the
Archbishop "on the morrow of the next Epiphany, with the King's assent,
elected the Abbot of St. Dogmaels, and a little before Christmas following
the Chapter solemnised the election made by the Archbishop."

To make matters now still more vexatious for Gerald, he was forthwith
cited to appear before the papal delegates to answer the charges of the Abbot
of St. Dogmaels, the Archdeacon of Carmarthen, and R. Foliot.

However, Gerald determined to summon a general synod on the morrow of Holy Trinity following, and caused the following letter to be sent "to the Abbot of St. Dogmaels, since he was unlearned and a despoiler of the temporalities of the bishopric, contrary to the disposal of the Lord Pope."

Charging him, by the authority of the Pope, to appear before " our Synod (which) will be solemnly held on the octave of Penticost, God willing, at Brecon." . . . . And that you restore to us "all the profits of the bishopric" which he had applied to his own use. "Moreover, on the second day, we enjoin on you the synodal sermon and word of exhortation and instruction as it were of a great and authoritative person who bears himself and calls himself the elect of St. David's."

This must have been a bitter pill to the Abbot, who could hardly fail to realise that he would never be able to get through this trial; the sermon, of course, he could get written for him, but in the verbal words of exhortation and instruction he would surely fail. Here follows the account of the first appearance of the Abbot in Gerald's own words : —

"And when the Abbot of St. Dogmaels who then for the first time appeared should be examined as to his learning the judges first offered him the letters of the lord pope to read containing the commission of the said business made to them. But those who spoke for him the clerks to wit and the accomplices of the Archbishop answered that he ought not to be proved by such letters to which he was not accustomed but rather by the ecclesiastical books. There was brought then a missal book with large and legible writing which was given him to read by the judges and to expound." Now after failing to read the Pope's letters he now "craved leave of the judges to retire for the purpose of consulting the Archbishop's clerks which being granted after a long and tedious delay he returned refusing both the reading and the exposition " . . . . and then withdrew.

One cannot help partly pitying the old fraud, though at the same time being glad that he was at last publicly exposed.

As will be foreseen, after this public failure of his to prove his ability to read even large and legible writing, his election to the Bishopric of St. David's was cancelled. When Gerald went to Rome to plead his own cause, he was subjected to many vexatious persecutions by his enemies, which to a man of his erudition and dominant disposition must have been exasperating. Among these was the accusation of the Welsh monk, of St. Dogmaels, Golwen, whom Gerald had formerly excommunicated, as a deserter from the Abbey, and as one who falsely without authority had gone through Wales preaching for gain.

This Golwen, together with a crowd of the like sort, came almost every day before the papal chamberlain, demanding a certain horse, and violently accusing Gerald of stealing it from him in Wales.

Gerald did not deny that a certain weak horse, scarcely able to carry Golwen, had been taken from him in Wales by one of his deans, with other spoils and false relics, without either his permission or authority, " But which horse, as compared with his horse, which was large and strong, and of no mean value, had nothing in common but the colour." Golwen, however, without any shame, continued to assert that the horse was his, and brought " a multitude of boys and ribalds of the opposite party who were all prepared to swear and testify" that the horse belonged to Golwen, and that they had seen it with him.

Golwen continuing to visit, the " papal chamberlain daily throwing himself with much weeping and sobbing at his feet, demanding his horse; the chamberlain, a simple man, ignorant of the law, and 'credulous,' sequestrated the horse, and caused it to be put in his own stable."

Gerald, therefore, seeing that these fellows "were prepared to testify anything, at the nod of their masters," and caring more for his own honour than ought else, and feeling that if they prevailed against him, his election to St. David's would fail, and also being both embarrassed and distracted by such a mean and frivolous attack, decided to resort to stratagem, in order to bring about their defeat. He therefore instructed one of his followers to get up in Court on a certain evening, when the parties were come before the Chamberlain, and address the Chamberlain as follows : —

" It is wonderful that a man than whom none viler none more treacherous in the world a deserter from his order can have a voice in this court to vex a good and honourable man. For this horse which was taken from him in Wales on account of his treachery and which he now falsely claims to be his was a Gelding but this one (Gerald's) is a whole horse."

Forthwith the rascal (Golwen) sprang up in the midst of them, and as he was hasty and bold, and ready to affirm or deny as occasion arose, turning to the spokesman, he said : —

" Surely thou liest for my horse was a whole horse which the lord Chamberlain can now judge and at once if it please him cause to be made clear which when he said the archdeacon and his party prayed that this testimony might be taken down word for word which was done."

The Chamberlain at once sent off one of his servants to inspect the horse in his stable, with the result that Golwen[1] was convicted of perjury, and of falsely

---

[1] Golwen was surnamed throughout Wales, Follus and Folleotus (fool and little fool), also another of the witnesses against Gerald in this case was Philip, a false deacon.

accusing Gerald. Universal laughter followed the report. That night, when relating the account to the Pope, who was convulsed with laughter and ordered the horse to be restored to Gerald, and silence to be imposed on the rascal.

"And so on the morrow when the adverse party were covered with confusion there was joy and exaltation throughout the court . . . . Now it happened in those days that the Pope was frequently wont to go to the Virgin's Fountain for the sake of recreation when times and circumstances allowed. It was a very beautiful fountain at no great distance from the Lateran on the southern side throwing up limpid and cool waters surrounded by walls of Parian marble from which flowed a pleasant and wide stream towards the country. And when it was known that the Pope was going both as the bells of the palace and report testified to his movements riding palfreys being made ready the elect of Bangor and his companion the Archdeacon (Gerald) followed in the wake of the Pope . . . . The Pope who sat apart by the steps of the fountain a little remote from the others as if in a room beyond a narrow path surrounded on all sides by the water with a few of his household . . . . Seeing Gerald he summoned him to come alone to his presence enquiring how he had progressed in the matter between him and the monk."

Gerald then related the stratagem by which he had won, and how by acute subtlety, as the breaking of a bladder by a small needle, he had easily shattered Golwen's evident falsehood, and how a monk named Roger, one of the four united with Golwen and the other rascals against Gerald, had publicly made witticisms and jokes against Golwen, Gerald remarked to the Pope that it was a pity the monks were not all geldings, as probably they would then attend better to their duties.

In process of time Gerald, seeing that his enemies still endeavoured by all means in their power to make out that the Abbot of St. Dogmaels was the first elected to St. David's, instead of Gerald, thus put his case before the Pope—

"Holy Father, that the election of the Abbot (St. Dogmaels) was not the first, as the adverse party lie in saying, we have supported by true statements with many presumptions and some proofs."

On behalf of the Abbot of St. Dogmaels it was stated that after the death of Bishop Peter (St. David's) two Archdeacons and four Canons of St. David's[1] were sent to Hubert, Archbishop of Canterbury, with letters of their Chapter, asking that he would elect them a pastor, giving three names, firstly, Gerald, and secondly, the Abbot of St. Dogmaels.

"But the Abbot of St. Dogmaels was quite illiterate as was proved both by the statement of the judges and by five or six witnesses of his own party at Rome."

[1] Gerald's "De Rebus a se Gestis," p. 94, Rolls Edition.

Gerald then accuses him of being such an ambitious man that though he knew Gerald's election was not cancelled, he consented to his own election, and intruded himself over Gerald. After this the three delegates nominated by the Pope, namely, the Abbot of Worcester, the Prior of Wenlock, and Master A. de Bromfield siding with the Abbot of St. Dogmaels, in spite of his illiteracy, condemned Gerald Archdeacon of Brecon, G of Llanthony, and J Prior of Brecon to pay one hundred marks. Forty of these to go to the Abbot of St. Dogmaels, thirty marks to the Archdeacon of Carmarthen, and thirty marks to Master G. Foliot, and that they were to put in their appearance before them on the eve of St. Matthew the Apostle, in the Church of Llandu, "if not we shall no less proceed to the execution of this order." In the end neither the Abbot of St. Dogmaels nor Gerald was ordained Bishop of St. David's, though the dispute had lingered on over several years. It has been already shown why Gerald was not made Bishop, and the Pope decided against the Abbot on the ground that he could not read. It is a pitiful story of lying and deceit, and a contemptible attack on a scholarly and able man.

The two following stories of Gerald's are examples of that time, and of the characters of the people who lived then.

"De Invectionibus," pp. 167 and 168 : —

A certain priest in those parts saw that a triformed beast such as he had never seen before pursued the Archdeacon whilst riding. At one time it appeared after the manner of a dog hanging on to the tail of his horse at another leaping towards the feet of the Archdeacon threatening to bite him.

When he was now overcome and worn out with fatigue and disgust one of his followers on foot at his command aimed an arrow at the beast and pierced it. When they saw that it was dead and had more carefully examined it the first part looked like a sheepskin with the wool[1] on the second like a wolf and the third like a fox. And it was thought that this beast represented the Archbishop who three times had transformed himself when he promoted the Abbot of St. Dogmaels the Abbot of Whitland and last Foliot.

The second is as follows :—

And there was a vision appeared to a boy at Ferentino . . . . wherein he saw three wolves one gray another white a third somewhat red and larger than the others the latter urging on the two others against the Archdeacon. And when the gray one savagely attacked him the Archdeacon meeting him boldly and thrusting his hand into his open mouth forcibly tore his jaws asunder and slew him. When the larger wolf still more angrily was urging him on the white wolf made a rush at the Archdeacon who boldly seizing him by the jaws in a similar manner broke them. And when the wolf the instigator of the affray saw this he was seen to retire in confusion

[1] "Melota."

with his tail between his legs. On which he beheld a most beautiful woman standing and following her a venerable old man carrying a very precious garment with which at the command as it were of the said lady he clothed and adorned the Archdeacon. And the boy beholding and wondering at these things enquired from one what they portended and received for answer that it was the Mother of Christ the Blessed Virgin and St. David the Patron Saint of Wales. So here it was seen that the Archdeacon shall have the victory for the two wolves are the two Abbots the first of St. Dogmaels the second of Whitland's and the third and large wolf that instigates the others is the Archbishop which can be regarded as the sentence of divine judgement.

Herein it is seen how certain Gerald was of success, for even these visions were interpreted as meaning his victory.

There is one more in which the Abbot of St. Dogmaels is mentioned, entitled—

The Anchorite Talks Through His Wicket.

When however not long after Gerald came to him for the sake of justifying himself for he willingly repaid the kindness of the religious man who among other sayings spoke thus through his lattice. It is very clear and manifest that God the Avenger regards traitors and the adversaries of the dignity of St. David with hatred and detestation especially those who ought to be sons (of the church) and faithful. For we now see the most wicked adversary of St. David the Abbot of Whitland deposed and deprived of all honour in the land and the foolish Abbot of St. Dogmaels your kinsman who owing to the vengeance of God and St. David the land will no longer sustain alive.[1]

In the patent rolls follows a letter of King John's relating to Gerald and the Abbot of St. Dogmaels. King John was shrewd enough not to wish Gerald to reign as Prince Bishop of St. David's, though at the same time he greatly admired him.

Pat. Roll. 3 John, m. 2, No. 2.

The King etc. to all etc. Know ye that G. Archdeacon of Brecon is manifestly acting against our crown and dignity in calling himself elect of St. Davids since we have never given our assent to his election.[2] And thereupon he has drawn into a suit W[alter] Abbot of St. Dogmaels to whose election we consented. The temporalities moreover of the See of St. Davids which at the vacancy of the See should be in our hand by the long and approved custom of the realm. Against our crown and dignity he has procured to be committed to himself and impudently acquiring these and other things against us such as no one since our coronation has

---

[1] All the quotations in this chapter have been translated direct from the Rolls edition of Gerald's Works.

[2] See Gerald the Welshman, by Henry Owen, p. 17. Wherein at Chinon John spoke to the deputation "in praise of Gerald, and accepted his nomination," this was shortly after the death of King Richard.

attempted against us. And whereas these things we can by no means endure. We charge you that as you love our honour and dignity which as our lieges you are bound to foster and maintain you will grant to the aforesaid G. Archdeacon in no way aid or assent for this purpose. And as far as you are able you shall resist the aforesaid Abbot of St. Dogmaels. And it is manifest that whoever does the contrary is an enemy to us and to our dignity.

Witness myself at the Rock of Golden Grove 10th April (1202).

In the "Papal Registers," edited by W. H. Bliss, Vol. iiij, p. 231, 29th April, 1346, is a mandate to the Bishop and Archdeacon of St. David's, and the Dean of Chichester, from the Pope, to carry out the ordinances touching apostates in regard to John Barett, a monk of St. Dogmaels.

Also in the same year, the 24th of May, dated Florence, in Vol. III, p. 23, is a mandate from the Pope to the Bishops of Ely and Worcester cancelling the "election of the Abbot (Walter) of St. Domuel (Dogmaels) and of G Archdeacon of Brecon to the see of St. David's, and they were to induce the canons to make an unanimous election; and if this is not done to promote some fit person and cause him to be consecrated by the Metropolitan."

Ancient Church and Cottage of the Abbey of Tiron.

CHAPTER VIII.

SILENT GROWTH.

IN the "Testa de Nevill," Henry III–Edward I, the Abbot of St. Dogmaels is mentioned among those holding knight's fees in the County of Devon, that he held a fourth part of a knight's fee in Wittokesdone, of Nicholas Fitzmartin, of his Barony of Dartington.

In 19 Edward I is seen, in the Taxatio of Pope Nicholas, the then value of St. Dogmaels Abbey.

Also in the "Exchequer T. R. Miscellaneous Books 72," 24 Edward I (F 55, Devon), the Abbot of St. Dogmaels holds Luscombe Barrudge, or Barnerd, for half a knight's fee of William Martin, of his Barony of Dartington. In the Memoranda Rolls, Michaelmas, 1320, Edward II, the Abbot had been taxed twice over for the same lands, both by the Archdeaconaries of St. David's and Cardigan. The £32 11s. 8d. taxed by St. David's being herein cancelled. Later, in the reign of Edward II, the Abbot and monks of St. Dogmaels beg the King in the Ancient Petition 4315, to confirm the gift made to them by David de la Roche,[1] of the Church of Maenclochog,[2] the monks pleading poverty from their lands having so often been laid waste by war in Wales. This petition is endorsed, "that the bill be shown to the Justices of Wales," the King also wishing to know the value of the church. Evidently the monks had been too precipitate in taking possession of this gift of David de la Roche, comprising an acre of ground, a garden and a parcel of land in Maenclochog, with the rights of patronage of the Church of St. Mary Maenclochog, and of the chapels annexed to this same church, before the King had confirmed the grant; however, in the Patent Roll of 14 Edward II, the King forgives the Abbot and monks their transgression in so doing, and confirms, at Westminster, the grant of David de la Roche.

---

[1] The same as "De la Rupe." [2] The Ringing Stone.

TESTA DE NEVILL, Hen. III—Edw. I, County of Devon.

p. 178. Names of those who hold knights' fees in the County of Devon and of whom they hold.

FEES OF THE ABBOT OF TAVISTOCK.

The Abbot of St. Dogmaels holds in Whittokesden a fourth part of 1 fee of the same.

p. 191. Inquisition of the fees and tenements in the Hundred of Staneburg made by the oath of William de Morlegh and others.

The Abbot of St. Dogmael in Wales holds in Whittokedone a fourth part of a knt's fee of the same [*i.e.* of Nicholas fitz Martin of his Barony of Dertingthon].

EXCHEQUER T. R., Miscellaneous Books 72, 24 Edw. I.

f. 55. Devon. Hund[1] of Staneberg.

The Abbot of St. Dogmaels holds Luscombe Barudge otherwise Barnerd for half a knight's fee of William Martyn as of his barony of Dartington.

Also in the "Calendar of Feudal Aids," Co. Devon, Hundred of Stanburg, 1284-1286, there is a similar entry to the above.

TAXATIO OF POPE NICHOLAS, 1291.

Devon.

	£	s.	d.
The Abbey of St. Dogmaels has at Rattre of Rent and other things taxed	13	9	8
Sum of the value of the tithes	1	6	11¾

St. David's.

	£	s.	d.
The Chapel of Mynachlog Ddu (belonging to the Abbey of St. Dogmaels)	2	13	4
The Church of Caldey (belonging to the Abbey of St. Dagmaels)	3	6	8

Temporalities.

	£	s.	d.
The Abbot of St. Dogmaels hath the town of St. Dogmael with its appurtenances; namely Crugau Gryffydd Mynachlog Ddu five carucates of land with rents of three mills for grinding and one fulling mill. The Revenues of the hundred Court together with other commodities	16	10	0
Also he has fisheries together with Grangistown[2] with rent of a mill perquisites and other commodities	11	15	0
Also he receives annually from the Priory of Pill	9	6	8
Also he hath at Caldey one carucate of land with rent of assize	1	10	0
The goods of the Abbey of St. Dogmaels	22	11	8

NOTE.—That this taxation of the goods of the Abbey of St. Dogmaels is hereby cancelled on this account because it is wrong as is clear in the memoranda of the fourteen years of King Edward son of King Edward in the Records of St. Michael's term.

There certainly are many omissions in this taxation of Pope Nicholas.

---

[1] Hundred.   [2] Granston.

MEMORANDA ROLLS, Mich. 14 Edw. II, m. 81.

For the Abbot of St. Dogmaels.

The Lord King has commanded here his writ of the great seal which is among the Communia of the 13th year in these words—Edward by the grace of God King of England Lord of Ireland and Duke of Aquitaine to the Treasurer and Barons of his Exchequer greeting. From a certain plaint of our beloved in Christ the Abbot of St. Dogmaels of the diocese of St. David's we have heard that although all the temporal goods of the said Abbot at the township of St. Dogmaels with their members in the Archdeaconry of Cardigan and other his temporal goods that are at ffisgard Grangestown and Caldey in the Archdeaconry of St. David's and a certain pension which the said Abbot receives from the Prior of Pulle in the same Archdeaconry of St. David's are part by part taxed for a tenth among the temporalities in the said Archdeaconry of Cardigan where the said Abbey is situated at £39 20d. and the said Abbot the tenth and other charges touching the clergy from his aforesaid goods according to the said taxation part by part made always hitherto has been wont to pay and has not ever had any other temporal goods than the aforesaid in the said diocese for which he ought to pay a tenth or any other such charge. Since however in the rolls of taxation of such temporal goods that are in the said diocese delivered into our Exchequer it is found that the temporal goods of the said Abbot at £32 11. 8. in the aforesaid Archdeaconry of St. David's are taxed in gross although such taxation in gross in the said Archdeaconry of St. David's is comprised in the aforesaid £39 20d. the collectors of such tenths granted to us in the aforesaid Archdeaconry of Cardigan account at our said Exchequer for the tenths of the said temporal goods after the rate of the said £39 20d. aforesaid and nevertheless to collectors of such tenths in the aforesaid Archdeaconry of St. David's are charged after the rate of £32 11. 8. of the aforesaid. And if the £32 11. 8. aforesaid in the aforesaid sum of £39 and 20d. are not included or comprised by pretext of which the aforesaid Abbot for the truth for one and the same thing to us is twice distrained to pay at the suit of the said collectors unjustly to the no little loss and charge of the said since it is not consonant with right that the said Abbot by such double taxation of his goods thus unjustly should be charged. We charge you that having made a scrutiny of the rolls and memoranda of such taxations which are at our Exchequer if by inspection of the same or by inquisition thereon if it shall be necessary to be made it shall appear to you that the temporalities of the aforesaid Abbot in the said Archdeaconry of St. David's at £32 11. 8. in gross as is aforesaid taxed within the sum of £39 and 20d. aforesaid are comprised and contained and that the said Abbot has not any other temporal goods than the aforesaid taxed at £39 and 20d. as above is expressed in the said diocese for which he ought concerning any tenth beyond the sum of £39 and 20d. aforesaid to be charged then the taxation of £32 11. 8. aforesaid shall be taken out and annulled from the said rolls of taxation and the aforesaid Abbot from that which is required from him of the tenth tax of £32 11. 8. aforesaid at our said Exchequer you shall cause to be exonerate and quit. Witness me myself at Westminster the 5th June the 13th year of our reign. By virtue of which writ the rolls being examined etc. it was found in the roll of taxation of the temporal goods of the clergy of St. David's diocese which is here in our treasury that the temporal goods of the said Abbot are taxed in the Archdeaconry of Cardigan part by part at £39 20d. And in

the Archdeaconry of St. David's at £32 11. 8. and that it does not appear by the
aforesaid taxation whether to wit the aforesaid £32 11. 8. are contained and comprised in
the aforesaid sum of £39 20d. as is above suggested in the writ aforesaid. It was
commanded the Bishop of St. David's that he should make an inquest of the truth
thereon to wit what temporal goods the aforesaid Abbot hath in the Archdeaconry of
Cardigan and in what townships and at how much such goods in the said Archdeaconry
of Cardigan part by part are taxed and also what temporal goods the said Abbot hath
similarly in the Archdeaconry of St. David's also if the temporal goods under the
name of the said Abbot in the said Archdeaconry of St. David's taxed are contained
and comprised within the taxation of his goods in the Archdeaconry of Cardigan and
what thereupon etc. he shall cause to be shown here without delay. Which said Bishop
now at the quindene of St. Michael sent here the King's writ upon the premises to him
directed which is among the writs executed for the King this 14th year endorsement
thus. By pretext of this mandate we have caused an inquisition diligently to be made
by trusty men of our diocese upon the contents in the mandate aforesaid who being
sworn say upon their oath that the Abbot of St. Dogmaels in the Archdeaconry of
Cardigan hath the township of St. Dogmaels with its members to wit Crugau Griffith
Menecregh the Black Grange five carucates of land with rents three grist mills and
one fulling mill and the perquisites of hundreds and courts and other commodities
which are taxed at £16 10s. Also they say that the said Abbot receives from the
priory of Pulle yearly which is in the Archdeaconry of St. David's £9 6. 8. Also at
ffishguard and Grangestown rents with a water mill and other commodities which are
taxed at £11 15s. in the aforesaid Archdeaconry of St. David's. Also he hath at
Caldey one carucate of land with rents and other things which are taxed at 30s. in the
same Archdeaconry. Also they say that the temporal goods of the said Abbot in the
aforesaid Archdeaconry of St. David's taxed as is premised are contained and comprised
within the taxation of the temporal goods of the said Abbot in the Archdeaconry of
Cardigan and that the said Abbot hath no other temporal goods in the Bishopric of
St. David's than those which are taxed in the aforesaid Archdeaconry of Cardigan.
And so it is considered that the taxation of the goods of the said Abbot which are
taxed in the Archdeaconry of St. David's at £32 11. 8. as is above contained shall be
cancelled and annulled in the Roll of Taxation and that the said Abbot shall be
exonerated from the tenth of aforesaid £32 11. 8. to wit 65s. 2d. yearly and is quit
by pretext of the mandate and inquisition aforesaid.

ANCIENT PETITIONS.
No. 4315.

To our lord the king pray his poor chaplains, the Abbot, and Convent of St.
Dogmaels for love of God if it please him to confirm by his charter the church of
Maenclochog in Cemaes in the lordship of Monsieur William Martin in the county
of Pembroke which David de la Roche has given them to their own use for love of
God and because they have been often laid waste by war in Wales.
Endorsed—

Let the Bill be shown to the Justices of Wales and let the King be advised also
of the value of the Church.

PATENT ROLL (153).   14 Edw. II, part I, m. 13.

1320.

The King to all those to whom etc. greeting.   Know that of our special grace we have pardoned our beloved in Christ the Abbot of the Monastery of St. Dogmaels in Kemmeys and the monks there abiding the transgression they committed in obtaining for themselves and their successors in fee of David de la Roche son and heir of Gilbert de la Roche one acre of land and one garden with a certain plot in the hamlet of Maencloghog as by landmarks and boundaries they are assigned with the right of patronage of the church of St. Mary of the same hamlet and of two chapels annexed to the aforesaid church and in entering upon them and in seizing and appropriating the aforesaid church with the aforesaid chapels for themselves and their successors forever after the publication of the statute concerning the non-bestowal of lands and tenements in mortmain issued by licence of the lord Edward formerly King of England our father which licence has not been superseded on our part willing and granting on behalf of ourselves and our heirs as far as in us lies that the aforesaid Abbot and monks may hold and have the aforesaid land garden plot right of the aforesaid patronage and likewise the aforesaid church thus appropriated for themselves and their successors forever without let or hindrance on the part of ourselves or our heirs Justiciars Escheators Sheriffs or other our bailiffs or our ministers soever the aforesaid statute notwithstanding save however the capital services thence due and customary to the lords of that fee.   In witness whereof etc. the King at Westminster on the 30th day of October.

P the King himself then Master Robert de Baldok.

+   +

In the fourteenth year of Edward II " Llewelyn ap Madoc was drowned in a certain pool near Glastir, in Cemaes."

William Martin, who succeeded his cousin, Nicholas Martin, as Lord of Cemaes, was seventh in descent from Martin of the Towers; he died in 1324, after being Lord of Cemaes for thirty-two years.   He was succeeded by his son, William, aged thirty, who died the year following, and was succeeded in the Lordship of Cemaes by James, son of Joan, sister and co-heir of this William Martin, and her husband, Nicholas Audeleigh.

In the inquisition held after the death of this last William Martin is enumerated : —

1st.   That " the Abbott of St. Dogmaells holdeth one knightes ffee called Cassia " etc. " valued at c^s."

7th.   " That the foresaid Abbott of St. Dogmaells owns half of the knight's fee of Kefen Chymwyrth."

George Owen writes under " Lords of Kemes," p. 459 : —

" Item. In the Recordes of the same yeere [6 Ed. II] it is written that Tangustel, the sonne of Keybour [Ceibwr] was indicted before the Steward of Pembroke, in his

Tour held at St. Dogmaells, for that he, for theft by him committed, fledd to the church of Nevearne in Kemeys, for wᶜʰ the towneshipp [St. Dogmaels] paid cˢ."

Thomas Warlaugh was also indicted for stealing a horse in St. Dogmaels; his wife, Joan, appeared and paid a fine of 6s. 8d. for him.

Later in the Calendar of Close Rolls it is noted that the Abbot of St. Dogmaels held a quarter of a knight's fee in Whittokesden, valued at 10s. yearly; this is the one referred to earlier in the " Testa de Nevill."

In 1330 (3 Edward III) William Martin having died, and James de Audeley, his heir, being a minor, Edward III, at Eltham, exercises the rights of the Barony of Cemaes, as guardian to the minor, on the death of the Abbot John de la Rede, namely, of putting in a warden to see that the monies belonging to the Abbey were not misapplied; but were spent on the Abbey, and also to receive the fealty of the new Abbot, when appointed. When such fealty was received, the warden was removed.

CARTÆ BARONIÆ DE KEYMES.
Extracts from the Roll of the County of Pembroke.

Also in the Rolls of the same year 6 Edw. II it is thus entered Tantustel son of Keybs was indicted before the Seneschal of Pembroke in his court held at St. Dogmaels for a theft he had committed he fearing for himself fled to the church of Nevern in Kemeys and afterwards fled the country before the coroner of Pembroke had taken his abjuration. Wherefore the township has paid for his escape 100s. and it is charged in the said rolls.

Also there comes the same year as appears in the roll of the county one Joan wife of Thomas Warlaugh a felon and gives to the said Earl for fine and forfeit of the land of the said Thomas in Morvill to have to wit 6s. 8d. And he was indicted for feloniously stealing a horse at St. Dogmaels etc.

CALENDAR OF CLOSE ROLLS. 20 Edw. II, m. 10-11.

Vol. 228, p. 595. To Robt. de Bikkemor Escheator in the Cos. of Devon Cornwall Somerset Order to deliver to Robt. de Watevill and Margaret his wife late wife of William son of Wm. Martin Tenant in chief the following knts fees which were the said William Martin's and assigned to her as dower . . . . Co. Devon . . . . a quarter of a fee in WHITTOKESDEN, which the Abbot of St. Dogmaels holds of the yearly value of 10s.

Assignment of kts fees made to James de Andele Kinsman and co-heir of the aforesaid William son of William . . . . a fee in CASSIA in Wales which the Abbot of St. Dogmaels holds of the yearly value of 100s. . . . a moiety of a fee in Wales which the Abbot of St. Dogmalls holds of the yearly value of 100s.

---

¹ White Oxen, in Dean Prior.

(Extracts.)

Of assignment of dower of knights fees which were of William son of William Martyn.

The King to his beloved Richard de Bikkemore his Escheator in the counties of Cornwall Devon Somerset and Dorset greeting. Know ye that of the knights' fees which were of William son of William Martyn deceased who of us held in chief and which on occasion of the death of the same were taken into our hand we have assigned to our beloved and trusty Robert de Watewill and Margaret his wife sometime the wife of aforesaid William fitzMartin the fees underwritten to wit . . . the fourth part of a knight's fee with appurtenances in Whittokesdon in the said county [of Devon] which the Abbot of St. Dogmaels holds and worth ten shillings.

Assignment of knights fees made to James de Audeley cousin and one of the heirs of aforesaid William fitzMartin . . . one knights fee with appurtenances in Cassia in Wales which the Abbot of St. Dogmaels holds and which is worth 100 shillings . . . the half of a knights fee with appurtenances in Wales which the Abbot of St. Dogmaels holds which is worth 100 shillings.

CLOSE ROLL. 3 Edw. III, m. 24.

For the Abbot of St. Dogmael in the land of Cemaes in Wales.

The King to his beloved and trusty Roger de Mortimer Earl of March Justiciar of the King in Wales or his lieutenant in South Wales greeting. Whereas we of late at the prosecution of our beloved in Christ the Abbot of St. Dogmaels in the land of Cemaes in Wales reporting to us that William Martin now deceased late lord of the said land of Cemaes and his ancestors lords of that land who for the time were the temporalities of the Abbey aforesaid at every vacancy of the same into their hands were wont to take and their ancestors aforesaid having received the fealty of the coming Abbot those temporalities of the said Abbey were bound to deliver without that we or our progenitors thereof in any vacancies of the said Abbey ought in anything to intermeddle and supplicating us that to the said Abbot the temporalities of such Abbot which late by the death of Brother John le Rede late Abbot of that place because the said land of Cemaes is in our hand by reason of the minority of James son of Nicholas de Audeley cousin and one of the heirs of aforesaid William who of the lord Edward late King of England our father held in chief were taken into our hands. We will shall be delivered and charge you that upon the estate which the said Abbot and his predecessors had in the Abbey aforesaid at the time of vacancy of the same and of other articles touching the premises you should make diligent inquisition. And by such inquisition by you the aforesaid lieutenant by our mandate made and into our Chancery returned it was found that from the time of the first foundation of the said Abbey the lords of the land of Cemaes founders of the said Abbey in times of vacancy of the same no issues from the temporalities of the said Abbey were wont to take or ought to take but that after the death of every Abbot there the founders of the said Abbey were wont to place a warden there on their behalf upon the temporalities of the said Abbey. So that the said Warden should take or ought to take nothing to the use of the founders but that he might see that the issues forthcoming of such temporalities were not dilapidated but were expended to the use of the aforesaid Abbey. And when the Abbot there was elected and confirmed having received the fealty of the same the aforesaid Warden retired without taking any issues from the temporalities aforesaid to the use of the said founders and that we and our progenitors aforesaid in any vacancies of that Abbey in anything have not intermeddled within the time of such custody by reason of the minority of the heirs of the lords of the land of Cemaes. We considering that we any other estate in that Abbey in the time of custody have not nor ought to have than the founders of the same when they are of full age have in the time of vacancy of the same charge you of the temporalities of the Abbey aforesaid being in our hand as is said if they are by reason aforesaid and not otherwise in our hand you further do not intermeddle, the issues if any therefrom you have levied to those whose they are you restore.

Witness the King at Eltham 1st May.
By writ of privy seal.

On November 26th, 1334, Edward II, at Westminster, confirms the renting of a mill and " 5 ferlings of land," with appurtenances at Rattre, Devon, to John Herbord, his heirs and assigns for the sum of four marks yearly.

Followed two years later on the death of William Martin by the assigning by Edward II of the fees of William Martin to Margaret, widow of William Martin, and her second husband, Robert de Watewill, amongst them the fourth part of a knight's fee in Whittokesdone (Co. Devon), held by the Abbot of St. Dogmaels at 10 shillings, and one knight's fee, in Cassia, in Wales, held by the same Abbot at 100 shillings, together with half another knight's fee held in Wales by the same Abbot at 100 shillings.

PATENT ROLL. 18 Edw. II, pt. I, m. 2.

For John Herberd.

The King to all to whom etc. greeting. The gift and grant which our beloved in Christ the Abbot and Convent of St. Dogmael by their charter made to John Herberd of a messuage and a mill and 5 " ferlings" of land with appurts in Rattre in the Co. of Devon. To have and to hold to the said John and his heirs at fee farm. Rendering therefrom to the said Abbot and Convent and their successors 4 marks per annum for ever ratifying and confirming the same for us and our heirs as far as in us lies we have granted and confirmed as the charter aforesaid reasonably testifies. Being unwilling that the aforesaid Abbot and Convent or their successors or the aforesaid John or his heirs . . . of the premises by us or our heirs, Justices, Escheators, sheriffs or other our bailiffs or ministers whatsoever should be hindered or burdened in anywise. In witness etc. Witness the King at Westminster 26th Nov. by fine of 100s.

In the reign of Richard II (1388), in the Registers of the Archbishopric of Canterbury, John Sampson was commissioned to visit the Abbey of St. Dog-maels and the Priory of Pill; but as there are no certificates of these visitations to be found in the registers, it is not known whether the visitation was carried out or no.

COURTNEY.

1388.

Commission by the Archbp to Master John Sampson to visit certain religious houses in the diocese of St. David's.

On the 4th May the Abbey of St. Dogmaels was visited.

On the 8th the Priory of Pulle (Pill).

The certificates of the above visitations are not entered in the register.

CHAPTER IX.

PALMY DAYS.

WITH the exception of a dispensation granted by Pope John XXIII, from St. Peter's at Rome, in the second year of his pontificate, and the year before the death of Henry IV, in the Papal Registers, Vol. VI, there is little concerning the Abbey till the reign of Henry VIII.

This dispensation was granted to Howel Lange, priest, Benedictine monk of St. Dogmaels, in the Diocese of St. David's, that notwithstanding his illegitimacy, as the son of an unmarried man and an unmarried woman, he may personally hold all dignities, perpetual administrations, offices, and benefices of his order, even if such dignities be abbatical, or be conventual priories.

There are about seven deeds ascribed to St. Dogmaels in the "Harleian MSS.," and in the "Originalia Rolls," etc.; these, however, refer instead to St. Dogwells, in Pebidiauk, so that at this period very little about the Abbey is known, beyond a dispute regarding tithes, under the heading of Devon, which apparently had not been paid in the reign of King Richard, and for which the Abbot of St. Dogmaels was summoned. He, however, pleaded that the King, Henry V, had already granted him a full pardon, and so he prayed for judgment, which doubtless he obtained, though no trace of it has been found. This abbot was probably Philip, who was abbot in 1415.

In a Patent Roll, 9 Henry VI, besides confirming the confirmation of nearly all the kings of England, since Henry I, of the grant of Robert Fitzmartin, the grant of William de Cantington to the Abbey is also confirmed.

MEMORANDA R. R. HIL TERM. 5 Hen. V, m. 4.

Devon.

Of the Abbot of St. Dogmaels late Collector of the second and third moieties of the tenth granted to King Richard the 2nd in the Archdeaconry of Cardigan summoned to render to the King account of the second moiety of the tenth aforesaid.

The Lord King hath commanded here his writ of his great Seal which is among the "Communia" of this term in these words Henry by the grace of God King of England and France and lord of Ireland to the Treasurer and Barons of his Exchequer greeting. Whereas on the first day of August in the third year of our reign of our special grace and with the assent of the lords spiritual and temporal and at the request of the Commons of our realm of England who were in our parliament at Westminster the 2nd year of our reign we pardoned and released Philip Abbot of St. Dogmaels or by whatever other name he is called and the convent of the same place all fines adjudicated amercements issues forfeitures reliefs scutages and all dues accounts profits arrears of farms and accounts to us on the 21st day of March the first year of our reign in whatever way due and pertaining. Also all kind of actions and demands which we alone against him or we conjointly with other persons or person may have or might have as in our letters patent thereupon made more fully is contained. We charge you that the said Abbot and Convent against the tenor of our aforesaid letters patent you shall not molest or burden in any way. Witness me myself at Westminster the 1st day of february the 4th year of our reign. And the tenor of the letters patent of which mention is made above in the writ follows in these words—Henry by the grace of God King of England to all his bailiffs and lieges to whom these present letters shall come, greeting Know ye that of our special grace and with the assent of the lords spiritual and temporal and at the request of the Commons of our realm of England who were in our last parliament we pardoned and released to Philip Abbot of St. Dogmaels or by whatever other name he may be called and the convent of the same place all trespasses offences misprisons contempts and impeachments by them before the 8th day of December last past against the form of the statutes concerning liveries of cloths and hoods made or performed and whereon punishment should fall in fine to redemption and in other pecuniary penalties or imprisonments the statutes aforesaid notwithstanding. So however that the present pardon and release shall not be to the damage prejudice or derogation of any other person.

And moreover of our mere motion out of reverence to God and by intuition of charity we have pardoned the said Abbot and Convent the suit of our peace which belongs to us against them for all kinds of treacheries rapes of women rebellions insurrections felonies conspiracies and other trespasses offences negligences extortions misprisons ignorances contempts concealments and deceptions by them before the 8th day of December in whatever way done or perpetrated murders perpetrated by them after the 19th day of November last past if there were any excepted upon which they are adjudged arrested or summoned. And also outlawries if any against them on these occasions have been promulged and thereon we have granted him our firm peace. While however the said Abbot and convent are not evildoers in the craft of money and multipliers of the coinage and washers of the gold and silver when coined in our Mint and clippers of our money common approvers and notorious thieves or felons who have made abjuration of the realm. So that however they stand to right in our Court if any shall prosecute them concerning the premises or any of the premises. And further of our more abundant grace we have pardoned and released the said Abbot and Convent all kinds of escapes of felons and chattels of fugitives outlaws and felons and all kinds of articles such as destructions of the highway and trespasses of vert and venison sale of woods within our forests and without and other things whatsoever before the said

8th day of December within our realm of England and the parts of Wales . . . upon which punishment shall fall by due demand or by way of fine and ransom or in other pecuniary penalties or in forfeiture of goods and chattels or imprisonments or amercements of counties townships or of any persons or in a charge of their free tenants who have never trespassed as of heirs executors land tenants Escheators sheriffs Coroners and others and all which to us against them should belong by the causes aforesaid. And also every kind of grant alienation and purchase by them of lands and tenements of us or our progenitors sometime Kings of England held in chief. And also grants alienations and purchases in mortmain made and had without our royal license. Also every kind of intrusion and entry by them in their inheritance in part or in whole after the death of their ancestors without duly sueing of the same out of our royal hand before the same 8th day of December done together with the issues and profits therefrom in the meantime taken. And also we have pardoned and released to the aforesaid Abbot and Convent all kinds of fines judgments amercements issues forfeitures reliefs scutages and all kinds of dues accounts prests and arrears of farms and accounts on the 1st day of March the first year of our reign in whatever way due and belonging. Also all kinds of actions and demands which we alone against him or we conjointly with other persons or person have or may have. And also outlawries against them promulged for any of the aforesaid causes. And moreover we have pardoned and released to the said Abbot and Convent all kinds of pains before the same 8th day of December forfeited before us or our council Chancellor Treasurer or any of our Judges for any cause and all other pains as well to us as to our most beloved father deceased for any cause before the same 8th day of December forfeited and to our use to be levied. And also all surieties of the peace before the same 8th day of December similarly forfeited. So that this our present pardon as far as concerns the premises or any of the premises shall not be to the damage prejudice or derogation of any other person that of us. In witness whereof we have caused to be made these our letters patent. Witness me myself at Westminster the 1st day of August the third year of our reign by the King himself. Upon which comes here on the morrow of St. Hilary this term the aforesaid Abbot by Richard Hutley his attorney and complains that he has been harshly distrained by the sheriff of the county of Devon as collector of the second and third moiety of a tenth and the moiety of a tenth to the lord Richard late King of England the second after the conquest from the clergy of the province of Canterbury in the church of St. Paul at London the 2nd day of March the 21st year of the said late King granted in the Archdeaconry of Cardigan. To render account to the lord King that now is of the 2nd moiety of the tenth aforesaid. And this unjustly because he says that the said lord King that now is has pardoned the aforesaid Abbot of St. Dogmaels all kinds of dues accounts due prests arrears of farms and accounts also all kinds of demands etc. As in the writ and abovesaid letters patent of the King more fully is contained. Whereupon the said Abbot does not think that the said lord King that now is will impeach him further in the premises. And he prays judgment etc.

There then occurs a long gap during the Wars of the Roses, when nothing about either St. Dogmaels or her cells can be gleaned, till, in 1504, in the reign of Henry VII, in the muniment room at Canterbury Cathedral, in the Registers

of that Archbishopric, occurs a record of the Visitation of the Deanery of
Cemaes, at Newport, Pembrokeshire, on the 14th July. Evidently by this the
secular priests had ceased to keep the outlying chapels belonging to the Abbey
in order, for we read of ruined chancels and damaged windows, though it is
noted that the Rector of Pill had restored his chancel. This is followed two
days later by a visitation at St. Dogmaels, held in the chapter house of the
Abbey, when the Abbot Dom Lewis Baron, and the Prior of Caldey, Dom
Nicholas, together with five other monks, are examined, who all agree that the
monastery was in good order and that they are free from debt.

These visitations took place while the see of St. David's was vacant, owing
to the death of John Morgan, the late Bishop, which is noted in these same
registers. The Abbey seems to have been prosperous at this time, as it was in
Henry VII's reign that the fan tracery roof was added, besides other
restorations.

THE REGISTERS OF THE ARCHBISHOPRIC OF CANTERBURY.
Warham,[1] f. 228.

The visitation of the Deanery of Cemaes in the Church of Newport, the 14th day of
the month of July, A.D. 1504.

The Abbot of St. Dogmaels impropriator of Llantood, Moylgrove, Eglwyswrw and
Monington appears by his proctors Dom Philipp Lawrence vicar of St. Dogmaels also
appears Dom Hugo Harris vicar of Llantood also appears Dom Phillip Lloyd vicar
of Eglwyswrw also appears, he is found guilty of incontinence, his chancel ruinous and
the windows not glazed.

Also at the visitation of the Deanery of Pebidiank from the same registers, we
find the Abbot of St. Dogmaels, impropriator of Fishguard, appears by his proctor of
good life Dom John ap Atho vicar of Fishguard also appears, he is found guilty of
incontinence.

Dom John Howell precentor of the Cathedral Church of St. Dogmells[2] also
appears—of good life.

Dom John Lowelin vicar there appears—of good life.

Dom Griffin Cedras vicar of Llanwnda also appears—of good life.

Now apparently from these two documents most of the priests appear to
have led good lives, with the exception of the Vicar of Eglwyswrw, and the
Vicar of Fishguard, both of whom had been convicted of immorality, and the
Vicar of Eglwyswrw also of neglecting to keep the chancel of his church in
good repair.

---

[1] Warham was Archbishop of Canterbury, and was the predecessor of Cranmer.
[2] ? St. Dogmaels.

The last three on the lists, if St. Dogwells is meant instead of St. Dogmaels, would have nothing to do with the Abbey; but it might be of interest to residents in these two places to know the manner of life their priests led at that date, and that it was good.

REGISTERS OF ARCHBISHOPRIC OF CANTERBURY.

Warham, f. 288, A.D. 1504, Henry VII.

Visitation of the monastery of Blessed Mary of St. Dogmaels made in the Chapter House there 16th day of the month of July of the year aforesaid.

Dom Lewis Baron Abbot there was interrogated and diligently examined of and upon the estate of his monastery who says that his monastery is in good estate and that it is not indebted to any one and that his brethren are of good and honest conversation and obedient to him at their free will.

Dom Nicholas Prior de Caldey being interrogated and examined agrees in all his statements with the Abbot.

Dom Phillip being interrogated and examined agrees with the Prior of Caldey above examined.

Dom Thomas Jevan Dom William Griffith Dom Thomas Baron Dom David . . being diligently and separately examined agree in all their statements with the Abbot and brethren above examined.

And the oath of canonical obedience by them to the lord Archbishop due being first received it was enjoined on the Abbot abovesaid that every day at dinner he should have read at the table by one of his brethren two or three rules of the Order of St. Benedict and he should so continue [to do] for the better instruction of his brethren.

SHAFT OF FAN TRACERY, ST. DOGMAELS ABBEY.

Photographed by Bishop Mitchinson, Master of Pembroke College, Oxford.

CHAPTER X.

THE DISSOLUTION.

THE original of this Acknowledgment of the King's Supremacy remains in the Chapter House, at Westminster, as also does the one signed by the prior and monks of Pill Priory, with their seal attached; it is signed by the abbot and eight of his monks, and has the COMMON SEAL of the Abbey attached to it, the impression being on red wax; it is oval, of moderate size, and somewhat flattened. The subject of it, corresponding with the dedication of the Abbey, is the Virgin Mary, seated under an ornamental arch, with the infant Christ in her lap. Below the arch is a monk praying, with the legend S. COMUNE. SANTI. DOG. . . LIS. DE. KEMMEYS., as will be seen by the impression hereafter given.

In the photograph of the Acknowledgment opposite, signed by the abbot and monks, it will be seen that the document is in one handwriting. The abbot signs his own name, as also does Dom Hugo Eynon, whereas the other seven names appear to have been written by the same hand, possibly that of Dom Robert Thomas, thus indicating how few of the monks could write even in 1534.

There is a noticeable fact regarding these signatures, every name being preceded by Dominus, so that the acknowledgment evidently was not signed by the ordinary fathers, if there were eight entitled to the title of "Dominus" there would be two or three times that number of monks in the Abbey, and not simply eight as quoted by fairly modern writers.

The honour given to Henry VIII's wife, Anne Boleyn, and the Princess Elizabeth, then one year old, will be noted in this act of supremacy.

In the Cotton MSS., Cleopatra, E. IV, f. 388, the Abbey is valued at £78 18s.

Acts of Supremacy.
Ch. H°, S. 3, 103.*

Since it is the interest not only of the Christian Religion and of piety but also the rule of our obedience that to our lord King Henry, the eighth of that name, to whom alone after Christ Jesus our Saviour we owe all things not only entirely but altogether in Christ and always the same sincere whole and perpetual devotion of soul faith observance honour worship reverence we should offer but also the reason of our said faith and observance as often as it shall be required we should give most willingly and openly to all if the matter demands and should testify. Let all to whom this present writing shall come know that we the Abbot and Convent of the house and monastery of St. Dogmael in the diocese of St. David's with one mouth and voice and with the unanimous consent and assent of all to this our deed given under our common seal in our Chapter House for us and our successors all and singular for ever we confess testify and faithfully promise and faithfully pledge ourselves and successors all and singular to whole inviolate sincere and perpetual faith observance and obedience we will always pay towards our lord King Henry the 8th and towards Queen Anne wife of the same and towards his offspring of the said Anne lawfully as well begotten as to be begotten and this same to the people we will notify preach and recommend wherever the place and occasion shall be due. Also that you hold always ratified and confirmed and for ever shall hold that the aforesaid our King Henry is head of the Anglican church. Also that the Roman bishop who in his bulls usurps the name of Pope and arrogates to himself the supreme Pontificate hath not any greater jurisdiction given to him by God in this realm of England than any other foreign bishop. Also that none of us in any sacred assembly privately or publicly held shall call the said Roman bishop by the name of Pope or Supreme Pontiff but by the name of the Roman bishop or [Bishop] of the Roman Church. And that none of us shall pray for him as Pope but only as Bishop of Rome. Also that to our said lord King alone and his successors we will adhere and his laws and decrees will maintain. For ever renouncing the laws decrees and canons of the Bishop of Rome which are found to be against the divine law and sacred scripture or against the rights of this realm. Also that none of us in any either private or public assembly shall presume to distort anything taken out of the sacred scripture to another sense but each one shall preach in a Catholic and orthodox way Christ and his words and works simply openly sincerely and according to the Canon or rule of the sacred scripture and of the true Catholic and orthodox doctors. Also that every one of us in his prayers and supplications made of custom first of all will commend the King as supreme head of the Anglican church to God and the prayers of the people then the Queen Anne with her offspring then last the Archbishops of Canterbury and York with the other orders of the clergy. Also that we all and singular the aforesaid and our successors firmly bind ourselves in conscience and by oath that all and singular the aforesaid faithfully for ever we will observe. In witness whereof to this our deed we have appended our common seal and with our own name each with his own hand we have subscribed.

Given in our Chapter house the 30th day of the month of July the year of our lord 1534.

William Abbot of the monastery of St. Dogmael

Dom Hugh Eynon

Dom Robert Thomas

Dom Philip Griffith

Dom John David

Dom William Bonne

Dom David William

Dom Lewis Laurens

Dom David Res

VALOR ECCLESIASTICUS, 26 Hen. VIII.

First Fruits Office.

Abbey of St. Dogmael in Cemaes, in the County of Pembroke.

William Abbot follower of the religion of St. Martin[1] and the convent of the same place holding the monastery or cell[2] of St. Dogmaels the town mills houses building orchard pastures granges lands and tenements besides the possessions below mentioned in towns places hamlets below mentioned for themselves and their successors in pure and perpetual alms together with the visé of frankpledge and the court to be held at the town of St. Dogmaels at their pleasure and the pleasure of their tenants fixed upon in accordance with the foundation and grant of Martin of the Towers.[3]

The Abbey of St. Dogmaels.

The manor or town of St. Dogmaels, and manors of Fish-
    guard and Grangistown with the appurtenances at the
    true value per annum of £16 13 4

Mynachlog Ddu with profits of free chapel at the same place
    per ann. 8 15 6

Lands and tenements in Haverfordwest per ann. 10 0

In Pembroke 1 6 8

In Menyth Tergh 1 6 8

[Total Receipts should be £28 12 2]

[However] the total Receipts are [given as] £28 7 2

Thence to be deducted at his Treasury Pembroke in any year whatever for the aforesaid lands as session dues and once only at the first entry of the said Queen[4] as

---

[1] Error, should be St. Benedict. Martin the founder again confounded with Martin the Saint.
[2] The Abbey was never a cell.   [3] Robert Fitzmartin.   [4] Anne Boleyn.

presents do give and grant to the said William a certain annuity or yearly pension of 20 marks sterling. To have enjoy and yearly to take the same 20 marks to the said William and his assigns from the time of the dissolution and suppression of the said late Abbey to the term and for the term of the life of the said William until the said William shall be promoted to one or more ecclesiastical benefices or other suitable promotion of the clear yearly value of 20 marks or more by us as well by the hands of the Treasurer of our aforesaid Court who for the time shall be. He shall be paid from our treasure in his hands from the aforesaid revenues happening to remain as by the hands of our Receivors of the particulars of our Revenues aforesaid of the said Revenues at the feasts of the Annunciation B V M and St. Michael the Archangel by equal portions. Because express mention etc. In witness whereof etc. Witness etc. at Westminster the 10th March the 28th year of our reign.

By the Chancellor and Council aforesaid by virtue of the warrant aforesaid.

PATENT ROLL, 35 Hen. VIII.
pt. 5, m. 9.

The King to all to whom etc. greeting. Know ye that we in consideration of four hundred and thirty nine pounds fourteen shillings of our good and lawful money of England paid to the hands of the Treasurer of our Court of Augmentations of the Revenues of our Crown to our use by our beloved Richard Savery of Totnes in our county of Devon gentleman of which said sum of four hundred and thirty nine pounds fourteen shillings we acknowledge that we are fully satisfied and contented and the said Richard his heirs and executors thereof quit and exonerate by these presents of our special grace certain knowledge and mere motion have given and granted and by these presents do give and grant to the aforesaid Richard Savery all that our lordship or manor of RATTRE and all that our Rectory and church of Rattre in our said county of Devon with all their rights members and appurts. now or late in the tenure or occupation of John Manisty or his assigns and late to the monastery of St. Dogmaels in South Wales in our County of Pembroke belonging and appertaining and late being parcel of the possessions and revenues of the same late Monastery also the advowson gift presentation free disposal and right of patronage of the vicarage of the church of blessed Mary of Rattre aforesaid. And also all that our wood or coppice of wood called Winterscomes Coppie containing by estimation two acres also all that our wood or coppice of wood called Hurtley Coppie containing by estimation one acre. And also all that our wood or grove called Commen Grove containing by estimation two acres. Also all that our wood or grove called Blakewell Grove containing by estimation one acre and all the land ground and soil of the same woods lying or growing in the parish of Rattre in our said county of Devon now or late in the tenure or occupation of the said John Manisty or his assigns and to the said late monastery of St. Dogmaels late belonging and appertaining. Also all and singular the messuages mills houses buildings lands etc. rents reserved upon certain leases and grants. And also woods underwoods furze heath moors commons ways waste grounds waters fishings fisheries Court-leets profits of Courts views of frankpledge etc. knights fees wardships marriages escheats reliefs heriots fairs markets tolls customs fairs free warrens goods and chattels waifs strays. And also glebes tithes etc. in Rattre aforesaid or elsewhere wherever in our said county of Devon to the said manor or lordship and Rectory or either of them in whatever way belonging or appertaining of same manor or lordship and Rectory now or late in the tenure or occupation of the said John Manisty or his assigns. We give also for the consideration aforesaid and of our certain knowledge and mere motion by these presents do grant to the aforesaid Richard Savery all that annual rent of twenty pounds upon lease to the aforesaid John Manisty to us reserved also all and singular other woods underwoods and trees of in and upon the premises or any parcel thereof growing or being. And also the reversion and reversions of the aforesaid manor or lordship and Rectory etc. with all their appurtenances in as ample manner and form as the last late Abbot and late Convent of the said late monastery of St. Dogmaels had held or enjoyed or ought to have had held or enjoyed and as fully and wholly and in as ample manner and form as the same all and singular to our hands by reason or pretext of the dissolution or surrender of the said late monastery or by reason or pretext of any charter gift grant or surrender by the said late Abbot and late Convent under their Conventual seal to us thereof made or by reason or pretext of any act of parliament in whatsoever way they came or should come and in our hands now are or ought to be. Excepting and to us our heirs and successors altogether reserved all and singular advowsons and rights of patronage to the said monastery or lordship and other the premises in whatever way belonging or appertaining excepting only the advowson of the vicarage of the church of the Blessed Mary of Rattre aforesaid. Which said manor or lordship rectory lands tenements and other the premises with their appurtenances in Rattre aforesaid extend to the clear yearly value of twenty pounds and not more. To have hold and enjoy the aforesaid manor or lordship of Rattre and the aforesaid Rectory of Rattre and the aforesaid messuages mills lands tenements glebes tithes meadows etc. advowson of the vicarage of Rattre aforesaid and all and singular the premises with all their appurtenances excepting the afore excepted to the aforesaid Richard Savery etc. for ever. To hold etc. by the service of a thirtieth part of a knight's fee. And rendering therefrom yearly to us our heirs and successors forty shillings of our legal money of England at our said Court of Augmentations of the Revenues of our Crown at the feast of St. Michael the Archangel every year to be paid by name of a tenth part of the premises for all rents services exactions and demands whatsoever therefrom to us our heirs or successors in any way to be rendered paid or done. And further we will and by our royal authority which we exercise by these presents have granted to the aforesaid Richard Savery his heirs and assigns that the said Richard etc. may and shall have hold and enjoy and to their own proper use convert the aforesaid Rectory and aforesaid tithes etc. as fully and wholly and in as ample manner and form as the last late Abbot and late Convent of the said late monastery of St. Dogmaels or any of their predecessors in right of the said late monastery the aforesaid Rectory and other the premises to the said Rectory belonging had held or enjoyed etc. We will also for us our heirs and successors for the consideration aforesaid and of our certain knowledge and mere motion by these presents have granted to the aforesaid Richard Savery etc. that the said Richard etc. shall have hold and enjoy within the aforesaid manor or lordship the Rectory and other singular the premises with all their appurts and within every parcel therefore so many such the same and similar Courts leet views of ffrank-pledge and all which to views of ffrankpledge pertain or in future may or ought to belong fines amercements assize and assay of bread wine and beer goods and chattels waifs strays free warren and all which to free warren belongs rights profits liberties privileges etc. which the said late Abbot and convent had held and enjoyed. And also we will for the consideration aforesaid and of our certain knowledge and mere motion by these presents have granted to the aforesaid Richard Savery his heirs and assigns that we our heirs and successors for ever yearly and from time to time will acquit exonerate and indemnify and keep as will the said Richard etc. who the aforesaid manor or lordship Rectory lands tenements and other the premises with all their appurtenances against us our heirs etc. of all and every kind of corrody rent fee annuity and sums of money whatsoever from the aforesaid manor or lordship rectory and other the premises or of any parcell thereof in whatever way issuing or to be paid or thereon charged or to be charged except the rent and service above by these presents to us reserved. Willing moreover and firmly enjoining charging as well our Chancellor and Council of our said court of Augmentations of the Revenues of our Crown for the time being as well all and singular our Receivers Auditors and other officers and ministers whatsoever of our heirs etc. that they and each of them upon the sole showing of these our letters patent or enrolment of the same without any other writ or warrant from us our heirs and successors in any way to be sought obtained or prosecuted full whole and due allowance default deduction and exoneration shown of all and every kind of corrodies rents fees annuities and sums of money whatsoever from the aforesaid manor or lordship and other the premises as aforesaid issuing or to be paid or thereon charged or to be charged shall make or cause to be made. And these our letters patent or inrolment of the same shall be yearly and from time to time as well to our said Chancellor and Council of our said Court of Augmentations etc. as well to our Receivers Auditors etc. sufficient warrant and exoneration in this behalf. And further we give for the consideration aforesaid and of our certain knowledge and mere motion by these presents have granted to the aforesaid Richard Savery all issues rents reversions and profits aforesaid of the manor or lordship Rectory and other and singular the premises with all their appurtenances from the feast of the Annunciation of the blessed Virgin Mary last past forthcoming or growing. To have to the said Richard of our gift without any account or any other provision to us our heirs and successors in any way to be rendered paid or made. And also we will and by these presents have granted to the said Richard Savery that he may have and shall have these our letters patent under our great seal of England in due manner made and sealed without fine or fee great or small to us in our hanaper or elsewhere to our use in any way to be rendered paid or made. Because express mention etc. In witness etc. Witness the King at Westminster 8th July.

By writ of privy seal etc.

Amongst the particulars for grants, Henry VIII, No. 160, dated March 10th, 1537, is the preliminary account of the Manor and property of the Abbey of St. Dogmaels, together with the Manor and Island of Caldey, followed by the charter of sale to John Bradshaw and his heirs, of Presteign, Radnorshire, and formerly of Lancashire, with the annual property, or King's tax thereon.

These deeds should be specially interesting to the present inhabitants of St. Dogmaels, owing to the family names, which are still mostly the same, and also the place names of various portions of land, lately belonging to the Abbey.

Among these " Potpitt," now " Poppitt," formerly the name for " Pwll-cam."[1]

" Dary or dareg," derived from " Deri " = " oak."

" Grige Pende " = " Crugiau[2] pen du " = the " crags of the blackhead."

" Parke Rolle " = " Parc y rheol " = " the roadside meadow."

" Arles " = a " great benefit," it was a meadow of about four acres, so it may be presumed it was so named on account of its excellence.

" Lalkerly " = " Llacharle " = " the bright place."

" ffunhone " = " ffynnon " = a " spring," a " source."

" The laundre " or " laundry " = Llandre = the house, or manor enclosure, this was evidently the Abbey enclosure, about forty acres, and where John Bradshaw lived.

" Haver Brokechelly " = " Hafn a firth "[3] = and if brokechelly can be taken as " brochell y lle," or " llys," it would then signify " the place or court of Tempest of the Firth."

" Briscwm " = " Brwys cwm " = " The fertile valley."

" Place pen Abounte " = " Plas pen y bont " = " The Place at the Head of the Bridge."

" Roosland " = " Rhos = a moor," therefore " moorland."

" Pen rallt " = " The head of the forest."

" Darne Parke " = " Dan y parke " = " Below the meadows."

John Bradshaw had to pay the yearly stipend of the Vicar of St. Thomas the Martyr's.

In 1538, 29 Henry VIII, there follows from the Aug[n] Min[rs] Accounts (155), the Compotus of John Bradshaw, with full description of the different places belonging to the late Abbey, and also of their values, together with arrears to the sum of £8 18s. 8d., also that it was let to farm to John Bradshaw for twenty-one years, who is here described as of Ludlow, in the County of Salop. It comprised all lands, buildings, etc., belonging to the Abbey in St. Dogmaels, with the site of the late Abbey, also the Rectory of the Church of St. Thomas the Martyr, Eglwyswrw, Caldey with appurtenances, also Bayvill, Moylgrove, Llantood, St. Nicholas Fishguard, Grangeston, and the Chapels of Penkelly vychan, Nantgwyn, Lisprant, and Newton, with appurtenances, and every conceivable right, as will be seen in the deed itself, only excepting the Manor of Rattre, which had been disposed of separately, and the Rectories of Maen-

---

[1] The crooked pool.   [2] Pronounced here Cri-ge.   [3] Danish.

clochog, Llandilo, Llancolman, and the Chapel of Mynachlogddu, and tenements at Haverford and Pembroke, which had belonged to the same Monastery.[1]

John Bradshaw had to pay the yearly rental of £90 9s. 8½d., also he paid the Chaplain of St. Dogmaels £4 yearly, and £3 13s. 6d. to the Chaplain of Caldey.

The King granting John Bradshaw for repairs, thatch, also hedgebote, firebote, ploughbote, and cartbote, that is wood for the making and repairing of ploughs and carts, the repair of hedges, firewood, but not timber. Then follows a similar account of the Lordship of Rattre, formerly part and parcel of St. Dogmaels Abbey, but now handed over to John Manisty.

Together with rents at Haverford and Pembroke, formerly belonging to the Abbey, amounting to thirty-six shillings and eightpence.

The Rectories of Maenclochog, Llandilo, and Llancolman, amounting to £8.

The rents of tenants at will in Mynachlogddu at a rental of 117 shillings and one penny.

The Chapel of Mynachlogddu at 100 shillings.

With mentions of the £9 6s. 8d. formerly paid to the last Abbot William Hire by the Priory of Pill, and a pension of sixteen shillings and eightpence formerly paid by the Priory of Glascareg, in Ireland, to the Abbot of St. Dogmaels; but which by the oath of William Hire, late Abbot, had not been paid for forty years and more.

In fees and wages, £4 2s.

Together with a few odd items belonging to the late Abbey.

In the Roll, 29 Henry VIII, Augmentation Office, the possessions of the Abbey are valued at £120 18s. 6d.; Rattre, £20; Glascareg, £3 6s. 8d.; Llandilo, Llancolman, and Maenclochog, £8, were not, however, let to Mr. Bradshaw, so that if £31 6s. 8d. is subtracted from this valuation, St. Dogmaels and the remaining possession as let to Mr. Bradshaw were only worth £89 11s. 10d.

PARTICULARS FOR GRANTS.

Hen. VIII, No. 160.   Mar. 10, 28 Hen. VIII, 1537.

The late Monastery of St. Dogmaels in the County of Pembroke.

By John Bradshaw.

Parcel of the possessions of the said late monastery in South Wales suppressed by authority of Parliament.

The site of the late monastery aforesaid with the demesne lands in the county aforesaid is worth in houses buildings barns gardens orchards and two mills which lay

---

[1] *See* deed.

Caldey Island, from Tenby Castle.

unoccupied before the suppression of the said late monastery x^s one close of arable
land called Parke Rolle containing 17 acres—11s. 4d. : one close of arable land called
the New parke containing 3 acres adjacent to the close called Parke Rolle aforesaid—
2s : a parcel of waste land called Grige pende 3s. 4d. : another parcel of waste land
called the Abbot's parke with a messuage called the Darey—3s. 4d. : one messuage
called the newer darey and one close of arable land called varn[1] parke containing
4 acres—2s. 8d. : one close of arable land called the medowe containing 1 acre—8d. :
one close called Potpitt[2] containing 15 acres adjacent to the seashore—6s. 8d. : one
close of arable land called Arles containing 4 acres—2s. : one close called the Great
close containing 4 acres—2s. : one close called doctor's parke containing 1 acre—8d. :
one close of arable land called free parke containing ½ acre 1 rood—8d. : one meadow
called the East meadow containing 1 acre—2s. : one meadow called lakerly containing
2 acres—10s. : one meadow called ffunhone containing 1½ acres—6s. 8d. Which said
premises are demised to John Bradshaw by Indenture under the seal of the lord King
of his Court of Augmentation of the revenues of the Crown under date 10th March
the 28th year of the reign of King Henry the 8th. To have the said site with the
parcels aforesaid to the aforesaid John and his assigns from the feast of St. Michael
the Archangel last past for the term of 21 years next ensuing and fully to be
completed rendering therefrom per ann. 74s.

Manor of St. Dogmaels otherwise the Laundre in the parish of St. Dogmaels aforesaid late Thomas Becket's Bishop in the county aforesaid with all the lands and
tenements to the aforesaid Laundry belonging.

The rents of divers tenements called Mill Broke with appurts : two tenements
with all their belongings called Haver Brekechelley : one burgage with a garden
annexed situate in the street called Landan within the township of St. Dogmaels : two
tenements with their appurts called Parke John Lloid and Wyott land : one burgage
with a garden and orchard adjacent late in the hands of Elizabeth Williams : two
acres of land lying in the East field of the township aforesaid with another small
piece of land to the same belonging : other two acres lying in a place called Briscum :
one tenement with appurts called Plas pen Abounte : one burgage called Arnard plas
Roos land : certain waste lands late in the tenure of James ap Powell Lloid : one
tenement with appurts late in the tenure of Owen ap Philip : one piece of land late
in the tenure of Robert ap Price ap Powell : one tenement with appurts situate by
Cardigan bridge : one tenement called Penralte : divers lands late in the hands of
William Hews : certain lands late in the hands of David ap Ieuan : one tenement
with certain lands to the same annexed late in the hands of Morice ap David :
one tenement with appurts late in the hands of Jenken Rogers j house with appurts late
in the hands of Jenken ap Ieuans j acre of land late in the tenure of Ieuan Powell
divers lands with a garden annexed late in the hands of John Sporrior j tenement with
appurts late in the tenure of John Mortimer. Which said land and tenements together
with the profits of court leets and views of frankpledge are demised to John Bradshaw
by Indenture above recited and a rent therefrom per ann. 8^{li} 2^s 5^d½.

Manor and island of Caldey with the chapel there and all the tithes, rents of
lands and tenements in the island aforesaid in the county aforesaid are worth in rents

---

[1] Varner in Dugdale.   [2] Poppitt of the present day.

and farms with all and every kind of tithe yearly growing in the island aforesaid late demised to divers persons and now in the tenure of aforesaid John Bradshaw by Indenture aforesaid per ann 116^s 10^d

17^{li} 3^s 3^{d}½ [1]

Reprises.

Namely in the stipend of a chaplain yearly celebrating divine service and having cure of souls in the chapel of Caldey per ann 73^s 6^d

And remaining clear 13^{li} 9^s 9^{d}½

ABSTRACT OF ROLL. 29 Henry VIII, Augmentation Office.

The late monastery of St. Dogmaels under the diocese of St. David's.

St. David's	St. Dogmaels	Manor Lands	...	...	...	3	4	0
		Rents	...	...	...	8	2	0½
			...	...	...	5	17	1
Devon—								
Manor of Rattre	...	...	...	...	...	20	0	0
Wales—								
Haverfordwest and Pembroke, Rents	...	...	...	...	1	16	8
Water Mill Fishguard	...	...	...	...	...	1	0	0
Rent in the town ,,	...	...	...	...	...	6	13	4
Grangiston rents	...	...	...	...	...	1	6	8
Caldey rents ...	...	...	...	...	...	5	16	10
Fishguard and Grangiston Rectories	...	...	...	...	10	6	8
Maenclochog House Llandilo and Llancolman	...	...	...	8	0	0
Mynachlog Ddu chapel	...	...	...	...	...	5	0	0
St. Thos. Rectory St. Dogmaels	...	...	...	...	20	0	0
Eglwyswrw	...	...	...	...	...	7	6	8
Nantgwyn Llysprant and Newton ...	...	...	...	7	6	8
Moylgrove Rectory	...	...	...	...	...	6	13	4
Llantood and St. Nicholas ...	...	...	...	...	6	13	4
Pill Late Priory	...	...	...	...	...	9	6	8
Glascareg (Ireland) rents	...	...	...	...	3	6	8
Penkelly Vychan	...	...	...	...	...	1	5	0

£120 18 6

AUGN. MINRS. ACCTS. 29-30 H. 8. 1538-9.

No. 155.

The late Monastery of St. Dogmaels within the Bishopric of St. David's.

Compotus of John Bradshaw Collector of Rents and farms of all and singular the lordships lands and tenements and other possessions whatsoever as well temporal as spiritual to the aforesaid late Monastery appertaining or belonging which to the hands of the lord King have now come and are and annexed to his Crown and of his heirs and successors the Kings of England in augmentation of the Revenues of the said Crown

---

[1] ? The addition; it is thus corrected in the Latin.

of England by virtue of a certain Act in his parliament held at Westminster upon prorogation the 4th Feb. [1537] the 27th year of the reign of the said lord King thereon published and provided as in the said Act among other things is contained to wit from the feast of St. Michael the Archangel the 29th year of the reign of the aforesaid King Henry the 8th until the said feast of St. Michael the Archangel then next ensuing the 30th year of the King aforesaid to wit for one whole year.

Arrears.

And of viij^{li} xviij^s viij^d of arrears of last Account of the year preceding as appears there.

Sum viij^{li} xviij^s viij^d

Site of the late monastery aforesaid with other things.

Of iiijx^{li} viij^s iij½^d forthcoming of divers parcels of land as well temporal as spiritual belonging to the late Monastery aforesaid he does not answer here because it is demised at farm to John Bradshawe by Indenture for term of 21 years settled under the seal of the lord King of his Court of Augmentations of the Revenues of his Crown as in the next title following more fully and particularly appears.

Sum nil.

ffirms.

But he answers of iiijx^{li} ix^s viij½^d of rents of the demesne land so demised to John Bradshaw by Indenture sealed with the seal of the Court of Augmentations of the Revenues of the Crown of the lord King the tenor of which follows in these words— This Indenture made between the most excellent prince and lord, the lord Henry the 8th by the grace of God King of England and France defender of the faith lord of Ireland and on earth supreme head of the Anglican Church of the one part and John Bradshawe of Ludlow in the County of Salop of the other part witnesseth that the said lord King by advice and consent of the council the Court of Augmentations of the Revenues of his Crown hath delivered granted and let at farm to the aforesaid John the house and site of the late Abbey or Monastery of St. Dogmaels within the Bishopric of St. David's by the authority of parliament suppressed and dissolved together with all houses edifices barns gardens orchards apple orchards ground and soil within the site and precinct of the said late Abbey etc. manor or lordship of Fishguard with appurts and a mill there with appurts to the said late monastery belonging and appertaining also the Rectories of the churches of St. Thomas the Martyr within the township of St. Dogmael, Eglwyswrw and Caldey with appurts Bayvill Moylgrove Llantood and St. Nicholas Fishguard Grangeston and the chapel of Penkelly Vychan Nantgwyn Lisprant Newton and Caldey with appurts to the said late monastery belonging and appertaining together with all tithes etc. whatsoever to the said Rectories and chapels or any of them belonging or appertaining and all messuages lands etc. and profits of Courts leet and views of frankpledge and other possessions and hereditaments whatsoever with their rights and commodities whatsoever in the township fields parishes and hamlets of St. Dogmaels Fishguard Grangeston Caldey Eglwyswrw Bayvill Moylgrove Llantood Penkelly Vychan Nantgwyn Lisprant and Newton to the said Monastery late belonging and appertaining. Excepting however and to the said lord King his heirs and successors altogether reserved the lordship and manor of Rattre and the Rectories of Maenclochog Llandillo and Llancoleman and the Chapel of Manoclog ddu and all the lands and tenements in Manochlog ddu Rattre Haverford and Pembroke to the said late monastery belonging and appertaining. And also excepting and reserved all wards marriages escheats reliefs great trees and woods and advowsons of the vicarages of the premises also well (illegible) and such edifices within the site and precinct of the said late monastery which the said lord King may in future command to be laid low and taken away. To have and to hold the site manors Rectories chapels lands etc. except the pre-excepted to the aforesaid John Bradshawe and his assigns from the feast of St. Michael the Archangel last past to the end of the term and for the term of 21 years then next ensuing and fully to be completed. Rendering therefrom yearly to the said lord King his heirs and successors Ninety pounds nine shillings and eight pence and one halfpenny of lawful money of England to wit for the aforesaid site lands meadows pastures rents and services in the township of St. Dogmaels aforesaid eleven pounds six shillings and five pence and one halfpenny and for the aforesaid lordship of Fishingard six pounds fourteen shillings and nine pence and for the aforesaid mill of Fishingard twenty shillings and for the aforesaid land and tenements in the township of Grangiston aforesaid twenty six shillings and eight pence and for the aforesaid Rectory of St. Thomas in the township of St. Dogmaels twenty pounds and for the aforesaid Rectory of Eglwyswrw seven pounds six shillings and eight pence and for the aforesaid Rectory of Bayvill four pounds thirteen shillings and fourpence and for the aforesaid Rectory of Molgrave six pounds thirteen shillings and four pence for the aforesaid Rectory of Llantood and St. Nicholas six pounds thirteen shillings and fourpence and for the aforesaid Rectories of Fyshguard and Grangiston ten pounds six shillings and eight pence and for the aforesaid Rectory or chapel and lands and tenements in Caldey one hundred and sixteen shillings and tenpence and for the aforesaid chapel of Penkelly Vychan twenty five shillings and for the aforesaid chapels of Nantgwyn Lisprant and Newton seven pounds six shillings and eight pence at the feast of the Annunciation of the blessed virgin Mary and St. Michael the Archangel or within one month of either feast of such feasts at the Court aforesaid by equal portions to be paid during the term aforesaid and the aforesaid lord King wills and by these presents grants that he his heirs and successors the said John Bradshaw and his assigns as well of four pounds yearly for the wage and stipend of a chaplain yearly celebrating the divine office and observing the care of souls in the church and parish of St. Dogmaels aforesaid. And of seventy three shillings and six pence yearly for the wage and stipend of a chaplain yearly celebrating the divine office and observing the cure of souls in the churches and parishes of Caldey aforesaid as of all rents fees etc. whatsoever of the premises or any of them issuing or to be paid except the rent above reserved against all persons whatsoever from time to time will exonerate acquit and defend and all houses and edifices of the premises in timber as in roofing of tiles and slate from time to time as often as shall be necessary and opportune will and sufficiently shall cause to be repaired sustained and maintained during the term aforesaid and the aforesaid John Bradshaw by these presents grants that he and his assigns roofing of thatch and all other necessary reparations of the premises except timber tiles and slate aforesaid from time to time as often as shall be necessary and opportune shall support and sustain during the term aforesaid and further the aforesaid lord King wills and by these presents grants that it shall be truly lawful to the aforesaid John Bradshaw and his assigns to take perceive and have competent and sufficient hedgebote firebote ploughbote and cartbote of in and upon the premises there and not elsewhere yearly to be expended and occupied during the term aforesaid. In witness whereof to one part of this Indenture with the said John remaining the aforesaid lord King his seal of the Court aforesaid appointed for the sealing of such deeds has commanded to be affixed and to the other part of the said Indenture with the said lord King remaining the aforesaid John has set his seal. Given at Westminster the 10th March the 28th year of the reign of the said lord King.

Sum iiijx^{li} ix^s viij^d ob.

The Lordship of Rattre in the County of Devon.

And of xx^{li} of rent of the whole lordship aforesaid with all its appurts and with all Courts etc. also all tithes of sheaves of the parish church of the Blessed virgin Mary of Rattre aforesaid so demised to John Manyssee by indenture sealed with the seal of the Court of Augmentations of the Revenues of the Crown of the lord King the tenor of which follows in these words—This Indenture made between the most excellent prince and lord the lord Henry the 8th by the grace of God King of England etc. and John Manysee of the other part witnesses that the said lord King by the advice and consent of his Council of the Court of Augmentation of the Revenues of the Crown hath delivered granted and at farm let to the aforesaid John the lordship and manor of Rattre with the appurts in the county of Devon together with the tithe of sheaves of the parish church of the Blessed Virgin Mary of Rattre to the said late Monastery of St. Dogmaels in South Wales by the authority of parliament suppressed and dissolved appertaining or belonging together with all messuages lands etc. and except however and to the said lord King his heirs and successors altogether reserved all wardships marriages escheats reliefs great trees and woods and advowsons of the vicarage of Rattre aforesaid. To have and to hold the manor and tithes aforesaid and other the premises with appurts excepting the before excepted to the aforesaid John and his assigns from the feast of St. Michael the Archangel last past to the end of and for the term of twenty one years then next ensuing and fully to be completed rendering therefrom yearly to the said lord King his heirs and successors twenty pounds of lawful money of England at the feasts of the Annunciation of the blessed virgin Mary and St. Michael the Archangel or within one month after either feast of those feasts at the Court aforesaid by equal portions during the term aforesaid and the aforesaid lord King wills and by these presents grants that he his heirs and successors the said John and his assigns of all rents fees feasts of Philip and James and St. Michael by equal portions. And of xxxvj^s viij^d of rent of one tenement with appurts situate in the township of Pembroke aforesaid demised at will to John Smyth to be paid at the terms aforesaid.

Sum xxxvj^s viij^d

Rectory of Maenclochog Llandilo and Llancolman.

And of viij^{li} of rent of the tithe of sheaves oblations and other profits there so demised to James Leche by Indenture sealed with the seal of the Court of Augmentations of the Revenues of the Crown of the Lord King of which the tenor follows in these words—This Indenture made between the most excellent prince and lord the lord Henry the 8th by the grace of God King of

England etc. of the one part and James Leche of la Hadden[1] in South Wales esquire of the other part witnesses that the said lord King by the advice and consent of his council of the Court of Augmentations of the Revenues of the Crown hath delivered granted and at farm let to the aforesaid James the rectories of Maenclochog Llandilo and Llancolman with appurts parcel of the late monastery of St. Dogmaels in South Wales etc. except however and to the said lord King his heirs and successors altogether reserved all great trees and woods of in or upon the lands of the premisses growing and being and the advowsons of the vicarages of Maenclochog Llandilo and Llancolman aforesaid. To have and to hold the rectories aforesaid with their appurts except the afore-excepted to the aforesaid James and his assigns from the feast of St. Michael the Archangel next coming to the end of the term and for the term of twenty one years then next ensuing and fully to be completed. Rendering therefrom yearly to the said lord King, his heirs and successors eight pounds of lawful money of England at the feasts of the Annunciation of the blessed Virgin Mary and St. Michael the Archangel or within one month after either feast or the feasts aforesaid at the Court aforesaid by equal portions and the aforesaid lord King wills and by these presents grants that he his heirs and successors to the said James and his assigns etc. And the aforesaid James has granted by these presents that he and his assigns roofing of thatch and all other necessary repairs of the premisses except repair of timber and roofing of tiles and slate aforesaid from time to time shall support and sustain during the term aforesaid and the aforesaid lord King further and by these presents grants that it shall be truly lawful to the aforesaid James and his assigns from time to time to take perceive and have of in and upon the premisses competent and sufficient hedgebote firebote ploughbote and cartbote there and not elsewhere yearly to be expended and occupied during the term aforesaid. In witness whereof to one part of this Indenture with the said James remaining the aforesaid lord King his seal of the Court aforesaid appointed for the sealing of such deeds hath commanded to be affixed. Given and to the other part of the said Indenture with the said lord King remaining the aforesaid James hath set his seal. Given at Westminster the 10th day of May the 29th year of the reign of the said lord King.

Sum viij[li]

Rent of tenants at will by copy and by Indenture in Manyghloke duy.

And of xiij[s] iiij[d] of rent of a tenement called Mynyth[2] terthe in the tenure of Parot's heir who holds freely To be paid at two terms of the year to wit at the feasts of the blessed Virgin Mary and St. Michael the Archangel by equal portions And of viij[s] iiij[d] of the rent of a tenement scituate and lying within the lordship aforesaid in the County of Pembroke and commonly called Mynachlog ddu y thache[3] which the abovesaid Howell now inhabits demised to Howell ap Thomas ap Owen by Indenture sealed with the Conventual seal of the late Monastery of St. Dogmaels aforesaid. Given the 8th day of October the 27th year of the reign of King Henry the eighth. To have to him and his assigns from the feast of St. Michael the Archangel last past before the date of these presents to the end of the term of 99 years then next ensuing and fully to be completed. Rendering therefrom as above to be paid at the feast of St. Michael the Archangel only as by one part of this Indenture with the Auditor remaining more

---

[1] Llawhaden.   [2] A mountain.   [3] Y ddachre = the beginning.

fully appears. And of v^s viij^d of rent of a tenement with appurts situate and lying within the lordship aforesaid in the county of Pembroke and commonly called Plas pant y Rege demised to Howell ap Owen ap Powell by Indenture sealed with the Conventual seal aforesaid given the 10th day of October the 27th year of the reign of Henry VIIIth. To have to him and his assigns from the feast of St. Michael the Archangel last past before the date of these presents to the end of the term of 99 years then next ensuing and fully to be completed. Rendering therefrom yearly as above to wit at the feast of St. Michael the Archangel only. And of x^s of rent of a tenement with all its appurts situate and lying within the lordship aforesaid in the County of Pembroke and commonly called Coine Karwyn[1] demised to David ap Ryce ap Owen by Indenture sealed with the Conventual seal aforesaid given the 12th day of October the 27th year of the reign of King Henry viijth. To hold to him his heirs and assigns from the feast of St. Michael the Archangel last past before the date of these presents to the end of the term of 99 years then next ensuing and fully to be completed. Rendering therefrom as above to be paid at the feast of St. Michael the Archangel only. And of xvj^s of the rent of two tenements with all their appurts situate and lying within the parish of St. Dogmaels in the lordship and county aforesaid and commonly called Landr[2] Mynachlog ddu demised to Lewis ap Ieuan by Indenture sealed with the Conventual seal aforesaid. Given the 10th day of October the 27th year of the reign of King Henry the viijth. To have to him his heirs and assigns from the feast of St. Michael the Archangel last past before the date of these presents to the end of the term of 99 years then next ensuing and fully to be completed. Rendering therefrom yearly to be paid at the feast of St. Michael the Archangel only. Rendering also and doing all other charges and services according to use and custom as other tenants there done and have been accustomed to do. And of iij^s iiij^d of rent of a tenement situate and lying within the lordship aforesaid at St. Julian's chapel demised by Indenture to Hoell ap Jenkyn ap Owen sealed with the conventual seal aforesaid which indeed he does not show. To be paid at the feasts of the Annunciation of the Blessed Virgin Mary and St. Michael the Archangel by equal portions. And of ix^s viij^d of the rent of a tenement with all its appurts situate and lying within the lordship aforesaid in the County of Pembroke and commonly called Pentr ithe[3] demised to Griffin ap Jevan ap Jenkyn by Indenture sealed with the Conventual seal aforesaid. Given the 9th day of October the 27th year of the reign of King Henry viijth. To have to him his heirs and assigns from the feast of St. Michael the Archangel last past before the date of these presents to the end of the term of 99 years then next ensuing and fully to be completed. Rendering therefrom yearly as above to be paid at the feast of St. Michael the Archangel only. Rendering also and doing all other charges and services according to use and custom as other tenants have done and have been accustomed to do. And of v^s viij^d rent of a tenement situate and lying within the lordship aforesaid in the county of Pembroke and commonly called Blaen y cowrse glethe[4] demised to Eynon ap David by Indenture sealed with the Conventual seal aforesaid. Given the 7th day of October the 27th year of the reign of King Henry viijth. To have to him his heirs and assigns from the feast of St. Michael the Archangel last past before the date of these presents

---

[1] Cwm Cerwyn, where the Abbey had had rights of pasturage for 5,000 sheep.

[2] Llandre = Home enclosure.   [3] Pentre uchaf = Upper chief house.   [4] The Cleddau.

to the end of the term of 99 years then next ensuing and fully to be completed rendering therefrom yearly as above to be paid at the feast of St. Michael the Archangel only rendering also and doing all other charges and services according to use and custom as other tenants there have done and have been accustomed to do as by one part of this Indenture with the Auditor remaining more fully appears. And of xj^s rent of three tenements with their appurts of which one lies at ybrone lase within the lordship of St. Dogmaels which Griffin ap David goes late held and the other two tenements lie at Hengurto as there by their metes and bounds they are limited and assigned and all other lands and tenements from the stream Blaenerth to Blaenban demised to Owen ap Powell and David ap Powell by Indenture sealed with the conventual seal aforesaid given the 9th day of July the 25th year of the reign of King Henry the 8th. To have to him his heirs and assigns from the feast of St. Michael the Archangel next coming after the date of these presents to the end of the term of 99 years then next ensuing and fully to be completed rendering therefrom yearly as above to be paid at the feast of St. Michael only. And of x^s. ij^d rent of a tenement with appurts demised at will to James ap Powell ap Bowen to be paid at the feast of the Annunciation of the Blessed Virgin Mary and St. Michael the Archangel by equal portions. And of iij^s viij^d rent of a tenement with appurts demised at will to Llewelyn ap Jevan Pickton to be paid at the terms aforesaid. And of v^s rent of a tenement with appurts demised at will to Jevan ap Powell ap Jevan ap David to be paid at the same terms. And of v^s viij^d rent of a tenement with appurts demised at will to Jenkyn ap Griffith to be paid at the same terms. And of 5^s rent of a tenement with appurts demised at will to Philip Thomas to be paid at the terms aforesaid. And of ij^s j^d rent of a tenement with appurts demised at will to David Willyams to be paid at the same terms. And of ij^s vj^d rent of a tenement with appurts demised at will to Thomas ap dio Gwil^{u}m to be paid at the same terms.

Sum cxvij^s j^d

Chapel of Mynachlog ddu.

And of c^s rent of the tithes of sheaves oblations and other profits so demised to Morgan John by Indenture sealed with the seal of the Court of Augmentations of the revenues of the crown of the lord King the tenor of which follows in these words—This Indenture made between the most excellent prince and lord the lord Henry the 8th of the one part and Morgan Johns of Llangadocke in the county of Carmarthen in Wales gentleman of the other part. Witnesses that the said lord King by the advice and consent of the council of the Court of Augmentations of the revenues of his Crown hath delivered granted and at farm let to the aforesaid Morgan Johns the chapel of Mynachlog ddu with all houses buildings tithes oblations and other profits to the said chapel belonging or appertaining which said chapel lately belonged to the monastery of St. Dogmaels in Wales etc. To have and to hold as well the said chapel with all houses buildings tithes etc. to the aforesaid Morgan his executors and assigns from the feast of the Annunciation of the Blessed Virgin Mary last past to the end of the term and for the term of 21 years then next ensuing and fully to be completed. Rendering therefrom yearly to the said lord King his heirs and successors c^s of lawful money of England at the feast of St. Michael the Archangel and the Annunciation of the Blessed Virgin Mary or within one month after either feast of such feasts at the Court aforesaid by equal portions to be paid during the term aforesaid and the aforesaid lord King wills and grants for himself his heirs and successors that they will allow yearly to the aforesaid Morgan four pounds for the stipend of a chaplain there yearly celebrating. In witness whereof to one part of this Indenture with the aforesaid Morgan remaining the aforesaid lord King his seal of the Court aforesaid appointed for the sealing of such deeds hath commanded to be affixed and to the other part of the said Indenture with the said lord King remaining the aforesaid Morgan hath set his seal. Given at Westminster the 12th day of May the 29th year of the reign of the said lord King.

Sum c^s

Pensions of the late Priory of Pulle.

Of ix^{li} vj^s viij^d rent of a pension yearly to be paid to William Hier[1] late Abbot of the Monastery aforesaid issuing out of the Priory of Pulle not answered for here because the aforesaid Priory is suppressed to the use of the lord King.

Sum nil.

Pension from Glascareg in Ireland.

Of xvj^s viij^d rent of a pension aforesaid for several years kept back and non paid for the space of forty years and more by the oath of the said William Hier late Abbot.

The whole sum with arrears

cxl^{li} ij^s j½^d Of which

Fees and wages.

Also he accounts in fees of the said Accountant Bailiff and Collector of Rents and farms abovesaid at iiij^{li} per ann and so in allowance this year for the whole time of this account finishing at the feast of St. Michael the Archangel the 30th year of the reign of King Henry the 8th—iiij^{li}. And in stipend for the Auditor's clerks writing this Account at ij^s per annum as the Auditor's clerks of the lord King of his Duchy of Lancaster are accustomed to be allowed in every account of the ministers there and so in allowance this year as in preceding—ij^s.

Sum iiij^{li} ij^s

Livery of monies.

And in monies delivered to Edward Watters Receiver of the particulars of the lord King of the issues of his office this year as appears by divers bills signed and sealed under the hand of the said Edward Watters and among the memoranda of this year remaining.

Sum cv^{li} xiiij^s ix½^d

In allowances and liveries aforesaid.

cix^{li} xvj^s ix½^d

And he owes xxx^{li} v^s iiij^d

Whereof

James Leche farmer of the Rectory of Myachlog above charged at viij^{li} per ann so of arrears behind half a year finishing at the feast of St. Michael the Archangel the 29th year of the reign of King Henry the 8th as appears there   iiij^{li}

The said Ferres for such monies by him received in the year preceding by colour of his office of Steward of the Court there at lxvj^s viij^d per ann which by right it is not known so upon him put until etc.   lxvj^s viij^d

---

[1] Hire.

Griffin Lloyd depute Archdeacon of St. David's diocese for such monies by him received in the preceding year for procurations and synodals issuing out of all the churches abovesaid late to the monastery aforesaid belonging at **xxxij**ˢ per annum by what right it is not known so upon him put until etc.   **xxxij**ˢ

John Vaghan doctor of laws farmer of the lordship or manor of Ratre above charged at **xx**ˡⁱ per ann to wit of his arrears this year behind   **xx**ˡⁱ

James Baskefelde farmer of a tenement in Pembroke above charged at **xxvj**ˢ **viij**ᵈ per annum to wit of his arrears this year behind   **xxvj**ˢ **viij**ᵈ

The same accountant of his own arrears behind this year   nil.

Drawn by H. Gastineau.

West end of Chapel of St. Dogmael's Abbey, & East end of previous Church.

CHAPTER XI.

THE OLD ORDER CHANGETH.

THE first record of the Abbey, found after the dissolution, is in the 35th year of Henry VIII's reign (1544), in Dugdale's "Monasticon." It is in the form of a memorandum, of the desire of John Bradshaw to purchase the late Abbey of St. Dogmaels, as follows:—

Num. IV.

Particular for Grant, 35 Hen. VIII, 12 June, 1544, Augmentation Office.

Memorandum that I John Bradshawe of Presthende in the county of Radnor Esquyer requyer to purchase of the kings highnes by vertue of the kings comyssion of sale the premisses beyng of the cler yerlie value of 25*l*. 16*s*. 6½*d*. the tenthe not deducted. In witnes whereof I have subscribed this bill with my hand and put to my seall the daye and yere in the said rate specified.

Per me. Joh'm Bradshawe.

Together with the parcels and possessions belonging to it in South Wales.

Hitherto one of the names, by which the Abbey enclosure or Llandre was known, has been omitted, namely, "The Llandre of the Bishop Thomas à Becket," who was Archbishop of Canterbury in the twelfth century. This is the more curious, as from the name it would be imagined that Thomas à Becket had either stayed at the Abbey, or was in some way connected with it; but so far as is yet known, no trace of such a connection has been found.

Following on this memorandum of John Bradshaw are items referring to St. Dogmaels and Caldey, the same as in the Charter following of 35 Henry VIII, with the addition of the three immediately following paragraphs, the first of which is audited by Edward Gostwycke.

Theis parcells before resyted be no parcell of any lordship of the clere yerely valew of 40*l*. nor doyth adjoyne to any of the kynges howses forrests or chases nor any fyne to my knolege hathe bene paid for the same, nether patronage advoyson nor

8

chauntre doyth unto theym belong nor any other valew made out for any parcell thereof and who wyll by the premisses the audytor knoweth not.

Per Edwardum Gostwyke auditorem.

xij^{mo} die Junii anno xxxv^{to} regni
regis Henrici octavi.
Pro Johanne Bradshawe.

Certen Parcells of the Possessions of the late Monasterye of Wigmore[1] and Sancti Dogmelis.

The clere yerelie value of the premisses, 25*l*. 16*s*. 6½*d*. Inde pro decima 2*l*. 11*s*. 8*d*. et remanet clare 23*l*. 4*s*. 10½*d*. which to be purchased after the rate of twenty-one yeres purchase amounteth to the some of 488*l*. 2*s*. 4½*d*. Add thereto for the woods 24*l*. 6*d*. and then the hole some is 512*l*. 2*s*. 10½*d*. To be paid in hand 300*l*. and the residewe within three monethes.

Memorandum the Kyng must discharge hym of all incumbraunces except the leasez and the rente before reservyd and also excepte 3*l*. 13*s*. 6*d*. for the stipende of the curate of Calde.

Memorandum to reserve all advowsons and patronages.

These memoranda are followed by Henry's charter to John Bradshaw and his heirs, wherein for the sum of £512 2s. 10½d., paid into the hands of the Treasurer of the Court of Augmentation of the Revenues of the Crown, he hands over to the said John Bradshaw and his heirs, all the lands and buildings, rights, etc., in St. Dogmaels and Caldey, formerly belonging to the Abbey of St. Dogmaels.

Next is a "Compotus" of John Bradshaw, dated February 4th, 1547, wherein the King receives back the 21 years lease of 1538-9, and grants a fresh lease for 21 years. In this deed the "arrears" have increased considerably, namely, £23 9s. 2d.

Whilst the Haverford and Pembroke rents are now valued at 2s. a year more, namely, on a tenement in Pembroke in the hands of John Smythe. The residue remains the same, except that there is no mention of either Pill, or Glascareg, and John Bradshaw has hereafter to pay a tenth yearly at the Court of Augmentation, amounting to twenty-six shillings and elevenpence halfpenny. In all other respects the two deeds are similar, and the necessity of this new deed was simply caused by John Bradshaw paying £512 2s. 10½d. three or four years previously, so that thereafter he simply paid a tenth of the yearly value to the King: a very similar tax to the income tax of the present day, only that it was then twice as heavy on landed property, it then being two shillings in the pound.

---

[1] Another property belonging to the Bradshaws.

PATENT ROLL.   35 Hen. VIII, pt. 4, m. 28, 1544.
Charter of John Bradshaw to him and his heirs.

The King to all to whom etc. greeting.   Know ye that we for the sum of five
hundred and twelve pounds two shillings and tenpence halfpenny of our good and
lawful money of England to the hands of the Treasurer of our Court of Augmentations
of the revenues of our Crown to our use paid by our beloved John Bradshaw of
Preston in our county of Radnor esquire of which said sum we acknowledge that we
are fully satisfied and contented and the said John his heirs and executors are thereof
acquitted and discharged by these presents of our special grace certain knowledge and
mere motion have given and granted and by these presents do give and grant to the
aforesaid John Bradshaw all that site enclosure circuit ambit and precinct to the late
monastery of St. Dogmaels in our county of Pembroke with all their rights and
appurtenances.   And also all and singular houses edifices structures barns stables
dovecotes orchards gardens pools vivaries waters fishings fisheries ground and soil being
within the said site enclosure circuit ambit and precinct.   Also all and singular
messuages mills houses edifices land tenements meadows fields pastures and other our
hereditaments lying or being in the township fields and parish of St. Dogmael
commonly called St. Dogmaels otherwise called Llandudock in our said county of
Pembroke to wit those two water mills with all their appurtenances.   And also all and
singular the pools ditches waters fishings fisheries rivers rivulets and water courses suits
ways liberties rights profits commodities and other our hereditaments whatsoever to the
said mills belonging or appertaining or with the same occupied and located.   Also all
that our close with appurtenances called the Parke Roll containing by estimation
seventeen acres.   And also all that our close called the Newe park with appurtenances
containing by estimation three acres adjacent to the said close called the Park roll.   Also
all that parcel of waste land called Grige pende.   And also all that other parcel of
waste land called the Abbots park.   Also all that our messuage with appurtenances
called the Dareg otherwise Over Dareg.   And also one other messuage with appurts
called the Nether Dareg.   Also all our close with appurts called Darne park containing
by estimation four acres.   And also all that our close called the Medowe containing by
estimation one acre.   Also all that our close called Potpyt[1] containing by estimation
fifteen acres adjacent to the seashore.   And also all that our close called Arlys containing
by estimation four acres.   Also all that our close called the Great close containing by
estimation four acres.   And also all that our close called Doctors park containing by
estimation one acre.   Also all that our close called ffres containing by estimation half
an acre one rood.   And also all that our meadow called The East meadow containing
by estimation one acre.   Also all that our meadow called Lakkerley containing by
estimation two acres.   Also all that our meadow called ffim containing by estimation
one and a half acres.   Also all and singular other messuages mills houses etc. known
by the names of the demesne lands to the said late monastery of St. Dogmaels
belonging and now or lately held or occupied by the said John Bradshaw or his assigns.
Also all that our manor of St. Dogmaels otherwise called the Llandre in our said Co.
of Pembroke.   And all that our manor of Caldey in the same county with its rights
members and all appurtenances now or lately held or occupied by the said John

[1] Poppit.

8 a

Bradshaw or his assigns and lately belonging and appertaining to the parcels possessions and revenues of the said late monastery. And also all and sundry messuages mills houses etc. with their belongings wardships marriages escheats reliefs heriots goods and chattels courtleets frankpledges and all things which pertain to it or can or ought to have regard to the future emoluments hereditaments and whatsoever of ours lies or exists in the aforesaid town fields and parish of St. Dogmaels or in the Island of Caldey in our said Co. of Pembroke or any other places in the same county in the said manors or members parts and parcels belonging and pertaining thereto now or lately in the tenure of the said John Bradshaw lately belonging and pertaining to the said monastery of St. Dogmaels also all and sundry messuages lands tenements burgages meadows fields pastures profits revenues and other hereditaments whatsoever in the said parish of St. Dogmaels namely two tenements with their appurtenances called Haver-berkchelley one burgage with a garden adjoining the same existing in the village called Laundau two tenements with their appurtenances called Parc y John Lloyd all those lands called Wyot a burgage with garden and orchard adjoining late in the tenure or occupation of Elizabeth Wills or her assigns two acres of land lying in the fields to the east of the town of St. Dogmaels one other piece of land belonging to and occupied with the same two other acres of land lying in a certain place called Briscwm one tenement with its appurtenances called Plas Pen Abounte one burgage called Arnarde one place or parcel of land called Rhos. All other waste lands late in the tenure or occupation of James ap Powell Lloyd one tenement with its appurtenances late in the tenure or occupation of Owen ap Philipp or his assigns one parcel of land late in the tenure or occupation of Robert ap Price ap Powell or his assigns one tenement with its appurtenances lying close to Cardigan Bridge one parcel of land called Penrallt. All other lands and tenements in the tenure of William Hughes or his assigns all other lands in the tenure or occupation of David ap Ieuan or his assigns one portion of land with its appurtenances lately held and occupied by Morris ap David one tenement with appurtenances lately held or occupied by Jenkin Roger or his assigns. One house with its appurtenances lately held or occupied by Jenkin ap Ieuan or his assigns. All those lands or tenements with their appurtenances and gardens adjoining in the tenure or occupation of John Sporier or his assigns. One tenement with its appurtenances lately held or occupied by John Mortimer or his assigns and also all other messuages bur-gages lands etc. in the parish of St. Dogmaels known and called by the name of the Landre lands lately in the tenure and occupation of the said John Bradshaw or his assigns and lately part and parcel of the monastery of St. Dogmaels. Likewise all and wholly our tithes arising and accruing therefrom or of whatsoever manors messuages lands tenements and other premises in the aforesaid Island of Caldey in our Co. of Pembroke lately in the tenure or occupation of the said John Bradshaw or his assigns and all and singular other messuages etc. in the said Island of Caldey held by John Bradshaw or his assigns etc. . . . We give for a certain sum aforesaid and of our own accord and certain knowledge by these our presents grant to the aforesaid John Bradshaw all that our wood called Abbots Wood otherwise the garden containing it is estimated five acres, lying on rising ground in the parish of St. Dogmaels part and parcel of the late monastery [here follows full list again] to hold and enjoy as fully and entirely as it was by the last Abbot and his predecessors before the dissolution etc. without prejudice to any reservations already thereon. Except that we reserve to our heirs and successors the tithes oblations obversions portions and other our special emoluments whatsoever etc. anyway belonging to the aforesaid and also reserving all the lead roofs and covering of any building soever of the late monastery the lead gutters and the lead in the windows, which said manor and other premises belonging to St. Dogmaels are to be held at the annual rent of £13 9. 9½. [here follow lands in Worcester belonging to John Bradshaw]. To have and to hold etc. [Here follows Presteign and Rhys Castle etc.] All tithes to be paid at the Court of the Augmentation of our Revenues at the Feast of St. Michaels yearly etc.

We will also and of our certain knowledge and suggestion for us our heirs and successors by these presents grant to the aforesaid John Bradshaw his heirs and assigns that the said John his heirs and assigns shall have hold and enjoy and may and can have hold and enjoy within the aforesaid site manor lands tenements and other singular the premises and within any parcel thereof as many as much as great and the same and similar Courts leet views of frankpledge and all things which pertain to frankpledge or in future may or ought to belong fines amercements assize and assay of bread wine and beer free warren and all which to free warren belongs goods and chattels waifs strays goods and chattels of felons and fugitives or in any other way condemned persons rights profits commodities emoluments privileges liberties and hereditaments whatsoever as many as much as great and such as the aforesaid Abbot of the aforesaid late monastery of St. Dogmaels in right of said late monastery or any Abbot of the said late monastery of Wigmore . . . . or any of their predecessors had held or enjoyed the same or should or ought to have had held or enjoyed the same in the aforesaid site manors lands tenements and other all and singular the premises above expressed and specified and within every parcel thereof by reason or pretext of any charter of gift grant or confirmation or of any letters patent by us or by any of our progenitors to the aforesaid late Abbots and these Convents or of either of them in any way made or granted or by reason or pretext of any prescription use or custom or otherwise in any way. We will also and of our certain knowledge and mere motion for us our heirs and successors by these presents grant to the aforesaid John Bradshaw his heirs and assigns that we our heirs and successors for ever yearly and from time to time will acquit discharge and keep indemnified as well the said John his heirs and assigns as the aforesaid site manors messuages lands tenements and other all and singular the premises and every parcel thereof against us our heirs and successors and other persons or person whatsoever of all and every kind of corrody[1] rent fee annuity and sums of money whatsoever excepting the pre-excepted from the aforesaid site manors messuages etc. except of the rent and service above by these presents to us reserved. And except of the annual pension of three pounds thirteen and sixpence yearly paid to the chaplain of Caldey aforesaid for his stipend. Willing moreover and firmly enjoining commanding as well our said Chancellor and Council of our Court of Augmentations of the revenues of our Crown for the time being that to all and singular our Receivors Auditors and other our officers and ministers whatsoever and those of our heirs and successors that they and each of them upon the sole showing of these our letters patent or upon the enrolment of the same without any other writ or warrant from us our heirs and

---

[1] Corody. *See* paragraph end of next deed.

successors in any way to be sought obtain or sued for upon payment of the said yearly rent to us by these presents above reserved full whole and due allowance default and clear discharge from all and every kind corrody rent fee annuity and sums of money whatsoever from the aforesaid site manors lands etc.   And these our letters patent or enrolment of the same shall be yearly and from time to time as well to our Chancellor and Council of the said Court of Augmentation as well to our aforesaid Receivors Auditors and other our officers whatsoever and of our heirs and successors sufficient warrant and discharge in this behalf.   We give also for the consideration aforesaid and of our certain knowledge and mere motion by these presents grant to the aforesaid John Bradshaw all the issues rents revenues and profits of the aforesaid site manors lands tenements and other all and singular the premises and of every parcel thereof from the feast of the Annunciation of the Blessed Virgin Mary last past forthcoming or growing to have to the said John of our gift without account or anything else therefrom to us our heirs or successors in any way to be rendered paid or made.   And also we will and of our certain knowledge and own accord by these presents grant to the aforesaid John Bradshawe that he may have and shall have these our letters patent under our great seal of England in due manner made and sealed without fine or fee great or small to us into our Hanaper or elsewhere to our use in any way to be paid or made.   Because express mention etc.   In witness etc.   Witness the King, the town of St. Albans the 10th day of November.

By writ of privy seal.

The late Monastery of St. Dogmaels in the county of Pembroke.   Feby. 4, 1547.

Compotus of John Bradshawe Bailiff of all and singular the lordships manors lands and tenements and other possessions whatsoever as well temporal as spiritual to the aforesaid late monastery belonging or appertaining.   Which to the hands of the lord King that now is have come and are in his hands and annexed to his Crown his heirs and successors of the realm of England in augmentation of the revenues of the said Crown of England by virtue of a certain act in his Parliament held upon prorogation at Westminster the 4th February the 37th year of the reign of the said King thereon issued and provided as in the same Act among other things is contained to wit from the feast of St. Michael the Archangel in the 34th year of the said lord Henry the 8th etc. to the same feast of St. Michael the Archangel then next ensuing the 35th year of the aforesaid King to wit for one whole year.

Arrears.

The same renders account of xxxij^{li} vij^s x½^d of arrears of last account the year next preceding.

Sum xxxij^{li} vij^s x½^d

ffarm of demesne lands.

The same answers iiijx^{li} ix^s viij½^d of the rent of the site of the late Monastery aforesaid together with all houses buildings barns gardens orchards land and ground within the site and precinct of the said late monastery and lordship of fyshyngarde one mill there with appurts also the Rectories of the Churches of St. Thomas in the township of St. Dogmaels, Eglwyswrw and Caldey Bayvil Moylegrave Llantood and St. Nicholas

THE HISTORY OF ST. DOGMAELS ABBEY.

Fishguard Grangiston[1] and the chapel of Penkelly Vychan Nantgwyn Lysprant Newton and Caldey with appurts. And all the messuages lands tenements mills meadows etc. in the townships fields parishes and hamlets of St. Dogmaels Fishguard Grangeston Caldey Eglwyswrw Bayvill Moylgrove Llantood Penkelly Vychan Nantgwyn Lysprant and Newton so demised to John Bradshawe by Indenture sealed with the seal of the Court of Augmentation of the Revenues of the Crown of the lord King given the 10th March the 28th year of the reign of the said lord King Henry the 8th. To have to him and his assigns from the feast of St. Michael the Archangel last past for the term of xxi years then next ensuing and fully to be completed. Yielding therefrom as above to wit for the aforesaid site land meadow pastures rents and services in the township of St. Dogmaels aforesaid xj^{li} vj^s v½^d and for the aforesaid lordship of Fishguard vj^{li} xiiij^s ix^d and for the aforesaid mill of Fishguard xx^s and for the aforesaid tenements in the township of Grangeton xxvj^s viij^d and for the aforesaid Rectory of St. Thomas in the township of St. Dogmaels xx^{li}, for the aforesaid Rectory of Eglyswrw vij^{li} vj^s viij^d Rectory of Bayvil iiij^{li} xiij^s iiij^d for aforesaid Rectory of Moylgrove vj^{li} xiij^s iiij^d for aforesaid Rectory of Llantood and St. Nicholas vj^{li} xiij^s iiij^d and for aforesaid Rectories of ffyshgard and Grangeston x^{li} vj^s viij^d, for aforesaid chapel and lands and tenements in Caldey cxvj^s x^d for aforesaid chapel of Penkelly Vychan xxv^s and for aforesaid chapels of Nantgwyn Lysprant and Newton vij^{li} vj^s viij^d at the feasts of the Annunciation of the Blessed Virgin Mary and St. Mary the Archangel equally. And the aforesaid lord King wills and by these presents grants that he his heirs and successors the said John and his assigns as well of iiij^{li} yearly for the wages and stipend of a chaplain yearly celebrating the divine offices and taking the cure of souls in the church and parish of St. Dogmaels aforesaid and of lxxiij^s vj^d yearly for the wages and stipend of another chaplain yearly celebrating the divine offices and taking the cure of souls in the church and parish of Calde aforesaid as of all the fees, rents, annuities, pensions, portions and sums of money whatsoever from the premises or any of them issuing or to be paid except the rent above reserved against all persons whatsoever from time to time will exonerate acquit and defend. And all the houses and buildings of the premises as well in timber as in roofing of tile and slate from time to time as often as shall be necessary and opportune shall cause well and sufficiently to be repaired sustained and maintained during the term aforesaid. And the aforesaid John and his assigns roofing of thatch and all necessaries for reparation of the premises except timber tiles and slates aforesaid which the lord King shall find from time to time as often as it shall be necessary and opportune shall support and sustain during the term aforesaid. And the aforesaid lord King further wills and by these presents grants that it shall be truly lawful to the aforesaid John and his assigns from time to time to take and have competent and sufficient hedgebote firebote ploughbote and cartbote of in and upon the premises there and not elsewhere yearly to be expended and occupied during the term aforesaid.

Sum iiijx̄x̄j^{li} ix^s viij½^d

---

[1] Granston.

Lordship of Rattre in the Co. of Devon.

And of xx^{li} of the farm of the whole lordship aforesaid with tithe of sheaves of the parish church of blessed Mary of Rattre and all messuages lands tents meadows fields pastures rents and services to the said lordship in any way belonging so demised to John Manesey by Indenture sealed with the seal of the Court of Augmentation of the Revenues of the Crown given the 20th March the 28th year of the reign of the aforesaid lord King. To have to him and his assigns from the feast of St. Michael the Archangel last past for the term of xxi years etc. And the aforesaid John and his assigns at their own proper costs and expense roofing of thatch and all other necessary reparations of the premises except the reparation of timber and roofing of tiles and slates aforesaid from time to time shall support and sustain during the term aforesaid. And the aforesaid lord King wills and by these presents grants that it shall be lawful to the said John and his assigns from time to time to take perceive and have of in and upon the premises there and not elsewhere yearly to be expended and occupied competent and sufficient hedgebote firebote ploughbote cartbote during the term aforesaid.

Sum xx^{li}

Rents at will in Haverfordwest and Pembroke.

And of x^s rent of j Tenement situate in the township of Haverfordwest in the hands of John therefrom as above to be paid at the feast of the Annunciation of the Blessed Virgin Mary and St. Michael the Archangel equally etc.

And of xxviij^s viij^d rent of j tenement scituate in the township of Pembroke aforesaid in the hands of John Smythe at the will of the lord to be paid at the terms aforesaid.

The Rectories of Maenclochog, Llandilo and Llancolman.

And of viij^{li} rent of the tithe of sheaves oblations and other profits there to the said Rectories or either of them belonging or appertaining so demised to James Leche by indenture sealed with the seal of the Court of Augmentations of the Revenues of the Crown of the lord King given the 10th May the 29th year of the reign of King Henry the 8th. To have to him and his assigns from the feast of St. Michael the Archangel next coming to the end of the term xx years then next ensuing etc. aforesaid James grants and that it shall be lawful to the aforesaid James and his assigns from time to time to take perceive and have from in and upon the premises competent and sufficient hedgebote firebote ploughbote and cartbote there and not elsewhere to be expended and occupied during the term aforesaid.

Sum viij^{li}

Rents of assize in the township of Manoglokdewe.

And of xiij^s iiij^d of rent of j tenement called Mynith Terth in the tenure of the heirs of parottes who hold freely to be paid at the feasts of the Annunciation of the Blessed Virgin Mary and St. Michael the Archangel equally. And of viij^s viij^d rent of a tenement in the township aforesaid called Maenochlog ddu y tharch so demised to Howell ap Thomas ap Owen by Indenture sealed with the convent seal given the viijth day of October the 27th year of the reign of King Henry the 8th. To have to him and his assigns from the feast of St. Michael the Archangel last past to the end of the term of 99 years then next ensuing and fully to be completed. Rendering therefrom as above to be paid at the terms aforesaid. And of v^s viij^d rent of a tenement with appurts called Plas pant y Rege in the hands of Howell ap Owen ap Powell by indenture sealed with the convent seal given the 10th Oct the 27th year of the reign of King Henry the 8th. To have to him and his assigns from the feast of St. Michael the Archangel last past for the term of 99 years then next ensuing and fully to be completed. Rendering therefrom yearly as above to be paid at the terms aforesaid equally. And of x^s rent of a tenement [called] Kome[1]-Kerwyn in the hands of David ap Ris ap Owen by indenture sealed with the convent seal given the 12th October the 27th year of the reign of King Henry the 8th. To have to him and his assigns from the feast of St. Michael the Archangel last past for the term of 99 years then next ensuing and fully to be completed. Rendering therefrom as above to be paid at the terms aforesaid. And of xvj^s rent of ij tenements with appurts called Lounder monoglok dwg in the hands of Ludovic ap Jevan by indenture sealed with the convent seal given the xth October the 27th year of the reign of King Henry the 8th. To have to him and his assigns from the feast of St. Michael the Archangel last past to the end of the term of 99 years then next ensuing and fully to be completed. Rendering therefrom as above to be paid at the feasts aforesaid. And of iij^s iiij^d rent of a tenement with appurts called Pentre gthe[2] in the hands of Griffith ap Ieuan ap Jenken by indenture sealed with the convent seal given the 9th Oct the 27th year of the reign of the same lord King. To have to him and his assigns from the feast of St. Michael the Archangel last past for the term of 99 years then next ensuing and fully to be completed. Rendering therefrom as above to be paid at the terms aforesaid. And of v^s iiij^d rent of a tenement called Blaen y Cowrse Glethe[3] in the hands of Evyon ap David by indenture sealed with the convent seal dated the 7th Oct the 27th year of the reign of King Henry the 8th. To have to him and his assigns from the feast of St. Michael the Archangel last past to the end of the term of 99 years then next ensuing and fully to be completed. Rendering therefrom as above to be paid at the terms aforesaid. And of xj^s rent of iij tenements in the hands of Owen ap Powell and David ap Powell by indenture sealed with the convent seal given the 9th July the 25th year of the reign of King Henry the 8th. To have to him and his assigns from the feast of St. Michael the Archangel then next ensuing and fully to be completed. Rendering therefrom as above to be paid at the feast of St. Michael the Archangel only. And of x^s ij^d rent of a tenement with appurts in the hands of James ap Powell ap Owen by indenture sealed with the Convent seal which indeed he has not shown to be paid at the feasts of the Annunciation of the Blessed Virgin Mary and St. Michael the Archangel equally. And of iij^s viij^d rent of tenement with appurts in the hands of Llewellyn ap Ieuan Pykton at the will of the lord to be paid at the terms aforesaid. And of v^s rent of another tenement in the hands of Ieuan ap Powell ap Ieuan David at the will of the lord to be paid at the terms aforesaid. And of v^s viij^d rent of j tenement in the hands of Jenkyn ap Griffith at the will of the lord to be paid at the terms aforesaid. And of v^s rent of another tent in the hands of Philip Thomas at the will of the lord to be paid at the terms aforesaid. And of ij^s j^d rent of a tenement with appurts in the hands of David Williams at the will of the lord to be paid at the terms aforesaid. And of ij^s vj^d rent of a tenement in the tenure of Thomas ap Dyo Guilliam at the will of the lord to be paid at the terms aforesaid.

Sum cxvij^s j^d

[1] Cwm Cerwyn = The Stags' Valley.   [2] Gith = The corn.   [3] Cleddau.

Chapel of Mynachlog ddu.[1]

And of c[s] farm of the Chapel in aforesaid [township] with all profits to the same belonging so demised to Morgan Jones by indenture under the seal of the lord King of his Court of Augmentation of the Revenues of the crown given the 12th May the 29th year of the reign of King Henry the 8th. To have to him and his assigns from the feast of the Annunciation of the Blessed Virgin Mary last past for the term of 21 years then next ensuing and fully to be completed. Rendering therefrom as above yearly to be paid at the feast of St. Michael the Archangel and the Annunciation of the blessed Virgin Mary by equal portions. And the aforesaid lord King wills and by these presents grants that he his heirs and successors will allow the said Morgan iiij[li] for the stipend of a chaplain celebrating within the aforesaid chapel. And the aforesaid Morgan grants by these presents that he and his assigns all the premises in all things and by all things will repair and sustain during the term aforesaid.

Sum c[s]

Perquisites of Court.

Of certain sums of money forthcoming of the perquisites of Courts held there this year he does not answer here because they are demised to John Bradshaw with the demesne as appears above.

Sum total with arrears clxiij[li] xj[s] iiij[d]

of which

ffees and wages etc. here follow.

Because our lord that now is Henry the 8th by his letters patent under the Great seal of England given the 10th Nov the 35th year of his reign gave and granted all and singular the premises to one John Bradshaw his heirs and assigns for ever. To hold of the said lord King and his successors in chief by the service of the twentieth part of a knight's fee. And rendering therefrom to the said lord King and his successors in name of a tenth part of the premises xxvj[s] xj¾[d] sterling at the Court of Augmentation of the Revenues of his Crown every year to be paid. To have to the said John Bradshaw from the feast of the Annunciation of the Blessed Virgin Mary last past forthcoming or growing of the same.

Which said tenth of xxvj[s] xj¾[d] is charged in the Account of the Receiver there under the tithe of the yearly tenth as is contained there and so in his allowance as above. And deduction of x[li] for the moiety of the rent of the lordship of Rattre and the Rectory of the same place.[2]

Corrody, or Corody, which appears in the grant of 35 Henry VIII, was formerly a right of sustenance, or of receiving certain allotments of victuals and provision for one's maintenance, in virtue of the ownership of some corporeal hereditament; specifically, such a right due from an abbey or a monastery to the king or his grantee.

In Pwyll, in the "Mabinogion," this giving of food is mentioned, though in those days they were more generous. Any one who applied for hospitality

---

[1] The Black Monastery.   [2] Here follows about Rattery again to the end.

was received. First they were washed, then they had food, night's lodging, and food again the next morning.

We also see that the night's lodging was given, as well as food, by many of the monasteries, for most of them had their "guest house."

A custom still holds good at the Hospice of St. Cross, Winchester, where anyone who applies is given a horn of beer and a piece of bread : all forms of corrody, the word corrody being derived from the middle Latin word corrodium, meaning, provision.

CHAPTER XII.

THE ABBEY'S RICHEST DAUGHTER.

THE Roches, who gave the Priory of Pill to the Abbey of St. Dogmaels, took their name of Roche, which means rock, from the rock on which Roche Tower or castle, as it is called, was built, though their name is Latinized in the charters as De la Rupe. They appear to have originally been Flemings, as, one Godebert, a "Fleming of Roose," dwelt in this part of Pembrokeshire in 1131; his grandsons, David, Henry, and Adam taking the name of De la Roche.

Adam was the first who lived at Roche Castle; he had acquired considerable property in that neighbourhood, and founded the Priory of Pill towards the end of the twelfth century, in honour of St. Budoc and the Blessed Virgin, giving to it, not only the lands on which the Priory was built, but lands in Roose and New Moat, together with the Churches of St. Cewydd (now St. Peter's) at Stainton, St. Mary of Roch, St. David (now St. Peter's) of Little Newcastle, and St. Nicholas of New Moat, with the assent and consent of his heir, his wife, Blandina, agreeing thereto, and granting it all, by his charter, to the monks of the order of Tiron, together with a mill, and the fisheries, with all rights, liberties, etc. The first witness to the grant was Andrew Abbot of St. Dogmaels.

Later, Thomas, son and heir of John de Roche, and his wife, Matilda, daughter of Thoms Wallensis, Bishop of St. David's, 1248-1256, confirms all the donations of Adam, the founder, and also grants two carucates of land, with all appurtenances, called Suthoc (South Hook), in the township of Herbiand (Herbrandston), given by his mother, Matilda, and three carucates of land, with all appurtenances in Sewant, with three parts of the mill there, also six bovates[1] of land in Stodhart (Studdolph), and five acres of land, with

---

[1] Three-quarters of a carucate. In the time of the Doomsday Book, and for three or four hundred years after, a carucate of land was called a hundred acres, though it was really six score, or one hundred and twenty acres; but in Queen Elizabeth's time a carucate of land was only sixty-four acres.

A Catch of Salmon, St Dogmaels.

half a carucate of land in the same parish, together with half a carucate of land in Strickemeres Hill (Dredgman's Hill), which is called Vyndessors (Windsor). Also six acres of land in Pill, formerly belonging to Richard Blakeman, and one mark of yearly rent with the lordship of Walter Baglas; also he grants all kinds of wreckage on the half carucate of land on which the Chapel of St. Cradoc of Neugol stands, as is witnessed in the charter of his father, John de Roche. He also grants two carucates of land with appurtenances, and one bovate of land in the township of John, which is called Monkestown, with patronage of the church there; two bovates of land in Castle Vydy, which seems to refer to Castle Hill, abutting upon Stainton Highway, mentioned among the possession of the Priory at the dissolution; two bovates of land in Thorneton, two bovates in Retford, with appurtenances; also he grants them land, tenements, and gardens, which they already have in Roche, in Hubert's township (Hubberstone), in Leddin's township (Liddeston), in St. Budoc, Redderch (Redberth), and all the meadows, which were returned after the death of his father, John de Roche, by the prior and monks, with right of patronage of St. David's, Hubberstone, and St. Madoc's, Nolton.

Amongst the witnesses were Sir Nicholas Fitzmartin (d. 1284), Sir Guy de Brian, etc.

Following this was a charter of confirmation by William Marshall, Earl of Pembroke, to the Priory of Pill, of one carucate of land called Roger's (Mortimer) land, half a carucate called Waffret, twenty and a-half acres called Seman Scopal Mill, the liberty of making a fishery in the creek by that mill, a burgage at Moat, eight acres at Bakerlineran, in the fee of Moat, and everything given by Adam de Roche, Phillip being Prior of Pill at this time. This was inspected and confirmed by Edward I, 1296. Among the witnesses being R. Archbishop of Canterbury, A. Bishop of Durham, W. Bishop of Ely, and R. Bishop of London, with Henry, elect of York, and Brother William, elect of Dublin, 13th July, 25 Edward I.

From this it appears that the Roches were the chief benefactors of Pill Priory, which was made by them a cell of St. Dogmaels.

John, the son of the above Thomas, seems to have died rather suddenly, as in making his will, in 1314, he notes at the end, he could not give any more thought to it, and his executors must dispose of the residue, but he willed that he should be buried at Pill Priory, and also bequeathed 40s. to the monastery. He was succeeded by his brother Thomas (d. about 1324).

In 1330 William, the son of the above Thomas, founded a chauntry in the chapel of St. Thomas the Martyr, by Pill Oliver, for the souls of his father and mother, and of his ancestors.

About 1383 there is an account by Llewellyn ap William, the Reeve, of the rents of two parts of the manor of Roche and Pill, after the death of Margaret, niece of William de la Roche, being daughter and heiress of his sister, Margot, and wife of Roger de Clarendon, who in her right held two parts of the Manor of Roche and Pill of the King by knight's service.

CHARTER ROLL, 25 Edwd. I.   July 13, 1294-5.
No. 8.

For the monks of Pill.

The King to his Archbishops etc. greeting. We have inspected a charter which Adam de Roche[1] made to God and St. Mary and St. Budoc and the monks of the order of Tiron serving God in the monastery of Pill in these words. Let all the children of Holy Mother Church present and to come know that I Adam de Roche having confidence of a heavenly reward for the exaltation of Holy Church founding a monastery in my land of Pill to the honour of the Holy Mother of God the ever virgin Mary with the consent and assent of my heir, my wife Blandina also agreeing for the health of our souls of our fathers and mothers and of our successors have given granted and by this my present charter confirmed to God and St. Mary and St. Budoc and the monks of the order of Tiron there serving God one carucate of land which is called Roger's land and half a carucate of land which is called Waffren land by the ancient bounds and twenty acres and a half in the land which is called Seman land near to the said monastery in meadow and in pastures and in all liberties which to them I can warrant and a mill which is called Stoppel mill and in Pill below the said mill the liberty of making and freely having a fishery in what place they will and in the township of the New Moat a burgage by the east gate and one burgage on the north side excepted with eight acres of land and in the same fee of the Moat all the land called Vachketerlmechan and of my woods about the said Moat to their own use as much as they will. Besides I have given to them and granted in their lands as is well known the duel gallows fire blood and all other rights and liberties which I have in my lands and whatever the free men of my lordship by inspiration of mercy of their lands have reasonably conferred with the aforenamed liberties I grant to them to hold I have given also to them common of pasture in my land with as many animals as their said land requires according to the custom of the country. So that my gabulars may have common of pasture with them. And because these donations to the building of the aforesaid monastery and to the good support of the aforesaid monks are not sufficient I have given to them and granted all the churches of my land to wit the church of St. Kewit[2] of Sternton and the church of St. Mary de Roche and the church of St. David of New Castle and the church of St. Nicholas of New Moat and all the churches of my whole conquest with all their appurtenances and liberties and the tithes of all my mills. These therefore aforenamed lands churches tithes and liberties I have given to them and granted in pure and perpetual alms free and quit from all

---

[1] Pill was founded before Glascareg; if 1173 is the correct date for the foundation of Glascareg, as given on the margin of the charter referring to it, then Pill must have been founded before that date. Allowing thirty years to a generation, Godebert's date being 1131, Adam, his son, probably founded Pill Priory between 1161 and 1170.
[2] St. Cewydd.

service and secular exaction as any alms can well and freely be bestowed. And that this my donation may remain firm and stable this present writing we have strengthened with the affixing of my seal. These being witnesses Andrew Abbot of St. Dogmael Richard Mangunel Richard de Huscart John son of Walter Henry son of Robert Maurice de Trenvan Stephen Lupo Henry Ruffo Richard Gundewin Adam the clerk Robert the clerk and many others.

We have also inspected a charter of confirmation which Thomas de Roche son and heir of John de Roche made to God and St. Mary and St. Budoc and the monks aforesaid in these words. Let all present and to come know that I Thomas de Roche son of John de Roche and heir for the health of my soul and of my ancestors and successors do give and grant and by this my present charter confirm all the donations which Adam de Roche the elder founder of the priory of Blessed Mary de Pill gave and granted to God and St. Mary and St. Budoc and the monks of the order of Tiron there serving and to serve God for ever as well in lands as in churches in houses and gardens as in mills in pools and weirs in meadows ways and paths in present rents. To have and to hold in pure and perpetual alms for me and my heirs or assigns for ever freely and quietly wholly peacefully and honorably without any secular exaction in all liberties and free customs as the aforesaid charters of Adam de Roche witness. And I the said Thomas de Roche for me and my heirs or assigns these donations aforesaid in form aforewritten I give and confirm together with two carucates of land with all the appurts which are called Suthoe[1] in the tenement of the township of Herbiand[2] as the charter of Matilda de Roche my mother witnesses and three carucates of land with all their appurts in the tenement of Sewant with three parts of the mill of the same township with their appurts. I grant also to the said monks six bovates of land with their appurts in the township of Stodliayt[3] and five acres of land with half a carucate of land in the same township. And half a carucate of land in the tenement in Strichemereshill[4] which is called Vyndessors[5] with appurts. And in Pill adjacent to the said Priory a weir in whatever place they will well and freely [to have] and six acres of land in the tenement of Pill with appurts which formerly were Richard Blakeman's and one mark of yearly rent with the lordship of Walter Baglas and his heirs or assigns with appurts. Moveover I grant to aforesaid monks all the land which they have with the houses and gardens in the tenement of Roche with six perches of land with appurts and every kind of wreck which happens or may happen in the half carucate of land in which the chapel of St. Caradoc of Neugol is situated as the charter of John de Roche my father witnesses. Moreover I grant to the said monks two carucates of land with appurts and one bovate of land in the tenement of the township of John with appurts which is called Munketun and the right of patronage of the church of the township of John with appurts and two bovates of the land in Castle Vydy with appurts and other two bovates of land in the tenement in Thornitun[6] with appurts. Also two bovates of land at Retford in the tenement of Dunant with appurts. I grant to the same monks all the land which they have in Hubert's township[7] and in Leddin's[8] township and in the land of St. Budoc with appurts together with eight acres of land at Redeberch[9] in the tenement of Robert's township with appurts. And all the meadows which were returned after the death of John de Roche my father by

---

[1] South Hook.   [2] Herbrandston.   [3] ? Studdolph.   [4] Dredgmans Hill.   [5] Windsor.
[6] Thorneton.   [7] Hubberstone.   [8] ? Liddistone.   [9] Redberth.

the prior and monks as their tenements besides their houses and gardens wherever they be I grant to the said monks saving the common of my Gabelers of Pull besides the hay when collected and carried. Moreover I grant to the said monks the right of patronage of the church of St. David of Hubert's township with appurts together with the right of patronage of the church of St. Madoc of the old township with one acre of land with appurts. And these donations abovesaid and grants to the prior and monks and their successors with all their appurts for me my heirs or assigns I have granted and quit claimed and by this present writing confirmed as the charters of their gifts or enfeoffments whatsoever witness. In witness whereof to this present writing I have set my seal. These being witnesses Sir Nicholas son of Martin Sir Guy de Brian Sir Robert de Val Sir Gilbert de Roche knts John Wogan Master Giles then seneschal of Pembroke Walter Malesaunt Richard de St. Bridget Radenor son of Philip and others. We have inspected also the charter which William Marshall sometime Earl of Pembroke made to the church of St. Budoc and the monks aforesaid in these words: William Marshall Earl of Pembroke to all to whom this present charter shall come as well present as to come greeting. Know ye that I by the inspiration of God and for the health of my soul and the Countess Isabella my wife and all my ancestors and heirs have granted and by this my present charter confirmed to the church of St. Budoc and the monks of the order of Tiron there serving God one carucate of land which is called Roger's land half a carucate of land which is called Wasfreit and twenty acres and a half in the land called Seman and a mill which is called Scopel mill and the liberty of making a fishery in Pull by that mill. And a burgage in the township of the Moat with eight acres of land and all the land which is called Bakerleneran[1] in the fee of the Moat and all the churches of the land of Adam de Roche with the tithes of his mills with pasture and with those things which are necessary to them to their own use in the woods of the said Adam about the said moat and the liberties and rights which the said Adam conferred on them in his lands which he held of my fee. Wherefore I will and firmly command that the aforesaid church of St. Budoc and the monks there serving God shall have and hold all the abovesaid with appurts in free pure and perpetual alms of the gift of aforesaid Adam as his charter which they had thereof witnesses. Saving all my right and service and of my heirs. And that this my grant may remain for all future time firm and unbroken this present charter I have strengthened signed with my seal. These being witnesses John de Erleng Henry son of Gerald Ralph Bloeb Ralph de Mortimer Walter Covenant John de Erleng the younger Ralph de Nevill Philip the clerk and many others. And we the grants gifts and confirmations aforesaid having ratified the same for us and our heirs as far as in us lies to our beloved in Christ Philip prior of the aforesaid church of blessed Mary of Pull and the monks of the aforesaid place and their successors have granted and confirmed as the aforesaid charters reasonably witness and as the said Prior and monks and their predecessors the priors and monks of the same place the aforesaid liberties have hitherto reasonably used and enjoyed. These being witnesses the venerable fathers R. Archbp of Canterbury primate of all England A. bp of Durham W. of Ely and R. of London Master Henry Elect of York and Brother William Elect of Dublin William de Beauchamp Earl of Warwick Hugh le Despencer Roger Brabazon Walter de Beauchamp steward of our household William

---

[1] Berllan.

de Bereford and others. Given by our hand at Westminster the 13th July the year etc. the 25th by bill of Exchequer.

MINISTERS ACCTS. (1383-4.)
1207-9.
Roche and Pille. 7-8 Rd. II.

The Compotus of Lllewellyn ap William the Reeve there of the issues of the aforesaid two parts of the manors of Roche and Pille falling to the lord King by the death of Margaret who was the wife of Roger de Claryndon who held of the King by Knight service to wit from the feast of St. Michael the 7th year of the reign of King Richard the 2nd to the 8th of August then next ensuing to wit the 8th year on which day the said two parts were delivered to Warren Archdeacon and Robert Verney heirs of the said two parts by letters of privy seal of the lord King to Hugh le Young his Escheator of Haverfordwest directed and in the account of the said Escheator of the 8th year noted as appears in the Court of the Forren of Haverford held there monthly on Wednesday next after the feast of the Translation of St. Thomas the Martyr the 8th year.

Free Rents.

The same answers for ij^s vij½^d part of v^s iij^d of 2 parts of the manor of Roche to be paid at the feasts of Easter and Michaelmas to wit for the term of Easter within the time of this account.

Sum ij^s vij½^d

Gablers Rents.

And of lxj^s j¼^d part of vj^{li} ij^s ij½^d received of Gablers rents there to be paid at the feasts aforesaid to wit for the term of Easter within the time of this account.

Sum lxj^s j¼^d

Sale of works.

And of xij^s xj^d part of xix^s iiij½^d received for winter works due at the feast of Easter within the time of this account besides the works of the Reeve there for the same time which are allowed to him for his office by custom of the manor. Of vij^s ij¼^d part of x^s ix½^d of summer works due at the feast of Michaelmas he does not answer for because they do not fall within the time of this account.

Sum xij^s xj^d

Farm of the demesne land.

And of xj^s j½^d part of xxij^s ij¾^d rent of Richard Moris for vij bovates of land so to him demised to be paid at the feasts aforesaid to wit for the term of Easter within the time of the Account. And of vij^s ix¼^d part of xv^s vj½^d received of David ap Morris for vij bovates of land so to him demised to be paid at the feasts aforesaid to wit for the term of Easter within the time of the Account. And for vij^s ix½^d part of xv^s vj½^d received of William Gay for vij bovates of land so to him demised to be paid at the feasts aforesaid to wit for the term of Easter within the time of this account. And of vij^s ix½^d part of xv^s vj½^d received of David ap Meurice William Gay and Richard Moris for the pasture of vij bovates of land so to them demised in le Wode to be paid at the feasts aforesaid to wit for the term of Easter within the time of the Account. And of ij^s ij½^d one half part of iiij^s v¼^d

9

received of the tenements of la Roche and Treffgarn so demised to be paid at the feasts aforesaid to wit for the term of Easter within the time of the account of the farm of a meadow called Castelmede he does not answer because it does not fall within the time of this account. Of the arable fields of Arnold the meadow of Rewan received from Tilbarg he does not account because it does not fall within the time of the account.

Sum xxxvj^s viij½^d

Farm of the mill.

And of xxvj^s viij^d part of liij^s iiij^d farm of the mill there to be paid at the terms aforesaid to wit for the term of Easter within the time of the account. And the lesser tolls he does not answer for because there are none.

Sum xxvj^s viij^d

Issues of the land remaining in the hands of the lord.

And of vj¾^d part of viij½^d received of Thomas ffox for ij bovates of land which Jevan ap Madoc sometime held to wit for the term of Easter within the time of the account. And the issues and profits of two bovates of land which Simon Sandre sometime held nothing because it does not appear within the time of this account.

Sum vj¾^d

Advowson.

Of the advowson there he does not answer because nothing falls within the time of the Account.

Sum Nil.

Perquisites of Court.

And of iiij^{li} xix^s received of pleas and perquisites of Court there within the time of the Account as appears by Court Roll upon this account delivered and examined.

Sum iiij^{li} xix^s

Sum total received xj^{li} xix^s vij^d of which there is paid to Philip Crabol the steward holding Courts there from the feast of St. Michael the 7th year of the reign of King Richard the 2nd to the 8th August then next ensuing at the rate of xxvj^s viij^d per ann. xxiij^s iiij^d And allowed to him what he has paid for parchment for Court Rolls there. And he owes x^{li} xiiij^s iij^d Which he has delivered to Hugh Young Receiver there by acknowledgment of said receiver. And he is quit.

Pulle.

Compotus of Philip Batton the Reeve of Pulle for the time aforesaid.

Free Rents.

The same answers for ix¼^d one half part of xviij½^d rents of free tenants there to be paid at the feasts of Easter and Michaelmas to wit for the term of Easter within the time of this account.

Sum ix⅜^d

Gablers Rents.

And of xij^{li} xiiij^s iiij¾^d part of xxv^{li} viij^s ix½^d of gablers rents there to be paid at the feasts aforesaid to wit for the term of Easter within the time of this account.

Sum xij^{li} xiiij^s iiij¾^d

Sale of work.

And of iiij^s vj^d part of ix^s received for winter works to be paid at the feast of Easter within the time of this account. And xij^s xj¼^d for summer works he does not answer because they do not fall within this account.

Farm of demesne land.

And of xxxvj^s viij^d part of lxxiij^s iiij^d farm of demesne lands so demised to be paid at the feasts of Easter and Michaelmas.

Sum xxxvj^s viij^d

The Mill.

Of the issues of the mill there he does not answer because it lies totally ruined and no profit therefrom can be taken for the time.

Sum nil.

Lands remaining in the hands of the lord.

And of xij^d part of ij^s received of David Hamlockes forthcoming of v acres and ½ of land remaining in the lord's hands so demised to be paid at the terms of Easter and Michaelmas to wit for the term of Easter within the time of this account.

And of vj^d part of xij^d received of Richard Thomas for the pasture of 5½ acres of land which were accustomed to pay ij^s vj^d To be paid at the feasts of Easter and Michaelmas for the term of Easter within the time of this account.

Sum xviij^d

Sum total received xiiij^{li} xvij^s x¼⅛^d

Arrears.

In arrears of rent of one messuage sometime Richard Coles v^s iiij^d to wit for the term of Easter ij^s viij^d And in arrears of rents of works of the tenants there part of xv¾^d—vij⅝^d because they could not be let this year. And in decay of the rent of a cottage sometime Richard Triggs part of ij^s—xij^d And in arrears of rent of x and ½ acres of land sometime John Philips part of ix½^d—iiij¾^d And in arrears of rent of one tenement sometime David Stodach's part of vij^s v¾^d— iij^s viij¾^d And in arrears of rent of the services of the tenants there sometime David Button's and David Jockyn's part of viij^s x¼^d—iiij^s v⅛^d And in arrears of rent of land sometimes John Davyston's part of xvj^d—viij^d And in arrears of the pasture of Walter Sandy part of ij^s—xij^d

Sum of arrears xiiij^s vj½^d

And he owes xiiij^{li} iij^s iij⅝^d which he has delivered to Hugh le Young Receiver of the said lordship by the acknowledgment of the said Receiver.

And he is quit.

In 1395, on July 19th, Richard II orders the investigation of some error that had occurred, by which Warrin, the Archdeacon, Robert Verney, and Eleanor, his wife, then of the Manor of Roche and Pill, had suffered great damage. David Fleming, who, together with Robert Verney, the plaintiff, Sir Warine, the Archdeacon, and Thomas de la Roche of Langum, represented the four daughters of the Thomas de la Roche, who died about 1324. His second daughter had married Sir David de la Roche, of Langum; they were sisters of the William de la Roche who founded the Chantry Chapel at St. Thomas the Martyr.

There appears, however, to be no record left of this suit.

PATENT ROLL.   19 Rich. II, pt. I, m. 27ᵈ
[1395.]
Of correcting an error.

The King to his beloved and trusty cousin Thomas de Percy and his beloved John Knightley Stephen White and Thomas Polsawe greeting.   Know ye that whereas in a record and process and also in the rendering of judgment of a plea which was before our beloved and trusty John Penros late our justice of South Wales at Haverford between us and David Fleming and Warrin Archdeacon and Robert Verney and Eleanor his wife of the manor of Roche and Pille within the lordship of Haverford in South Wales a manifest error occurred to the grave damage of them Warrin Robert and Eleanor as by their plaint we have heard.   We the error if there is any now willing duly to be corrected and full and speedy justice to be done on this behalf have assigned you three and two of you of whom you the aforesaid Stephen we will to be one to survey the record and process of the plaint aforesaid if judgment thereupon was given and the errors if there are any or in the giving of the judgment aforesaid shall happen to be found to correct and amend and the aforesaid Warrin Robert and Eleanor full and speedy justice thereon to cause to be done according to law and custom of the aforesaid parts.   And so we charge you concerning the premises you diligently apply yourselves and cause the same to be examined in form aforesaid.   Saving etc.   And you the aforesaid Thomas de Percy[1] at certain etc. which etc. of which etc. for this purpose you shall provide the record and process of the plaint aforesaid with all touching the same in your custody as it is said before you etc. you shall cause to come warning the aforesaid David that he be then there to hear the errors if there are any in the record and process aforesaid or in the giving of judgment of the plea aforesaid shall happen to be found and further to do and receive that by us etc. of which etc. it shall be considered in the premises.   In witness whereof etc.   Witness the King at Westminster the 19th day of July.

By writ of priory seal.

[N.B.—There appears to be no record of this suit.]

From the following ancient petition in Norman French the later Roches do not appear to have been so piously disposed as Adam and Thomas, for here is a complaint from the poor Prior of Pill that David, son of Thomas de la Roche, has laid waste their possessions, and seized his monks, and begging the king to cause him to come before the Justices of the King's Bench to answer for his trespass.

ANCIENT PETITIONS.
No. 3301.

To our lord the King and his Council shows his poor Prior of La Pulle how David who was the son of Thomas de la Roche has laid waste the goods of their house

---

[1] ? Sheriff.

and seized his monks to his great damage and fines them at his will whereupon he begs the favour that he will cause him to come before the Justices of the Kings Bench to answer for the trespass since our lord the King has cognizance of all trespasses which his tenants in chief commit.

In the calendar of entry in the Papal Registers are a few entries about this date.

CALENDAR OF ENTRY IN PAPAL REGISTERS.

Petition Vol. X, 1347, 5 Clement VI, f. 43d.

Richard Vaughan, late the King's envoy, on behalf of John Henry of the diocese of St. David's, for a benefice with cure of souls, value thirty marks, in the gift of the prior and hospital of St. John of Jerusalem in England, notwithstanding that he expects a benefice *in forma pauperum* in the gift of the Benedictine Prior and convent of St. Mary Pille, order of Tiron, in the said diocese. Granted at Avignon Kals. February.

PETITIONS. Vol. XXXIII of the same, p. 383 & 4, 9 Innocent VI.

John Philip, Clerk. For confirmation of the collation by the ordinary of the Church of St. Swithin, London, Void by the death of Ralph Nicol, nothwithstanding that he expects a benefice in the gift of the Prior and convent of St. Mary Pille, order of Tiron, in the diocese of St. David's.

Granted Avignon, May 22.

PETITIONS. Vol. XXXVII of the same, p. 428, 1 Urban V, 1363.

Thomas Parnel, a poor priest of the diocese of St. David's for a benefice in the gift of the Prior and Convent of Pill (Pulla Tironensium).

These are followed, in 1405, from Vol. VI of the Papal Registers, by a mandate from the Pope to the Prior of Pill.

PAPAL REGISTERS. Vol. VI. 1405.
4 Non, Feb., St. Peter's, Rome.

To the Prior of Pill in the Diocese of St. David's. Mandate to collate and assign to John Heywarde, canon of St. David's, if found fit the canonry and prebends of Penfoos in St. David's, value not exceeding 20 marks, void by the free assignation of Robert Wermyngton to Bishop Guy; notwithstanding that John holds another canonry and a cursal prebend of St. David's and the church without cure of St. Martin Pomeroy (in Pomerio) London the value of both of which does not exceed 40 marks. Upon obtaining the said canonry and prebend of Penfoos he is to resign his said canonry and cursal prebend.

Next follows, in 1553-4, a valuation of the rents of Roche and Pill, taken by Thomas Parker, collector, which may be interesting, together with the former compotus, to those living in that neighbourhood, and for the mention of a coal mine.

Min. Accts. 651, 10532. 31-2 H. VI.

Roche and Pulle.

Compotus of Thomas Parker Collector of Rents there for the time abovesaid.

Arrears.

The same answers of **xxxvj**ˢ of arrears of last account of the year preceding as appears at the foot there.

Sum **xxxvj**ˢ

Free rents and Gablers.

And of **xxiij**ˡⁱ **viij**ˢ **ij**ᵈ of free rent of the gablers there at the terms of Easter and St. Michael equally. And of **xx**ˢ rent of v acres of land of new rent so demised to John Tonker at the same terms. And of **lxvj**ˢ **viij**ᵈ of the farm of a coal mine there at the same terms. And of **v**ˢ **iiij**ᵈ increased rent of one plot and land at Annablepull, which he answers to pay **xiij**ˢ **iiij**ᵈ per ann.

Sum **xxvij**ˡⁱ **xxij**ᵈ

Perquisites of Court.

Of perquisites of Court there this year nothing because no courts were held there this year by the oath of the accountant.

Sum nil.

Sum of receipts with arrears **xx**ˡⁱ **xvij**ˢ **x**ᵈ

Of which there is allowed to him **iiij**ˡⁱ **xviij**ˢ **viij**ᵈ of decayed rent of divers tenants there remaining in the hands of the lady the Queen for default of tenants as may be proved by examination thereof made and as was allowed in preceding account. And to the same **xx**ˡⁱ **xix**ˢ **ij**ᵈ of money delivered to aforesaid Receiver by acknowledgment of the said Receiver upon the Account. And he owes **lx**ˢ.

Which are respited to him to wit **xxxvj**ˢ thereof above charged under the name of arrears and **xxxiiij**ˢ above charged under the name of rents of Gablers in the total of **xxiij**ˡⁱ **viij**ˢ **ij**ᵈ of decayed rents of divers lands and tenements there being in the hands of the lady the Queen by default of tenants as here testified by the homage and ministers and here respited until etc. And nothing beyond this in respite.

Dugdale's account of Pill Priory is so very erroneous that it is not worth quoting the first part of it; he falls into the old error of mixing up Martin of the Towers, Lord of Cemaes, with St. Martin of Tours, and makes Thomas de la Roche of the second charter, son of Adam, instead of his being one or two generations later. The Priory at Pill was subordinate to St. Dogmaels Abbey from first to last, and paid a yearly sum to St. Dogmaels up to the dissolution, as we see by valuation of St. Dogmaels Abbey, in which £9 6s. 8d. is put down as the sum yearly paid by Pill Priory. This should set at rest once and for ever any doubts of this kind. It naturally had its own revenue as all cells did, so that its revenue being assessed 26 Hen. VIII at £67 15s. 3d. gross, but £52 2s. 5d. net,[1] in no way rendered it independent of St. Dogmaels, as Dugdale assumes. Also the assertion that the convent of Pill " in time forsook that strict rule, and became ordinary Benedictines," as quoted by Dugdale, Regner and Stevens is exceedingly doubtful. St. Dogmaels Abbey was nominally of the order of Tiron to the last, therefore her cells must have been the same; but that either the abbey or her cells kept to the strict Rule of St. Bernard of Tiron, any more than, as we have seen, the Convent of Tiron herself did, is absurd.

Leland also falls into the error of describing Pill as being in Caldey Island, thus making two cells into one. Speed also falls into the same error, possibly through taking Leland for his authority. There is no date to these two charters of Adam and Thomas, but Adam was a son of Godebert, a Fleming of Roose, who held land there in 1131. Adam's charter was therefore certainly before 1200, whilst the grant of Thomas was probably 80 years later. Nicholas Martin, who was one of the witnesses of the latter charter, did not succeed to the Barony till 1216, and died in 1284. Also Thomas's father, John, held the land in 1251. Roger Mortimer granted Thomas a carucate of land at Pill Rhodal, in 1274. So that evidently his charter, which was in all probability made on his death bed, was after 1274, but before 1284, when Nicholas, one of the witnesses, died.

In the fifth year of Henry V is a similar deed to the one under St. Dogmaels Abbey, in which Henry grants full pardon to the Prior and Convent of Pill for whatever misdeeds they may have committed, amongst other things remitted to them were " deodands ";[2] in English law, from the earliest times, this had been a personal chattel, which had been the immediate occasion of the death of a human being, and for that reason was " given to God "—that is, forfeited to the king to be applied to pious uses, and distributed in alms by his high almoner. Thus if a man was killed by a cart, the cart was by law forfeited as a deodand, and the coroner's jury required to fix the value of the forfeited property. Deodands were not abolished till 1846. The pious object of this forfeiture was soon lost sight of, so that kings might, and often did, cede their right to deodands, within certain limits, as a private perquisite.

Henry V's deed continues that no one was in any way to harass, or molest, the prior and convent. However, in spite of this, the prior appears by his attorney, John Brokholes, and complains that he had been hardly distrained

---

[1] The Cotton MS., Cleopatra, C. IV, f. 388. St. David, Priory of Pill, gives gross value at £72 11s. 5d. and the net value at £49 5s. 9d.

[2] From the Latin Deo dandum, a thing to be given to God.

by Roland Leynthole Knight, Lord of Haverford, for a subsidy to the king. A day being fixed to hear the Prior of Pill's case, he was exonerated by the king's deed from paying the sum demanded.

MEMORANDA K. R. EASTER TERM. 5 Hen. V, m. 5. 1418.

Wales. Letters patent of the King made to the Prior and Convent of la Pille of the order of St. Benedict enrolled.

The Lord King has commanded here his writ under his great seal which is among the "Communia" of this term in these words Henry by the grace of God King of England and France and lord of Ireland to the Treasurer and Barons of his Exchequer greeting. Whereas of our special grace and with the assent of the lords spiritual and temporal and at the request of the Commons of our realm of England in our parliament held at Westminster the 2nd year of our reign we have pardoned and released the Prior and Convent of la Pille otherwise called Pull otherwise called the Prior of Pulla of the order of St. Benedict collector of a tithe and a moiety of a tithe to the lord Richard late King of England the second after the Conquest granted by the clergy of the province of Canterbury the 21st year of his reign in the Archdeaconry of St. David's in the diocese of St. David's and collector of a subsidy to the lord Richard late King of England granted from the clergy of the province of Canterbury in the church of St. Paul at London the 10th day of May the 7th year of his reign to wit 6s. 8d. from every chaplain secular or religious also of the order of mendicants stipendiary or hired, taking a salary or stipend. And from every chaplain or warden of chantries and every other beneficed person or other beneficed persons or officials for tithe or tithes to our said father granted not accustomed to pay. Also from all vicars whatsoever or other beneficed persons in Cathedral and collegiate churches and Rectors and Vicars of Churches whatsoever to such tithe not accustomed to pay in the Archdeaconry of St. David's in the diocese of St. David's all kind of trespasses offences misprisons contempts and suits by them before the 8th day of December the said 2nd year against the form of the statutes of liveries of cloth and . . [1] made or perpetrated. Upon which punishment shall fall by way of fine and ransom or in other pecuniary penalties or imprisonments the statutes aforesaid notwithstanding. So that the present pardon and release shall not be to the damage prejudice or derogation of any other person than ourself. And moreover of our mere motion out of reverence to God and by intention of charity we have pardoned the said prior and convent the suit of our peace which to us against them belonged for all treacheries murders rapes of women rebellions insurrections felonies conspiracies and other trespasses offences negligences extortions misprisons ignorances contempts concealments and deceptions by them before the said 8th day of December the said 2nd year in whatever way done or perpetrated, murders by them perpetrated after the 19th day of November the aforesaid year if there are any excepted. Whereupon they are adjudged arrested or summoned. And also outlawries if any against them on these occasions have been promulged and our firm peace to them we have granted. While however the said prior and convent are not evildoers in the craft of money multipliers of the coinage washers of gold and silver

---

[1] Illegible.

coined at our Mint clippers of our money common approvers and notorious thieves or felons who have made abjuration of the realm. So that they stand to right in our Court if any shall prosecute them concerning the premises or any of the premises. And further of our more abundant grace we have pardoned and released to the said prior and convent all escapes of felons chattels of felons and fugitives chattels of outlaws and felons deodands, wastes suits and all articles such as destruction of the highway and trespasses of vert and veneson sale of woods within our forests or without and other things whatsoever before the said 8th day of December within our realm of England and the parts of Wales . . .[1] whereupon punishment should fall in due demand or in fine and ransom or in other pecuniary penalties or in forfeiture of goods and chattels or imprisonments or amercements of Counties townships or other persons or in charge of their free tenants who have never trespassed as heirs executors or land tenants Escheators sheriffs Coroners and others and all which to us against them may belong for the causes aforesaid. And also all grants alienations and purchases in mortmain made or had without our royal license. Also all intrusions and entries by them in their inheritance in part or in whole after the death of their ancestors without duly sueing out the same of our Royal hand before the said eighth day of December done together with the issues and profits therefrom in the meantime taken. And also we have pardoned and released to the said Prior and Convent all fines judgments amercements issues forfeitures reliefs scutages and all dues accounts prests and arrears of farms and accounts to us on the 21st day of March the first year of our reign in whatsoever way due and belonging. Also all actions and demands which we alone against them or we conjointly with other persons or person have or may have. And also outlawries against them promulged for any of the aforesaid causes. And moreover we have pardoned and released to the said prior and convent all pains before the said 8th day of December forfeited before us on our Council Chancellor treasurer or any of our judges for any cause and all other pains as well to us as to our most dear father deceased for any cause before the said 8th day of December similarly forfeited and to our use levied. And also all sureties of peace before the said 8th day of December forfeited as in our letters patent thereof made more fully is contained. And since the aforesaid prior and convent have found before us in our Chancery sufficient surety of bearing themselves well towards us and our people from this time according to the form of the statute for that purpose published and provided. We charge you that the said prior and convent against the tenor of our letters patent you do not molest or harass in any way. Witness me myself at Westminster the 1st of May the 5th year of our reign by the King himself. And the tenor of the letters patent of which above in the writ mention is made follows in these words . . [Letters patent repeated] . . .

Upon which comes here now at the quindene of Easter this term the aforesaid Prior by John Brokholes his attorney and complains that he has been harshly distrained by Roland Leynthole Knt lord of Haverford to render account to the King of the tenth and the moiety aforesaid as of the subsidy aforesaid and this unjustly because he says that the said lord King pardoned inter alia all dues and accounts and all actions demands etc. as in the letters patent of the King more fully is contained. And

---

[1] Illegible.

the said Prior does not think that the said lord King will further sue him concerning the premises against the force and effect of the letters patent and writ of the King aforesaid. And because the Court wishes further to deliberate on the premises before that further etc. A day is here given to the aforesaid Prior of la Pille to the morrow of St. John Baptist upon which deliberation being had by the Barons it was considered by them that the aforesaid Prior as far as the accounts to be exacted from him to the King is exonerated by pretext of the letters patent and writ of the King aforesaid. Saving action of the King if otherwise etc.

The Ruins of Ely Priory

CHAPTER XIII.

HER DECLINE AND FALL.

FOR nearly a hundred years no records of Pill are found till in the visitation of the Deanery of Cemaes, July, 1504, from the Canterbury Registers, Warham, f. 228, held in the Church of Newport, the Prior of Pill, as Rector, was reported to have restored the ruined chancel of Pill, and that it was in good order; also on f. 234 of the same registers, in the visitation of the Deanery of Roos, held in the chapter house of Pill Priory, September 10th, 1504. Dom David here says that he has five monks all obedient to him, that the monastery was not in debt, and that he had sufficient means to keep it up, that they held services in the accustomed manner, and at due hours, according to the rule of St. Benedict, and that as far as he knows all the brethren were honest and chaste.

Amongst the names of the monks given is Dom William Watt, who was prior at the dissolution, and Dom William Hyre (Hire) shortly after Abbot of St. Dogmaels.

All the brethren being examined after Dom David Luce gave similar testimony.

WARHAM, f. 234.

Visitation of the Deanery of Roos begun in the monastery of Pulle in the Chapter House there the 10th day of September 1504.

Dom David Luce prior of the Priory of Pulle produces a certificate in writing. And the said Prior was examined as to how many monks he had in number and he says that he has five and that they are obedient to him. Further interrogated of the letting of his benefices he says that he hath not any church let at farm until the feast of St. James next coming. Interrogated concerning the estate of his monastery he says that the said monastery is not charged with any debt but that he hath wherewith he can satisfy and keep up the estate of the said monastery.

Further interrogated concerning divine worship he says that he and his brethren observe divine worship in the accustomed manner and at the due hours according to the foundation of the said monastery and the rule of St. Benedict. Also he says that his brethren keep themselves honest and chaste as far as he knows.

Names of the monks there Dom John Castell, Dom John Dore, Dom William Watts, Dom William Hyre whom the lord has diligently examined concerning the estate of the monastery who being examined and interrogated agree in all their statements with the lord prior abovesaid.

The oath of canonical obedience from them as is customary being received the lord commissary admonishes the prior and Convent abovesaid that they should so govern themselves in future that they might please God and these things being done the lord Commissary dissolved his ordinary visitation.

Thirty years later they agree to call the Pope by no other name than Bishop of Rome, and to pray for him only as such, and to reject his laws, decrees, and canons, unless according to divine law, scripture, and the laws of England. They agreed also to preach according to the Scriptures, not distorting their meaning, and also in the commendatory prayers, after the king as head of the Church, his Queen Anne, and their offspring, to commend the Archbishops of Canterbury and York, together with the rest of the clergy. William Watt, now prior, alone remaining of the five monks whose names are given in 1504.

The original Act is at Westminster.

In the " Lansdowne MS.," 165, the County of Pembroke, is the account of a mill in Dennant belonging to the Priory of Pill, its yearly rental being six shillings and eightpence. Now come the last days of the priory, for there is nothing more to be found till a deed taken from Rymer, which is in reality the Act of Supremacy, in which Henry VIII is acknowledged by the Prior and Convent of Pill as head of the Anglican Church, and they render allegiance to him as such, and next to his wife, Anne Boleyn, and to their infant daughter, Elizabeth, then about a year old, and to other legitimate children of theirs.

Rymer XIV.
CLOSE ROLL. 26 H. VIII, m. 15^d and m, 9^d. July 20, 1534.

Since it is a matter not only pertaining to the Christian religion and piety; but also a rule for our obedience, that we ought to give to our Lord Henry eighth king of that name, to whom alone after Christ Jesus we owe [all things], not only entirely but altogether in Christ, and always the same sincere, undiminished devotion of soul, fidelity, esteem, honour, worship, and reverence; but also with the same fidelity and esteem we render an account, as often as it may be demanded, and bear witness openly to all most willingly, if the matter calls for it. Let all men know to whom this present writing comes, that we the Prior and Convent of Pill in the diocese of St. David's, with one mouth and voice assent to all by this our deed. Given under the common seal in our chapter house, on behalf of ourselves and our successors, all and singular for ever. We profess, testify, and faithfully promise and pledge, that we aforesaid, our successors all and singular observe whole, inviolate, sincere and perpetual esteem and obedience towards our lord the King Henry VIII, and towards Anne the Queen, his wife, and towards his offspring of this same Anne, as well legitimately begotten as to be begotten.

And that we shall notify, proclaim and recommend these same things to the people wheresoever place and occasion permit.

Item. Also that we consider as confirmed and ratified, and always and for ever will thus consider that, the aforesaid King Henry is head of the Anglican Church.

Item. Also that the Bishop of Rome, who in bulls usurps the name of Pope, and arrogates to himself the position of sovereign pontiff, has not any greater jurisdiction, conferred on himself by God in holy scripture in this kingdom of England, than that of an outside Bishop.

Item. Also that not one of us, in any sacred meeting to be held privately or publicly, will call the same Bishop of Rome, by the name of Pope, or sovereign Pontiff; but rather by the name of Bishop of Rome or of the Romish Church; and that none of us will pray for him as Pope, but as Bishop of Rome.

Item. Also that we will adhere to the said lord King alone, and to his successors, and will maintain his laws and decrees, renouncing for ever the laws, decrees and canons of the Bishop of Rome, which may be found to be against divine law and holy scripture, or against the laws of this kingdom.

Item. Also that none of us in any private or public assembly shall presume to twist anything taken from sacred scripture to another meaning; but each one of us will preach Christ, his words and deeds simply, openly and sincerely by "*Norm*," or rule, of holy scriptures, and by true catholic and orthodox teachers in a catholic and orthodox manner.

Item. Also that each one of us in his orisons and supplications, according to general use, shall first commend to God and the people the King, as the supreme head of the Anglican Church, then Queen Anne with their offspring, and lastly the Archbishops of Canterbury and York with the rest of the ordained clergy as seems fit.

Item. Also that we, all and singular, the aforesaid Prior and Convent firmly bind ourselves and our successors by an oath, that all and singular the aforesaid shall faithfully observe for ever.

In witness whereof, to this writing we append our common seal and we have subscribed our names each with his own hand.

Given in our chapter house the twentieth day of the month of July, 1534.[1]

Wyllym Watt, Prior of Pill.

Dñs Mauricius Ieũn, Monk of the same.

Heliseas Pecocke, Monk of the same.

---

[1] This has been corrected by the acknowledgment of supremacy of Pill at Westminster.

Attached to this is the "Common Seal" of the Convent (see illustration) representing the Virgin with Christ in her right arm, and a sceptre in her left hand; underneath is a full-length figure of a monk, with the inscription round —Sigillium commune prioratus B. V. Marie De PULLA.

Here follows the Valor Ecclesiasticus, Hen. VIII (1535):—

Priory of St. Mary the Virgin of Pill.

Of the order of Tiron.

Priory of Pill.

	£	s.	d.
William Watt, prior of this same priory, founded by Adam de la Roche, held his aforesaid priory church and mansion with lands of his lordship, pastures, building, etc. with one carucate of land at the yearly value of		xxvj^s	viij^d
Also at Steynton one manor and a carucate of land „ „ „	iiij^{li}		
Also one tenement in Haverford. viij^{li} which was valued in common years at		ij^s	x^d
Also at Southoke one carucate of land valued per ann.		lxvj^s	viij^d
Also at St. Badock „ „ „ „		liiij^s	
Also at Stedogh half a carucate of land „ „		xxvj^s	viij^d
Also at Monckheton ij carucates of land „ „		xx^s	
Also at Thornton ij bovates of land „ „		x^s	
Also at Dennant ij carucates of land „ „		xxxij^s	
Also at Deplesmore a tenth of a carucate of land „ „			xij^d
Also at Ketyngeston a tenth of a carucate of land „ „		x^s	
	£	s.	d.
Total	xvj	x	x

	£	s.	d.
The same prior held a tenement in Ledameslton iiij^s iiij^d			
The rent of one carucate of land in Hubberstone xj^s			
Subject by Philip Steven in the cure of Steynton			
And subject by William Vychan in Ketyngeston. xiij bovates of land.			
Free rent per ann. for ward marriages etc. ij^s			
And subject to and in the occupation of Thomas Hichets in Stedogh iiij bovates of land.			
Add one half years rent.			
And five carucates of land with appurtenances in the lordship of Maria Herle widow relict of James ap Owen in Kethingeston etc. xviij			
	£	s.	d.
Total Value	xx	xv	iij

Rebates fees fines etc. etc.

	£	s.	d.
John Wogan of Dennant		xj	
John Longton of Thornton			ii½^d

John Wogan of Dennant · · · · xj

John Longton of Thornton · · · · ii½^d

And also John Langton for house in Roch and
    Castle Walwin and Southhook · · · iij^s iiij^d

And for great Pill Hubberston and Roch · · iij^s

And cure ditto · · · · · · xij^d

And the fee of Henry Catherine Esq. etc. · · xiij^s iv^d

To John Fisher Bailliff per ann. during his life · vj · viij

	£	s.	d.
	xiij	iij	ij

Fees etc. · · · · · · x^s

And annuity to the Abbot of St. Dogmaels · lx^{li} vj^s viij^d

	£	s.	d.
Sum clear	vij	xij	j

The Churches belonging to the Priory.

Steynton, with vicarage · · · · xxx^{li}

Roch with vicarage one tenement, one bovate of land
    and 10   belonging to it · iiij^s

Fruits and emoluments xj^{li} with xxxx^s glebe

Church of New Castle in Cemaes with glebe · ·iiij^{li}

    ,,   New Moat · · · · xlv^{li}

Fees etc. Archidiaconal · · · · xxiij^s

    ,,   ordinary · · · · xxvj^s viij

	£	s.	d.
There remains clear	xliij	x	iij

Pensions.

The same Prior receive as pensions annuity as rector
    of Hustard · · · · · xxvj^s viij

From the Church of Hubberstone · · · iij^s iiij^d

    ,,   ,, Nolton and the rent of an acre
    of land · · · · · · iiij^s

From the Church of Pentvayne · · · iiij^d

    ,,   ,, Johneston · · · vj^s viij

Sum of Pensions xl^s

	£	s.	d.
Clear value of the sum total	lij	ij	v
Tithe		ciiij	iij

Churches etc. belonging to Pill Priory

Hubberstone.

Church of the same under the Priory of Pill.

Thomas Parrish is rector, with house and glebe

Total value in common years	vj^{li}	xiij^{s}	iiij^{d}
Yearly Pension to the foresaid Prior		iij^{s}	iiij^{d}
Visitation fees every 3^{d} year			xx^{d}
Visitation Synodal etc. fees	v^{s}		ix^{d}

	£	s.	d.
There remains clear	vj	ii	vij
Tithe		xij	iij¼

Hustarde.

Church of the same under the Priory of Pill.

Xerpofer Taylour clerk is rector and has a house

yearly value of the fruits of this Benefice	xx^{li}	
Year pension to the Prior of Pill	xxvj^{s}	viij^{d}
Archidiaconal and Synodal etc. fees	v^{s}	ix
Ordinary Visitation each third year		xiij

	£	s.	d.
There remains clear	xviij	vj	vj

Nolton.

Church of the same The Prior of Pill is patron.

Thomas Wogan is rector and has a house

Value etc. yearly	iiij^{li}	xiij^{s}	iiij^{d}
Pension to the Prior of Pill		iiij^{s}	
Ordinary Visitation each 3rd year			xij
Archidiaconal Visitation etc.	v^{s}		ix^{d}

	£	s.	d.
There remains clear	iiij	ij	vij
Tithe		viij	iij½

Rupe.

Vicarage of the same under the said Prior of Pill.

John Barbour, clerk, is vicar has a small house
and glebe

Value in common years	iiij^{li}	
Ordinary Visitation fees every 3^{d} year		xiiij½
Archidiaconal fees etc.	v^{s}	

	£	s.	d.
There remains clear	iiij	xiiij	ix
Tithe		ix^{s}	iiij½

Pontvayne.

Church of the same under the Priory of Pill.

Gryffyn Lloid is rector	Value, common years	lxvj^{s}	viij^{d}
	Tithe	vj^{s}	viij^{d}

Decanatus   Deanery of Donegleddy.
                               Archdeaconry of St. David.

    New Moat

The Priory of Pill hold the rectorship of this church himself
He has one manor with certain lands of vj viij yearly value etc.
    with fruit fees etc.   of the total clear value xliiij^s vij^d
                            Tithe iiij^s v½^d

Decanatus   Parishes Church in the Deanery of Rhos.

    Freystroppe
           Parish Church under the Priory of Pill.

Thomas Stephen is Rector.   The Rectory with land and fruits
    is valued at vj^{li}
Ordinary Visitation fees every 3rd year viij^d
Archidiaconal Visitation and Synodals etc. v^s ix^d
                        Clear value cxiij^s vij
                        Tithe xj^s iiij½

            Steynton Vicarage.
    The Vicarage of the same under the Priory of Pill.

Richard Coyre is vicar   Total value x^{li}
Visitation fees every 3rd year   vj^d
Archidiaconal Visitation Synodals etc.   ij^s iiij^d

                      £ s. d.
            Clear value lx xvij ij
            Tithe   xix viij¾

         Johneston.
      Church under the Priory of Pill.

Mr. Thomas Johns is rector with house and land
               Value in common years liiij^s iiij^d
Ordinary Visitation every 3rd year fees   viij^d
Archidiaconal Visitation Synodals etc.   v^s ix^d
Pension from the rectory to the foresaid Prior of Pill vj^s viij^d
                      Clear value xl^s iij
                      Tithe iiij ½

Then follows, in 1536, the king's grants of a pension to William Watts, the late Prior of Pill, of the yearly value of ten pounds, and two years later is an account of the value of the possessions of the late Priory of Pill, by John Wogan, collector of rents, taken from the Exchequer Augmentation Office, together with another valuation, taken four years later, in which the " arrears " have considerably increased. The first of these two valuations, of John Wogan, contains an interesting account of a messuage, etc., and a rabbit warren, let by John Prior of Pill to Morris Butler, called " Le Monckton," at xx shillings a year, containing 2⅛ carucates of land with the warren, on a forty years lease, given July 4th, 1517, in which lease it was agreed that it was lawful for the Prior and convent to hunt in the aforesaid warren, three times a year, and also to have a rick of rushes every year, cutting and carting them at their own expense, besides other rights. These two indentures also occur again in the next deed, from the Exchequer Augmentation Office, Vol. 232, f. 52.

EXCHEQUER AUGMENTATION OFFICE. Vol. 232, fol. 52. 20 Mar., 1536.

The King to all to whom etc. greeting. Whereas the late Priory of Pulle in South Wales by the authority of parliament is suppressed and dissolved. And whereas one William Wattes at the time of such dissolution and long before was Prior thereof. We willing that a reasonable yearly pension or adequate promotion for the said William should be provided to better maintain him in food and sustenance. Know ye that we in consideration of the premises of our special grace certain knowledge and mere motion by the advise and consent of the Chancellor and council of our Court of Augmentations of the Revenues of our Crown have given and granted and by these presents do give and grant to the said William a certain annuity or yearly pension of ten pounds sterling. To have enjoy and yearly to take the same ten pounds to the said William and his assigns from the time of the dissolution and suppression of the said late Priory to the term and for the term of the life of the said William or until the said William to one or more ecclesiastical benefices or other adequate promotion of the clear yearly value of ten pounds or beyond by us shall be promoted as well by the hands of the Treasurer of our aforesaid Court who for the time shall be from our treasure in his hands of the revenues which happen to remain in his hands as well by the hands of the Receivers of the particulars of the revenues aforesaid of the said revenues at the feasts of the Annunciation B V M and St. Michael the Archangel by equal portions to be paid. Because express mention etc. In witness whereof etc. Witness etc. at Westminster the 20th day of March the 28th year of our reign.

By the Chancellor and Council aforesaid by virtue of the warrant aforesaid.

AUGMENTATION MINISTERS ACCOUNTS. 29-30 Hen. VIII, 153. 1538-9.

The late Priory of Pylle within the Bishopric of St. David's.

Compotus of John Wogan Collector of Rents and farms of all and singular the lordships manors lands and tenements and other possessions whatsoever temporal as well as spiritual to the aforesaid late priory appertaining or belonging which came to the hands of the lord King that now is and is annexed to his Crown and that of his heirs and successors the Kings of England in augmentation of the revenues of his said Crown of England by virtue of a certain act in his parliament held at Westminster on its prorogation 4th Feb. the 27th year of the reign of the said lord King published and provided as in the said Act inter alia is contained to wit from the feast of St. Michael the Archangel the 29th year of the reign of the aforesaid King Henry the 8th to the same feast of St. Michael the Archangel then next ensuing the 30th year of the aforesaid King to wit for one whole year.

Arrears.

And of xxxvij[s] of arrears of the last account of the year preceding as appears there.

Sum xxxvij[s]

Site of the late priory of Pille with other things.

Of xlj[li] xij[s] ij[d] forthcoming of divers parcels of land as well temporal as spiritual to wit the site of the late Priory aforesaid lxxiij[s] iiij[d] Southoke[1] lxxvj[s] viij[d] Seynt Baddocke[2] xxvj[s] viij[d] Lodameston lv[s] iiij[d] Great Pulle x[s] ij[d]   The Rectory of Staynton xxx[li] not answered for here because demised at farm to John Wogan by Indenture for term of xxj years sealed under the seal of the lord King of his Court of Augmentations of the revenues of his Crown as in the next title following more fully and particularly appears.

Sum nil.

Farms.

But he renders account of xlj[li] xij[s] ij[d] of rent of demesne lands with divers parcels of land and with the Rectory of Staynton demised by Indenture to John Wogan sealed with the seal of the Court of Augmentations of the Revenues of the Crown of the lord King of which the tenor follows in these words—This Indenture made between the most excellent prince and lord the lord Henry the eighth by the grace of God King of England and France defender of the faith and lord of Ireland and on earth supreme head of the Anglican church of the one part and John Wogan of the other part witnesseth that the said lord King by advice and consent of the Council of the Court of Augmentation of the Revenues of his Crown hath delivered granted and let at farm to the aforesaid John the house and site of the late Priory of Pulle within the Bishopric of St. David's by authority of parliament suppressed and dissolved together with all houses edifices barns gardens orchards dovecotes ground and soil within the site and precinct of the said late Priory and five small orchards and one small wood and one meadow there abutting upon Davye Harryes wood to the same late priory belonging and appertaining also one parcel of arable land called Castell Hill there abutting upon Steynton Highway and two acres of waste land there.   And also one other parcel of waste land in the field aforesaid abutting upon the way of the waste land on the one side and Staynton highway on the other side also all the grain mill with appurts there together with the pool and all the watercourse running to and belonging to the same which said premises to the said late priory belonged and appertained and further the said lord King has delivered granted and let at farm to the aforesaid John all the messuages lands tenements meadows fields pastures with appurts in Southoke[1] Saint Badocks[2] and Ledemaston to the said late priory belonging and appertaining and which in the hands and proper occupation of the late prior of the said late priory at the time of the dissolution of that priory were reserved and occupied.   And also four bovates of land in Great Pulle to the said Priory similarly belonging and appertaining which Philip Webbe late had and held at farm by a yearly rent of ten shillings and two pence and further the said lord King by the advice and consent of his council aforesaid hath delivered granted and let at farm to the aforesaid John the Rectory of the parish Church of Staynton with appurts to the said late priory belonging and appertaining together with lands glebes tithes etc. whatsoever to

---

[1] South Hook.   [2] St. Budoc.

10 a

the said Rectory appertaining and belonging except however and to the said lord King heirs and successors altogether reserved all great trees and woods of the premises and advowsons of vicarages and chapels all kinds of buildings within the said site and precinct of the late priory which the said lord King shall command to be thrown down and carried away. To have and to hold all and singular the premises with the appurts excepting the preexcepted to the aforesaid John and his assigns from the feast of the Annunciation of the Blessed virgin Mary last past to the end of the term and for the term of 21 years then next ensuing and fully to be completed rendering therefrom yearly to the said lord King his heirs and successors forty-one pounds twelve shillings and two pence of legal money of England to wit for the aforesaid site mill orchards wood lands meadows and pastures except the said lands and tenements in Southoke St. Badoks Ledemaston and aforesaid four[1] bovates of land in Great Pulle and the said Rectory of Staynton seventy three shillings and four and for the said lands and tenements in Southoke sixty six shillings and eight pence and for the aforesaid lands and tenements in Saint Badoks twenty six shillings and eight pence and for the aforesaid lands and tenements in Lodesmaston fifty five shillings and four pence and for the aforesaid four bovates of land in Great Pulle ten shillings and two pence and for the aforesaid Rectory of Staynton thirty pounds at the feasts of St. Michael the Archangel and the Annunciation of the Blessed virgin Mary or within one month after either feast of those feasts at the Court aforesaid by equal portions to be paid during the term aforesaid. And the aforesaid lord King wills and by these presents grants that he his heirs and successors the said John and his assigns from all rents services fees annuities pensions portions and sums of money whatsoever of the premises or any of them issuing or to be paid except of the Rents above reserved against all persons whatsoever from time to time will exonerate and defend and all houses and buildings of the premises as well in timber as in roofing of tile and slate from time to time as often as shall be necessary and opportune will and faithfully shall cause to be repaired sustained and maintained during the term aforesaid and the aforesaid John grants by these presents that he and his assigns roofing of thatch and all other necessary repairs of the premises except timber tiles and slates aforesaid from time to time shall support and sustain during the term aforesaid and the aforesaid lord King further wills and by these presents grants that it shall be lawful to the aforesaid John and his assigns to take perceive and have from time to time of in and upon the premises competently and sufficiently hedgebote firebote ploughbote and cartbote there and not elsewhere to be expended and occupied during the term aforesaid to one part of this present indenture with the aforesaid John remaining the aforesaid lord King his seal of the aforesaid Court appointed for the sealing of such deeds has commanded to be affixed and to the other part of the same Indenture with the said lord King remaining the aforesaid John has affixed his seal. Given at Westminster the fifth day of July the 29th year of the said lord King.

Sum xlj[li] xij[s] ij[d]

Rents of tenants at will in the manor of Staynton.

. And of x[s] of rent of one tenement with divers lands to the same annexed demised to Rotherothe ap John at the will of the lord to be paid at the feasts of SS. Philip and

---

[1] ? Eight bovates in the later and former deeds.

James and St. Michael the Archangel by equal portions. And of viij^s of rent of one burgage demised at will to David Bordde[1] to be paid at the terms aforesaid. And of xiij^s of Rent of one tenement demised at will to William Phillip to be paid at the terms aforesaid. And of xx^s of Rent of one messuage demised at will to Phillip Meller to be paid at the terms aforesaid. And of v^s of rent of one tenement with appurts demised at will to William Hay to be paid at the terms aforesaid. And of xx^s of rent of one tenement demised at will to John Bull to be paid at the same terms.

Sum lxxvj^s

Rents of tenants by indenture and at will in Devant.

And of xx^s of rent of one tenement with appurts lying within the lordship of Haverford West demised by Indenture to Richard Davye sealed with the conventual seal of the Priory of Pille of which the tenor follows in these words—Thys Indenture etc. [as given in Latin copy] . . . . And of xxj^s viij^d of one tenement and 6 bovates of land with all and singular their appurts in the tenement of Devant demised by Indenture to Richard ffisher sealed with the conventual seal of the late priory of Pylle which indeed he has not shown to be paid at the feasts of Easter and St. Michael the Archangel by equal portions. And of xvj^s of rent of one tenement with appurts demised at will to Robert Pers to be paid at the terms aforesaid. And of xij^s of rent of one tenement with appurts demised at will to John Hoell to be paid at the terms aforesaid.

Sum lxix^s viij^d

Saint Baddocks.[2]

And of xxvj^s viij^d of rent of one messuage and one carucate of land with all and singular their appurts which they have in the township and fields of St. Badocks within the lordship of Haverford which said messuage and carucate of land with all and singular their appurts one William Rowe late held there as by certain metes and boundaries to the said Hugh are assigned and limited now demised to Hugh Nutt by Indenture sealed with the Conventual seal aforesaid given the 4th April the 16th year of the reign of King Henry the 8th To have and hold To have and hold to him and his assigns from the day of the making of these presents to the end of the term of 60 years then next ensuing and fully to be completed rendering therefrom yearly as above to be paid at the feast of SS. Philip and James and St. Michael the Archangel by equal portions. And the aforesaid Hugh wills and grants for him and his assigns the aforesaid messuage with all buildings to the said messuage belonging with all their appurts he will repair sustain and maintain at his own proper costs and expense during the term aforesaid and at the end of the term aforesaid the said messuage with other buildings to the same belonging with appurts well and decently shall surrender and leave and suit of Court etc.

Sum xxvj^s viij^d

Rents of free tenants by Indenture in Stedolph.[3]

And of j^d of rent of one tenement in the tenure of Thomas Hytes who held freely To be paid at the feast of St. Michael the Archangel only. And of xxxvij^s viij^d of rent of one messuage and seven bovates of land with appurts in the township and fields of

---

[1] Byrde in the Latin compotus.   [2] St. Budocs.   [3] Studdolph.

Stedolph aforesaid as by metes and bounds are assigned and known demised to William Hill by Indenture sealed with the Conventual seal aforesaid given the 19th day of December the 27th year of the reign of King Henry the 8th. To have and to hold to him his heirs and assigns from the feast of the Nativity of our Lord next coming after the date of these presents to the end of the term of 95 years then next ensuing and fully to be completed. Rendering there from yearly as above to be paid at the feasts of St. Michael the Archangel and Easter by equal porcions and the aforesaid William Hyll wills and grants for himself his heirs and assigns by these presents the aforesaid messuage with appurts he will repair sustain and maintain and at the end of the term aforesaid in good repair according to the custom of the lordship of Haverford will surrender and leave etc.

Sum xxvij[s] ix[d]

Mounckton.

And of xx[s] of Rent of one messuage with appurts and with warren of conies demised to Moris Butler by Indenture sealed with the Conventual seal of the late Monastery aforesaid the tenor of which follows in these words This Indenture made between John Prior of Pulle and convent of the same and by their assent and consent have delivered granted and at farm let to the aforesaid Maurice one messuage called Le Monckton containing two carucates one bovate of land with warren of conies in the tenement of Johnstone aforesaid as by certain metes and bounds there are assigned and limited. To have and to hold to the aforesaid Maurice and his assigns from the feast of St. Michael the Archangel next coming after the date of these presents until the end of the term of forty years of 40 years then next ensuing and fully to be completed under the form and conditions following to wit to render and do to the chief lord of that fee the rents and services therefrom due and accustomed and to render to us the aforesaid Prior and convent and our successors during the term aforesaid a yearly rent of xx[s] of silver of lawful money of England at two terms of the year to wit at the feast of the Holy Apostles Philip and James and St. Michael the Archangel by equal portions to be paid and if it happen the aforesaid rent or any part of the same to be behind unpaid in part or in whole at any feast at which it should be paid that then it shall be lawful to the aforesaid Prior Convent and their successors into the aforesaid messuage and lands with their appurts to enter and distrain and the distraints so and there taken from thence to take carry drive away and retain until of the whole aforesaid rent and every part of the same if there shall be any they shall be satisfied and moreover the aforesaid Maurice wills and grants that if it happen the aforesaid rent to be unpaid for one whole year and a day through default of the aforesaid Maurice or his assigns. So that sufficient distress in the aforesaid messuage and lands with appurts shall not be found by which the aforesaid Prior Convent and their successors shall be able to distrain that then it shall be lawful to the aforesaid Prior Convent and their successors the aforesaid messuage and lands with their appurts to re-enter and their former estate therein to have again without any impeachment; and the aforesaid messuage with appurts he shall repair sustain and maintain and at the end of the term aforesaid in good and sufficient repair according to the custom of the lordship of Haverford shall surrender and leave. Moreover know ye that I the aforesaid Maurice for me and my assigns [do grant] that it shall be lawful to the aforesaid Prior Convent and their successors during the term aforesaid into the warren aforesaid three times a year to enter and there to hunt and there to hold their Courts to wit within the feast of all Saints the feast[1] of the Nativity of our Lord and the feast of the Purification of the Blessed Virgin Mary without any impeachment and conies or rabbits there and then take for the use of their household or quest house to take have and with them from thence to carry away without distress of the said warren. And also if "Rushes" grow upon the land aforesaid then the aforesaid Maurice wills also and grants for himself and assigns that the aforesaid Prior and Convent may have of such "Rushes" one rick every year at their own costs and expense to be paid done and carried away besides other rights unless it is required for the use of the household of the said Maurice or his assigns if the aforesaid Rushes shall be sold. In witness whereof to one part of these Indentures with the aforesaid Maurice remaining the aforesaid Prior and Convent their common seal in the chapter house of Pulle have procured to be affixed and to the other part of these indentures with the aforesaid Prior and Convent remaining the aforesaid Maurice has affixed his seal. Given the 4th July A.,D. 1517 and the ninth year of the reign of King Henry the 8th after the conquest of England.

Sum xx[s]

Rents at will in Thorneton.

And of x[s] of rent of one tenement with appurts demised at will to John Day to be paid at the feasts of Philip and James and St. Michael the Archangel by equal portions.

Sum x[s]

Deplesmore.

And of xij[s] of Rent of one tenement with all and singular its appurts demised by Indenture to Hugh Barnard sealed with the Conventual seal of the late Priory of Pylle the tenor of which follows in these words—This indenture made between William Watts prior of Pulle with the assent and consent of his Order, the convent and chapter of the said house of the one part and Hugh Barnard of Camrose of the other part witnesses that the aforesaid prior and convent with unanimous assent and consent have delivered and let at farm to aforesaid Hugh one tenement and all the lands meadows messuages and pastures with all their appurts called Deplesmore in the tenement of Ketingeston being within the lordship of Haverford as by certain metes and bounds are assigned and limited To have and to hold the said messuages and all other the premises with appurts to the aforesaid Hugh and his assigns during the term of 40 years next ensuing and fully to be completed the term beginning at the feast of the Annunciation of the Blessed Virgin Mary next ensuing after the date of this Indenture to be rendered made and paid therefrom to us the aforesaid Prior Convent and our successors a yearly rent of twelve shillings sterling and services there accustomed as the tenants there have been wont to hold render and pay to be levied and satisfied by all kinds of distraints as shall be just and we the aforesaid Prior and Convent and our successors the aforesaid messuages and tenements aforesaid with their appurts etc. to the aforesaid Hugh and his assigns during the term aforesaid against all men will warrant and defend by these presents. In witness whereof the aforesaid Prior and Convent to one part of this Indenture with the said John remaining the common seal

---

[1] "Within the feast." ? Would this include the octave=three weeks hunting per year.

of the said house order and chapter have affixed and to the other part of this Indenture with the said Prior and Convent remaining the said Hugh for the performance of this said agreement has set his seal. Given at Pulle the 28th May the 26th year of the reign of King Henry the 8th.

Sum xij^s

Rents of free tenants and by Indenture in Kethingston.

And of ij^s of Rents of marriages and reliefs there in the tenure of William Vaghan who holds freely. To be paid at the feasts of Philip and James and St. Michael the Archangel by equal portions. And of xviij^s of rent of 5½ carucates of land with appurts in the tenure of Dame Owyn widow who holds freely to be paid at the terms aforesaid. And of x^s of rent of one tenement with a plot of land to the said tenement belonging lying there demised by Indenture to William Gyliat sealed with the conventual seal of the late monastery of Pylle which said [indenture] he does not show. To be paid at the terms aforesaid.

Sum xxx^s

New Castle.

And of viij^s of rent of one tenement with its appurts demised at will to John Stephen to be paid at the feasts of Easter and St. Michael the Archangel.

Sum viij^s

Rents at will in Windsore.

And of xiij^s iiij^d of rent of one tenement with appurtenances demised at will to David Guy. To be paid at the feasts of Easter and St. Michael the Archangel by equal portions.

Sum xiij^s iiij^d

Ratford.

And of vj^s viij^d of rent of one bovate of land with appurts demised at will to John Mellor to be paid at the feasts of the Annunciation B V M and St. Michael the Archangel by equal portions.

Sum vj^s viij^d

Free Rents in Roche and Huberstone.

And of iiij^s of rent of a piece of land in the tenure of William Giliat who holds freely to be paid at the feast of St. Michael the Archangel only. And of xj^s of rent of divers lands and tenements lying in Huberstone aforesaid to be paid at the feasts of Philip and James and St. Michael the Archangel by equal portions.

Sum xv^s

Neugold.[1]

And of ij^s iiij^d of rent of divers lands and tenements lying and being in the parish of Roche and the chapel called St. Cradok's Chapel demised by Indenture to John Phillips Esquire sealed with the Conventual seal aforesaid which he does not show. To be paid at the feasts of the Annunciation B V M and St. Michael by equal portions.

Sum ij^s iiij^d

---

[1] Neugol.

Rectory of Newmote.

And of c^s of Rent of the tithe of sheaves and other profits there with appurts of the aforesaid Rectory demised to John Phillips Esquire by Indenture sealed with the Conventual seal of the late Monastery aforesaid as is said to be paid at the feasts of Philip and James and St. Michael the Archangel by equal portions.

Sum c^s

Rectory of New Castle and Roche.

And of xv^{li} of the Rents of tithe of sheaves and all other profits forthcoming of the Rectory aforesaid demised to Edward Lloyd by Indenture sealed with the seal of the Court of Augmentations of the Revenues of the Crown of the Lord King the tenor of which follows in these words—This Indenture made between the lord Henry the 8th of the one part and Edward Lloyd yeoman of the houshold of the lord King of the other part witnesses that the said lord King by the advice and consent of the Council of the Court of Augmentations of the Revenues of his Crown hath delivered and let at farm to the aforesaid Edward the Rectory of New Castle and Roche with the appurts to the late Priory of Pulle within the Bishopric of St. David's by the authority of Parliament suppressed and dissolved together with all tithes oblations profits and emoluments whatsoever of the said Rectory, belonging and appertaining [to the late Priory] excepting however and to the said lord King his heirs and successors altogether reserved all great trees and woods of and upon the premises growing and being and the advowson of the vicarage of New Castle and Roche aforesaid. To have and to hold the Rectory aforesaid and other all and singular the premises with the appurts excepting the pre-excepted to the aforesaid Edward and his assigns from the feasts of the Annunciation of the Blessed Virgin Mary last past to the end of the term and for the term of 21 years then next ensuing and fully to be completed rendering therefrom yearly to the said lord King his heirs and successors fifteen pounds of lawful money of England at the feasts of St. Michael the Archangel and the Annunciation B V M or within one month after either feast of those feasts at the Court aforesaid by equal portions to be paid during the term aforesaid and the aforesaid lord King wills and by these presents grants that he his heirs and successors the said Edward and his assigns from all pensions portions and sums of money whatsoever of the premises or any of them issuing or to be paid except the rent above reserved against all persons whatsoever from time to time will exonerate acquit and defend and all houses and buildings of the premises as well in timber as in roofing of tiles and slate from time to time as often as shall be necessary and opportune well and sufficiently shall cause to be repaired sustained and maintained during the term aforesaid and the aforesaid Edward grants by these presents that he and his assigns roofing of thatch and all other necessary repairs of the premises except repairs of timber and roofing of tiles and slate aforesaid from time to time will support and sustain during the term aforesaid. In witness whereof to one part of this Indenture with the aforesaid Edward remaining the aforesaid lord King his seal of the Court aforesaid appointed for the sealing of such deeds has commanded to be affixed and to the other part of the said Indenture with the said lord King remaining the aforesaid Edward has affixed his seal. Given at Westminster the 14th May the 29th year of the said lord King.

Sum xv^{li}

Pensions.

And of xxvj^s viij^d of rent of a pension from Huscard there yearly paid to William Watts late prior there at the feast of St. Michael the Archangel only. And of iij^s iiij^d of rent of a pension from Hubertston there yearly paid to the aforesaid William Watts late prior there at the feast aforesaid. And of vj^s viij^d rent of a pension from Jannston[1] there yearly paid to the aforesaid late prior at the feast aforesaid. And of xij^d rent of a pension from Norlton there yearly paid to the late prior aforesaid at the feast aforesaid only.

Sum xxxvij^s viij^d

Perquisites of Court.

Of any profit forthcoming of perquisites of Court held there this year he does not answer here because none have fallen this year within the time of this account by the oath of the said Accountant.

Sum nil.

The whole sum total with arrears.

iiijj^{li} iiij^s iij^{d}[2]

Of which

Fees and wages.

The same accounts in moneys paid to John Phillips Esquire steward of the Court there at 40s. per ann as appears by letters patent sealed with the Conventual seal as in the account of the year preceding more fully appears and so in allowance this year as in the preceding—xl^s And in fee of Henry Cathern Clerk of the Court of Stanton granted to him for the term of his life at xiij^s iiij^d per ann. and so in allowance this year as in preceding—xiij^s iiij^d And in fee of the aforesaid Accountant by reason of his collection of rents and farms abovesaid at xxxvj^s viij^d per ann. and so there shall be an allowance for the whole time of this account at the feast of St. Michael the Archangel the 30th year of the King aforesaid—xxvj^s viij^d And in the stipend of the Auditor's clerk writing this account at ij^s per ann as the clerks of the Auditor of the lord King of his Duchy of Lancaster were accustomed to be allowed on every account of the Ministers and so in allowance this year as in preceding—ij^s

Sum iij^{li} ij^s

Rents resolute.

And in moneys paid to the heirs of Malesant issuing out of the late priory aforesaid for a certain rent resolute at xl^s per ann. to be paid at the feast of St. Michael the Archangel only and so in allowance at such feast of St. Michael the Archangel this year as in preceding—xl^s And in similar moneys paid to the heirs of James Bowen issuing out of the manor of Staynton for a certain rent resolute at vj^d per ann. to be paid at the feast aforesaid only and so in allowance this year as in preceding vj^d And in similar moneys paid to Thomas Llamesfelde for a certain rent resolute issuing out of tenements in Denante and Southeoke at 2½d. per ann. To be paid at the feast aforesaid only and so in allowance this year as in preceding 2½d.

Sum xl^s viij½^d

---

[1] Johneston.　　[2] £81 4s. 3d.

Livery of moneys.

And in moneys delivered to Edward Watters Receiver of the particulars of the lord King of the issues of his office as appears by divers bills thereof delivered and among the memoranda of this year remaining.

lxiij^{li} viij^s vj½^d

Sum of allowances and liveries aforesaid lxix^{li} xj^s iij^d

And he owes xj^{li} xiij^s

Whereof—

Lewis ap Bowen Archdeacon of the diocese of St. David's as holding of moneys by him received in the year preceding for procurations and synodals issuing out of all the churches to the late priory aforesaid belonging at xxxvij^s per ann. which by right of inquisition therefore charged upon him as well for this year as for the year preceding as soon as it was decreed and determined by the Chancellor and Council of the Court of Augmentations of the Revenues of the Crown of the lord King   lxxiiij^s

John Phillips for rent of a tenement as above charged at vj^s viij^d per ann to wit of his arrears this year behind   vj^s viij^d

The same John for rent of another tenement as above charged at vj^s viij^d per ann. to wit of his arrears this year behind   ij^s iiij^d

John Stephens for rent of a tenement as above charged in New Castle at viij^s per ann. to wit of arrears this year behind   viij^s

Owen Tewe for rent of a tenement above charged at iiij^s per ann to wit of his arrears behind this year   iiij^s

The Rector of the parish church of Hus Kard for rent of his pension as above charged at xxvj^s viij^d per ann. to wit of his arrears this year behind   xxvj^s viij^d

Sir Thomas Jones, priest Rector of the church of Janeston as above charged at vj^s viij^d per ann to wit of his arrears behind as well for this year as for the year preceding by the oath of the said Accountant   xiij^s iiij^d

EXCHEQUER AUGMENTATION OFFICE.   34-35 Hen. VIII, 215.   1142-3.

County of Pembroke.

The late Priory of Pylle in the county aforesaid.

Compotus of John Wogan Collector of Rents of all and singular the hereditaments belonging to the said late priory by authority of Parliament suppressed and dissolved.

Arrears.

The same answers for l^{li} xiij^s xj^d of arrears of last account of the preceding year as at the foot of the same more plainly appears.

Sum l^{li} xiij^s xj^d

Farm of the site of the late priory aforesaid same value as in previous account etc. and the same only less full till we come to the following—

Within the Site of the aforesaid late Priory this year as appears by bill of parcels thereof made and before the Auditor shown examined and approved and among the Memoranda of this year remaining and so in allowance as above. And he owes c^{li} vij^s v^d

John Phillips for rent of a tenement above charged at vj^s viij^d per ann being in arrears for three years ending at the feast of St. Michael the Archangel the 32nd year of the reign of the King aforesaid whereof of Arrears xx^s John Stephen for the farm of a tenement above charged under the title of New Castle at viij^s per ann being in arrears for the said time and not yet paid whereof of arrears xxiiij^{s1}

The Rector of Uskard rent of a pension issuing there at xxvj^s per ann being in arrears for the same time   iiij^{li} (xxvj^s and viij^d)
_{last time}

The Rector of Janyston for rent of a pension issuing there at vj^s viij^d per ann being in arrears for five years finishing at the feast aforesaid in the 33rd year
_{last time}
iiij^{li} (xiij^s and iv^d)

John Phillips farmer of the Rectory of Newmote is charged at c^s per ann being in arrears for the whole time of this account and not yet paid whereof of arrears   c^s

Edward lloyd farmer of the Rectory of New Castle and Roche is above charged at xv^{li} per ann. being in arrears as well for this year as for the preceding year and not paid   xxx^{li}

The Archdeacon of St. David's and Cardigan for monies by him received from the accountant aforesaid for procurations and synodals in the 32nd year of the King aforesaid issuing out of divers churches aforesaid at xxiij^s pen ann and disallowed by counsel of the Court aforesaid and not yet paid whereof of arrears   xxiij^s

John Young clerk depute to the Bishop of St. David's for similar monies by him the same year received and by counsel of the court aforesaid disallowed as in preceding and not yet paid whereof of arrears   xvij^s ix^d

The heirs of Mallesant for monies by them of the aforesaid accountant received for rent resolute issuing out of the manor of Staynton at xl^s per ann and by counsel aforesaid disallowed   xl^s

John Griffith deputy farmer of the site of the late Priory aforesaid with others above charged at xl^{li} xij^s ij^d per ann whereof arrears on behalf of the said rent this year and not yet paid   xxxiij^{li} xiij^s vj^d

The said Accountant of his arrears of the last in the preceding year   xviij^{li} xv^s ix^d

The Rector of Norlias for rent of pension yearly paid to the late priory aforesaid at xij^d per ann so of his arrears behind to wit as well for this year as the year preceding   ij^s

The said accountant for his own arrears behind   iiij^{li} xvj^s

Total of above xj^{li} xiij^s

" Pill," as seen in Camden, as well as by the maps of the present day,

"Otherwise called Pill Roose, was a house of monks of the St. Dogmaels order, standing in Roose country four miles above Arford West [Haverfordwest] upon the further shore of the Haven of Milford. It was founded about 1200 by Adam de Rupe for Monks of the Order of Tyron."

It is in the parish of Stainton, about one and a-half miles north-east of Milford.

---

[1] Increased from viijs.

There is an indenture between the King and Edward Lloyd yeoman of the Royal Household, 14th May, 29 Henry VIII, 1538, regarding the Rectory of Newcastle and Roche.

After the dissolution, Pill Priory was granted to John Barlow with its possessions. Later, in 31 Charles II, there was a dispute in the Parish of Stainton, Jordan v. Field, relating to tithes and similar to the one we shall give under Fishguard, and in 8 James II another, Hook v. Meare, regarding tithes in Monckton, both formerly part of the old Priory of Pill.

Fenton writes : —

The church of Little New Castle was, by the endowment of Adam de Rupe annexed to the priory of Pill, which latter also belonged to St. Dogmaels. About a mile from the village of Hubberston Mr. Le Hunt, an Irish gentleman, built a house on the site of the old chapel of St. Budoc, descending into the valley at the extremity of Hubberston Pill, one suddenly comes on the small remains of Pill Priory ; there is little more standing than the east side of part of the tower wall, yet enough to inform us that the building was cruciform, the tower in the centre forming the choir supported on arches, one of which remains entire, a little pointed, but very plain and rude, without the least trace of sculptured ornament anywhere. Yet this principal fragment, together with the lesser ones scattered round the cottages among the ruins, and the mill backed by the prettily wooded hill of Ledelmston, groups into no unpleasing landscape. This religious establishment owed its foundation to Adam de Rupe or de la Roche. . . . A few years ago, in digging a garden adjoining the ruins of the priory church, the workmen fell upon the spot that had been the burying place of the monastery, and uncovered several gravestones ; one of which I have seen broken in two, with an inscription round the rim in flowery characters in a gentleman's yard in the town of Milford ; though much effaced, there was still enough left to prove it the gravestone of one of the early priors of the house. . . . With an endowment of the best land round the spot, a right of fishery not restricted, and various other privileges, in a retirement made more desirable as it was visited twice a day by the sea bringing fresh air and health with its tide ; if monks were capable of happiness, surely those of Pill might have felt themselves so.

Fenton had in his possession a charter of William de la Grace, Earl of Pembroke, Earl Marshal of England, confirming the endowment of Pill Priory not mentioned by Dugdale, which was incorporated in Charter Roll 25 Ed. I already given.

In Nicholas Carlisle and Tanner are the following extracts, which are not altogether correct, as at the dissolution Pill was still a cell of St. Dogmaels and by the Cartulary of Tiron we know that in 1516 St. Dogmaels belonged to Tiron, so that there must be an error in the statement of several of these later authors, who relate that the Priory of Pill forsook the order of Tiron and became common Benedictines.

Pille, in the Cwmwd of Ys Garn, Cantref of Rhos (now called the Hundred of Rhos), Co. of Pembroke. In the Parish of Stainton—"Adam de Rupe founded a Priory here, about A.D. 1200, and placed Monks in it of the Order of Tyron, who in time forsook that strict Rule, and became common Benedictines. This House was dedicated to St. Mary and St. Budoc, and is said to have been subordinate to St. Dogmaels, but was found 26 Hen. VIII, to have distinct Revenues of its own to the value of £67 15. 3. per annum in the whole, and £53 2. 5. clear; and was granted, 38 Hen. VIII, to Roger and Thomas Barlow." N. Carlisle.

Also as already seen though Pill had her own Revenues, as was usual with cells, she still paid a certain sum yearly to the mother Abbey of St. Dogmaels to the end, which proves conclusively that she was subordinate to St. Dogmaels. Dugdale also falls into exactly the same two errors; and as St. Dogmaels remained under Tiron, one fails to see how Pill could have left that order.

Even the learned Dom Gasquet, till lately Abbot President of the English Benedictines, falls into the error of mixing up the Saint and the Seigneur in his description of Pill, or Pylle, or Pulle, as he describes it in his "English Religious Houses." It is there noted as an alien priory, cell to *St. Martin of Tours*, instead of cell to St. Dogmaels and of the order of Tiron, reformed Benedictine.

CHAPTER XIV.

ERIN'S TRIBUTE.

IN continuation of the benefactions of the Roches to the Church, notably by the foundation and endowment of Pill Priory, a cell of St. Dogmaels, is the foundation of another priory by them in Ireland for the monks of Tiron, and given by them also to St. Dogmaels Abbey.

The Priory of Glascareg, in the diocese of Ferns, Co. Wexford, was founded by Griffin Condon and Cecilia Barry, his wife, also her father, Rinoc Barry, Roberic Borke, David Roche, Richard Carrin, and John Fitts, of Arcalon, these granted all their lands, viz., woods, meadows, pastures, with a mill in their special lands of Consinquilos and Trahir, with the long marsh, fisheries, and salvage of wrecks, it being near the sea, in the Barony of Ballaghkeen, six miles from Gorry, in honour of the Abbey of St. Dogmaels, in Pembrokeshire, of the order of St. Bernard of Tiron. One of the MSS. calls him St. Benedict of Tiron, but this is an error mixing up St. Bernard, founder of the Benedictine Order of Tiron, with St. Benedict, the founder of the Benedictines, a similar error to that between the Sieur Martin of the Towers and St. Martin of Tours, and almost the same number of centuries in each case between the two men. There is also another mistake in the Additional MS. 4,789, for in it the founders of Glascareg claim to have been founders of St. Dogmaels, instead of the Priory of Pill, a *cell* of St. Dogmaels. They specially ordain that the Priory of Glascareg is to be subject to the Abbey of St. Dogmaels, whose Abbot was always to present one of his monks to succeed on the death of each prior of Glascareg. Raymond, Lord Barri, gave the Church of St. Patrick, Dormaghyn, with the Chapel of St. Mary Magdalen, also the Church of St. Barburga of Leytmagh; Lord Griffin Condon and his wife gave the Church of Temple[1] Landecan, and the free chapel of Templeboyne;[1] Lord Barry and Lord Robert

---

[1] ? Co. Tipperary.

Burgh gave the Church of Inleyn, with the Chapel of Joram, otherwise called Lagen; the Church of St. Leatrina de Nayt, was given by Lord David Roch, also the Church of St. Patrick, by the marsh near Clonenan, in the lordship of the Lord David Roch; William and Raymond, sons of Lord Condon gave, in Ferramuige, in the diocese of Cloyne, Co. Cork, the Church of St. Mary, in Magnomia, in Clonendon the Church of Letrom, and the Church of[1] ——; Richard Carryn and his brothers gave the Church of Laceria Delturaon, with the Chapel of St. Brigid, the Church of St. Mary of Clongossy[2] with the Chapel of St. Mary, the Church of St. Synell with the chapel of St. Peter, the Church of St. Leyre of Baston with the Chapel of St. Mary in the diocese of Leighlin, Co. Carlow. John Fynelte gave the Church of St. Brigitte of Tinagh in the diocese of Glendalough (Co. Wicklow) with all the tithes thereto belonging. This charter was confirmed by Thomas Den, who was Bishop of Ferns from 1363 to 1400, and again confirmed by Patrick Barrett, Bishop of Ferns (he died in 1415), and by the then Bishop of Ferns, 1501, by Chas. McMurgh, Prior and the Convent of Glasgareg.

On the Feast of St. Katherine, 5 Edward VI,[3] Dermit, the Prior (then last), was seized of the following rectories of Lorome (in that town and Killmalapoke), Kilreny Kilerat, and Cormore, also of Templebodigane, Kiltenen, and Clonygosse (? Co. Carlow), and of Ballane, Castelgrace, Balledyne, and Keppoghe.

One has only to compare the list given in the first grant with this list of Edward VI to see how many of their old possessions had passed away from the convent, and that they had acquired many new possessions in their place.

There is also a seventeenth century transcript of the original charter, and its confirmation in 1501 by the then Bishop of Ferns to the venerable and religious man Charles McMugh, Prior of Glascareg, from the Harleian MSS.; unfortunately it is in some places illegible. Charles McMurgh was Prior 35 Hen. VIII.

ADD. MS. 4789, f. 71 (205).

Know ye present and to come that we Griffin Condon and Cecily Barry and Rinoc Barry father of Cecily my wife Robric Borke and David Roch Richard Karrin John Fitts of Arcalon lords, led by our free will and piety have granted given delivered and mortmained all our lands woods meadows pastures with a mill in those our special lands of Consinquilos and Traher with their appurts and the long marsh and right of fishing and goods cast on the shores by fortune of the sea as it appears that we have there to found a monastery in honour of the blessed virgin Mary in the place which is called Glascarge for our souls and for our ancestors and for the

---

[1] Illegible.   [2] ? Clongall, Co. Carlow.   [3] After the dissolution in England.

St. Dogmaels from the Netpool, Cardigan.

souls of our wives and children and in honour of the monastery of blessed Mary of
St. Dogmael in Pembroke in Wales of the order of St. Benedict of Tiron of which
monastery our predecessors were founders giving these from the well by the chapel of
St. Patrick and by the marsh " rectar " as far as garve and right over to Clonenan and
by Clonenan direct towards the great wood being part of the township of Pemery
and so to the sea by a circuit with all the liberties without any secular service which
now we have given for ever and liberally have bestowed in aid of charity and for our
souls and our predecessors to build the aforesaid monastery or cell of the blessed Mary of
Glascarig in the diocese of Ferns.

Glascarrig.

Archdale's " Monasticon Hibernicon."

In the barony of Ballaghkeen on the seaside and six miles south-east of Gorey
Griffin Condon and Ceclia Barry his wife and Roberic Borke her father[1] together with
David Roche, Richard Carrin and John Fytte of Arcolon granted all their lands in
Consenquilos and Trahir with the long marsh fishery and salvage of wrecks for the
purpose of founding this priory for Benedictine monks in honour of the monastery of
the blessed Virgin Mary of St. Dogmael in Pembrokeshire Wales of which their pre-
decessors were founders, this house to be subject to that of St. Dogmaels whose abbot
was always to present one of his monks to succeed on the death of the prior of
Glascarrig. We find the following churches and chapels granted to this priory; by
Raymond lord Barry the church of St. Patrick of Dormaghyn, with the chapel of St.
Mary Magdalen and the Church of St. Barburga of Leytmagh; by Griffin Cordon and
his wife the church of Temple Laudecan and the free chapel of Templeloyne; by the
Lord Barry and the Lord Robert Burgh the church of St. Inleyn with the chapel of
Joram otherwise called Lagen, the church of St. Leatrina de Nayt, and the church of
St. Patrick in the lordship of the Lord David Roch; by William and Raymond sons
of the said Lord Condon in Ferramuige and in the diocese of Cloyne, in Magnomia the
church of the Virgin Mary, in Clonendon the church of Letrom, and the church of . . .
by Richard Carryn and his brothers the church of Laceria Delturaon with the chapel of
St. Brigid, the church of St. Mary of Clongossy with the chapel of St. Mary, the
church of St. Synell with the chapel of St. Peter, the church of St. Leyre of Baston
with the chapel of the blessed virgin in the diocese of Leighlin; and by John Fynette
the church of St. Brigitte of Tinagh in the diocese of Glendalogh with all the tithes
thereunto belonging. This charter received the approbation of Thos Den who
succeeded to the Bishopric of Ferns in the year 1363 he died in 1400.

[Here is given briefly the survey of 32 Hen. VIII.]

N.B.—A very imperfect transcript of the charter to Glascarig—a short preamble
says it was exhibited for confirmation in 1501 to the Bp of Ferns at his visitation by
Charles McMurgh[2] and his convent.

On the deed are some not very legible notes.

Largit^r intuitu cavitat A^o ab incarnatione dm 1172.[3]

---

[1] Rinoc Barry, *see* add. MS. 4789.

[2] A faulty 17th century transcript, in some places illegible; the original was no doubt destroyed.

[3] If Glascareg was founded in 1172, then Pill Priory was founded earlier still, as it was founded
by Adam de Roche some years before David de Roche went to Ireland.

Confirmed by the Lord Thomas Dem by the grace of God Bishop of Ferns (1363).

Patrick Barrett Bishop of Ferns confirms this charter.

This Patrick died A.D. 1415, and was buried at Kemlas, where he was formerly a canon.

HARL. 4789, fol. 205.[1]

In the name of God Amen by this present public instrument let it evidently appear to all that in the year from the incarnation of our Lord according to the course and computation of the church of England and Ireland 1501 in the first Indiction of the Pontificate of our most hold father in Christ and Lord Julius by divine providence pope the 2nd in the monastery of the Blessed Virgin Mary of Glascarge of the order of Tiron in the diocese of Ferns to the Reverend Bishop of Ferns in the course of his visitation in the aforesaid monastery the venerable and religious man Charles McMurgh by the sufferance of God prior of the aforesaid monastery with his convent exhibited a certain charter concerning the land possessions names of benefices and confirmations of liberties before made to the monastery under the rule of ancient ordinaries almost consumed by age and by moths bearing date the month of January and the [1]   day in the presence of me the notary public personally appointed and witnesses underwritten for this purpose specially summoned and called by the organ of voice of the said prior and convent have caused to be read [1]

and that it would quickly pass from the memory of transitory men which to us and our successors would [1]   damage since things conveyed by the ear more slowly impress minds than those submitted to the eye have requested for the faithful that in this matter of my merit they should be pleased the aforesaid charter or ancient deed should be reduced into public form which in the presence of them and of the said bishop and [1]   in the order which follows I have thought fit to be described.

Know ye present and to come that we Griffin Condon and Cecilia Barry and Rinoc Barry father of my wife Cecilia Roboric Borke and David Roch Richard Karrin John Fytte of Arcalon lords all of their free will and free piety have given granted bestowed delivered and mortmained all our lands meadow fields pastures with the mill in those special places of Consinquilos and Trahor with their appurtenances and the long marsh and the right of fishery and things cast on the land by good fortune of the sea as to us it plainly appears to have been for the founding a monastery in honour of the Blessed Virgin Mary in the place which is called Glascarge for our souls and of our fathers and for the souls of our wives and children and out of honour of the monastery of Blessed Mary of St. Dogmael in Wales in Pembrokeshire of the order of St. Benedict of Tiron of which monastery our predecessors were founders giving these lands from the well by St. Patrick's chapel and by the marsh . . as far as Garve and right on to Clonevan and by Clonevan direct to the great meadow being part of the township of Pomery and so to the sea by a circuit with all liberties or any secular service which [1]   we have given for ever and have freely bestowed in aid of charity for our souls and our predecessors towards the fabric of the aforesaid monastery or cell of Blessed Mary of Glasarg in the diocese of furnes for the reverence profit and

---

[1] Illegible.

honour to endure to future times of the lord almighty and the blessed virgin Mary of Glasarg and the priors of St. Dogmael in Wales and the sustenance of the convent [1] the rights of jurisdiction churches chapels in which we have perpetual proprietary [rights] by the foundation and special [ordinances] of the Roman pontiffs bishops and archbishops with all their rights and appurts so that the house or cell of Glasarg shall always by monks of St. Dogmaels [be served] that it be not defrauded of due observances and divine suffrages and the memory of the founders in [1] be forgotten or [their names] removed from the martyrology and lest a rapacious wolf should invade the learned flock after the death of the prior [1] the lord Abbot shall present another monk of his convent to govern the priory or cell of blessed Mary and these churches with the chapels of the gift of Raymond lord Barry of St. Patrick of Dormahyn with the chapel of St. Mary Magdalene the church of St. Barbarge de Leyttnach with rights and appurts of the pious donation of Lord Griffin Condon and his wife Cecilia Condon the church of Temple Landecan with his free church of Tempelboyne and of the gift of Lord Barri and Lord Robert Borg the church of blessed Bridget of . . . with the chapel of Lanven the church of St. Merleyn decul and fosse with the chapel of St. Joram aforewritten which is otherwise called Lacryne the church of St. Leatrine of Naigt [1] with their rights and appurts the church of blessed Patrick of the lordship of Lord David Roche of the gift of the lord of Roche with its appurts. These are contained in the diocese of Ferns of the gift of William and Raymond[2] sons of aforesaid Condon in ferranige (?) in the diocese of Cloyne in Magnonia the church of Blessed Mary of Clovendan the church of Letrom the church of [1] with its rights and appurts of the gift of Richard Carryn and his brothers the church of Lascria deleuraon with the chapel of St. Bridget of [1] the church of Blessed Mary of Clongossy with the chapel of [St. Mary the] virgin the church of St. Synell with the chapel of St. Peter the church of St. Leyre of boscun with the chapel of Blessed Mary with its rights and appurts in the diocese of Leiglen the church of St. Bridget of Tinagh of the gift of Lord John ffyutte in the diocese of Glendalogh with all rights tithes oblations fruits forthcoming of the premises . . . freely given and sealed etc. Archdale adds " This Charter received the approbation of Thos Den, who succeeded to the bishopric of Ferns in 1363 and died in 1400."

" Chas McMortho was prior 35 Hen. VIII."

[abstract of inquisition given]

" On the feast of St. Katherine 5 Edw. VI, it was found that Dermit, the last prior, was seized of the following rectories in this county, appropriated to him and his successors ; Lorome, which extendeth into the towns of Lorome, Kilmalapoke, Kilreny, Kilerat and Cormore ; Templebodegane Kiltenen and Clonygosse which extend into Kiltenen Clonygosse Balledonagh, Killenerlde Bollyncollen and Killemonde ; and the rectories of Ballane and Templemallyne which extend into Templemallyne, Ballane Castlegrace Balledyne and Keppoghe."

---

[1] Illegible.   [2] ? Raymond, Lord of Barry.

In the Papal Letters, Vol. V, 1397, 12 Kal December, from St. Peter's at Rome, there is a mandate concerning Ymar Odinyd (or Odoymd or O'Dowd) a Benedictine monk in priest's orders, of a Scotch monastery in Vienna, of the Cistercian Abbey de Benedictione Dei (?Bective) in the Diocese of Meath. This Ymar Odwynd appears later appointed Abbot of Benedictione Dei (? Bective), though he seems never to have been accepted as Abbot, whether through his never going there, or through the convent for some reason objecting to receive him, for it is curious that the Pope, after appointing him to be Abbot, then gives him the Priory of Glascareg instead of the Abbey, though Glascareg was not even a free priory, but was subordinate to St. Dogmaels, so that it looks as if there were something objectionable in this Ymar Odwynd. Whether he was received or not at Glascareg is not known; by the foundation charter the appointment of Prior rested with the Abbot of St. Dogmaels, and not with the Pope; ten years later than Odwynd's appointment the Prior, Henry of Wales, had just died. After Henry's death the Pope again intervened and appointed Andrew Occuryn, a priest's bastard, to Glascareg; but there are no further MS. apparently to prove whether this appointment was confirmed by the Abbot of St. Dogmaels or not.

In the Papal Letters 1401, February 15th, from St. Peter's, Rome, in the 12th year of Pope Boniface IX, is found a mandate to the Bishops of Tivy and Clonfert and Eugene O'Maershayn, Canon of Killaloe, to collate and assign to the above Ymar[us] Odwynd Cistercian abbot de Benedictione Dei, in the diocese of Meath, the Benedictine Priory not exceeding 40 marks, conventual, with cure and elective, of Glascareg in the diocese of Ferns—upon his obtaining possession, they are to transfer him from Benedictione Dei, of which he is Abbot, under a provision which the pope recently ordered to be made to him, but of which he has not got possession, and which he is, as he has offered, to resign upon obtaining Glascareg.

In Vol. VI of the Papal Letters, ten years later (1411), from Bologna we find a mandate from the Pope to the Abbot, as he is called, of St. Mary's Ferns dependent upon the Monastery of St. Dogmael, and to the Archdeacon of Leighlyn, relating to the Priory of Glascareg being void by the death of Henry of Wales, so that Ymar Odwynd could not have been Prior long, or Henry either, and referring to the appointment of Andrew Occuryn, a bastard.

PAPAL LETTERS. Vol. VI, p. 235. 1 John, xxiij.

1411 3 Kal Feb Bologna.

To the Bishop of Civitaten (sic) the Abbot of St. Mary Ferns and the Archdeacon of Leighlin Mandate to collate and assign to Andrew Occurryn, priest monk of St. Stephen's Bologna of the order of St. Benedict—who lately, then a secular clerk, received Papal dispensation as the son of a priest and an unmarried woman to be

promoted to all even holy orders, and hold a benefice even with cure under the priory
of St. Mary Glascarraig of the said order [of St. Benedict] in the diocese of Ferns
which has cure and is not conventual is dependant on the monastery of St. Dogmael
[of the order of] Tiron (Tyronen) of the same order [of St. Benedict] in the diocese
of St. David's and is wont to be governed by monks thereof, and whose value does not
exceed 40 marks void by the death of Henry of Wales (de Wallia) Andrew hath hereby
the necessary dispensation Religionis zelus vite etc.

In the State Papers of Ireland some idea is gained both of the acreage and
value of the possessions of this Priory after the dissolution, 27th January, 1541,
wherein the old Priory Church was then used as a parish church, and that within
the precincts of the late Priory were three small thatched buildings of no
value, but might be useful to the farmer there.

In the township of Kylynghill they had possessed 120 acres of land worth
six shillings, and twenty-four flagons of beer worth four shillings, but laid
waste by war this year and of no value.

In the township of Kylinagte sixty acres of land lately worth half an ox
or three shillings here may be noticed the value of an ox in those days; this
also was laid waste.

In the township of Ballenemonery sixty acres of the same value, also laid
waste.

In the township of Smytheston and Templederry the same amount of land
in each of the same value, also laid waste.

The Rectory of Ardemayne, lately worth 20s., but now waste.

The Rectory of Killemagh[1] was worth 6s., laid waste.

The Rectory of Lorome[2] was worth 13s. 4d., advowson now belonging to
the King.

The Rectory of Kylmoch Irysshe was worth 26s. 4d., now worth only
13s. 4d.

The Rectory of Kylpatrick[3] was worth 26s. 4d., now worth only 4s.

Two Rectories in Munster[4] not named worth 13s. 4d., now waste.

The total worth now, except the land laid waste, xxx^s viij^d

STATE PAPERS IRELAND. Fol. Vol. III.

Extent of Glascarrig.

The possessions to the late Priory of Glascarrig belonging.

County of Wexford. Extent of all and singular the lands and possessions to the
late priory of Glascarrig in the county aforesaid belonging being in the hands of the

---

[1] ? Killenaule, Co. Wexford.   [2] ? Laurencetown, Co. Tipperary.
[3] Between Bandon and Inishannon, Co. Cork.   [4] Munster.

lord King by the dissolution of the said late Priory made at Arcclo 27th Jan. the 32nd year of the reign of the lord King that now is before the aforesaid John Mynne one of the Commissioners of the lord King and assisting him William Brabazon and Patrick Dowdale then and there present by the oath of Thomas fitz Henry Walter Devereux · and other good and lawful men of the county aforesaid Who say upon their oath that the church of the said late priory is the parish church for the parishioners there to hear the divine offices.   And there are within the precinct of the said late priory three small buildings covered with thatch which are necessary and convenient for the farmer there and of no value per annum beyond the reparations.

Township of Kylynghell.

And there are there 120 acres of land which late were worth one mark value 6s. and 24 flagons of beer value 4s.—in all 10s. now being waste by reason of the Rebellion and the wars by the Irish and the Kavaners and of no value per year.

Township of Kylmayte.

And there are there 60 acres of land which late were worth per ann half an ox value 3s. now being waste for the reason as above.

Township of Ballenemonery.

And there are there 60 acres of land which late were worth half an ox value 3s. now being waste for the reason as above.

Township of Smytheston.

And there are there 60 acres of land late worth half an ox value 3s. now waste for reason as above.

Township of Templederry.

And there are there 60 acres of land late yearly valued when they were let at 3s. now waste for reason as above.

The Rectory of Ardemayne.

And that the Rectory there to the said late Priory belonging and late worth 20s. now waste and worth nothing per annum.

The Rectory of Kyllenagh.

And that the Rectory there was late worth when the lands were sown 6s. 8d. now waste and of no value per ann.

Rectory of Lorome.

And the Rectory of Lorome is worth in 2 parts of the tithes there beyond the third belonging to the vicarage 13s. 4d.   And the gift and advowson of the vicarage there belongs to the lord King by reason of the dissolution of the said late priory.

The Rectory of Kylmock Irysshe.

And that the Rectory aforesaid is worth when the lands there are sown 26s. 8d. but now worth only—13s. 4d.

The Rectory of Kylpatryk.

And that the Rectory aforesaid when the lands there are sown are worth 26s. 8d. but now only 4s.

Mounster.

And there are there two Rectories of the names of which the Jurors aforesaid are altogether ignorant which are worth when the lands are sown—13s. 4d. but now they are waste and worth nothing per ann.

Sum of the whole extent of all the possession besides those in waste   xxx^s viij^d

This laying waste of the lands of Glascareg by war had evidently occurred some years before the dissolution as is seen by the valuation of St. Dogmaels Abbey, wherein the late Abbot states that nothing had been received from the Priory of Glascareg for some years past, instead of the annual payment formerly sent of £3 6s. 8d.

In the "Monasticon Hibernicon" we find, under "Benedictines," on p. 152, in the Co. of Wexford—

Glasscarick Abbey[1] [? Priory].

"At Glasscarrick, a small town on the Coast, was an Abbey founded by some English in the twelfth century, cell to St. Dogmaels, order of Tiron."

Glascareg evidently was not really dissolved till the reign of Edward VI, for Dermit was the last Prior, 5 Ed. VI, 1552.

All the Priors yet discovered are as follows:—

Ymar Odwynd (appointed by the Pope)	1397
Henry of Wales (died)	1410
Andrew Occuryn (appointed February)	1411
Charles McMurgh	1501-1544
Dermit (the last)	1551

The Priory continuing to this date is the more extraordinary owing to it being dissolved by the King according to the State Papers of Ireland at Arcelo, the 27th January, 1541.

---

[1] A clerical mistake for Priory.

CHAPTER XV.

GEVA'S GIFT.

ALDEY, as already shown by the grant of Robert Fitzmartin, was given by Robert to his mother, Geva, who in her turn granted it to the Abbey of St. Dogmaels.

It had been, like St. Dogmaels, an old British Religious House, at one time under the rule of the still well-known Dubricius (Dyfrig), who was afterwards Bishop of Llandaff, and who at an extremely advanced age retired to Bardsey Island, where he died at the reputed age of 130.

In the Island is a well-known Ogham Stone, with the inscription, MAGL . . DUBR . . INB, the rest broken, which reads so far,[1] as Maglia Dubracuna, i.e., of the slave of Doborchon. Mr. Law, however, gives it in his " Little England beyond Wales " as " Magolite Bar Cene," and mentions that there is also an imperfect Ogham inscription on the other side of the stone. This same tombstone has been used again for a later inscription in Latin, to one " Catuocomus " or Cathen, who lived in the latter half of the seventh century; he was name-giver to Llangathen, and to the hundred of Catheiniog, and may have been one of the early Priors or Heads of the Religious House of Caldey.

It is a fine old stone of red sandstone, 5 ft. 10½ in. long, by 1 ft. 2¾ in. wide at its narrowest point, and four inches thick; above the inscription to Catuocomus is an inscribed Latin cross.

The British name for Caldey was Ynys Pyr (the Island of Pyrus), Pyrus being the name of an ancient and almost mythical King of Britain; his name is retained also in Manorbier (Manor Byr = Pyr or Pyrus) the House of Pyrus.

The name Caldey is derived from the Norse, kald = cold, and eye = island. It was specially celebrated for its barley.

The island was purchased by Mr. John[2] Bradshaw after the dissolution.

---

[1] The rest of the Ogham character is too broken to decipher.

[2] George Owen calls him " *Roger* " Bradshaw, and father to John Bradshaw, sen. ? but according to the Grant it was bought by John Bradshaw at the same time as St. Dogmaels Abbey.

From the date of its being granted to St. Dogmaels Abbey by Geva, the wife of Martin, we know little of its history; its seal is no longer to be found, neither is there at Westminster any Act of Supremacy signed by the Prior and monks of Caldey. It may be that it was such an out of the way Priory that it was never dissolved separately from St. Dogmael. It is averred by a Roman Catholic now living that the monastery continued to exist early in 1700, and

CALDEY CHURCH.

that it was the last place in Great Britain where mass was celebrated, excepting in private chapels. In the Valor Ecclesiasticus, 1535, its yearly value is given as £5 10s. 11d.; tithes, 11s. 1½d. At the present time the island is owned by the Rev. D. Bushell, D.D., lately a master at Harrow School, who has established a so-called Anglican Benedictine Monastery there. He has written a booklet containing the ancient British history of Caldey Priory, when

Dubricious was Prior, before he was translated to Llandaff, as well as other interesting points in its history.

George Owen describes Caldey in his "History of Pembrokeshire," p. 110, as "an Iland, as I shold judge, a mile long, and halfe as broade, yt standeth ij miles from the mayne, seated opposite the town of Tenby. . . . There was in yt in times past a Priorie . . . a parish church and a chappell . . . yt did belonge to the Abbey of St. Dogmells, and was purchased by Mr. Roger Bradshawe, at the dissolution, father to the last Mr. John Bradshawe and grandfather to Mr. John Bradshawe, that nowe ys, who about foure yeares past sould the same to Mr. Water Philpin of Tenby, whose inheritance now yt is, the Iland is verie fertile and yeldeth plentie of corne, all their plowes goe wth horses, for oxen the inhabitantes dare not keepe, fearing the purveyors of the pirates, as they themselves told me, who often make their provisions there by their owne commission, and most commonlie to the good contentement of the inhabitantes when conscionable theeses arrive there, the Iland is of viijᵗ or xᵉⁿ housholdes, and some parte of the demesnes annexed to the ruines of the Priorie, the Lord keepeth in his handes, yt is nowe growne a question in what hundred of Pembrokeshire this Iland shold be, whether in Kemes as parcell of St. Dogmells, to which it appertayned, or parte of the next hundred of the maine, and, untill this doubte be decided, the inhabitantes are content to rest exempt from anie payementes or taxacions wth anie hundred."

Camden, in his "Britannia" (Gough edit., 1789), p. 696, under "Islands to the West of Britain," states that "The next Island is Caldey, in British Inispir, very near the shore."

And in Vol. II, p. 517, "Against Manober, or between it and Tinby, lieth Inispir, I.E. Insula Pirrhi, alias Caldey. There was in Caldey or Pyr island, a cell of monks of St. Dogmail."

Rees in "Beauties of England and Wales," Vol. XVIII, also gives a similar account of Caldey, to that which one has had already, and also of St. Dogmael's, p. 867, and of Pill Priory, p. 815. Also Donovan, in his "Excursions through South Wales," in 1804, Vol. II, p. 379, gives an account of an excursion to Caldey as follows: "Proceeding up the Island, we could not avoid observing it to be thinly inhabited, and so far as we went, at least, in a meagre state of cultivation. Formerly it was represented as being very fertile, and yielding corn in plenty, but so infested by pirates that they dared not plough with oxen lest the marauders should carry them off with other booty in their occasional visits. There are scarcely more than half-a-dozen houses on the island, a tract of land extending . . . a mile in length and half a mile in breath . . . Wild rabbits are everywhere abundant on this spot beyond conception . . . . . so numerous were they that the sale of their skins realized more than sufficient to pay half the yearly rental of the island." Woodward speaks of "a sort of black marble found in Caldy island. Upon the shore I (Rees) picked up many fragments of coarse granite, calcareous spars, fossil madrepores, etc. A course granite of a reddish colour prevails through many parts of the island."

On p. 251 of Fenton one finds "Every insulated rock off the coast (of Tenby) had its cell and its anchorate; and Caldey a much larger establishment, a priory subordinate to the Abbey of St. Dogmaels. . . . In company with my friend Sir Richard Hoare, I took boat from the pier of Tenby to visit Caldey; the day was pleasant, and the voyage not too long to excite any dread of that most horrid of all disorders—sea sickness; for by the help of a gentle favourable breeze, enough to fill our sails, we were soon wafted across, and landed in a little bay just under the principal mansion, which by a gentle ascent from the water, we soon reach. It consists of a handsome modern building joined to a curious aggregate of miscellaneous masonry, the greater part being evidently of the age of the first monastic pile, enlarged by additions of a later date, though very old, and some of a castellated form. The ancient tower of the priory church crowned with a stone spire, still remains entire, and all the lower apartments of the old house and its offices are vaulted, and seemingly coeval with it. In the room, which, from its position, must have been the chancel of the priory church, the tracery of the great east window, though now stopped up, may be followed, and the present kitchen, which in all probability had been their refectory, has a very curious arched roof with many intricate odd-shaped doors opening from it, which might have led to the dormitory. In the ruins of the priory was dug up many years ago a gravestone, now lying in Mr. Kynaston's garden, with an inscription in very rude characters and much effaced, but I plainly read—' ORENT PRO ANIM CADUOCANI ' (pray for the soul of Cadwgan[1]). Sufficient to ascertain that it was inscribed to commemorate one of the early priors of the name of Cadwgan, this stone, after its removal from its first position, had served the office of lintel to a window, and in this capacity it was last found."

" The priory was founded, as we presume, by Robert, the son of Martin of the Towers, soon after the date of the charter of endowment to his Abbey of St. Dogmaels, to which it was annexed. In that charter Robert recognizes the grant of the Island of Caldey by his mother to the monastery of St. Dogmaels, and confirms it, and it is supposed that the priory was founded here soon after. To the right of the road going down to the beach there is an old chapel, in which, till lately, there stood an old baptismal font. At the dissolution it (Caldey) was held to be of the value of five Pounds ten shillings and eleven pence. The island is about a mile in length, and half as broad; it consists of six hundred and eleven acres, two hundred of which are enclosed and in good cultivation; the west end of the island is all limestone, and the opposite a red drab. . . . In William of Worcester's time it had thirty houses on it, and in the time of George Owen eight or ten. William of Worcester, writing of it says, the island of Caldey is situated next to Shepey Island . . . and has about thirty inhabited houses and one with a chapel to St. Mary above the seashore, and the church of the priory of Caldey."

" To the south-west lies the Island of little Caldey, which is usually rented by Lord Milford to the occupier of Caldey." (Fenton.)

" At the dissolution, the Island, together with the Abbey of St. Dogmells and its appurtenances, was purchased by George[2] Bradshaw." (ibid.)

In the October number of the " Archaeologia Cambrensis " for 1855, and in the October number 1880, are both plates and description of the Caldey Island Ogham Stone, which in 1855 was built into a window-sill of the Priory there, which was a

---

[1] Cathen.   [2] John.

cell to St. Dogmael's. The name of the person recorded on the stone is " Catuoconus," possibly the Latinized form of " Cathen," the founder of Llangathen, Carmarthenshire, and from whom the hundred of Catheiniog, in the same county, is supposed to derive its name; this account is given by " J. O. Westwood, of Hammersmith"; in October, 1880, Prof. Rhys had more recently examined the stone and had " found traces of Oghams all round the upper part of the stone." In his " Lectures on Welsh Philology," he, however, gives the reading of the Ogham as Magolite Bar-Cene. The stone was thus evidently used twice, as Mr. Westwood gives the probable date of the Latin inscription as between the seventh and ninth centuries, the Ogham inscription being several hundred years older. Mr. Romilly Allen also gives this stone in his " Catalogue of the Early Christian Monuments in Pembrokeshire." In April, 1896, Professor Rhys writes as follows: " I had failed to read the Ogam inscription; but the late Dr. Haigh, who saw the stone after it had been taken out of the wall, suggested the reading Mogolite Barcene. I agree with him as to most of the consonants, but he seems to have erred in not observing that the whole of the top of the stone is gone. . . . My reading is: " Magl Dubr Inb," the rest is not legible. The vocable beginning with Dubr is probably to be completed as Dubracunas or Dubracuna, that is Duborchon; the whole name would be Maglia-Dubracuna; that is " of the slave of Doborchu."

Tanner writes under Caldey :—

The Abby of St. Dogmael had this fmall^a island by the gift of Robert FitzMartin's mother[b], and before the diffolution had a cell here of the yearly value of 5^l 10^s $11^{d\,c}$

Dugdale's " Monasticon."
Caldey.

This is indexed to iv. 132 mentioned under St. Dogmaels Abbey at p. 129. Caldey in Pembrokeshire, situated in the island of its name was a Cell to St. Dogmael. So Leland, *ibid*, V, 14, " Ther was a celle of the order of monks of St. Dogmaels in Caldey Island now suppressed."

As will have been seen in previous chapters, Caldey being in the Archdeaconry of Cardigan, for all visitations, etc., its prior attended in the chapter house of St. Dogmaels Abbey and signed his name after the Abbot of St. Dogmaels, therefore in the signature to the Act of the Acknowledgment of the King's supremacy Dom Hugh Eynon may have been Prior of Caldey.

Corbett, in his " Abbeys and Priories, etc., confiscated at the Reformation," gives Caldey as a Tyrone [Tiron] cell, the gift of Robert Fitzmartin's mother; rents, £5, now worth £100.

---

a. For though they had the whole island, the Lincoln taxation saith the Abbey of St. Dogmaels had a cell at Caldey (in the Archdeaconry of Cardigan) and one carucate of land of the yearly value of xls.

b. My mother gave to these same monks to hold the island of Pyr otherwise named Caldey—R. Fitzmartin's Charter, Mon. Angl. Vol. I, p. 445.

CHAPTER XVI.

QUEEN ELIZABETH.

THE extract, from Bundle 225 of the Augmentation Office leases, is interesting as giving full particulars of the estates of the late monastery rented to Mr. John Bradshaw, and afterwards to his son, with certain portions reserved to the Crown.

The portions rented to Mr. John Bradshaw are as follows:—

The Rectories and Churches of
- St. Thomas' St. Dogmaels
- Eglwyswrw
- Bayvil
- Moylgrove
- Llantood
- St. Nicholas Fishguard
- Grangistown

And all the Chapels of
- Penkelly Vychan
- Nantgwyn
- Lylsvrayne[1]
- Newton

With all appurtenances, rights, etc., also all houses, lands, tenements, mills, meadows, fields, pastures, moors, marshes, rivers, fishings, etc. With the exception of the Lordships and Manors, etc., of Rattre (Devon).

The Rectories of Maenclochog, Llandilo, Llancolman, the Chapel of Mynachlogddu, and all lands, etc., in Mynachlogddu, Haverford, and Pembroke, all great trees, woods, underwoods, marriages, reliefs, escheats, mines, quarries, advowsons of churches, chapels, etc.

This property is leased to Mr. John Bradshaw, Jun., at £66 11s. 8d. per annum, payable at Lady Day and Michaelmas.

---

[1] Llysprant.

The Queen exonerating Mr. Bradshaw from the payment of £4, the stipend of the Chaplain of St. Thomas Church, St. Dogmaels, etc., and of all repairs to the chancels, etc. This latter item as to the exonerating of John Bradshaw from the repairs of the chancels, is singular, as he owned the Rectorial Fees. However, this special clause may have been inserted, owing to all the chancels being in a more or less state of great disrepair. It hardly seems likely that this would have come to pass so rapidly unaided, yet St. Dogmaels Abbey is described as a ruin by George Owen, and he was born only five years after the death of Henry VIII.

There is no mention of Caldey in this document, though in the post mortem inquisition on John Bradshaw, Senr., who died only two months later, he was seized for Great Caldey. This renting of the Abbey and its possessions to John Bradshaw, the younger, before the death of his father, would show that the father had left St. Dogmaels, and was living elsewhere, most likely at Presteign, and had handed St. Dogmaels over to his eldest son to live in; but still retaining the ownership of it.

In the post mortem inquisition, John Bradshaw had two tenements in Nevern and one in Moylgrove, as well as Caldey and St. Dogmaels.

The writ for this inquisition was given Nov. 14th, 1567, within three days of the completion of the 9th year of the reign of Queen Elizabeth. Therefore the inquisition, taken at Haverford, followed early in the tenth year of her reign; the day and month are, however, illegible.

AUGMENTATION OFFICE LEASES.

Bdle. 225, No. 69. 9 Queen Elizabeth, 23 July, 1567.
County of Pembroke.

Parcel of the possessions of the late Monastery of St. Dogmaels in the county aforesaid.

Farm of the whole mill in Fishguard and of all the Rectories and Churches of St. Thomas within the township of St. Dogmaels Eglwyswrw, Bayvill, Moylgrove, Llantood, and St. Nicholas Fishguard and Grangiston and of all the chapels of Penkelly[1] Vychan Nantgwyn Llysvrayne[2] and Newton with all their rights and members and appurtenances in the said County of Pembroke or elsewhere within the Bishopric of St. David's to the said late Monastery of St. Dogmaels belonging together with all tithes profits obventions commodities and emoluments whatsoever to the said Rectories and chapels or to any of them belonging or appertaining. Also of all messuages lands tenements mills meadows fields pastures commons moors marshes Rivers fishings and fisheries Reversions pensions portions tithes oblations obventions fruits profits and commodities and other possessions and hereditaments whatsoever in the townships fields

---

[1] Pengelly.   [2] Llysprant.

parishes and hamlets of St. Dogmaels, Grangiston, Eglwyswrw, Bayvill Moylgrove
Llantood St. Nicholas Fishguard Pengelly Vychan Nantgwyn Llysvrayne and Newton
aforesaid in the said county of Pembroke or within the Bishopric of St. David's with
all their rights and appurts to the aforesaid late Monastery of St. Dogmaels sometime
belonging. All which and other the premises were late demised to one John Bradshaw
senior of Preston in the county of Radnor and so now demised to John Bradshaw junr
by letters patent of the lady Elizabeth now Queen given at the town of St. Albans the
23rd July the 9th year of Her Majesty's reign. Except and altogether reserved the
lordship and manor of Rattre and the rectory of Maenclochog Llandilo and Llancolman
and the chapel of Mynachlog ddu. And all the lands and tenements in Mynachlog ddu
Rattre Haverford and Pembroke. And also excepted and similarly reserved all great
trees woods underwoods Wardships Marriages Reliefs escheats mines and quarries of
the premises. And advowsons of churches and chapels whatsoever to the
premises or to any of them in any way belonging. To have from the
feast of the Annunciation of the blessed Virgin Mary last past for the term of
21 then next ensuing and fully to be completed. And the aforesaid lady the Queen
shall exonerate the aforesaid farmer as well of £4 for wages and stipend of a chaplain
to celebrate divine service in the parish church of St. Dogmael as of all other rents
fees annuities pensions portions and sums of money all things whatsoever to the
premises or any of them being parcel repairs of the Chancels aforesaid and of all the
premises at the charge of the farmer timber only excepted with a clause of forfeiture of
the lease aforesaid for non-payment of rent for the space of 40 days after any feast
of the usual feasts as in the same letters patent more fully appears. Rendering therefrom yearly to our said lady the Queen her heirs and successors of in and for the
aforesaid mill of Fishguard with the appurtenances 20s. And of in and for the
aforesaid lands and tenements in Grangiston with the appurtenances 26s. 8d. And of
in and for the Rectory of St. Thomas in the township of St. Dogmaels with the
appurtenances 20ˡⁱ And of in and for the aforesaid Rectory of Eglwyswrw with the
appurtenances 7ˡⁱ 6ˢ 8ᵈ And of in and for the Rectory of Bayvill with appurtenances
4ˡⁱ 13ˢ 4ᵈ And for the Rectory of Moylgrove with the appurtenances 6ˡⁱ 13ˢ 4ᵈ for
the Rectory of Llantood and St. Nicholas 6ˡⁱ 13ˢ 4ᵈ And for the Rectory of Fishguard
and Grangiston 10ˡⁱ vjˢ viijᵈ for the Rectory of Pengelli Vychan with the appurts 25ˢ
for the chapels of Nantgwyn Llysvrayne and Newton with appurtenances 7ˡⁱ 6ˢ 8ᵈ In
all reaching [the sum] among them at the feasts of the Annunciation of the Blessed Virgin
Mary and St. Michael the Archangel equally per ann 66ˡⁱ 11ˢ 8ᵈ

[The rest in English.]

Make a lease of the premises unto the said John Bradshaw the ffather of William
and James Bradshawe, his sonnes for the term of their lyves successively yelding to
the Q Matie the sayd rent and ffyne. The lease to have comencemts from Michas last
past Th'excepçõns covennte and condiçõns to be such as in like cases are appointed.
The clere yerely value of the premises being   lxvjˡⁱ xjˢ viijᵈ
The ffyne thereof ys rated at fortie marks   xl marks
to be paid in hand.

Evidently John Bradshaw, Senr., died September 30th. The date of this
lease, according to the post mortem examination being two months later. In the

next document the Queen issues a writ for his post mortem inquisition, which is followed by the inquisition itself.

WRIT FOR POST MORTEM INQUISITION ON JOHN BRADSHAW. 14 Nov., 1567.

Elizabeth by the grace of God of England France and Ireland Queen Defender etc. To her beloved John Rastell esq John Barlow esq Rice ap Morgan esq Greeting. Whereas it hath been given us to understand that John Bradshaw esq who held of us in chief hath closed his last day as we have heard. We having great confidence in your fidelity and provident circumspection have assigned you or two of you to enquire by the oath of good and lawful men of the county of Pembroke as well within the liberty as without by whom the truth of the matter shall be better known what lands and tenements the aforesaid John Bradshaw or any other or others to the use of the said John Bradshaw held of us in chief as in demesne as in service in the county aforesaid on the day he died and how much of others and by what service and how much such lands and tenements are worth per ann in all issues. And on what day the said John Bradshaw died and who is his next heir and of what age. And to take and seize the said lands and tenements into our hands and concerning other articles and circumstances of the premises whatsoever more fully the truth. And so you or two of you we charge that at certain days and places which you or two of you for this purpose shall provide diligently upon the premises to make inquisition and it distinctly and openly made to us in our Chancery under your seals or of two of you and the seals of those by whom it shall be made without delay you send and these our letters patent. And we charge by the tenor of these presents our sheriff of the county aforesaid that at certain days and places which you or two of you shall cause him to know he cause to come before you or two of you so many and such good and lawful men of your bailiwick by whom the truth of the matter in the premises shall be better known and inquired into. In witness whereof we have caused to be made these our letters patent. Witness me myself at Westminster the 14th Nov. the 9th year of our reign.

INQ. P. M. Chan. Vol 148, No. 48. 1567.

Inquisition indented taken at Haverford in the tenth year of our lady Elizabeth by the grace of God of England ffrance and Ireland Queen defender of the Faith. Before John Barlowe and Richard Morgan esqrs. commissioners of our said lady the Queen by virtue of a commission of our said lady the Queen to the same and John Rastell directed and annexed to this Inquisition by the oath of Morgan ap Owen gent. James Lewes gent John Griffith gent Matthew Thomas gent William ap Rice Junior gent Rice Davyd Powell ap Owen, Matthew Jenkin Jevan Davyd de Molgrove Lewes David Jacob Jevan Rice ap . . . Howell llen[1] ap David Lewis David de Whitchurch Thomas ap Rice and William Stephen. Who being sworn and charged say upon their oath that John Bradshaw in the said Commission named was seized in his demesne as of fee on the day he died of the lordship or manor of St. Dogmaels with appurts in the said county of Pembroke which is worth per ann. in all issues beyond reprises 12^{li} (?) 6^s 8^d and of two tenements in the parish of Neverne in the county

---

[1] Llewelyn.

aforesaid which are worth per ann 8ˢ And of a parcel of one tenement in Moylgrove in the county aforesaid which is worth per ann. 5ˢ which said tenements are parcels of the said lordship or manor of St. Dogmaels. And they say by their oath that aforesaid John Bradshaw was seized in his demesne as of fee on the day he died of an island called Great Caldey in the said county of Pembroke which is worth per ann. in all issues beyond reprises 3ˡⁱ ¹ . . . And further they say upon their oath that the aforesaid John Bradshaw died the last day of September the 9th year of the reign of our said lady the Queen. And also that John Bradshaw esquire is his son and next heir and on the day of the death of aforesaid John his father was 48 years old and more. In witness whereof as well John Barlow and Richard Morgan commissioners as the aforesaid jurors to this Inquisition have alternately put their seals. Given the day and year aforesaid.

In 1579 this lease of 1567, granting St. Dogmaels and part of its possession to John Bradshaw, Jun., is cancelled, a new lease being granted for the balance of the 21 years of the old lease, and an additional 21 years, with remainder, to his son, William Bradshaw, his heirs and assigns, for their lives. At his death, or the deaths of either or each of his sons, William and James, provided that James inherited the property after William, the best beast belonging to the deceased was to be surrendered and paid to the Queen "in name of heriot." Also in this fresh lease, the Bradshaws were responsible for keeping the various chancels, houses, mills, etc., in repair, and the land clear of gorse, and also were bound to pay the stipend, £4, of the Chaplain of St. Thomas', St. Dogmaels. In return, they were allowed to have sufficient timber from the woods for all repairs of tenements, hedges, for making and repairing carts and ploughs, and for firewood, with large timber for the repairing of chancels, houses, mills, etc., from the steward or under-steward. In the Pembroke Rolls, Augmentation Office, the same day and year, is a similar, but curtailed deed.

In the 40th year of Queen Elizabeth, in the "Lansdowne MS.," 445, February 18th, 1598, the Vicarage of St. Dogmaels was granted to Gryffyn Johnes, Clerk of the Diocese of St. David's, with a net yearly value of £4 15s. 11d. In the following year, on the 10th July, 1599, the Vicarage of St. Dogmaels was granted to Nicholas Davies, Clerk of the diocese of St. David's, through the resignation of the last incumbent, by the Lord Keeper of the Great Seal.

PATENT ROLL. 23 Eliz. Pt. , m 29 (21). 16 Dec., 1579.

Of a grant for John Bradshaw and others. The Queen to all to whom etc. greeting. Whereas we by our letters patent made under our great seal of England bearing date

---

¹ Radnor lands here.

at the town of St. Albans the 23rd July the 9th year of our reign. We delivered granted and at farm demised to one John Bradshaw junr all the mill in Fishingard and all the tithes of the churches of St. Thomas within the towns of St. Dogmaels and Eglwyswrw Bayvil Moylgrave Llantood and St. Nicholas Fishguard and Grangiston. And all the chapels of Penkelly Vychan Nantgwyn Lisprant and Newton with all their rights members and appurtenances in our County of Pembroke or elsewhere within the bishopric of St. David's to the said late monastery of St. Dogmaels as it is said sometime belonging and appertaining and formerly being parcel of the possessions thereof together with all the tithes profits obventions commodities and emoluments whatsoever to the said Rectories and chapels or any of them belonging or appertaining also all messuages lands tenements mills meadows fields pastures commons moors marshes waters fishings fisheries fruits profits and commodities. And our other possessions and hereditaments whatsoever in the townships fields parishes and hamlets of St. Dogmaels Grangiston Eglwyswrw Bayvil Moylgrave Llantood St. Nicholas Fishguard Penkelly Vychan Nantgwyn Lisprant and Newton aforesaid in our said County of Pembroke or within the said bishopric of St. David's with all their members and appurts to the late monastery of St. Dogmaels sometime belonging and appertaining as parts or parcels of the premises or either of them before then usually by a separate rent in our said letters patent reserved being acknowledged accepted used or occupied. Except however always and to us our heirs and successors altogether reserved the lordship and manor of Rattre and the Rectories of Maenclochog Llandilo and Llancolman and the chapels of Mynachlogddu and all the lands and tenements in Mynachlogddu Rattre Haverford and Pembroke aforesaid to the late Monastery of St. Dogmaels as is aforesaid belonging and appertaining. And also except and in a similar way reserved all great trees woods underwoods wardships marriages reliefs escheats mines and quarries of the premises and advowsons of churches and chapels whatsoever of the premises or any of them in any way belonging appertaining falling or emerging. To have and to hold the aforesaid mill rectories chapels messuages lands tenements meadows fields pastures tithes rents pensions portions and other all and singular the premises with all their appurts except the pre-excepted to the aforesaid John Bradshawe junior his executors and assigns from the feast of the Annunciation B V M then last past to the end of the term and for the term of 21 years then next following and fully to be completed. Rendering then yearly to us our heirs and successors of and for the aforesaid mill of Fishingard with appurts 20s. And of and for the aforesaid lands and tenements in Grangiston with appurts 26^s 8^d And of and for the aforesaid rectory of St. Thomas in the township of St. Dogmaels with appurts 20^{li} And of and for the aforesaid Rectory of Egglwyswrw with appurts 7^{li} 6^s 8^d And of and for the aforesaid Rectory of Bayvill with appurts 4^{li} 13^s 4^d And of and for the aforesaid Rectory of Moylgrave with appurts 6^{li} 13^s 4^d And of and for the aforesaid Rectory of Llantood and St. Nicholas with appurts 6^{li} 13^s 4^d And of and for the aforesaid Rectory of Fishguard and Grangiston 10^{li} 6^s 8^d And of and for the aforesaid Chapel of Penkelly Vaughan with appurts 25^s And of and for the aforesaid chapels of Nantgwyn Lisprant and Newton with appurts 7^{li} 6^s 8^d of lawful money of England as by the same our letters patent more fully appears. Which said letters patent and all the right estate title term of years and interest of and in the premises our beloved John Bradshaw esq having and enjoying surrendered and restored to us to be cancelled with the intention however that we other letters patent and a lease of the premises to the said John Bradshaw remaining to William and James Bradshaw sons of the said John Bradshaw for term of their lives and of either of them longest living in form following we have thought fit to make and grant. Which said surrender we have accepted by these presents. Know ye therefore that we as well in consideration of the surrender aforesaid as for a certain sum of money of lawful money of England at the receipt of our Exchequer paid. We have delivered and granted and let at farm and by these presents do deliver grant and let at farm to the same John Bradshaw all that our aforesaid mill in Fishguard. And all those our aforesaid Rectories of churches of St. Thomas within the township of St. Dogmaels and Eglwyswrw Bayvil Moylgrove Llantood and St. Nicholas Fishguard and Grangiston and all the chapels of Penkelly Vychan Nantgwyn Lisprant and Newton with all their rights and appurts in our said county of Pembroke or elsewhere within the said bishopric of St. David to the said late monastery of St. Dogmael as is aforesaid sometime belonging and appertaining and formerly parcel of the possessions thereof together with all tithes profits obventions commodities and emoluments whatsoever to the said Rectories and chapels or any of them belonging or appertaining also all messuages lands tenements mills meadows fields pastures commons moors marshes waters fishings fisheries rents pensions portions tithes oblations obventions fruits profits and commodities and other our possessions and hereditaments whatsoever in the townships fields parishes and hamlets of St. Dogmaels Grangiston Eglwyswrw Bayvil Moylgrove Llantood St. Nicholas Fishguard Penkelly Vychan Nantgwyn Lisprant and Newton aforesaid in our said County of Pembroke or within the said bishopric of St. David's with all their rights and appurts premised by these presents aforegranted or any of them in any way belonging or appertaining or with the same or either of them for a separate yearly rent as below by these presents reserved being before this demised placed used or enjoyed. Except however always and to us our heirs and successors altogether reserved the lordship and manor of Rattre and the rectories of Maenclochog Llandilo and Llancolman and the chapels of Mynachlogddu and all the lands and tenements in Mynachlogddu Rattre Haverford and Pembroke to the said late Monastery of St. Dogmaels late belonging and appertaining. Also except and in a similar way reserved all great trees woods underwoods wardships marriages reliefs escheats mines and quarries. And advowsons of churches and chapels whatsoever of the premises. To have and to hold the aforesaid mill rectories chapels messuages lands tenements tithes pensions portions and other all and singular the premises by these presents demised with all their appurts excepting the pre-excepted to the aforesaid John Bradshaw and his assigns at the term and for the term of the life of him John and after the decease surrender or forfeiture of the said John Bradshaw then the aforesaid mill rectories chapels lands tenements tithes pensions portions and other all and singular the premises by these presents demised with all their appurts excepting the pre-excepted wholly to remain to the aforesaid William Bradshaw and his assigns at the term and for the term of the life of him William and after the decease surrender or forfeiture of either aforesaid John and William Bradshaw then the aforesaid mill rectories chapels lands tenements tithes pensions portions and other all and singular the premises by these presents demised with all their appurts except the pre-excepted shall wholly remain to aforesaid James Bradshaw and his assigns at the term and for the term of the life of him James.

12 a

Rendering yearly to us our heirs and successors of and for the aforesaid mill of Fishguard with appurts 20^s And of and for the aforesaid lands and tenements in Grangiston with appurts 26^s 8^d And of and for the rectory of St. Thomas in the township of St. Dogmael with appurts 20^{li} And for the aforesaid Rectory of Eglwyswrw with appurts 7^{li} 6^s 8^d And for the aforesaid Rectory of Bayvil with appurts 4^{li} 13^s 4^d And for the aforesaid rectory of Moelgrove with appurts 6^{li} 13^s 4^d And for the aforesaid Rectory of Llantode and St. Nicholas with appurts 6^{li} 13^s 4^d And of and for the aforesaid rectory of ffischard and Grangiston 10^{li} 6^s 8^d And of and for the chapels of Penkelly Vychan with appurts 25^s And for the aforesaid chapel of Nantgwin Lisprant and Newton with appurts 7^{li} 6^s 8^d of lawful money of England at the feast of the Annunciation B V M. and St. Michael the Archangel at the Receipt of our Exchequer, or to the hands of the Receivors or Bailiffs of the premises for the time being by equal portions to be paid during the several terms aforesaid by these presents granted. And after the decease of the said John Bradshaw then to be rendered and paid to us our heirs and successors the best beast of him John by name of heriot. And after the decease of the said William Bradshawe if the said William Bradshaw shall survive the said John the best beast of him William by name of heriot. And after the decease of the said James Bradshaw if the said Bradshaw shall survive the said John and William Bradshaw the best beast of him James by name of heriot. And we will and by these presents grant to aforesaid John William and James and their assigns that we our heirs and successors the said John William and James and their assigns as well of 4^{li} yearly for the wages and stipend of a chaplain yearly celebrating divine service and observing the cure in the church and parish of St. Dogmael aforesaid as of all rents fees annuities pensions portions and sums of money and all whatsoever of the premises or of any parcel thereof in any way issuing or to be paid or as above charged or to be charged except the several rents as above by these presents reserved. And except all such payments and sums of money which any farmer of the premises or either of them before this were accustomed to support and pay if any there were against all persons whatsoever from time to time will exonerate and acquit during the term aforesaid. The aforesaid however John William and James Bradshaw and their assigns all chancels mills houses and edifices and all hedges ditches inclosures shores banks and sea-walls and all other necessary reparations of the premises in all and by all from time to time as often as it shall be necessary and opportune at their own costs and expense shall well and sufficiently repair scour purge and maintain during the term aforesaid. And the premises sufficiently repaired shall leave at the end of the term aforesaid. And we will and by these presents grant to the aforesaid John William and James Bradshaw and their assigns that it shall be truly lawful to them from time to time to take perceive and have growing of in and upon the premises competent and sufficient housebote hedgebote firebote ploughbote and cartbote there and not elsewhere yearly to be expended and occupied during the term aforesaid. And that they may have timber growing in the woods and lands of the premises to and for the reparations of the chancels mills houses and edifices of the premises by the assignment and survey of the steward or under-steward or other our officers our heirs and successors there for the time being during the term aforesaid. Provided always that if it shall happen that aforesaid several rents or any of them should be in arrear and not paid in part or in whole for the space of forty days after any feast of the feasts aforesaid as it is aforesaid they should be paid. That then and from then this present lease and grant shall be void and shall count for nothing anything in these presents to the contrary notwithstanding. Any statute, etc. In witness whereof. Witness the Queen at Westminster the 16th day of December.   By writ of privy seal.

PATENT ROLL (1589).   34 Eliz., pt. 10, m. 12.

Of a grant at farm for William Bradshaw his wife and others.

The Queen to all to whom etc. greeting. Whereas we by our letters patent sealed with our great seal of England bearing date at Westminster the 16th day of December the 23rd year of Our reign delivered granted and let at farm to our beloved John Bradshawe Esq. all that our mill in Fishguard and all those Rectories of the churches of St. Thomas in the vill of St. Dogmaels and Eglwyswrw Bayvil Moylgrave Llantood and St. Nicholas Fishguard and Grangiston. And all the chapels of Penkelly Vychan Nantgwyn Lisprant and Newton with all their rights and appurtenances in our county of Pembroke or elsewhere within the Bishopric of St. David's with all their rights and appurtenances to the late Monastery of St. Dogmael sometime belonging and appertaining and parcel of the possessions thereof sometime being together with all tithes profits obventions commodities and emoluments whatsoever to the same Rectories and chapels or any of them belonging or appertaining also all messuages lands tenements mills meadows feedings pastures commons moors marshes waters fisheries fishings rents pensions portions tithes oblations obventions fruits profits and commodities and other our possessions and hereditaments whatsoever in the vills fields parishes and hamlets of St. Dogmaels Grangiston Eglwyswrw Bayvil Moylgrave Llantood St. Nicholas Fishguard Penkelly Vychan Nantgwyn Lisprant and Newton aforesaid in our said County of Pembroke or within our said Bishopric of St. David with all their rights and appurtenances premised by the said letters patent demised or any of them in any way belonging or appertaining or with the same or any of them by several yearly rents in the said letters patent reserved before then demised let used or enjoyed. Except however always and to us and our successors altogether reserved the lordship and manor of Baare and the Rectory of Maenclochog Llandillo and Llancolman and the chapel of Maenclochog and all the lands and tenements in Maenclochog Baare Haverford and Pembroke to the said late Monastery of St. Dogmaels late belonging and appertaining also excepted and likewise reserved all great trees woods underwoods wards marriages reliefs escheats mines and quarries and advowsons of churches and chapels whatsoever of the premises. To have and to hold the aforesaid mill Rectories chapels messuages lands tenements tithes pensions portions and other all and singular the premises by said letters patent demised with all their appurts except the pre-excepted to the aforesaid John Bradshawe and his assigns at the term and for the term of the life of him John. And after the decease surrender or forfeiture of the said John Bradshawe then the aforesaid mill Rectories lands tenements tithes pensions portions and other all and singular the premises by said letters patent demised with all their appurts except the pre-excepted shall wholly remain to William Bradshawe and his assigns at the term and for the term of the life of him William and after the decease surrender or forfeiture of either of the aforesaid John and William Bradshawe then the aforesaid mill Rectories chapels lands tenements tithes pensions portions and other all and singular the premises by said letters patent demised with all their appurts except the pre-excepted shall wholly remain to James Bradshawe and his assigns at the term and for the term of the life of him James. Rendering yearly to us our heirs and successors of and for the aforesaid mill of Fishingarde with appurts 20s. and of and for the aforesaid lands and tenements in Grangiston aforesaid with appurts 26s. 8d. And of and for aforesaid Rectory of St. Thomas in the vill of St. Dogmaels with appurts £20. And of and for the aforesaid Rectory of Eglwyswrw with appurts £7 6s. 8d. And for the aforesaid Rectory of Bayvil with appurts £4 13s. 4d. And for the aforesaid Rectory of Moylgrove with appurts £6 13. 4. And for the aforesaid Rectory of Llantode and St. Nicholas with appurts £6 13. 4. And for the aforesaid Rectory of Fyshgard and Grangeston £10 6. 8. And of and for the aforesaid chapel of Penkelthie Vaughan with appurts 25s. And of and for the aforesaid chapels of Nantgwyn Llisprant and Newton with appurts £7 6. 8. of lawful money of England at the feasts of the Annunciation B. V. M. and St. Michael the Archangel at the receipt of our Exchequer or at the hands of our bailiffs or receivers of the premises for the time being by equal portions to be paid during the several terms aforesaid by our said letters patent granted as by the said letters patent more plainly appears. Which said John Bradshaw and James Bradshawe are dead as we have certain knowledge thereof. And the aforesaid William Bradshawe is in full life having and enjoying the whole right estate title term and interest of and in the premises by virtue of the letters patent aforesaid as to all and singular the said premises with appurts except the premises in Nantgwyn aforesaid which he surrendered restored and gave to us with the intent however that we other letters patent and another demise of all and singular the premises except of the premises in Nantgwyn aforesaid to the said William Bradshaw for term of his life remainder thereof to Elizabeth his wife for term of her life remainder thereof to Edmund Bradshawe their son for term of his life in form following we thought fit to make and grant. Which said surrender we have accepted by these presents. Know ye therefore that we as well in consideration of the surrender aforesaid as for a fine of £20 of lawful money of England at the receipt of our Exchequer to our use by the aforesaid William Bradshawe Elizabeth his wife and Edmund Bradshawe their son paid with the advice of our beloved and trusty councillors William Baron of Burghley our Treasurer of England and John Fortescue esq our Chancellor and Sub-treasurer of our Court of Exchequer have delivered granted and let at farm and by these presents do deliver grant and let at farm to the aforesaid William Bradshawe Elizabeth his wife and Edmund Bradshaw all that aforesaid mill in Fishingarde and all those aforesaid Rectories of the churches of St. Thomas in the vill of St. Dogmaels and Eglwyswrw Bayvil and Moylgrave Llancode alias Llantode and St. Nicholas Fyshgard and Grangiston and all the aforesaid chapels of Penkelthie Vaughan Llisprant and Newton with all their rights and appurtenances in our said County of Pembroke and elsewhere in the said Bishopric of St. David's to the said late Monastery of St. Dogmaels as is aforesaid sometime belonging and appertaining and being sometime parcel of the possessions thereof together with all tithes profits obventions commodities and emoluments whatsoever to the same Rectories and chapels or to any of them belonging or appertaining also all messuages lands tenements mills meadows feedings pastures commons moors marshes waters fisheries fishings rents pensions portions tithes oblations obventions fruits profits and commodities and other our possessions and hereditaments whatsoever in the vills fields parishes and hamlets of St. Dogmaels Grangiston Eglwyswrw Bayvil Moylgrove Llantood St. Nicholas Fishguard Penkelly Vychan Lisprant and Newton aforesaid in our aforesaid County of Pembroke or within the said Bishopric of St. David's with all their rights and appurtenances premised by these presents demised and granted or any of them in any way belonging or appertaining or to the same or any of them by several yearly rents by these presents reserved before this demised let used or enjoyed. Except however always and to us our heirs and successors altogether reserved the lordships and manors of Baare and Rectories of Maenclochog Llandillo and Llancolman and the chapels of Maenclochog and all the lands and tenements in Maenclochog Baare Haverford and Pembroke to the said late Monastery of St. Dogmaels late belonging and appertaining also excepting and in likewise reserved all great trees woods underwoods wards marriages reliefs escheats mines and quarries and advowsons of Churches and chapels whatsoever of the premises. To have and to hold the aforesaid mill Rectories and Chapels messuages lands tenements tithes pensions portions and other all and singular the premises by these presents demised with all their appurts except the pre-excepted to aforesaid William Bradshawe and his assigns at the term and for the term of the life of him William. And after the decease surrender or forfeiture of aforesaid William Bradshawe then we will and by these presents grant that aforesaid mill Rectories lands tenements tithes pensions and other all and singular the premises by these presents demised with all their appurts except the pre-excepted shall wholly remain to aforesaid Elizabeth wife of aforesaid William and their assigns at the term and for the term of the life of said Elizabeth. And after the decease surrender or forfeiture of the said William and Elizabeth Then we will and by these presents grant that the aforesaid mill Rectories lands tenements tithes pensions portions and other all and singular the premises by these presents demised with all their appurts except the pre-excepted shall wholly remain to aforesaid Edmund Bradshaw and his assigns at the term and for the term of the life of him Edmund. Rendering yearly to us our heirs and successors of and for the aforesaid mill of Fishgard with the appurts 20s. And of and for the aforesaid land and tenements in Grangiston aforesaid with appurts 26s. 8d. And of and for the aforesaid Rectory of St. Thomas in the vill of St. Dogmael with appurts £20. And for the aforesaid Rectory of Eglwyswrw with appurts £7 6. 8. And for the aforesaid Rectory of Bayvil with appurts £4 13. 4. And for the aforesaid Rectory of Moylgrove with appurts £6 13. 4. And of and for the aforesaid Rectory of Llantood alias Llancode and St. Nicholas Fishguard with appurts £6 13. 4. And of and for the aforesaid Rectory of Fishguard and Grangiston £10 6. 8. And of and for the aforesaid chapel of Penkelly Vychan with appurts 25s. And for the aforesaid chapels of Lisprant and Newton with appurts £7 of lawful money of England at the feasts of St. Michael the Archangel and the Annunciation B. V. M. at the receipt of the Exchequer of us our heirs and successors at Westminster or at the hands of our bailiffs and receivers of the premises for the time being by equal portions to be paid during the several terms aforesaid by these presents aforegranted. And after the decease of the said William Bradshaw then to be rendered or paid to us our heirs and successors the best beast of said William in name of heriot. And after the decease of said Elizabeth wife of aforesaid William if the said Elizabeth shall survive the said William the best beast of the said Elizabeth in name of heriot. And after the decease of said Elizabeth Bradshawe if the said Edmund survive the said William and Elizabeth the best beast of the said Edmund in name of heriot. And we will and by these presents grant to aforesaid William Elizabeth his wife and Edmund and their assigns that we our heirs and successors to the said William Elizabeth and Edmund and their assigns as well of £4 yearly for the wage and stipend of a chaplain yearly celebrating divine service and serving the cure [of souls] in the church and parish of St. Dogmaels aforesaid as of all rents fees annuities pensions portions and sums of money and charges whatsoever from the premises or any parcel thereof in any way issuing or to be paid or thereupon charged or to be charged besides of the several rents above by these presents reserved and besides of such payments charges and sums of money which any farmer or farmers of the premises or any of them before this have been accustomed to support and pay if there are any against whatsoever persons from time to time will exonerate acquit and defend during the term aforesaid. And the aforesaid William Bradshawe Elizabeth his wife and Edmund Bradshawe and his assigns the chancels mills houses and buildings and all hedges ditches inclosures shores banks and sea-walls also all other necessary repairs of the premises in all and by all from time to time as often as is necessary and shall be opportune at their own charges and expense shall well and sufficiently repair support sustain scour purge and maintain during the term aforesaid. And the premises sufficiently repaired and maintained at the end of their term shall demise. And we will and by these presents grant to aforesaid William Bradshawe, Elizabeth his wife and Edmund Bradshawe and their assigns that it shall be lawful for them and each of them from time to time to take perceive and have from and upon the premises growing competent and sufficient houseboote[1] hedgeboote fyreboote ploughboote and cartboote there and not elsewhere yearly to be expended and occupied during the terms aforesaid. And that they may have timber in the woods and lands of the premises growing for and towards the repair of chancels mills houses and buildings of the premises by assignment and survey of the steward or understeward or of other officers of us our heirs and successors there for the time being during the term aforesaid. Provided always that if it happen the aforesaid several rents or any of them shall be in arrear and not paid in part or in whole for the space of forty days after any feast of the feasts aforesaid on which as is aforesaid they should be paid and not paid at such day and place days and places as by proclamation within the County aforesaid by the Sheriff of the same to be made as by warrant of the Receiver for the first moiety of the year also of the Auditor and Receiver for the last moiety of the year were appointed. That then this present demise and grant so far as the estate and interest of him who so shall default in payment of the several rents aforesaid. And so far as such part and parcel of the premises whereof several rents above by these presents reserved are so in arrear unpaid shall be void and of no effect. Anything in these presents to the contrary thereof notwithstanding. Any statute etc. In witness whereof etc. Witness the Queen at Westminster 21st day of July.   By writ of privy seal.

---

[1] Bote = wood.

The Bradshaws held St. Dogmaels for three or four generations, the first being the John Bradshaw who died September 30th, 1567. His son, John, succeeded him, dying May 31st, 1588, and was buried in the Abbey burial ground; part of his old tombstone is still to be found, with the inscription " Hic jacet Johannes Bradshaw Armiger, qui obiit ultimo die Maii Anno Domino 1588," aged 59.

This John was the father of William and James Bradshaw. He was Sheriff of Pembrokeshire in 1570. Lewis, in his " Topographical Dictionary," states " that it was of this family of Bradshaw that the Bradshaw who presided at the trial of Charles I came."

The Bradshaws came to St. Dogmaels in 1537, and in 1645 were still living there. John Bradshaw, the regicide, was born at Stockport, in Cheshire, in 1602, and died in London, 1659; evidently he was not in the direct line, and as far as is ascertainable the Bradshaws were only connected with Lancashire years before coming to St. Dogmaels, afterwards with Shropshire, and then Radnorshire and Pembrokeshire; however, Lewis is often incorrect—witness the " Sagranus " stone which he describes as " Acrani." William Bradshaw succeeded in 1588; he was the father of Joan, who married Alban Owen of Henllys, in 1591. His wife's name was Elizabeth, and he had also a son named Edmund. He was one of the jurors at the post mortem inquisition held at Haverfordwest, May 4th, 1614, after the death of George Owen. On April 13th, 1613, by commission of that date, he was made a Justice of the Peace for Pembrokeshire, and his name is in the list as a Justice of the Peace for Pembrokeshire, in 1620. James Bradshaw married Alice, daughter of James Rhys of Mynachlogddu, but died early, before or during 1589, and his widow married Edmund Winstanley, who had been Sheriff of Pembrokeshire in 1590. The re-grant of St. Dogmaels, etc., to William, his wife, Elizabeth, and their son, Edmund, in Patent Roll, Elizabeth, July, 1592, was probably caused by the death of James, who had in the former grant been noted as next heir after William.

St. Dogmaels continued in the Bradshaw family till 1646, when it was sold to David Parry of Noyadd Trefawr.

The Parrys lived at St. Dogmaels, at Plas Newydd, and the old house of the Abbey seems to have entirely disappeared.

After 1646 they owned the Abbey. Thomas ap Harry,[1] of Blaenpant and Noyadd Trefawr, County Cardigan, married for his second wife, about 1560-1570, Margaret, sole heiress of Rhydderch ap Rhys Vychan, Lord of Towey, of

---

[1] I am indebted for this pedigree to Mrs. Tyler, of Glanhelig.

St. Dogmaels. Her grandmother was daughter and co-heiress of Owen Cwri, ap Ieuan, ap Nicholas of Tredafed, and second wife of Rhys Vychan, Lord of Towey. Margaret brought Thomas ap Harry as her dowry, Plas Newydd and its appurtenances; their eldest son, Stephen Parry, lived at Plas Newydd, and was Sheriff for Cardiganshire in 1629. His eldest son, Thomas,[1] by his first wife, Joan, daughter of Morgan Lloyd, of Llanllyr, also lived at Plas Newydd. By his first wife, Bridget, daughter of James Owen, he had one son, Stephen, who died without issue, and two daughters; Elizabeth, the elder, married her second cousin, David Parry, of Noyadd Trefawr; he died in 1621, leaving two sons, the elder also named David. Now it is the second of these Davids who became owner of the old Abbey property. John Parry, one of the Commissioners in 1691 in the tithe dispute, was the brother of this last David; he was Archdeacon of Cardigan, and Vicar of Troedyrawr, and died in 1727. His elder brother, David, was Sheriff for Cardiganshire in 1684, and died without issue in 1711, and was buried at Llandygwydd. His second sister, Susan, inherited the St. Dogmaels property; she married her cousin, William Parry, of Brethyr, about 1748; in 1753 they inherited Noyadd Trefawr, through the death of her elder sister. At the present day Mrs. Brenchley, of Glaneirw, owns some of the old Abbey lands, whilst the rest of it has been sold in plots to the various owners.

In the dispute regarding the tithes, Matthew Thomas, aged 57, born and bred in St. Dogmaels, and others, testify in 1693 David Parry, Esq., is the right owner and proprietor of the Abbey.

---

[1] This Thomas Parry married, as his second wife, Anne, daughter of Hector Phillips, of Cardigan Priory, they had, however, no issue.

Entrance to Old Harbour and River Gwayne, Fishguard.

CHAPTER XVII.

A LITTLE RIFT WITHIN THE LUTE.

IT has already been seen that certain lands, etc., at Fishguard were granted to the Abbey by William of Cantington, son of Jordan, son of Lucas de Hoda, Martin's chief knight.

From the phraseology used in the grant, that is, making the abbot and monks his heirs, it appears to have been a death-bed grant, and that William wished to make his peace with Heaven by bestowing this property on the Church. It is part of this property then given, shortly after the pillaging of the Abbey by the Irish, under the four Welsh princelings, that forms the subject of the following dispute in the reign of James I, concerning the ownership of a certain field, and that a mill belonging to the Bradshaws, and formerly to St. Dogmaels Abbey, was not used by the tenants of the Bradshaws, as it should have been, for the grinding of their corn.

In the " Lansdowne MS.," 443, 1-24 Elizabeth, in the first book of presentations, is noted the appointment of Owin Parker, clerk, to the Church of Fishguard, 10th May, 1571, void by death, at a salary of £4 os. 5d.

In the second book of above MS., 444, 25-33 Elizabeth, is noted the appointment of Rowland Jones, clerk, 13th October, 1599, to the same church, at the same salary, again void by death.

And in 165 of the " Lansdowne MSS.," fol. 5, is a notice of Fishguard mill, in the County of Pembroke, of the yearly value of xx⁵.

In the Book of Extracts from the Records of the Church of St. David's, the tithe of the Vicarage of Fishguard is noted as viij⁵ and a halfpenny.

In the reign of James I, William Bradshaw was the owner of this property, as well as of St. Dogmaels Abbey and Caldey, in Pembrokeshire, in this document following William Bradshaw contended that Owen Phillip had encroached on his land, and that his tenants were sending their corn to be ground at another mill, instead of to his water-mill as agreed, together with the question of the rent and repairs of the same mill, which we see by the extract above given was valued at twenty shillings yearly. And also as to the Vicar of Llanunda for the time being, who " quietly and without any gainsaying " carried off the tithe hay, growing on the land in dispute, and the extent of the parish of Fishguard.

First there is James I's command for an Inquisition to be held at Fishguard by James Thomas, gent., Edward Powell, gent., Owen Pickton, gent., and Alban Lloyd, gent., with a list of eight interrogations appended, followed by the deposition of the witnesses for the plaintiffs, taken at Fishguard on the 19th of August of the same year, by virtue of the King's writ from the Court of Exchequer, at Westminster, again followed by the depositions of the witnesses for the defendants.

In 35 Charles II, 1695, there were again disputes relating to this mill, under Owen *v.* Stefford, and the following year the same dispute between the same parties; however, space forbids the giving of these later deeds, but should anyone desire to see them, they will now know where they may be found.

DEPOSNS.   14 Jas. I.
Writ.   Court of Exchequer.

James by the grace of God King of England Scotland France and Ireland defender of the Faith etc. to our beloved James Thomas gent Edward Powell gent Owen Pickton gent and Alban Lloyd gent greeting. Know ye that we having full confidence in your fidelity industry and provident circumspection in the conduct of our affairs have given and by these presents do give to you or three or two of you full power and authority to diligently examine any witnesses whatsoever of and upon certain articles or interrogatories as well on behalf of William Bradshaw esq plaintiff as on behalf of Owen Phillips Griffin Nicholas and Robert Llewellyn defendants to you three or two of you to be shown or delivered. And therefore we charge you that at ffishingard in our county of Pembroke at such day or days as for this purpose you shall provide or three or two of you shall provide you shall cause and summon the witnesses aforesaid to come before you or three or two of you and the said witnesses and each of them by themselves of and upon the articles or interrogatories aforesaid upon their oath before you or three or two of you upon the holy Gospels of God corporally to be taken you diligently examine and you shall receive their examinations or three or two of you shall receive and shall reduce them into writing on parchment and when the same are so taken you shall send to the Barons of our Exchequer at Westminster from the day of St. Michael in fifteen days next coming under your seals or of three or two of you enclosed or three or two of you shall send together with the interrogatories aforesaid and this writ provided always that one of the defendants shall have warning by the space of 14 days of the first day of your sessions about the execution of this our writ. Witness Laurence Tanfield Knt at Westminster 19th June the 14th year of the reign of our reign of England France and Ireland and of Scotland the 49th.   by the Barons.

Endd. Execution of this writ appears in certain schedules attached to this writ.

Upper and Lower Town of Fishguard.

Interrogatories mynistred by Owen Phillips Robert Llewellyn and Griffith Nicholas deff[s] to examine their witnesses against William Bradshaw esquier complt.

1 Imprimis. Do you knowe the plt[f] and deffendants and doe you know one water mill lyeing in the parish and lordship of fishgard held by the plt[f] or his under ffearmour by lease from the late Queenes Ma[tie] and doe you knowe one parcell of medowe grounde claymed by the plaintiffe to be held from the late Queenes Ma[tie] by lease and howe longe have you knowne the said water mill and meadow grounde.

2 Item. Do you knowe or have you credibly hard that the deff[ts] Robert Llewellen and Griffith Nicholas and others who have heretofore dwelt in the howses and enjoyed the lande w[ch] the said deffendants now hould are and during your memorie were tenants unto one William Williams of mardnawen gent and to those whose estate he hath, and have alwaye during your memorie ground all the corne growing upon their said tenemente at mardnawen mill and seldome or never but at their oone pleasure have ground at the pltffs mill—declare your knowledge herein at lardge.

3 Item. Doe you knowe that the said deffendts Robert Llewellin and Griffith Nicholas are bounde by covenantes in their leasez made between them and their landlord to grind all their corne and graine growing upon their said tenements in their landlords mill called Mardnawen mill—declere your knowledge herein at lardge.

4 Item. Doe you knowe that the mill of fishgard is by the negligence of the miller or fearmour there much decayed and not attended as it ought to be and doe you knowe that this notwithstanding the complaynant receyveth about six pounds rent yerely for the same mill w[ch] hath heretofore bene sett at xx[s] rent—declare your knowledge herein at lardge.

5 Item. Do you know that he deff[te] Owen Phillip is seized in his demesne as of ffee of and in one messuage or tenement of land called the Drym in the parish of Llanunda within the county of Pembroke. And doe you know the said percell of meadowe grounde claymed by the pltf and adjoining unto the said deffts lande declare the quantity and the bounds thereof at lerdge uppon your othe.

6 Do you knowe a great brooke or river runing uppon the Southeast side of the said deff[te] Owen Phillips land called the Drym declare the name of the said river and doe you knowe that the same river hath for all the time of your memorie bene reputed and taken all the waye of the course thereof to the sea to be the landscare and division between the parishes of fishgard and Llanunda and between the hundred of Kemes and Dewesland and how longe have you knowne the said river and doth not the same nowe runne on the channell that you have ever knowne it to run declare the truth herein uppon your othe.

7 Item. Declare uppon your othe within what parish you doe believe the said percel of meadow grounde to be and unto whom do you beleeve in your conscience the same to belonge of right and what resons have you soe to beleeve declare the truth herein at lerdge uppon your othe.

8 Item. Doe you know that the tythe heye growing uppon the said percel of ground hath beene carried away by the vicar of Llanunda for the time being quietlie without anie gainesaying and for howe many yeres have you knowne the same soe to

be. And have you known or have you overhard for truth that the lordship or parish of fishgard have or do extend to the Northwest any further than the said river—declare what you knowe or beleeve to be the truth therein uppon your othe.

DEPOSITIONS. 14 Jas. I.
Pembroke. Mich. 24.

Interrogatories ministred by William Bradshaw esquier complaynant to examine his witnesses against Robert ħein Griffith Nicholas and Owen Phillips defendants.

1 Imprimis dooe you know the said parties and dooe you knowe the menor or lordship of fishingard in the countie of Pembroke and one water mill within the said menor being the Kings Maties mill and one meadow called y weirglodd dan y goyed grodig and one perte thereof called Garth y Gwenyn lying and being in the lordship and perishe of fishingard in the said county of Pembroke. What quantitie of ground dothe the said medowe conteine. And dothe it not conteine one welsh acre or more. And how longe have you known the said manor and lordship mille and percel of meadowe.

2. Item dooe you knowe the water grist mille of William Williams gent called Melin manor nawon. And how long is it sithence the same hath benne first erected. And is not his Maties said mille an auncient mille and hath had contynuance tyme out of mynd and long time before the erecting of the said William Williams mille.

3. Item dooe you knowe or have you heerd that our late soverayne lady Elizabeth late Queene of England was seased in her demesne as of fee in the right of her crown of England of and in the said percel of meadowe as percel of the lands belonging to the said manor or lordship of fishingard. And doth not the same meadowe lye within the perish of fishingard and doth not the teyth have thereof issuing and due ben yerely from tyme to tyme thereof the memorye of man is not to the contrary payed to the farmor for the tyme beinge of fishingarde.

4 Item. Doo you know or heve you heerde that all the tenaunts which hold of the said lordship and manor of fishingarde as well those which inhebit or dwell within the borough as those which dwell without the borough within Tregoes and elsewhere within the hundred of Kemes tyme out of mynd whereof the memorie of man is not to the contrary have from tyme to tyme and at all tymes used and accustomed to grind their several corne and graine growne uppon their several lands at his Maties said Myll and at no other Myll. And that they have ben accustomed so to doe. And are not the said Robert ħen and Griffith Nicholas tenants inhabiting within his Maties said lordship of Fishingard.

5 Do you knowe have you hard that the father of the said Robert ħen and the former inhabitants of the lands as well where the said Robert ħen as of the tenement that Griffith Nicholas dwelleth on have bene ever accustomed and used to grind all their corne and graine at his Maties Mylls at ffishgard and at noe other Mylls and hath not the said Robert ħen and Griffith Nicholas of late within these fewe years withdrawne their suit from his Maties mylles of ffishgard unto the myli of one William Williams. And howe far is it distant from the Kinge's mill. And is it not in another lordship and out of the same hundred wherein the King's myll is declare your knowledge herein at lerdge.

6 Item. Do you knowe or hard that the said Robert Hen and Griffith Nicholas doe severally hold divers messuages landes and tenements of the said Manor or lordship of fishgard. And that by reason of their several tenures they ought to doe suit to his Maties myll. And at his Maties said myll to grind all their said corne growing upon the said severall tenements and not at any other myll declare your knowledge herein at lerdge.

7 Do you knowe that there is yerelie payd out of all the tenements and landes within the mannor of fishgard an yerelie rent to his Maties use at May and Michaelmas. And that the occupants of the same tenements and landes doe paye their yerelie rent. And that all the tenaunts and occupants have used and accustomed tyme out of mynd to grind all their griste at his Maties said myll. And have not the said defendants Robert Hen and Griffith Nicholas heretofore. And those that hold their severall landes and tenements before them dooe suit at his Maties mylls.

8 Do you knowe or hard that the said defs Robert Hen and Griffith Nicholas have of late withdraune their suit from his Maties said myll and have not brought their corne thether to be ground. And that they have carried the same to ther mylles. And that the plaintif and his . . tenaunts have had greate hindrance and losse therebye declare your knowledge.

9 Item. Do you knowe or hard that the deffs Owen Phillips being seased of certain landes adjoininge his Maties said meadowe hath of late encroached upon the said meadowe and altered the meres and bounds of the same. And his Maties said landes cannot be knowne from his the said Owen Phillips lands. And so entendeth to gaine the said whole meadowe or at least some part thereof. And hath directed out of his course a ryver that in parte dyd meere and devyde between the said meadowe and said defs owne landes.

Item doe you knowe or have you hard that upon complaint made about iiij yeres past to the steward of the said mannor and to the great Inquest at a Leet Court there for the said manor houlden that the def Owen Phillip had then encroched upon the said meados whereupon the said Inquest repayred to the said meadowe and viewed the same and the meres and boundes thereof and did not the said Inquest upon evident and good proof then made by divers witnesses before them fynd and present that the said def Owen Phillips had then encroched upon the said medowe and turned the said water out of his course. And also fynd and present that Garth y Gwenyn was perte and percell of the said medowe. And weare you one of the said Jurie yea or noe or weere you then present when the Jurie soe found declare your knowledge thereon at lardge.

DEPOSITIONS. 14 Jas. I.

Pembroke. Mich. 24.

Witnesses on the part of the plaintiff.

Depositions of witnesses taken at ffishingard in the county of Pembroke the 19th day of August the year of the reign of our lord James by the grace of God of England Scotland France and Ireland King defender of the faith etc. to wit of England France and Ireland the 14th and of Scotland the 50th. Before James Thomas gent Edward

Powell gent Owen Picton gent and Alban Lloyd gent by virtue of the King's Maties write of Commission to them directed from his Maties Courte of Exchequer at Westm̃ for examination of witnesses in a matter depending at issue in the said Courte. Betweene William Bradshawe esquier plantief and Owen Phillips Gryffith Nicholas and Robert Lloid deffs for one[1] the behalff of the said plaintieff.

Owen Johnes of Tre[2] Coon in the Com̃ of Pembroke gent of the age of Threascore and fifteen yeares or thereabouts sworn and examined upon the interrogatories hereunto annexed one the said plaintieffs behalff deposeth and sayeth as followeth. To the first interrogatorie he sayeth that he knoweth both perties and the menor or lordship of fishingard in the Com̃ of Pembroke and one water mill within the said menor being the King's Matie mill and knoweth the medowe in that interrogatorie mencioned nowe in question between the said plaintief and said deffs Owen Phẽes[3] wch he always hath hard called and knowne by the name of y Weir glodd[4] dan goed y drym. And sayeth that one part thereof is called Garth y Gwenen. And this deponent sayeth that about seven and ffortie yeres past viz in or aboute the tenth yere of the reigne of the late Queen Elizabeth late Queen of England there was a commission awarded from her Matie then . . . . Suth Wales to Edward Powes esquier and Thomas George Bowen esquier authorising and requirring them by the othe of a sufficient Jurie of the then freeholders of the said maner to view and take a survey of her Maties then said manor or lordship of fyshyngard and of all her then lands and possessions within the same. By vertue of wch commissions the said Commissioners did swaere and cherge in that behalf a Jurie of the then best and substantiell ffreeholders of the said manor, of wch Jurie this deponent was foreman and sixteen or thereabouts more of the then freeholders of the said manor were of the said Jurie wch are nowe all dead saveing this deponent. And the defendant Owen Phillips grandfather was of the said Jurie. And this deponent and the rest of the Jurie then viewing the said medow did then find that the same did lie within the manor or lordship of Fishyngard in the parish of Fishingarde. And the said then Jurie found the said medowe to containe in quantitee two acres or thereabouts. To the third interrogatorie he sayeth that he knoweth that our said late sovereign lady Elizabeth late Queene of England was seased of those percels of medowe as percel of the lands belonging to the said manor or lordship of fishyngard. And the Jurie aforesaid found that the same did lie within the said manor of fishyngard. To the nyneth interrogatorie he sayeth that of the said medowe found by the Jurie aforesaid and wch by the then prooff and report of old men was found to be her said late Maties medowe. The said defendant Owen Phillips hath sithence the said surveye taken, encroched and drawen to his grounde a part of the said medowe called Garth y Gwennen. And the def Owen Phillips himself hath confessed that he did and dothe occupie the same and mowe haye thereupon but claymeth the same to be his. And he this deponent sayeth that the course of the water that did mere[5] and divide between the said medowe and the lands of the said defendant Owen Phillips in perte is everted out of that course where it was found by the said Jurie it sholde be wch course of the water was then found by the jurie upon report and proof of olde men to be the mere between the said medowe and the lands of the said def Owen Phillips. To the tenth interrogatorie he sayeth that he hath heard by credible report that about

---

[1] On.   [2] Tre Cwm.   [3] ? Phillippes.   [4] The meadow under the wood on the ridge.   [5] Bound.

fower yeares past the inquest in that interrogatorie mentioned did view the said medowe and found and presented that the defs Owen Phẽes[1] had encroched upon part thereof and heard how the said inquest found and presented that Garth y Gwennyn was part of the said medowe. And further doth not depose.

David Johnes of fishingard in the Coṁ of Pembroke Clre[2] of the age of ffortye three yeeres or thereabouts alsoe sworne and examined upon the interrogatories aforesaid one the said pltfs behalfe deposeth and sayeth as followeth. To the first interrogatorie he sayeth that he knoweth both parties and the manor or lordship of fishingard in the Coṁ of Pembroke and the water mill lying in the said manor being the King's Ma[ties] mill and knoweth the medowe in that interrogatorie mentioned by the name of the King's Ma[ties] medowe and knoweth one part thereof to be called Garth y Gwenyn and he sayeth that about three yeares or somewhat more nowe last past this deponent being then a layman and one of the inhebitants of the said manor was of a jurie sworen in at a leet before the deputie steward of the said manor and upon Complaint then made touching the encrochement of the said medowe this deponent and others the rest of the then jurie repayring to the said medowe and viewing the same did upon the othe and testimonie of certaine witnesses and the reporte of certain olde men find and present that the said medowe nowe in question was lying wthin the perish and manor of fishingard and therefore by the same testimonie and proof then made before the said jurie this deponent taketh it that the said medowe lyeth within the manor and parish of fishgard. To the third interrogatorie he sayeth that he knoweth that our late sovereign lady Elizabeth late Queen of England was seazed of the said percel of medowe pert of the lands belonging to the said manor of fishingard. And for the reason by him in his answer to the first interrogatorie layed down he thinketh it and taketh that the said medowe lyeth within the perish of fishingard. And he sayeth that the tieth haye thereof for the space of these two and twenty yeeres nnowe last past hath yerely for ought this deponent knoweth to the contrary ben payed to the farmour for the time being of fishingard. To the seventh interrogatorie he sayeth that there is yerelie payen out of all the tenements and lands within the said manor of fishingard oon yere chieff rente to his Ma[ties] use at Maye and Michaelmas and thoccupants of the said tenements and lands do paye the same chief rents yerelie. To the ninth and tenth interrogatories he sayeth that the deff Owen Phillips doth holde and occupie one percel of the said meadow called Gerth y Gwennyn w[ch] upon proof made on he this deponent and the rest of the jurie [torn] in this deponents answer to the first interrogatorie. This deponent and the rest of the said jurie did find and present upon hearinge of the said pruff and view of the said meadowe. And for further reason of their said prsent[mt] this deponent sayeth that one William John Hewes came before this jurie and made pruff upon his oath that about eighteen yeres past he this William and one Thomas John Meredith did mowe this meadow and that pert thereof called Gerth y Gwennin for one John Germin whoe then was tenant of those medowes to the pl. or to John Bradshaw esquier the pls nephew. And that as they were mowinge that pte of the said medowe called Garth y Gwennin Phee Gr[yffydd] the deft Owen Phillips father then holding the defs lands came to the said mowers and never made any clayme then

---

[1] ? Phillippes.   [2] Clericus, clerk.

to Gardd y Gwennen or contradicted them in mowing but intreated them to come to mow him a plott of medowe in another place and further doth not depose.

John Dawes of ffishingard in the Com of Pembroke gent of the age of threescore and five years or thereabouts alsoe sworne and examined upon the interr aforesaid one the said Compls behelff deposeth and sayeth as followeth. To the first interrogatorie he sayeth that he knoweth both perties and the menor or lordship of fishingard in the Com of Pembroke and knoweth the water mill within the said manor being the King's Maties mill and knoweth the medowe in that interr specified nowe in question. And sayeth that the same is called Y Weirglodd dan goed y drym[1] and knoweth that parte of the said medowe wch is in question is lying and being in the lordship and parishe of fishgard in the county of Pembroke and he sayeth that in or about the tenth yeere of the reigne of our sovereign lady Elizabeth late Queen of England upon a survaye teken of the said lordship there was a Rent roule[2] of and for the King's lands and rents within the said menor made which rent roule this deponent diverse tymes hath seene and perused and by the same rent rolle it appereth that the said medowe lieth in the lordship and parish of fishgard and dothe contayne two acres and the names of the iurie that did soe survaye the said manor and layed downe in the said Rent rolle and as by the same rent rolle appereth one Gr[yffydd] ap Ieūn ap Rees grandfather to the deff Owen Phēe was one of the said Jurie sworne upon and for the survayinge of the s^d manor. To the second interr he sayeth that he knoweth his Maties said mill is an auncient mill and has had continuance tyme out of mynd. To the third interr he sayeth that he knoweth that o^r late sovereign lady Elizabeth late Queen of England was seized of and in the said medowe as percel of the lands belonging to the said menor or lordship of fishingard. To the iiijth vth and vjth interr he sayeth that the severall messuages lands and tenements wch the deffs Robert Hen and Griffith Nicholas doe holde and are tenants of . . the lands of William Williams gent and the same or moste pert thereof were purchased by Ieūn ap William gent late father of the said William Williams. And he sayeth that before the said purchase the owners and occupiers of the said messuages tenements and lands wch the said two deffs nowe doe holde and occupie did use to grinde their corn and griest in his Maties said mille except the same happened to be out of repaire or to want water. But whether they were bounde to do suit to the said mill he doth not knowe and he sayeth that all other the tenants wch holde of the said of the said lordship or manor of fishgard as well those that doe inhabit and dwell within the borough as those that dwell without the borough within tregroes and ells where within the menor of fishgard as farr as he knoweth have always during all the tyme of this deponents remembraunce used to grind their seuerall corne and graine growing upon the seuerall tenements at his Maties said mill. But whether they ought soe to doe he knoweth not. To the seventh interr he sayeth that there is yerelie payed out of all the tenements and lands within the said manor an yerelie chief rent to his Maties use at Maye and Michaelmas and the occupante of the same tenants did paye the same rent yerelie. To the eighth interr he sayeth that the said two deffs Robert Hein and Griffith Nicholas have of late brought their corne to be ground to the mill of the said William Williams at some tymes and at some other tymes to his Maties said mill. To the nyneth and xth interr he sayeth that

---

[1] The meadow under the wood on the ridge.   [2] Roll.

about iiij yeeres now last past upon complaint made on the nowe pls behelff at a Leete Court holden for the said manor [torn] that the def Owen Phẽes had encroched upon pert of the said meadow [torn] great inquest sworne at the said leete repayred to the said medowe [torn][1] where divers witnesses whereof this deponent was one were examined thereon. Who proved what they knew themselves and what had ben . . [1] and reported to them touching the meeres of the said meadow . . [1] the same and the lands of the said deff Owen. And as the same meeres . . . [1] shewed and proved by witnesses upon their oune knowledges . . [1] they hard of other old men before it appered and soe it was found by the said jurie that the said deffs Owen had encroched and drawen to his land the said medowe and further dothe not depose.

John Mendus of fishgard in the county of Pembroke weaver of the age of lx yeres and upwards alsoe sworne and examined upon the interr aforesaid on the said Complts behalffe deposeth and sayeth as followeth. To the first interr he sayeth that he knoweth both pties and doth knowe the moste part of the Lordship of fishingard in the Cõ of Pembroke and the water mill within the said manor being the King's Maties mill and the medowe nowe in question wch he knewe and heard call by the name of Y Weyrglod dan goed y dryn and one part thereof called Gardd y Gwenyn[2] wch medowe as this deponent taketh it and as it hath bene shewed him and as he was informed by olde people doth lye in the lordship and parish of fishingard in the Com of Pembroke. And he hath knowen the same premises for the space of these 43 years or thereabouts. To the second interr he sayeth that he knoweth the mill of William Williams gent in the same interr menconed but doth remember when it was bilt but knoweth the Kings Ma[ties] said mill hath had continuance tyme out of mynde. To the third interr he sayeth that when he was a boye repayring to the churche of ffishgard many yeres past he sawe then there a company of the men of the said lordship. And as then he heard it said and repeated they were a jurie sworn to survey the said Lordship. And the lands thereof. And then it was reported that they found the said medowe to be parcel of the said lordship. And that our late lady soueraigne lady Elizabeth late Queene of England was then seased thereof as parcel of the said manor. And it was then reported that the said jurie found this medowe to be lyinge in the lordship and parish of ffishingarde. And he sayeth that he knoweth that his this deponents father was one of the said jurie. And he sayeth that the first yere that the said medowe bare haye and was tornd[3] for meadow was about 20 yeres past and that yere this deponent took to rent the 4th part of the said meadow and three others of his neighbours tooke the other three parts at 6d parte and that yere John Jermyn then farmer of fishgarde had the tithe heye of the said medowe. To the 4th interr he sayethe that aboute fortie yeres past and for certein yeres then after all the freeholders and tenants of the said lordship of ffishingarde did from tyme to tyme use and accustome to grinde their corne and grist. w[ch] grewe upon the growndes and tenements at his Ma[ties] said mill of the s[d] lordship excepte the mill were decayed or wanted water but sithence some dwellinge out of the s[d] lordship have purchased certein tenements in the said lordship and some of those purchasers caused theire tenants of those tenements to withdrawe their suite from his Ma[ties] said mill and to bringe theire corne to the said purchasers owne mills and by the then reporte it was thought and reported that all the tenants of the said

---

[1] All torn or illegible. [2] The bees' garden, or enclosure. [3] Turned.

Lordship ought to doe suite to his Maties said mill. To the vth interr he sayeth that Ieũn ap William of Manor Nawen did heretofore purchase the tenemts and lands nowe in the occupacon of the deffs Robert ꝉꝉein and Griffith Nicholas. And they for a long time after sale thereof made and did suite and brought theire corne to his Maties said mill except the same were out of repaire or wanted water. But after the death of the said Ieũn ap Wm they were drawen by William Williams their landlord to his mill. To the rest of the interr he can say noe more than formerlie he hath answered and further dothe not depose.

James Phillips of Ste Edryns in the County of Pembroke husband man of the age of 60 yeres or thereabouts also sworn and examined upon the Interr aforesaid on the said Complts behalf deposeth and sayeth as followeth. To the 1st interr he sayeth that he knoweth both parties the manor or lordship of Fishingard in the Com̃ of Pembroke and the Kings Maties mill within the said manor and hath known the same these 48 yeres nowe last or thereabouts to all the rest of the interr he sayth that he was borne in the parish of ffishingard and dwelt there wth his father at tree yeres until he was aboute xxtie yeres of age and then being about fortie yeres past removed thence to Ste Edryns some 6 miles thence. And doth not knowe any thinge of the said mill since. But before this deponents removeable out of the said parish of ffishgard this deponents father being a freeholder dwelling at Tregroes[1] in the said lordship of ffishingard and brought his corne to his Maties said myll allwayes excepte the same was oute of repaire or wanted water. And further doth not depose.

John David Walker of ffishingard in the Com̃ of Pembroke husbandman of the age of lxxvij yeares or thereabouts alsoe sworne and examined upon the interr aforesaid on the said pltfs behalf deposeth and sayeth as followeth. To the first interr he sayeth that he knoweth both parties and the manor of ffishingarde aforesd and his Maties mill within the said manor and hath knowne the same for the space of these 60 yeres nowe last past or thereabouts to all the rest of the interr he sayeth that allwayes from tyme to tyme duringe all this deponents memorie all the tenants and freeholders of the said lordship or manor of fishingard as well those that inhabited and dwelt within the borough as without the borough in tregroes and ells where within the said manor have used and accustomed to grind their several corne and graine growing upon their several tenements at his Maties said mill and at noe other mill except his Maties said mill shold happen to be out of repair or want water untill that Jevan ap William of Maner Nawen did purchase the lands nowe in the occupation of Robert ꝉꝉien and Griffith Nicholas and after the said purchase drewe them to his mill. And farther doth not depose.

Depositions of witnesses taken at fishingard in the Com̃ of Pembroke the xixth day of August the 14th year of the reign of our lord James by the grace of God of England France and Ireland King defender of the Faith etc. Before James Thomas gent Edward Powell gent Owen Picton gent and Alban Lloyd gent. By virtue of the King's Maties writte of Commission to them directed etc. for and on behalf of the Defendants.

---

[1] The Cross house.

Witnesses on the part of the Defendts Moris David of the parish of Llanunda in the Com̃ of Pembroke yeoman aged four score and six yeares and upwards being sworn and examined on the defts behalf upon the Interrogatories annexed deposeth and sayeth as followeth. To the 1st Interrogatory he saieth that he knoweth both parties plaintiff and defts and knoweth the water mill leyeing in the parishe and lordship of fishgard in that interrogatorie named held by the plaintife or his under tenante by lease from the late Queenes Matie and knoweth the parcel of meadow ground claimed by the plaintife to be held from the said late Queen by lease and hath knowne the said mill and parcell of meadow grounde this threescore and fifteene years or thereabouts. To the 5th 6th 7th and 8th interrogatorie this deponent sayeth that the said deft Owen Phillips in that interr named is seased in his demeasne as of ffee of and in the messuage or ten^{t} of lands therein mentioned called the Dryne[1] and that part therein adjoined to the plaintiffs lands being less than an acre by this deponents estimation. And sayeth that the River called Goodige for all the time of this Deponents memorie hath bene reputed and taken to be the Landscare[2] and division between the parish of fishgard and betwene the hundreds of Kemes and Dewsland and knoweth that the course of the said River hath bene as nowe it is this threescore and fifteen years and sayeth that the said percel of meadow grounde lieth in the parish of Llanunda and the reason of his knowledge herein is that he this deponent heretofore about eight or nine yeares past bought the teyth hay growing uppon the said parcel of meadow of Sir Hugh Īīen[3] clerk Vicar of Llanunda and caried the same home. And sayeth that the said vicar had and enjoyed the said teyth haye to his owne use during all his life tyme without contradiction to this deponents knowledge. And sayeth that he never knewe or hard that the Lordship or parish of fishgard doth or did extend to the Northwest anie further than the said river and further dothe not depose.

Philip Jenkin of the parish of Llanunda in the Com̃ of Pembroke mason adged fourscore and six yeares and upwards sworne and examined on the defendants behalf deposeth and sayeth as followeth. To the first interrogatorie this deponent sayeth that he knoweth both parties plaintiffs and defendants and knoweth the parcell of meadow grounde claymed by the plaintife to be held from the late Queen's Matie by lease and hath known the same verie nigh this fourscore yeares past. To the 5th 6th and all the rest of the Interrogatories this deponent sayeth that the defft Owen Phillipes in the 5th interr named is seazed on his demeasne as of fee of and in the messuages tenements and lands in that interr named called Drym in the perish of Llanunda and adjoyneth to the plaintiffs lands. And sayeth that a great brooke or river running upon the South east of the said Owen Phē's lands called the Drym which river is called the River of Goodige which is and for all the time of this deponents memorie hath bene reputed and taken (all the waye of the course thereof to the sea) to be a Landscare and division between the parishes of fishgard and Lanunda and betweene the hundred of Kemes and Dewsland and sayeth that the said River dothe nowe runne and during all the tyme of this deponents memorie did runne the self same waye into the Mayne sea without change or alteration of his course. And sayeth that the said parcell of meadow grounde lieth in the parish of Llanunda and that part thereof doth belonge to the pltf by vertue of his lease from the late Queen's Matie and another parte to the defendant Owen

---

[1] The ridge.   [2] Landscare = Boundary.   [3] Llewelen.

Phillipes. And sayeth that the parishe or lordship of fishgard doth not nor never did to this deponents knowledge extend to the Northwest anie further than the said river. And further doth not depose.

John Hughe of the parish of Llanunda in the Coñi of Pembroke yeoman aged threescore and sixe yeares or thereabouts sworne and examined on the defendants behalf deposeth and sayeth as ffolloweth.   To the 1st interr he sayeth that he knoweth both parties plaintiff and defendants and knoweth the water mill in that interr named and the parcel of ground in variance and hath known the said percel of ground this threescore yeeres or thereabouts. To the 5th and all the rest of the interr this deponent sayeth that the defendte Owen Phillips is seazed in his demeasne as of fee of and in the messuage ten^{ts} and lands in the Vth interr mentioned called Drym and knoweth the said parcell of meadow claymed by the pltf to be within the parish of Llanunda (for ought this deponent knoweth). And sayeth that the river called Goodige is and for ought he knoweth hath bene tyme out of mind the Landscore and division betweene the parishe of fishgard and Llanunda and between the hundreds of Kemes and Dewsland. And this deponent remembreth that the course of the said river doth now runne in the channel that yt hath used to passe this 60 yeers together without change or alteration of his course. And further dothe not depose.

A Salmon Fishing Fleet, S.t Dogmaels.

CHAPTER XVIII.

RELICS.

OWARDS the end of the seventeenth century discontent with the Established Church of England gained ground, finally culminating in such disturbances over the religious question that in some places troops had to be called out to quell the riots. It was about this time that the old parish Church of St. Dogmaels became involved in the trouble, and was partly pulled down, a window and a portion of a wall were left, and formed part of one of the cottages built on its site; several other cottages were also built in the churchyard, all signs of tombstones being removed.

According to old deeds, "St. Thomas the Apostle," the old parish Church of St. Dogmaels "lay between two mills," near the present National Schools in Davies Street. One of these mills is still in existence, the other was in ruins some years ago.

In 1905 two of these old cottages, both rented by widows, and belonging to a sea captain, were pulled down, in order that he might build himself a comfortable house to retire to. The builder excavating at the site of the southern cottage, expecting to find sand for building, came upon some ancient stone coffins[1] in good preservation, some still containing skeletons, the head of one of the skeletons lying just beneath the usual seat of one of the old widows, as she sat beside her hearth. In all there were about sixteen coffins found; four of these were of slate slabs joined together, the others having only loose slabs at the two sides, ends, and top.

In pulling down the other cottage, the ancient stone framework of a Gothic window was found, and some remains of the old church wall, built of an exceedingly hard stone, reddish in colour, probably the same " Redd Stone "

---

[1] For this information I am indebted to Capt. Jones, " Cardigan Bay," and the builder, there being no remains of coffins and bones left when the author visited the spot.

mentioned by George Owen in his "Description of Pembrokeshire," and described as a—

"Kynde of freestone, which for fynes and collor passeth all other yet spoken of, which is a bludd red stone, and will be hewen very well, and make fine worke, this is very perfect red myxt with some brownesses and will serve to make faer and lardge windows, mantell trees and all other hewen work both within and without the house & against weather is most durable . . . . I find it in many places in the ruins of the Abbey of St. Dogmaels. Yt is founde in Moelgrove in the Cornefieldes . . . and also in the sea clyffes there."

There is also a quarry of this stone on the Pantsaeson Estate.

These remains undoubtedly belong to the ancient Church of St. Thomas, as these cottages lay in the position indicated between the two old mills. The north cottage was undoubtedly part of the church, whilst the south cottage was built over part of the graveyard. The site of this old church adjoins the present National School. The account taken from the *Tivyside Observer* the week after here follows, dated October 20th, 1905 : —

INTERESTING ANTIQUARIAN FIND AT ST. DOGMELLS.

—:—

On Tuesday last, at Shingrig, St. Dogmells, an interesting discovery was made that points to olden times in connection with the village. Messrs. H. O. Davies and John Bowen, contractors, having recently been engaged in building a new house just below the National School, and in the course of clearing away the rubbish of some out-buildings, discovered three stone-lined graves apparently of considerable antiquity. Two of them were empty, with the exception of dust and fine ashes at the bottom, but the third contained a quantity of human bones, thoroughly decayed, but still recognisable. It is said the old building pulled down was a portion of the ancient Church of St. Dogmells, and pronounced by Fenton, the historian of Pembrokeshire, to have existed long before the present parish church was built. Fenton, nearly a century ago, stated that the old church of the parish stood between two mills, and such is the case with the old building, now pulled down, as it stood between an old mill opposite the Cardigan Bay Inn, and the present mill, occupied by Mr. Gwynne. The building now demolished had two pine ends, one of comparatively modern date, but still of old formation, and the other was evidently a portion of the old church, as it contained the remains of a window with grooves for glass in the stonework, which points to its being really the eastern window of the ancient edifice, and appears to be coeval with the Abbey itself, the formation of the window being in red stone similar to those now extant in the abbey ruins. This supposition may be ratified by the fact that there is nothing to show that the present St. Dogmells Churchyard dated further back than the seventeenth century, and the present find, if equal in antiquity to the abbey, would go back to some date between the eleventh and seventeenth centuries. Probably we may hear something more upon the matter.

A little further up the hill were the ruins of the old Vicarage.

In a dispute relating to the lay rectorship of St. Dogmaels, and the claiming of rectorial tithes, October 15th, 1691, many of the old witnesses deposed to remembering an ancient chapel belonging to the Abbey, and still visible, and recently used for "divine service," and to seeing a pulpit still remaining, made of green stone. This pulpit, as related elsewhere, was made of greenish porphyritic granite, the same as used for the Ogham stone; also Anne Davies testifies that she also saw a tombstone of this green stone, and a baptismal font within the said chapel. This was evidently St. Thomas's Church, still standing in 1691, but apparently no longer used. The deed will doubtless be of special interest to all those who live in St. Dogmaels, the farms still bearing the same names that they did 216 years ago, and some of the same family name still surviving in and around St. Dogmaels. Thomas Lloyd, one of the Commissioners, was undoubtedly then living at Hendre, where they still lived in 1741, his descendants soon after moving to Cwmgloyne. Mr. Parry, another of the Commissioners, has descendants in the female line still living in the neighbourhood.

The farm herein mentioned as Manaian Fawr, where an ancient stone was found in 1904, used as a gate-post, and removed last year to the Abbey grounds for safety, inscribed with a long floreated cross intersected by a St. Andrew's cross, and having circles also inscribed between the arms of the cross fleuré.

Sayings and Depositions of witnesses taken sworne and examined upon their corporall oathes at the towne Hall of Cardigan the 15th Oct 1691 by and before Thomas Jones gent Roger Philips gent Thomas Lloyd esq and John Parry Commissioners etc. for the defendants behalf.

JAMES GRIFFITH of the perish of Bayvill aged 80 years and upwards sayth that he knoweth the Abbey or Monastery of St. Dogmells and the close and site and all that belongs to the same for the space of 20 years last past and further sayth that he doth not know nor ever heard of any manner of tith or any other decimal duty or anything else in lieu thereof payed or rendered by or from the inhabitants or landholders that inhabited or dwelt or held occupied or enjoyed or manured any messuage lands tenements pieces closes or parcels of land that is or lyes within the site or close wall now in the possession of the said defendants neither did this deponent know of any manner of tithe or anything else in lieu thereof claimed or demanded by the said plaintiff or by any other person or persons of or from such person or persons as did any time hold occupy manure or enjoy any lands closes pieces or percels of land that is or lye within the said site or close wall. And the reason of this deponents knowledge herein is for that he inhabited and dwelt as a husbandman or Dairyman for the space of three years in a certain tenement of land of David Parry Esq called Menion Vawe[1] under Robert Lloyd who rented the same of said Mr. Parry or his agent and likewise five years more as Dairyman or husbandman in another tenement of land of the said Mr. Parry called Ty Hyr[2] under the said Robert Lloyd and five or six yeers more under one James Griffith who rented the same from the s^d Mr. Parry both wch s^d tenements doe lye and are within the wall and site close belonging to the said Abby or monastery of St. Dogmells. And during all the time that the Deponent dwelt and inhabited in the s^d tenements and sowed ploughed manured and reaped in and upon the said premises there was no manner of tith or any other decimal duty claimed or demanded of or from this Deponent from the Rector or impropriator of St. Dogmells or his agent neither was there any manner of tithe corne or grayne or any other titheable duty or anything else in lieu thereof payed or rendered for such corn or grayne as was plowed sowed reaped or raised in and upon s^d premises by this Deponent etc.

JAMES GRIFFITH of the town of Cardigan gent aged 60 years sayth he knoweth the Abby of St. Dogmells for about 60 years last past and likewise knows all the messuages etc. within the site close wall or precinct of the said Abbey and that all the messuages lands tenements etc. in the s^d def^{ts} possession that is or lyes within the s^d close or site of the said Abby by some Auncient custome or usage is and hath beene freed dischardged and exempted of and from paym^t of tythes or any other decimal dutye to the Rector or Impropriator of the parish of St. Dogmell neither was there any manner of tythes or tenths paid or rendered or claimed or demanded from landholders within the said site for the space of 60 yeers last past nor of or from one particular field or close called Arlaise. And the reeson of this deponents knowledge herein is for that he was imployed and concerned for Abell Griffith gen^t deponents father in his life-time as agent or steward to his said father who held several messuages within the said site called Menian Vawr and Ty Hyr[2] and did usually sowe or look after the sowing dividing and threshing of all or most of the corn or grayne that did yeerely grow in and upon the said severall premises for severall years while he this deponents said father held the said premises and likewise sayeth that Mathew Griffith this deponent's brother succeeded his s^d father in the enjoyment of the said premises as tenant to David Parry esq.

THOMAS PHILIP HENRY of the parish of Neverne Co. Pembroke husbandman aged 80 saithe that he knows the Abby of St. Dogmells and the Parke Close site wall etc. And that there was an old chappell belonging or appertaining to the said Abbey and hath known the same premises with its appurts for the space of sixty five years last past and upwards and further sayth he knoweth all and every the severall

---

[1] Manaian Fawr ? Man eigion = the place by the sea.   [2] The long house.

messuages tenements lands etc. within the said park and that the same was and time out of mind hath been exempted and discharged of and from payment of tith or tenth or any other decimal duty or annything else in lieu thereof to the Rector or Impropriator of St. Dogmells or to his agents or servants for the time being and saith that he was credibly informed by his Mother who lived and dwelt with some of her relations in the time of her virginity upon a certain tenement within the said site and close wall or precinct called Menian Vawr that all the messuages and within the s^d close by some Auncient custom or usage time out of mind wherof the memory of man not to the contrary was and hath beene freed exempted and discherdged of and from the payment of any tithe or tenth and the reason of this Deponents knowledge was and is that he was born and bred in the parish of St. Dogmells called the Great parish and was and hath been a covenant servant unto Abell Griffith gent who took to rent or ffarm the s^d premises that lyes within the site etc. called Menian Vawr and this deponent was plowing sowing and reaping upon the s^d premises and never heard of any tith or tenth ever claimed or demanded and deposeth that it is usually and anciently called the little parish. And he did follow plow etc. upon severall tenements within the close and particularly upon a certain piece called Arlaise and no manner of tithe was paid or rendered for the same. And further sayth that there is a certain tenement of land called Clawdd Cam[1] now in the possession of the def^t Anne Martine, that some part thereof is and lyes within the said close and some other part without etc. and for such as is or lyes within the s^d Park close etc. no manner of tithe was ever payd or rendered or claymed and for such pert of the said premises as lyes without the said close was and is tithable.

MATHEW THOMAS of the parish of St. Dogmells Husbandman aged 57 saith that he hath known the Abbey of St. Dogmells and the close etc. since he came to any knowledge he being bred and born in the said parish and believes that David Parry esq is the right owner and proprietor of the said Abby and further deposeth that there was and is an auncient chappell that belongs and lyes within the s^d Abby or Monastery where this deponent supposeth and believes might be a place of Divine worship or prayers in the time of the Ancient Abbotts and likewise believes that all and every the severall messuages lands etc. that is and lyes within the s^d site was the Auncient demesne belonging and appertaining to the same and to the Abbots thereof and further sayth that all and singular the messuages etc. within the s^d site hath been ever since this deponents remembrance freed exempted and discharged of and from the paying or rendering of any manner of tithe or tenth etc. and this deponent was ever since his nativity an inhabitant and dwells to this day within aforesaid parish of St. Dogmells and hath been often Reteyned and employed by the owners and proprietors of the said Rectory of St. Dogmells to gather and collect tithes within the said Rectory and more particularly in gathering tith of corn and grayne that grew upon the messuages bordering on such site and deposeth that there is a certain tenement called Clawdd Cam some part thereof without the site pays tith etc. And further sayeth that there is one field close or piece of land grounde called Parke le Cleg[2] that is and hath been Reputed deemed or taken to be within the precincts or demesne there and

---

[1] The crooked ditch.   [2] Cleg = a hard mass, a lump.   The field of the place of the hard mass.

that the same is likewise freed discharged and exempted of and from paying or
Rendering any manner of tithe etc.

OWEN JAMES of the parish of St. Dogmells husbandman aged 79 sayth that
he knows the Abbey of St. Dogmells for the space of 60 years and sayeth that Mr.
Bradshaw was the owner or proprietor of the same when first this depon[t] knew it and
believes the same is now the right inheritance of David Parry esq and that all the
messuages etc. within the site is usually called Parke yr Abbot or Litte Parish and
reputed to be the demesne lands of the said Abby and that there hath been and yet is
an Ancient chappell within the said Monastery where this deponent verily believes and
was likewise credibly informed was a place anciently used and imployed for the
Abbottes and others the owners and proprietors of the said Abby for the reading of
Divine service and exercising Divine worship and Religion and the reason of this
deponents knowledge and belief herein is for that he this Deponent hath seen the
ancient reading seat or pulpit anciently used there for that purpose and that part of
the said reading desk or pulpit is yet to be seen for the confirmation of this Depon[ts]
knowledge herein and further sayeth that all the messuages etc. within the said site
have been time out of mind exempt from paying of tithe. And there is a percel called
Clawdd Cam [deposeth as the other witnesses] . . . and sayeth that there is two
several closes or percels of land called Parke Pen y Gragge[1] and Parke y Hinen[2] now
in the possession of the def[t] William Parry by the grant of David Parry Esq which did
always pay tithe to the Rectory of St. Dogmells and two other closes or parcels of
ground called Parke y reese[3] and Parke y Coed[4] now in possession of s[d] William
Parry is not nor hath been tithable in regard that the same did belong as part of the
demesne land belonging to the s[d] Abby.

JOHN BEYNON of the parish of St. Dogmells labourer aged 78 saith he
knoweth the said Abbey site etc. for 55 years last past and that the messuages etc.
within the said site hath been time out of mind exempt from tithe and this deponent
heard or believes that the reason that the s[d] severall premises was and is exempt and
discharged from the payment of tithe for that the said ancient Abbots or owners of
the s[d] Abby keepe annuite for the reading of Divine service and exercising of Divine
worship and Religion in a certain old chappell that was and yet is within the s[d] Abbey
in w[ch] s[d] chappell there was an ancient pulpit or reading seat and yet remaines part
thereof for that purpose as this deponent veryly believes . . [deposeth as before as
to Clawdd Cam etc.]

JOHN MORRIS of the town of Cardigan alderman a witness formerly produced
for plaintiffs knoweth the Abby and site and never heard if any tithe paid from
messuages within said site and about 35 yeers since was Agent for James Phillips esq
for getting the tithes of St. Dogmell and doth not remember any tithe paid or rendered
out of the premises mentioned and sayeth that he is a tenant of S[r] John Cope Knt
impropriator of Mount and Llechrid Co. Cardigan and that the chapelries of
Llechryd pays assessmt as of the Rectory or parish of Llangoedmore notwithstanding

---

[1] Crugiau = Crags.   [2] ? Eithinen = Gorse, the gorse field.
[3] Rhys' field.   [4] The field of the wood.

that the Rector or parson of Llangoedmore doth not nor hath not receaved any manner of tithe out or from the messuages etc. within the s^d chapel of Llechryd or the inhabitants thereof.

ENGHERARD[1] GRIFFITH of the parish of St. Dogmells widow aged 70 sayth that she knows the Abbey and precinct for 60 years past and the messuages etc. within the site have been time out of mind exempt from tith, she was bred and born in St. Dogmells [and deposeth as the others].

THOMAS JONES of the parish of Menerdivy[2] Co. Pembroke gent aged 57 sayth that he hath heard of the Abbey and believes the same to be the inheritance of David Parry Esq and that the said David Parry Esq of two parts out of three parts the whole into three parts divided of the two severall and respective impropriations or Chapelry of Kilsy[3] Vawr and Llangolman penbeador[4] in the Co. of Pembroke and the tythes arising out of the same. And that William Jenkins gent is intitled to the s^d other third part of the said premises and the tithes and profits arising from the same and further sayth that the said chapelry of Kill y Vawr pays all manner of taxations and impositions excepting Church rates as of the same were part and parcel of a certain rectory or parish adjoining and bordering to the said chapel of Kill y vawr called the Rectory of Manerding and that the s^d chapel of Llangolman Penbeador likewise lyeth and bordereth upon the rectory of Llannyhangell Penbeador and notwithstanding that the inhabitants of the said chapelry of Llanfyhangell[5] penbeador doe always pay all manner of tithe to the s^d Mr. Parry and Mr. Jenkins the inhabitants and landholders of the said chapelry of Llangolman[6] penbeador doe and time out of mind hath been by some ancient custom charged with all manner of offices and lyeable to taxations etc. as if they were residing within the said Rectory of Llanfyhangell penbeador aforsd etc.

MARGARET RICHARD of the parish of St. Dogmells widow aged 66 hath known the Abbey and precinct for 55 yeers and that there is an ancient chappel in or near the said Abby and now visible and that all the messuages within the ring or precinct called Parke y Abbot have been time out of mind exempt from payment of tithe as she hath been credibly informed by her ancestors and several of the ancient people that heretofore were bred and born in the said parish and vell knew of the ancient customs and usages. And she was bred and born in Menian Vawr now or late in the tenure or occupation of George Lewis one of the defendants.

MORGAN BOWEN of the parish of Verwick Co. Cardigan husbandman aged 70 knoweth the monastery or site etc. and that there was and yet is an ancient chapell[7] now visible which was anciently used for the reading of Divine service and for burying and interring of the dead that should dye within the precincts of the said Abbey and verily believes that without doubt the tithes and tenths of the said Abby landes was imployed intended and apply'd for the said Abby and the messuages etc within the precinct have been ever exempted from paying tithe [and further deposeth as the rest].

---

[1] Angharad.   [2] The Teify Manor.   [3] Cilfawr.   [4] Penbedw = Head of the birches.
[5] The angels' enclosure.   [6] St. Colman's enclosure.   [7] St. Thomas.

ANNE DAVIES of the town of Cardigan widow aged 80 yeers knoweth the Abby and the ancient chappell that is within and belonging to the said Abby and that she did see a tombe or grave one made of Green stone and likewise a baptizeing ffont and alsoe a pulpitt for the reading of Divine service within the said chapel. And that all and singular the lands and tenements that did anciently belong to the said was by some ancient right or custom time out of mind exempted from payment of tithe. And that the tithes of such lands was intended and imployed for the use of the said Abby or chappell as this deponent was credibly informed. And that certain fields and closes now the inheritance of David Parry esq was formerly in the tenure or occupation of this deponent viz one field or Close called Parke glas[1] and another called Park y ffryer[2] and another called Park weirglodd[3] vaier all which premises were tyme out of mind exempt from payment of tithe etc.

At Michaelmas, 1691, 3 William and Mary, the King and Queen jointly commanded four Commissioners, namely, Thomas Jones, gent., Roger Philipps, gent., Thomas Lloyd, Esq., and John Parry, or two of them, to hold an inquisition on behalf of Julius Deeds, Esq., plaintiff, and of the ten defendants named in the inquisition, respecting the disputed lay rectorship, Mr. Deeds claiming the rectorial tithes, whilst the defendants refused to pay them, claiming exemption from tithes, owing to the lands named having previously belonged to the Abbey. Mr. Deeds' witnesses, however, claimed to have previously paid the rectorial tithes to Mr. Deeds, and an assessor asserted that he had collected them. It was no unusual thing in those days for the Lord of the Manor to let out the lay rectorship. There are several examples of this in the old deeds belonging to Cardigan Priory. Apparently at this time Mr. David Parry owned the greater part of St. Dogmaels. The previous examination of the defendant's witnesses should follow this, but for the sake of the evidence therein, respecting the old parish Church of St. Dogmaels, it has been placed next to the account of the old church, the examination of the plaintiff's witnesses following this order of William and Mary.

On the same day in the same year, 3 William and Mary, is an examination as to the "Tithes of St. Dogmaels," in the Exchequer Depositions, taken at the Town Hall in Cardigan, before the same four Commissioners mentioned in the last case, wherein Julius Deeds, Esq., is the plaintiff, and claims the rectorial tithes of St. Dogmaels.

The first witness, James Griffiths, states that "he did pay church rate and poor rate," and also "did pay to his landlord [David Parry] for his share of tythe," which was "the fourth part of all Corn, Woole, Lambes, and other tythable things," and that he did not know the plaintiff.

---

[1] The green field.   [2] The friar's field.   [3] St. Mary's meadow.

The next witness knows all the defendants and the plaintiff, and believes the Rectory Impropriate belongs to Julius Deeds, he having been "Sessor" within the parish of St. Dogmaels, and had charged Julius Deeds, as Impropriator, in the said rates, and they had been paid; and that Julius Deeds, or his agent, received the tithe both great and small of the said parish, many other witnesses testifying to the same, especially John Morris, gentleman, of Cardigan, whose evidence is fuller and more interesting.

This is followed on the 13th February, probably 1692, by a decision of the three Judges, Sir Nicholas Lechmere, Sir John Turton, and Sir John Powell, Knights, three of the Barons of the Court of Exchequer, at Westminster. The verdict was in favour of the plaintiff, Mr. Julius Deeds, and the defendants were ordered to pay the rectorial tithes to him.

EXCH. DEPOSITIONS. William and Mary. Mich. 12.

(Writ.)

William and Mary by the grace of God King and Queen of England Scotland France and Ireland defenders of the faith etc. to our beloved Thomas Jones gent Roger Philipps gent Thomas Lloyd esq and John Parry greeting. Know ye that we having full confidence in your fidelity industry and provident circumspection in the conduct of our affairs have assigned you or two or more of you and do give and commit to you full power and authority by these presents diligently to examine any witnesses whatsoever of and upon certain articles and interrogatories as well on behalf of Julius Deeds esquire pltf as on behalf of George Lewis David Thomas William Parry Hector Gambold John Gambold William Rees Anne Martin Alice Rowland David Griffith and David Howells def^ts before you or two or more of you to be exhibited or delivered. And so we charge you that at such a day and place or days and places as you for this purpose shall provide the aforesaid witnesses before you or two or more of you you summon and cause to come and the said witnesses and every of them by themselves separately of and upon the articles or Interrogatories aforesaid upon their oaths before you or two or more of you by the holy gospels corporally to be taken you shall diligently examine or two or more of you shall examine and the examinations you shall take you shall reduce into writing on parchment and etc. when you shall have taken the same to the Barons of our Exchequer at Westminster from the day of St. Michael next ensuing in one month under your seals or two or more of you enclosed you send or two or more of you send together with the Inetrrogatories aforesaid and this writ Provided that John Woolley shall have warning by the space of fourteen days of the day and place of your first session about the execution of this writ. Witness Robert Atlyns Knt Given at Westmr the 1st July the third year of our reign

by the Barons.

Provided that before the within named defendants shall examine any witnesses by virtue of this commission they shall first pay or cause to be paid to the within-named pltf or his solicitor 9s. 4d. half of the fee for this writ.

Endd. Execution of this writ appears in certain schedules to this attached.

Thos Jones.
Ro Phillips.
Tho Lloyd.
John Parry.

Exchеq. Deposns.　3 Will. and Mary.　Mixed Counties. Mich. No. 12.
Tithes of St. Dogmael's.

Sayings and depositions of witnesses taken sworn and examined at the town-hall of Cardigan in the County of Cardigan by virtue of their Majesties Commission unto us Thomas Jones Roger Phillips Thomas Lloyd Esqrs and John Parry gent directed from their Ma^{tles} Court of Exchequer for the swearing and examining of witnesses in a matter or cause depending at issue in the said honorable Courte. Wherein Julius Deeds Esq is plaintiff and George Lewis David Thomas William Parris[1] Hector Gambold John Gambold William Rees Anne Martin Alice Rouland David Griffith and David Howells are defend^{ts} the 15th Oct 1691 and that on the plaintiffs behaulfe as followeth.

JAMES GRIFFITH of the parish of Bayvill in the county of Pembroke yeoman aged eighty years or thereabouts. To the first interrogatorie this deponent sayeth that he doth not know the plaintiff Julius Deeds in the title or heading in the said Interrogatorie named by doth know George Lewis William Parry Hector Gambold John Gambold Anne Martin Alice Rouland David Griffiths and David Howells in the said Interrogatorie named defendants. To the third interrogatorie and all the rest this deponent sayeth that he knoweth several pieces or parcels of ten^{ts} in the severall possessions of the defendants lyeing or reputed to lye within the scite close wall or precinct of the late dissolved monastery and that he hath lived for some years in Ty Hir and Manegan as dayrieman to one Robert Lloyde and this deponent sayeth that the severall pieces or parcels of land the scite close or wall was reputed and taken to be part and parcel of the parish of St. Dogmaels and did always beare offices and pay rates as pert and parcel of the said parish and that he this deponent did pay church rate and poor rate during the tyme he lived in the tenement aforesaid towards the Church and poore of the perish of St. Dogmaels and this deponent further sayeth that during the tyme that he lived in the said lands which was three years this Deponent did pay to his landlord for his share of tythe which was the fourth part of all the Corn Woole Lambes and other tythable things and this Deponent likewise sayth that the tythe of ty Hir and Manegan was some yeares worth five poundes and some yeares three poundes and further deposeth not.

JAMES ROWLAND of the parish of St. Dogmells Co. Pembroke gent aged fifty years or thereabouts deposeth that he knoweth all the defendants and hath heard of the plaintiffs. To the 2nd interrogatorie he sayth that the Rectory Impropriate of

---

[1] Parry.

St. Dogmells and doth verily believe that Julius Deeds Esq is Impropriator or Rector of the said parish and the reason of this deponents belief herein is that he this deponent hath several times been Sessor within the said parish and that he did charge the said plaintiff in the said Rate as Impropriator and that the said Rates were accordingly paid and that the said plaintiff and his agents do receave the tithe of the said parish both great and small. To the 3rd Interr he sayeth that he knoweth severall pieces or parcels of land belonging to the said Abby of St. Dogmells for about twenty years ago which is the tenements which was and is in the possession of George Lewis one of the defendants and that he heard that one Howell Thomas was leading tithe from part or parcel of the said Abby land called Arlish and that the tithe arising from the said Abby land is worth per ann four or five pounds : to the 5th and all the rest of the interrogatories saith that he knoweth the percels of land within the site close wall or precinct of the said Abbey in the possession of the said defendants doe lye or have been reputed to lye within the parish of St. Dogmells during this Deponents memorye and that the said lands was always taxed and assessed within the parish of St. Dogmells and did likewise pay all manner of Church rates and all other rates whatsoever and that the defendants which lived or doe live within the site close wall or precinct did and doe beare all maner of offices as lyeing within the said parish of St. Dogmells and to noe other parish.

JOHN GEORGE of the perish of ffishgard Co. Pembroke yeoman aged 50 yeers or thereabouts. To the first Interrogatorie sayth he hath heard Julius Deeds Esq is Impropriator. To the 2nd and all the rest of the interrogatories he sayth that he was informed that the manor or impropriation of ffishgard always held under the Abby of St. Dogmells and all the inhabitants of the parish of ffishgard doe now and always did pay all manner of decimal duties and tithes in kind to the Impropriator of the said perish ever since this deponent remembers.

OWEN JAMES of the perish of Monington yeoman aged 40 yeers saith that he knoweth the site close or wall belonging to the said Abby and that the plaintiffs agents did sett the tithe of the parish of St. Dogmells and did receave the proffitts thereof but not from the site close wall and precincts of the Abbey and sayth that if the tithes were duely and constantly payd from the lands belonging to the said Abbey it would be really worth five or six pounds per ann. to this deponents knowledge and the reason of this deponents knowledge herein is that this Deponent did live for some tyme in the premises in the pleadings mentioned viz. Ty Hyr and Manegan and his father bieng tenant in aforesaid premises about 20 years ago during the time that he continued tenant did always and yeerely pay for his share or profit of the tenth of the fourth part accrueing from the said tenement which was the fourth of all the profits unto his landlord one Robert Lloyd who held same from David Parry Esq or his predecessors and that the inhabitants residing within the said site close or wall of the Abbey of St. Dogmells have been always assessed and taxed and were alwayes reputed and taken to be part and percel of the parish of St. Dogmells and that the said Inhabitants residing within the limits aforesaid bore all manner of offices which they were charged with as inhabitants of the said parish of St. Dogmells ever since this Deponent doth remember.

JAMES MATHIAS of the perish of St. Dogmells yeoman aged 53 sayth that he knowes the impropriation or Rectory of St. Dogmells 33 years and upwards and hath heard say that the plaintiff or his agents doth receeve the tyth both great and small within the said parish excepting such messuages tenements and lands within the site close or wall in the possession of defendants and of the tythe or titheable matters accrueing from the said defend¹ were payd yeerly it would be worth four or five pounds and the reason of his knowledge is that he hath lived with his father in one of the tenements called Manegan Vawre for 7 yeers and ever since he knewe the parish of St. Dogmells the inhabitants living within the site wall or close did alwayes beare offices and payd all manner of Rates and taxations as well to the parish church of St. Dogmells as to the poor of the said parish without any distinction or separation more than other parishioners or inhabitants of the said parish.

JOHN MORRIS of the town of Cardigan gent aged 60 years sayth that he hath known the Rectory impropriate of St. Dogmells for four or five and thirty years past and doth know that the plaintiff is Impropriator or Rector of the said perish and doth and did enjoy the said parish or Rectory of St. Dogmells for 9 or 10 years past and that the said impropriation or Rectory doth extend throughout the whole parish of St. Dogmells and the reason of this deponents knowledge herein is for that the plaintiff is always assessed and taxed with the tenth part of all assessments which are imposed upon the whole perish as well within the site close wall or precinct of the said Abbey as otherwise and that the said plaintiff or his agents doth and did alwayes as often as it was charged pay the tenth part of all manner of assessments whatsoever which are imposed uppon the said parish: he knoweth the tenements called Manegan and Ty Hyr and several other percels of land in the pleading mentioned which doe not pay any tithe and which doe lye in the little parish usually soe called and that the said tenements pieces or percels of lands doe conteine above four score acres and that the said land is sowed with wheat Rye barley Pease and oats as this deponent is informed and that there are several tenements or parcels contiguous or neare to the pretended exempted lands from paying of tithe now and formerly belonging to the Abbey and called and reputed to lye within the little parish soe usually called which always pay their full tithe in kind and further sayth that he would give for the tithe or decimal duties of or from the pretended land exempted from tithe in the pleadings mentioned the sum of five or six pounds yeerely and would take a lease if graunted of one and twenty years upon the same upon the same rate. And saith that all those person living or residing on the pretended exempted lands from tith did and doe alwayes pay all manner of Rates assessments and taxations within the parish and Rectory of St. Dogmells and did or doe likewise pay all Church rates to the parish church or Rectory of St. Dogmells and did and doe beare all manner of offices as residing within the parish without any distinction whatsoever and sayth that he about two yeers ago as agent for the plaintiff did claim and demand the tith in kind from the defendant George Lewis or his wife who then held the tenements called Ty Hyr and Manegan Vawre and this deponent further sayeth he did there was a lease granted from Henry the eighth in the eight and twentieth yeer of his reign to one John Bradshaw gent conveying in it the Abbey of St. Dogmells and the manner of ffishgard among other things which manner of fishgard pey their tith or decimal duties in kinde as this deponent is credibly informed.

JOHN AP JOHN of the town of Cardigan yeoman aged 49 sayth that there are several tenements lying and being within the Little parish soe commonly called which pay their tith corn in kind and the reason of his knowledge herein is that he hath been leading and gathering of tith Corn in a certain hamlet called the Little parish hamlett to the plaintiff or his agent's use.

EXCHEQ. BOOK OF DECREES. Lib. IV, No. 15.

13th Feb. Hillary Term. William and Mary.

Whereas Julius Deeds Esq pltf did in Michaelmas Terme in the 2nd year of their now Maties reigne exhibit his English Bill in this courte against George Lewis David Thomas William Parry Hector Gambold John Gambold William Rees Anne Martin Alice Rowlande David Griffith David Howell def^ts thereby setting forth that the pltf for term years last before the exhibiting of the bill had been lawfull owner and proprietor of the Rectory and personage of St. Dogmells in the county of Pembroke and thereby had bene intituled to all tithes both great and small yeerly happening within that Rectory or parish or ye titheble places thereof and that ye defts had yearlye during the said tyme severally occupyed great quantities of land within the said parish of St. Dogmells and had thereon yearly great quantityes of corne hay and other tythable matters ye tithes of wch they ought partly to have paid the pltf in kind or some satisfaction for the same wch they had severally refused pretending an exemption from payment of any manner of tithes their said lands formerly belonging to some Abby or by some otherwayes or meanes were discharged of tithes whereas if their lands did formerly belong to some Abby at ye dissolucon thereof yet by ye law of ye land their lands ought not to be discharged of tithes ye said Abbey being one of ye lesser Abbies. Therefore that ye def^ts might sett forth ye pticular cause of their exemption and might satisfie ye pltf for ye values of their said tithes was ye scope of ye said bill. To wch bill the saied def^ts having appeared put in two severall answers and thereby said that they had held for ye respective tymes therein sett forth severall percells of land as tenants under David Parry esq and had heard and believed that part of their said land were percells of ye possessions of ye late dissolved Abby of St. Dogmells enjoyed by the Abbots thereof and within the gate or wall of the Abby and always in their own manurance and said yt some part of their lands wch lyeth out of ye close wall or precinct of ye said Abby of St. Dogmells doth lye within the said Rectory of St. Dogmells and thet tithes have bine constantly paid for the same but ye def^ts said thet other part of their lands doe lye within the site wall close or precinct of the said Abby and for such part thereof noe manner of tithes or anything in lieu thereof were ever paid or demanded for the same but have alwayes bine exempted or discharged from tithes either by real Composicion or by some usage law custom pscription or by some other wayes or meanes and the def^ts did by their said answers severally sett forth ye valewes of ye tithes of suche part of their lands as lye within the scite close wall or precinct of ye said Abby. To wch answer the pltf replyed and the def^ts rejoyned and divers witnesses being examined in ye said cause and duly published ye said cause came this day to be heard in ye Exchequer Chamber at Westmr before Sr Nicholas Lechmere Sr John Turton and Sr John Powell Knts three of ye Barons of this Court where upon opening of ye said bill by Mr Dodd and of the def^ts answer by Mr Lloyd and heareing Mr Ettrick and ye said Mr Dodd for the pltf and of Sr Robert Sawyer Knt and ye said Mr Lloyd for ye def^{ts} and on debate of ye matter for asmuche as ye def^{ts} insisted that ye lands in question were ye lands lyeing within the scite close wall or precinct of the said Abby of St. Dogmells and were always thought to be exempted from ye payment of tithes or anything in lieu thereof ye same being part of ye possessions of ye said Abby of St. Dogmells at ye dissolucon thereof and always in ye manurance of ye Abbots thereof but it appearing to the Court that ye said Abby was one of ye lesser Abbyes and was dissolved by ye statute of ye 27th of Henry ye 8th the Court was therefore of opinion thet though it did not appeare thet the said lands had for many years past paid any tithes yet thet ye said lands in question ought and are by law lyable to ye payment of tithes to ye pltf as Impropriator of ye said parish of St. Dogmells. It is therefore ordered adjudged and decreed by ye Court thet ye said def^{ts} do severally accompt and pay to ye said pltf for ye values of their tithes ariseing upon ye said lands lyeing within the scite close wall or precinct of ye said Abby for ye respective tymes and according to ye respective values in their said answers sett forth the said pltf being willing to accept the same at those values to witt ye said def^t George Lewis the sum of £2 5s. the said def^t David Thomas the sum of 12s. the said def^t William Parry the sum of 4s. 8d. the said def^t Hector Gambold the sum of 12s. the said def^t John Gambold the sum of £1 10s. the said def^t William Rees the sum of 15s. the said def^t Anne Martin the sum of £5 the said def^t Alice Rowland the sum of 10s. The said def^t David Griffith the sum of 15s. And the def^t David Howells the sum of tenn shillings.

CHAPTER XIX.

SIDELIGHTS.

S T. MARY'S ABBEY, St. Dogmaels, when restored after the Irish invasion of 1138, must have been a fine building. In 1118 there were twenty-six monks and an abbot, also doubtless many lay brothers. Their numbers must have increased considerably, as the remains show that the buildings were both large and numerous.

In 1188 the Abbey was sufficiently large to house Archbishop Baldwin, Gerald, and their retinues, and their cuisine was such that they were able to entertain them well. The steps closed in the time of Mr. Vincent's predecessor,[1] which were reputed to lead down to the golden coffin, in which, legend states that, an Irish Princess, who came over with her followers from Ireland, was buried, really led to large ovens, situated in all probability close to the old kitchen of the Abbey, now buried under the debris of centuries. The adventurous man,[1] who descended these steps, in order to find out what was there, unhappily died three weeks later, poisoned by the foul air of this long-unused stairway and passage. Unhappily the then vicar closed this stairway, so as to prevent any further misadventures; it is represented as having been in the middle of the orchard, which now flourishes, among the ruins of the old abbey.

When digging a grave,[2] some sixty years ago, opposite the vestry door of the present church, and about eight to ten feet distant, a large hole was discovered which led down to some part of the old buildings. A similar hole was also found on the south side of the church, and a stone arch was discovered, about nine years ago, five feet below the surface at the west end of the church, when digging a grave.

The enclosure surrounding the Abbey contained about forty acres.

---

[1] Capt. Jones, of "Cardigan Bay," to whom I am indebted for this account, was a friend and next-door neighbour of this man.

[2] I am indebted to Capt. Jones, of Bryn Teify, for this and the two following items of information.

Half of the gravestone of Mr. John Bradshaw, Junr., now rests at the end of the rockery in the vicarage garden, the inscription being as clear as on the day it was cut.

The old altar slab stands on end in the orchard; at each corner of the slab there is a cross chiselled.

Evidently from the broken bits of carved stone lying about, and forming the before-mentioned rockery, these Tironian Benedictines excelled as stone-masons. It is highly probable that they were also as skilful in the carving of wood, though of this there is now no proof remaining, so that the old Abbey may be regarded as a fine group of buildings, standing in a lovely wooded valley. Its present ruinous condition is more likely to be due to the ruthless hand of man than to the ravages of passing years.

A stone lately found, used latterly as a gate-post at Manaian fawr, has been placed near the old Sagranus stone in the Abbey grounds. This stone has in all probability been removed, like the Sagranus stone, from the old burial ground of St. Dogmaels Religious House.

According to an early rent roll, "the Abbey at its foundation"[1] owned one hundred and five houses, and a yearly revenue of £95 os. 2d. in St. Dogmaels.

There still remain of the ruins, the west and north walls of what was the north transept, and of various buildings attached to the east wall. The chapel was evidently cruciform in shape, and had a very large choir.

In the west wall are remains of a large window (see photograph), but all the tracery has now fallen away.

The door in the west end of the north wall has a jamb moulding, and this had formerly a ball flower moulding round it, an ornament peculiar to the decorated style of architecture (1272-1377). Other additions must have been made to the Abbey during this period as well as in Henry VII's time. The north wall has also recesses, at one time containing the tombs of the abbots, probably either destroyed at the dissolution or else by Cromwell's soldiers. Formerly within the choir there were two canopied recesses, which are reported to have contained the effigies of Martin and his son, Robert, who, as is already known, were buried in the middle of the choir.

In the south wall were recesses, apparently used as sediliæ,[2] and the remains of a piscina,[2] also a recess about five feet deep by fourteen feet long, in the centre of the wall, probably used as a confessional.

---

[1] The author thinks this "foundation" is probably an error for "dissolution."   [2] Fenton.

Fenton writes " that the North transept has undergone considerable alterations at a later period, and had been used as a lady chapel, and has the same kind of recess (sepulchral) on each side of the altar, some rich key stones, ornamented with a winged lion and an angel holding an escutcheon." The roof is described as " of stone, and of a good design of fan tracery groining, springing from richly ornamented corbels, only a few feet however of the springers of this rich groining remain. The windows of this transept are of the same date and character as of the roof, namely, the reign of Henry VII. On the south side there remains part of the cloister walls, and the south wall of the refectory, this portion is very interesting, having the stairway constructed in the wall leading to the remains of the pulpit, which had a window at the back. . . . On the same line about one hundred and fifty foot east of the refectory is another building in more perfect preservation 38 foot long by 20 ft. 6 inches wide, it seems to have been another chapel having remains of a piscina, sediliæ, etc. It seems to have been of an earlier date than the larger cruciform chapel and built of better masonry, it has alternate lines of dark and light stone, the roof also being of stone in the form of a pointed arch; but without ribs, and has been ingeniously constructed to avoid all outward thrust of the walls. Over the panel of the east window is a corbel, supported by an angel."

The refectory is still perfect; it is used as a barn; it was formerly well lighted by a " handsome end window, as well as side ones of fine tracery," and had a " lofty vaulted roof." Over this end window is a stone with a date cut, which, owing to its height and the lack of light, is difficult to make out.

The church of Fenton's day was, Fenton writes: "Evidently raised from the ruins of the Abbey," as the stonework of " the windows of the chancel exhibit remains of workmanship that could never have been meant originally to furnish such an edifice."

The fragments, formerly among the ruins, consisted of Norman, transition, early English, decorated, and perpendicular styles, proving that the Abbey was enlarged or embellished from time to time. In the grounds are a mutilated coffin lid, with an early Greek cross, and another slab with the shaft of a cross, both leaning against the wall, near the Sagranus stone. The present church was built in 1847. In Fenton's time the ruins of St. Thomas' Church could still be traced, and it was then called " Yr hen Eglwys."

Fenton was in error as to his reading of the date of Mr. Bradshaw's death as 1538, it being 1588. He continues:

" In Queen Elizabeth's time it (St. Dogmaels) was deemed a corporation, and had at the first establishment of it, one hundred and five houses, as may be gathered from an ancient rental of the town. It was governed by a portreeve, yearly elected at the leet court after St. Meigan's Fair, and William Bradshaw was then lord thereof, with all the power and priveledges of the abbot. His mansion-house was the abbey. This magnificent pile was charmingly situated on a gentle elevation, in a richly wooded and watered dingle, bounded by high hills on every side, but that which admits of an opening to the navigable Teivy whose every tide administered to the luxury of the convent. . . . ."

On page 301 of Fenton one reads " Nor must I omit here to enumerate amongst the other insignia of royalty of this lordship marcher (Cemaes), and peculiar to it alone, the patronage of the bards, with the adjudication and disposal of the silver harp, an honour, except in this province, confined to the prince's palace, and one of the brightest gems in his diadem, yet here supposed immemorially to be suffered to attach to the reguli of Dyved, and their later descendants the nobles of Cemaes, many of whom had themselves been bards of eminence, such as Gwynvardd and his son, Cuhylin Vardd, names to which the people were so endeared, that the Normans from pride as well as policy could do no less than comply with and continue a custom sanctioned by the heads of that tribe, whose subjection he took pains to conciliate. The silver harp in the absence of the lord was placed in the custody of his monastery of St. Dogmaels, the abbot being his representative at the Eisteddfod, whenever he was summoned to parliament or to the field."

The after history of this harp cannot be traced, though there are rumours that it was found fifty or sixty years ago, together with other hidden silver. George Owen also notes this silver harp as belonging to the Barony, and that it was deposited at St. Dogmaels Abbey for safe custody during the absences of the Lords of Cemaes.

In the " Register Book of Kemeys "[1] is a post mortem inquisition on William Martin, by order of Edward II, King of England, held at the Court at Newport, Cemaes, by John of Hampton, Escheator to the King, May 14th, 10 Edward II. Amongst the thirteen sworn were John Peverel and William Picton; all declared on oath that William Martin held from the King in chief, the day he died, twenty knights' fees in Cemaes, of which the Abbot of St. Dogmaels held one called Cassia, valued at 100 shillings; also Adam de Roche held three fees of the same William, namely, Maenclochog, valued at one hundred shillings; Monington, eighty shillings; and Randykaith (?), three pounds. This is followed by another very similar document.

In a deed 14th June, 37 Edward III, the King confirms a grant of James, Lord Audeley, one of the witnesses being the Lord John Abbot of St. Dogmaels, who also did homage to the Lord of Cemaes, at Newport, on the feast of St. Barnabas, June 11th, 37 Ed. III.

---

[1] George Owen.

The following list of Abbots contains all that are so far traceable : —

Fulchardus (first abbot)   1118
Hubert   ...   . after   1138
Andrew   ...   . before   1188
Walter (kinsman of Gerald the Barri)...   before and after   1200
John Le Rede   ...   . died   1330
John (did homage at Newport)   1364
Phillip   ...   . about   1415
Walter   ...   .   „   1429
Lewis Barron   1504
John Wogan   ...   . died before   1520
William Hire (last abbot)   1520-1536

Of the Priors of Pill, so far only three have been discovered—

Phillip Prior   ...   . about   1200
David Luce   1504
William Watt (last Prior)   ...   .   till   1534

Whilst Nicholas, 1504, is the only Prior of Caldey recorded, so completely have all traces of the history of the island vanished.

In October, 1357, in the Papal Registers, the Vicarage of St. Thomas the Martyr is recorded as given to Philip Henry.

There is little fresh in " The Acta Sanctorum," 23rd June, Vol. III, of the Bolandus, beyond the fresh spelling of Rammaes for Cemaes, and that the Barony contained three towns,[1] twenty military stations,[2] and twenty-six parishes. Also that Bernard, Bishop of St. David's, was a Norman by birth, Chaplain to Henry I, and was consecrated Bishop of St. David's July 12th, 1115; but the account given therein of Tiron is erroneous as regards dates.

An interesting bit of information is found in the Dimetian Code, namely, that there were seven Bishops' houses in Dyved (Pembrokeshire), the sixth being at Llan Deulydog,[3] and that " the Abbot of Teulydog[4] should be graduated in literary degrees."

Referring again to George Owen's " Pembrokeshire," under his description of the geology of the county, and that of Cemaes and St. Dogmaels in particular, it is noted that—

There is a " kynde of freestone which for fignes and collor passeth all other yet spoken of " [found in many parts of Moylgrove and at Pantsaeson] " which is a blood red stone, etc.," next " slates & tylinge stones black and blewe." Then there is a

---

[1] Of which two belonged to the Abbey.   [2] Knights' fees.
[3] Llandudoch or St. Dogmaels.   [4] St. Dogmaels.

" russet stone, more lardge and roughher than the other two, but more profitable to the owner, soe his house be tymbered thereafter, and the lattes (laths) and nayle agreable. This stone is digged verye lardge, three foote & some fowre foote longe and layed on of that biggnes cleaveth more roughe then the rest, and therfore the lyme taking better hold then betweene the smoeth stone dureth the longer on the house . . . . with these the great fratry [refectory] at St. Dogmells is covered many yeres seethence ; the best stones of this kinde are found at Pont y gwen undy [Pant y Grwndy = valley of the ridge house] Coom Degwell [Cwm Tegwell = Valley of St. Dogmael] Llantood Henllys [The Old Court—The home of George Owen Lord of Cemaes] and almost in every quarry between the ryver of Nevarne [Nevern] and the sea." ·

Nearly all the houses, cottages, outbuildings, and walls were built of this stone in St. Dogmaels, and around in the sixteenth century, " It is founde to lye in great flakes alwaies leanninge to the South "; and now follows a curious explanation which George Owen gives : —

" This is thought to be doon by the violence of the generall flood, which at the departinge thereof breake southward and tare the erthe in pieces, and seperated the Ilandes from the Contynent, and made the hills and valleies as we now find them."

Further on in a chapter on the chief rivers of the shire we come to the exact whereabouts of the River Bryan.

From Aberych[1] forward the river Teify " is the lanskarre[2] between Pembrok & Cardigan Sheers . . . & soe passinge down under Leghrid[3] bridge a little beneath receiveth a brooke from the south called Morgeney."

The name of this brook is exceedingly interesting, dating from the time of Howel dda. It takes its name from Morganeu, or Morgenau, the judge summoned by Howel dda, with six of the wisest laymen, etc., when he made his " book of the law " in Dyfed, and this book was compiled by Morganeu and his son, Cyfnerth, two of the wisest men in the kingdom.
After receiving the Morganeu—

" It approacheth Killgarron[4] betweene great deepe and narrowe hills, over which is frame the weare of Killgarron strongly built of stone and tymber worke, where abaundance of most excellent & sweet salmons are taken . . .a little beneath, it receaveth from the southwest a rillet called Pliskogh and there hence proceedeth downewards by the Forest . . . where at the lower part it receaveth the brooke Bryan coming from Diffrin [Dyffryn] Breyan, which there parteth the hundreds of Kemes & Killgarron . . . before it cometh to the barre yt receaveth in a rill Meynian Moore [Manaian Marsh] & so to the sea."

---

[1] Abercych.   [2] Boundary.   [3] Llechryd.   [4] Cilgerran.

It is between this Manaian Marsh and the sea that the " Poppit " lays, mentioned as " Potpit "[1] in one of the grants; the sands also on the same side of the river are called the Poppit Sands.

George Owen in his notes on the Tallage for redemption of the great Sessions in old times, within the County of Pembroke, writes : " I finde also in the auncient booke of Receipts of Pembrokeshire of my father William Owen at the feast of St. Michael 18 Henry 8 " . . . as to the paying of knights fees " and this way payed by the Knightes Fees as followeth at the rate of ix[s] a knightes fee every paiement of the five paiements " [about fifteen entries]
" Abbey of St. Dogmaels v shillings.
" Lordship of Monachlog v shillings.
" This Tallage was paied in five paiementes, twice every yeare at Michaelmas & Easter as appeareth by my fathers booke of Receipts 18, 19 & 20 Hen. 8."

So that the Abbot of St. Dogmaels had to pay tallage for his knight's fee of Cassia.

In the " Dale Castle MS.," a William de Cantington is mentioned as Lord of the Manor of Eglwyswrw, in 1200.

In the Lords of Kemes tracts it is recorded :

" 1st. That the Abbott of St. Dogmaells holdeth one knightes ffee called Cassia by giving of free alms[2] and yeeldeth nothinge to the lord, and that the same is worth yeerely to the Abbott in all issues c[s]."

This Manor of Cassia is mentioned in " Pembrock and Kemes," fol. 3a, as one of the eight " meane fees holden of the Baronye " which were manors subject to the High Court of Kemes.

In the " Carte Baroniae de Kemes," p. 29, it is stated that Cassia belonged to the Abbot of St. Dogmaels, " is like to be a knightes ffee of one Alen," mentioned in the grant of Robert Fitzmartin, and further " that the foresaid Abbott of St. Dogmaells holdeth half of Kefenlhymwyth [Kenth limuth, in the Parish of Llanfair nant y Gof], alias Fishgard by ffree almes geeveinge & yieldeth nothinge to the Lord out of the same yeerely."

There were two chapels belonging to the Abbey in St. Dogmaels, " Chappell Cranok " and " Chappell Degwel." These two chapels were " pilgrimage chapels," and were also used for solemn processions on holy days. Whether " Capel Cranok " was the name of the chapel at Hendre, which belonged to the

---

[1] Potpit is given as another name for Pwllcam (the Crooked Pool) in Elizabeth's time.

[2] The tenure in frank-almoign (or free alms) was expressly excepted from the abolition of feudal tenures by 12 Car. II, cap. 24, and still exists in a modified form. By it the religious houses and parochial clergy held lands by the service of praying for the souls of the donor and of his heirs. *Vide* note by Dr. Henry Owen in George Owen's " Pembrokeshire."

Abbey, is not so easy now to know for a certainty, though Hendre appears to be far larger than a pilgrimage chapel. St. Dogmaels was divided into four hamlets—Bridge End, Abbey, Pant y groes, and Cipyn, the two former being now in the Municipal Borough of Cardigan. The ancient and conventional division of St. Dogmaels was " Y Plwyf Mawr (the great parish) and Y Plwyf Bach (the small parish)," by a line drawn from Cwm Iôn to Cwm Deifo, through the lands of Trewidwal, Pen y Wern, Tirion Uchaf, Pantirion, etc., all the land between this line and the sea being called Y Plwyf Bach. At a vestry, July 15th, 1741, held in the Parish Church, St. Dogmaels, a separate account was brought for Y Plwyf Mawr; and according to a pamphlet of Mr. Vincent's, called Pwll y Granant, " the inhabitants of ' Y Plwyf Bach ' have then (1856) a right of summer pasture for their young cattle on the Manor of Mynachlog Ddu, which formerly belonged to the monastery, and afterwards to Mr. John Bradshaw."

In 1599 St. Dogmaels, in Cemaes hundred, had, according to George Owen's " Taylors Cussion " : —

Population.	Househoulders.	Plowes.	Dairies.	Cartes or Truckles.
1,370.	510.	510.	120.	0.

From the number of householders compared to the population, one would gather that only adults were included, as there is only an average of $2\frac{7}{10}$ persons to each house. The larger houses and farms, where there would be grown-up sons and daughters, and also servants kept, would easily account for these few extra adults. The population in 1801 was 1,379; the parish rates in 1803, £400; the parish contains about 6,000 acres of land, also there is a chalybeate spring.

Salmon Fishing. Drawing in the Seine on the Poppitt Sands

CHAPTER XX.

"FISHERIES AND FISHINGS."

HAVING now finished the history of the Abbey, it may be interesting to notice some of the products of the neighbourhood shortly after the dissolution.

The fisheries, mentioned in various grants to the Abbey, were undoubtedly the same as the salmon and sewin fisheries of to-day; also it is most probable that the very same kind of seine or shot fawr was used by the monks at the Abbey, as is used by the fishermen at St. Dogmaels to-day.

Further, in the grants will be noted that besides the "Fisheries," "fishings" were also granted; by this may be gathered, the herrings, mackerel, gurnards, whiting, soles, turbot, plaice, lobsters and crabs, that are caught in the bay, together with the silver bass, grey mullet, and eels that are caught in the tidal waters of the river, of all of which George Owen gives such a delightful account, especially his quaint quotation from Darion (? Claude Dariot) regarding the lobster.

The principal industry of St. Dogmaels is this salmon and sewin fishery, which, in fact, gives a name to the village, which is often called "the fishing village" of St. Dogmaels. The Teify ranks as one of the best salmon rivers of Great Britain, except at Christchurch, Hants, there is no salmon that can compare with it, for the excellence of its taste, in all Great Britain. In the photograph appended some of the St. Dogmaels fishermen will be seen drawing in their net, whilst a man in the boat is holding up a small salmon, already taken.

Near where the Bryan enters the Teify, the men fish in a more primitive manner, namely, two men, each in a coracle, paddle down the river with a net spread between the two coracles. The Teify has been celebrated for the flavour of its salmon for many hundred years; even in the twelfth century Gerald, the Welshman, mentions that the Teify was famous for salmon, beavers, and otters; the beavers, however, are long since extinct.

Many lobsters and crabs are still caught off Cemaes Head, which was within the domains of the old Abbey; herrings and mackerel, in their season, come in large shoals along the coast, and are caught by the St. Dogmaels fishermen; the mackerel come in so close to the beach[1] even, that they could be caught with a prawning net from the sands, being most probably scared into such shallow water by the dog fish that are so numerous off this coast.

George Owen writes of the shoals of herrings as follows:—

" Also there is the great aboundance of heringes taken all alonge the coast round about the whole sheere, as if the same were enclosed in with a hedge of heringes which beinge in great store & sold to partes beyond sea procureth also some store of money."

George Owen writes in his "History of Pembrokeshire" that—

" Lamperies also used to be found in the Teify. Lobsters and crabbes are also found in the sea klyffes and other places, and are verye sweete and delicate meate, and plentie liken. The lobster sayeth Darion (probably Claude Dariot, a French physician, A.D. 1594) sent whole on the table hath iij special qualities, for saith he, he yieldeth exercise, sustenance and contemplacion; exercise in crackinge his legges and clawes, sustenance by eatinge his meate, contemplacion in beholdinge the curiouse worke of his compleate Armour both in hue and workmanship by tasses (tassel the upper thigh) vambraces (upper arm plate) powldrons (shoulder plate) cousbes (thigh plate) gauntlettes (iron glove) and gorgettes (throat guard) curiously wrought and forged by the most admirable workman in the world also shrimps, mussels and limpets etc. Lastly I will end my fish meale with the iij strange nature fishes that is the seale or sea calfe, the porpoise and the thorne pole (grampus)."

In another place he writes regarding the market that used to be held in St. Dogmaels that:—

" There hath been in times past diverse marketts used in diverse other places, and by reason of the powertie of the townes, and inaptness of the places altogether decayed." Among these townes that formerly had markets he mentions St. Dogmaels, and continues: " Where [St. Dogmaels] by reporte of auncient men, marketts have beene kept in old time."

St. Dogmaels is not only no longer a Borough, but is also no longer a market town, so greatly has it decayed since the time of Henry VIII. Two of the eight Boroughs of Cemaes were held by the Abbey, namely, St. Dogmaels and Fishguard.

The upper parts of Pembrokeshire, as Cemaes and Cilgerran, used, in the time of Queen Elizabeth, to sell their wool each week at Cardigan market; it

---

[1] So close, in fact, that on the Poppit sands the author has seen them in water of the depth of five inches, and has known of 278 being caught in half an hour with two prawning nets in one of the pools among the rocks further up the coast.

was bought by north Welshmen, and by them woven into white cloths, which they again sold to men from Shrewsbury. At the same period were sold in Cemaes, corn, cattle, butter, and cheese, the cheese being sometimes sent to Ireland for the use of the Queen's garrisons there.

Butter is still sent away weekly to Bristol and Cardiff; but the cheese now made is used locally. Pigs are from time to time sent to England. There is also an annual Wool Fair, held in Cardigan, to which the St. Dogmaels farmers bring their wool.

Also in Queen Elizabeth's reign great droves of sheep and lambs were driven into England to be sold, and also droves of pigs, which brought money into the country.

Now it is chiefly cattle that are sent to England to be fattened.

Amongst other products of Cemaes, George Owen again writes :—

" It also uttereth store of hides, tallow, and sheepe skinnes and lambe skinns ; this last commoditie litle regarded but such as the trade thereof hath enriched divers men, neither will I here laye down what somes of money as I have hard hath ben paied in these three sheeres for lambeskinns in one Maie by Londoners."

Numbers of excellent and sturdy cobs and mountain ponies are largely bred on the lands formerly belonging to the Abbey, as well as in Cardiganshire, being chiefly sold at Wrexham.

ORGAN
SHIRE.

Towy Haven
S. Ismaels poynt

IA
s
VM.

INDEX.

Abbéville, 31
Abbot of Glastonbury, 60
—— President of the English Benedictines, 158
—— of St. Dogmaels, Andrew, 70, 124, 127, 217
—————— Dom Lewis Baron, 91, 92, 217
—————— Fulchardus, 42, 47, 217
—————— Hubert, 52, 53, 217
—————— John de la Rede, 84, 85, 217
—————— The Lord John, 216, 217
—————— Philip, 89, 217
—————— Walter, 68, 69, 71, 72, 73, 75, 76, 77, 78, 217
—————— Walter, 217
—————— William Hire, 95, 97, 98, 102, 111, 217
—— of St. Cyprian, Raymond, 31
—— of Tavistock, 80
—— of Tiron, Bernard (Bernardus), 17, 30, 31, 32, 33, 34, 35, 36, 37, 41, 42, 57, 59, 139, 159
—————— Charles de Ronsard, 36
—————— Geoffrey le Gros, 31, 32, 36, 37, 42
—————— John, 36
—————— John II of Chartres, 35, 37
—————— Hippolyte d'Este, Cardinal of Ferrara, 36
—————— Lionel Grimault, 35
—————— Louis le Crevaut, 35
—————— René de Laubier, 36
—————— Stephen, 35
—————— William, 2nd Abbot, 31, 37, 38, 42, 43, 44, 45, 46, 47, 55
—————— William, 4th or 5th Abbot, 35
—— of Whitland, Peter, 69, 70, 77
—— of Worcester, 69
Abbot's Parke, 103, 115
Abbot's Wood, 116
Abercych, 218
Abergwayne, 28
Aberteivi (Cardigan), 49, 66, 67
Aberystwyth, 12
Acrani, 185
Acta Sanctorum, 217
Act of Supremacy, 94, 96, 140, 169, 172
Adam, the Clerk, 127
Adela, daughter of William the Conqueror, 34

Adelaide (Adeleya), Queen of Henry I, 44, 46, 47
Advowson, 130
Alan, 47, 219
Alen Basset, 58
Ales, 25
Alfordi, Michael, 13
Alfred de Bennevilla (? Bayvill), 47
Allen, Romilly, Catalogue of Early Christian Monuments in Pembrokeshire, 172
Altar Slab, 214
Amsterdam, 9
Anaraud, 49
Anchorite, The, 77
Ancient Petitions, 52, 79, 82, 132
Angels' Cairn, 12
Angharad, daughter of Gerald de Windsor, 66
Angharad, daughter of Rhys ap Gryffydd, 26, 56
Anglesey, 62
Annable Pull, 134
Annales Cambriae, 24, 49, 64
Anne, Queen of Henry VIII, 10, 94, 95, 96, 140
Antiquarian Find, 200
Arcalon, 159, 160, 161, 162
Arcelo, 166, 167
Archæologia Cambrensis, 15, 16, 20, 170
Archbishop of Canterbury, Baldwin, 66, 67, 213
—————— Becket, Thomas à, 113
—————— Courtney, 86
—————— Cranmer, 91
—————— Hubert, 75
—————— R, 125, 128
—————— Warham, 91, 92, 139
—————— 68, 69, 70, 72, 73, 77, 95, 140, 141
—— Dublin, Brother William, elect of, 125, 128
—— Rouen, 57, 58
—— York, Henry, elect of, 125, 128
—— York, William, 48, 95, 140, 141
Archdeacon of Brecon (Gerald), 75, 76, 77, 78
—— Buckingham, 69, 71
—— Cardigan, 79, 81, 82, 156, 172
—— Carmarthen, 72, 76
—— Leighlyn, 164

Archdeacon of St. David's, 78, 79, 81, 82,
        112, 136, 155, 156
Archdeaconry of Cardigan, 79, 81, 82, 88, 90
—— St. David's, 145
Archdale's Monasticon Hibernicon, 161, 163
Arcisses, 33, 34
Arcol Llaw Hir, 19
Ardmayne, 165, 166
Arlaise, 202, 203, 209
Arles (Arlys), 101, 103, 115
Arnard plas Roos, 103, 116
Arnold, 130
Arrears, 118, 131, 134, 146, 155
Arthur, 14, 28
Atlantic, The, 12
Atlyns, Robert, Knt., 207
Audeleigh, James, 83, 84, 85, 216
—— Nicholas, 83, 85
Audleys, 57
Augmentation Ministers' Account, 101, 104
—— Office Leases, 173, 174
—— Rolls, 177
Augustine, The Prior, 53
Avignon, 133
Azor, son of Totus, 61

Baare, Manor of, 181, 183
Baglas, Walter, 125, 127
Bakerlineran, 125, 128
Baldwin (see Archbishop of Canterbury).
—— Count of Albimare, 58
—— de Riverius, Earl of Exeter, 60
—— The Chaplain, 58
Ballaghkeen, 161
Ballane, 160, 163
Balledyne, 160, 163
Ballenemonery, 165, 166
Ballflower Moulding, 214
Ballydonagh, 163
Bandon, 165
Bangor, The elect Bishop of, 75
Barbour, John, 144
Bardsey Island, 12, 168
Barlow, ex-Monk of St. Dogmaels,
        John, 176, 177
—— Roger, 158
—— Thomas, 158
Barnard, Hugh, 151, 152
Barnstaple, 56
Baronia de Kemes, 50, 53, 219
Barony of Ballaghkeen, 159
Barony of Cemaes, 24, 25, 27, 57, 84, 135,
        217, 219
Barret, John, 78
Barry (Barri), Raymond, Lord, 159, 161, 163
Barry, Cecilia, 159, 160, 161, 162
Barry Island, 66
Barry, Rinoc, 159, 160, 161, 162
Bartholomew, Bishop of Exeter, 29
Baskerfelde, James, 112
Basset, Allen, 58
—— Thomas, 58
Battle Abbey Rolls, 22, 23, 50
Battle of Hastings, 23
Batton, Philip, Reeve of Pill, 130

Bayeux, 56
Bayvill, 201
—— Church of, 96, 101, 105, 106, 118, 119,
        173, 174, 175, 178, 179, 180, 181, 182,
        183
Beance, 30
Beatrice, mother of Count Rotrou, 33
Beauchamp, Wm., Earl of Warwick, 128
—— Walter de, The King's Steward of the
        Household, 128
Benedictines, 55, 157, 158, 167
Benedictione Dei (? Bective) Abbey, 164
—— Reformed, 17
Ber in Grenebi, 61
Bereford, William de, 129
Bernard, Abbot of Tiron, 17, 30, 31, 32, 33,
        34, 35, 36, 37, 41, 42, 57, 59, 139, 159
—— Bishop of St. David's, 45, 47, 52, 53,
        55, 217
Bernadite, 17
Beynon, John, 204
Bishop of Bath and Wells, R of, 47, 52
—— Chartres, 32, 34
—— Civitatem, 164
—— Clonfert, 164
—— Durham, A of, 47, 125, 128
—— Ely, Eustach of, 58, 69, 71, 72, 78
—— Ely, W of, 125, 128
—— Exeter, Bartholomew of, 29
—— Ferns, Thomas Den, 160, 161, 162, 163
—— Hereford, 69
—— Llandaff, D of, 168
—— London, R of, 125, 128
—— Norwich, W of, 48
—— Rome, 95, 140, 141
—— St. David's (1281), 54
—— —— Bernard, 45, 47, 52, 53, 55, 217
—— —— David, 77
—— —— Guy, 133
—— —— Peter, 75
—— —— Thomas, 47
—— —— Thomas Wallensis, 124
—— Saverino, 58
—— Tivy, 164
—— Winchester, J, 47, 48
—— Worcester, 69, 72, 78
Black Grange, Nigra Grangia, 169
Black Marble, 174
Blaen, 9
Bleanban, 110
Blaenerth, 110
Blaenpant, 185
Blaen y cowrse glethe, 107, 121
Blakeman, Rd., 125, 127
Blakewell Grove, 97, 98
Blandina, wife of Adam de Roche, 124, 126
Bliss, W. H., 78
Bloeb, Ralph, 128
Blois, 34
Bolandus, 217
Boleyn, Anne, 10, 94, 95, 96, 140
Bologna, 164
—— St. Stephen's, 164
Bollyncollen, 163
Bonkommes, Priory of, 55

Book of Extracts, Records of St. David's, 187
Book of Receipts of Pembrokeshire, 219
Bordde, David, 149
Borke, Roberic, 159, 160, 161, 162
Boundaries of the Abbey lands, 45
Bourgo de Neville, 53, 54
Bourne and Deeping Lordship, 43
Bowen, James, 154
—— James Bevan, 28
—— John, 200
—— Morgan, 205
—— Thomas George, 192
Brabazon, Roger and William, 128, 166
Bradshaws, 107
Bradshaw, Alice, 185
—— Edward, 181, 183, 184, 185
—— Elizabeth, 181, 182, 183, 184, 185
—— George, 170
—— James, 175, 177, 179, 180, 181, 182, 185
—— Joan, 183
—— John, Sen., 49, 100 to 107, 113 to 119, 122, 168 to 170, 173 to 177, 185, 210, 220
—— —— Compotus of, 101, 104, 114
—— —— Postmorten Examination of, 174, 176
—— John, Jun., 169, 173, 174, 175, 177, 178, 179, 180, 181, 182, 185, 212
—— John, the Regicide, 185
—— John, William's nephew, 193
—— Roger, 168, 169
—— William, 175, 177, 179, 180, 181, 182, 183, 184, 185, 187, 188, 189, 204, 215
Branwen, 62
Brecon, 73
—— John, Prior of, 76
Brenchley, Mrs., 186
Brian, Guy de (6 Guys in succession), 46, 125, 128
Briscwm (Brwyscwm), 101, 103, 116
Bristol, 223
Brokholes, John, Attorney, 135, 137
Bromfield, Master J of, 76
Brut Ieuan Brechfa, 24
Bryan (Braian, Broyan) River, 28, 45, 46, 62, 218, 221
Brychan Brycheiniog, 11, 12
Brynach, 12
Buckfastleigh Abbey, 41
Buckinghamshire, 60, 61
Bull, John, 149
Burghley, Wm., Baron 182
Bushell, The Rev. D., D.D., 169
Butler, Morris, 150, 151
Bulton, David, 131
Bwlch Pant y groes, 17

Cadell, 49
Cadwaladr, 49
Cadwgan, 170
Caen, 22, 58
Caeran, Traditions of, 18, 19
Caldey,
—— Chaplain or Curate of, 102, 114, 117, 119
—— Church of, 80, 104, 105, 118, 119

Caldey Island, 28, 45, 47, 82, 100, 103, 104, 105, 106, 113, 115, 116, 119, 135, 168, 169, 170, 171, 174, 177, 187
—— Prior of, Dubricius, 169
—— —— of Dom Nicholas, 91, 92, 217
—— —— Hugh Eynon, 172
—— Priory of, 96, 168, 169, 172
Calendar of Close Rolls, 84
—— of Documents (France), 41, 44, 57, 58
—— of Entry, Papal Registers, 133
—— of Feudal Aids, 80
Cambrian Archaeological Meeting, 20
Cambrian Register, 63
Camden's Britannia, 169
Camrose, 151
Canterbury, 70, 90, 136
—— Cathedral Muniment room, 90
—— Registers, 88, 91, 92, 139
Cantington, Jordan de (son of Lucas de Hoda), 20, 49, 50, 51, 88, 187, 217
—— William de, 49, 50, 51, 88, 187, 217
Cantref (or hundred) of Cemaes, 27
—— —— Cilgerran, 46, 218
—— —— of Rhos, 158
Capel Cradog, 219
Caradoc, 71
Cardiff, 223
Cardigan, 52, 66, 204, 206, 207, 210, 211, 222, 223
—— Bay Inn, 200
—— Bridge, 103, 116
—— Co. of (or Shire), 12, 22, 185, 186, 204, 205, 208, 218, 223
—— Priory of, 62, 206
—— Town Hall of, 201, 206, 208
Carlisle, Nicholas, 157
Carmarthenshire, 46, 110, 172
Carn Engli, 12
Carswell, 59, 60
Cartae Baroniae de Keymes, 84
Carrin, Richard, 159, 160, 161, 162, 163
Cassia, 83, 84, 85, 86, 216, 219
Castell, Grace, 160, 163
Castell, ION, 18
—— Nevern, Description of, 20, 25, 26, 29
Castle Hill, 125, 147
—— Martin, 51, 52
—— Vydy, 125, 127
—— Walwin, 143
Cath (Caedes, Lat.), slaughter, 23
Catherine, Henry, 143
Cathern, Henry, clerk, 154
Catheiniog, 168, 172
Cathen, 168, 170, 171
Cathmais (Chamais), 13, 23, 24, 37, 38, 39, 42, 43, 62, 64
Catuocomus (Caducani), 168, 170, 171
Ceibwr (Keybour), 83
Celtic, 163
Cemaes, Cemmaes, Cames, Kameys, Kemeys, Camoys, etc., 23, 24, 42, 43, 46, 54, 56, 62, 63, 64, 65, 68, 82, 83, 85, 95, 143, 169, 216, 217, 222, 223
—— Deanery of, 91, 139
—— Head, 221

Cemaes, High Court of, 219
—— Lords of, 216
Ceredig, 11
Chapel (Capel) Cradoc, 219
—— Degwell, 219
—— at Hendre, 20, 219
—— Sidan, 67
Charles I, 10, 185
—— II, 188, 219
—— Prince of Wales, 10
Chartres, 30
—— Bishop of, 32, 34
—— Canons of, 35
—— Chapter of, 34, 35
—— Church of Notre Dame of, 35, 36
—— Diocese of, 37
—— John of, 35
Chalybeate Spring, 220
Chapters, Canterbury, 72, 75
—— Pill, 139, 141
—— St. David's, 69
—— St. Dogmael,
—— Tiron, 38
Charters of Martin, 40, 42
—— —— Robert Fitz, 46, 57, 60, 172
—— —— Nicholas Fitz, 50, 51
—— Baldwin de Riverius, Earl of Exeter, 60
—— Charles I, 185
—— Charles II, 188, 219
—— Edward I, 126
—— Edward III, 41, 45, 46, 50
—— Henry I, 45, 58
—— Henry II, 59, 60
—— Montacute, 59, 60
—— John Bradshaw, 114, 115
—— Totnes Priory, 43
—— William de la Grace, Earl of Pembroke,
        Earl Marshal of England, 157
Cheshire, 185
Chichester, Dean of, 78
Chinon, 77
Christchurch (Hants), 221
Cilgerran (Kilgerran), 218, 222
—— Church of, 46
—— Hundred of, 218
Cistercian Abbey, 164
—— Abbot, 164
Clairveaux, The Rev. C., 30, 37
Clare, Gilbert de (Cousin of William the
        Conqueror), 22
—— Strongbow, Earl of, 10
Clarendon, Roger de, 126, 129
Clawdd Cam, 203, 204
Cleveland, The Duchess of, 56
Clonenan, 160, 161, 162
Clonendon, Church of Letrom and another,
        160, 161, 163
Clongosse, Rectory, 160, 163
Clongossy, Church of St. Mary, 160, 161, 163
—— Chapel of St. Mary, 160, 161, 163
—— —— St. Peter, 160, 161, 163
—— Church of St. Synell, 160, 161, 163
Cloyne, Diocese of, 160, 161, 163
Cluny, 33, 34
Clyddau River, 28, 45, 47, 109

Cnwc y Celwydd, 19
Cockington, 28, 29, 40, 41
Coed y Wynog (Coed y Winoke), 63
Coel Godebog (King Cole), 11
Coffin lid, 215
Coffin, The Golden, 60, 213
Colchester, 11
Coles, Richard, 131
Combe Martin, 22, 23
Comore, 160, 163
Condé, Prince de, 36
Condon, Cecelia, 163
—— Griffin, 159, 160, 161, 162
—— wife of Griffin, 159
—— Lord, 159, 161, 163
—— Raymond, 160, 161, 163
—— William, 160, 161, 163
Conquest of Cemaes, 22, 24, 25, 26, 27
Consinquilos, 159, 160, 161, 162
Constantine, 11
Constantius, 11
Cope, Sir John, Knt., 204
Corbett, Abbeys and Priories, etc., 172
Cornwall, Co. of, 84, 85
Coracle, 221
Corody, 100, 117, 118, 122, 123
Cotton MSS., Cleopatra, E. IV (see MSS.).
Co. Cardigan (see Cardiganshire).
Co. Carlow, 160
Co. Cork, 160, 165
Co. Pembroke (see Pembroke Co.).
Co. Wexford, 159, 165, 167
Co. Wicklow, 160
Covenant, Walter, 128
Court of the Exchequer, 188, 192, 207, 208
—— —— Barons of, 207, 208, 211
Coyre Road, 145
Crabot, Philip, 130
Criccieth, 12
Croes Bigog, 18
Cromwell's Soldiers, 214
Crugiau Cemaes, 25, 26
Crugiau Griffyth (? Treriffith), 80, 82
Crugiau Pen du, 101
Cuhelyn, The Regulus, 19, 27, 216
Cunedda Wledig, 9, 14, 64
Cwm Carw (or Cerwyn), 28, 45, 47, 64, 109,
        121
Cwm Deifo, 220
Cwm Gloyne, 20, 201
Cwm Ion, 220
Cwm Tegwell, 218
Cwmwd of Ys Garn, 158
Cwri, Owen ap Ieuan ap Nicholas of
        Tredafed, 186
Cyfnerth, 218
Cymraeg, 63
Cymry (Lat. Cambria), 63
Dairies, Number of, 220
Danegeld, 60
Danes and Danish, 14, 24
Dareg (Dary Dairy), 101, 103, 115
Darne Parke (Dan-y-Parke), 101, 115
Darion (Claude Dariot), 221, 222
Dartington, Barony of, 79, 80

Dartington, Lords of, 29
David de Barry, 51
David ap Ieuan, 103, 116
—— ap Powell, 110, 121
—— ap Ryce ap Owen, 109, 121
—— John, 194
—— King of Scotland, 31
—— Lewis, 176
—— Lewis de Whitchurch, 176
—— Morris, 197
—— William, 121
—— de Wydeurze, 51
—— St. (see St.).
Davies, Anne, 201, 206
—— H. O., 200
Davyd Rice, 176
—— Jevan de Moylgrove, 176
Davye, Richard, 149
Davyston, John, 131
Day, John, 151
Dean Prior, 84
Deeds, Julian, 206, 207, 208, 209, 211
De Invectionibus (Geralds), 69, 76
Dennant (Devant, Dumant), 127, 142, 143, 149, 154
—— Mill, 140
Deodands, 135, 136
Deplesmore, 142, 151
De Rebus a se Gestis (Geralds), 67, 75
Despencer, Hugh le, 128
Devereux, Walter, 166
Devon, Devonshire, 22, 23, 26, 28, 40, 41, 45, 47, 57, 59, 79, 80, 84, 85, 86, 88, 90, 96, 97, 98, 104, 107, 120, 173
Dewesland Hundred, 189, 197, 198
Dimetian Code, 217
Dinas, and Dinas Head, 12
Dives, 22
Doctors Parke, 103, 115
Dodd, Mr., 211, 212
Dogfeiliog (part of Denbighshire), 11, 14
Dogmael ap Cunedda, 9, 14
Dogmael, meaning of, 13, 14, 15
—— (Dogfael), St., 11, 12, 13, 14
Dogmaels St. Cemaes, 42, 44, 45, 49
—— Abbey of, 37, 38, 39, 40, 41, 42, 43, 49, 50, 51, 52, 53, 54, 56, 58, 59, 66, 73, 79, 80, 81, 82, 84, 85, 86, 88, 89, 90, 91, 93, 94, 95, 96, 97, 98, 99, 100, 101, 102, 104, 105, 108, 110, 113, 114, 115, 116, 117, 118, 134, 135, 157, 158, 159, 161, 162, 164, 167, 168, 169, 170, 172, 174, 175, 178, 181, 182, 183, 185, 186, 187, 192, 200, 201, 202, 203, 204, 205, 206, 209, 210, 211, 212, 213, 215, 216, 219, 221, 222, 223
—— Abbots of, 29, 37, 38, 42, 48, 50, 51, 52, 55, 62, 66, 68, 78, 79, 80, 81, 82, 83, 84, 85, 86, 88, 89, 90, 91, 92, 94, 95, 96, 116, 117, 139, 143, 159, 161, 163, 164, 167, 169, 170, 203, 211, 212, 213, 215
—— Ancient Church of, 45, 46, 49
—— Borough of, 28, 222

Dogmaels, St., Cathedral Church of, Dom John Howell, Precentor, 91
—— —— Dom John Lowelin, Vicar, 91
—— Chaplain and Vicar of, 101, 102, 174, 175, 177, 180, 184
—— Dissolution, 94, 96, 97, 114
—— Fishermen of, 221, 222
—— Four Hamlets of, Abbey, 220
—— —— Bridge End, 220
—— —— Cipyn, 220
—— —— Pant y groes, 220
——Foundation of Abbey, 1118, 28, 38, 41, 42
—— Grants to, 40
—— Manor of, 53, 54, 95, 100, 103, 110, 115, 176, 177, 220
—— Market of, 222
—— Old Religious House of, 41, 214
—— Parish of, 84, 91, 92, 100, 109, 116, 181, 183, 200, 201, 203, 204, 205, 206, 207, 208, 211, 215, 217, 218, 220
—— Present Church of, 215, 220
—— Priors of, 160
—— Priory of, 37, 54, 58, 62, 64
—— Rectory, Vicarage, or Church of St. Thomas, Apostle and Martyr, 96, 101, 104, 105, 106, 118, 119, 173, 174, 175, 177, 178, 179, 180, 181, 182, 183, 199, 200, 201, 202, 203, 204, 205, 206, 210, 211, 215, 217, 220
—— Remains, Description of, 214, 215
—— Township of, 81, 95, 105, 106, 107, 114, 119, 174, 175, 179, 186
—— Vicars of, Dom Philipp Lawrence, 91, 92
—— —— Gryffyn Jones, 177
—— —— Nicholas Davies, 177
—— —— Henry J. Vincent, 15, 16, 19, 20, 213, 220
—— —— Philip Henry, 217
—— 28
Dogwells, St., 88, 92
Dom Gasquet, 158
Donovan's Excursions through S. Wales, 169
Donegleddy Deanery, 145
Domesday Book, 23, 60, 124
Dormaghyn Chapel of St. Mary Magdalene, 159, 163
—— Church of St. Patrick, 159, 161, 163
Dorset, 60
Dowdale, Patrick, 166
Drym, 189, 197, 198
Duborchon, 168, 172
Dubricius (Dyfryg), 12, 168, 169
Dupont, Mons. Emile, 23, 58, 61
Dyfed, 27, 216, 217, 218
Dyfryn Braian, 218

East Brent, 41
Edgar Hubert, 53
Edmund, Brother of Edward III,
Edward the Confessor, King of England, 61
—— I, King of England, 46, 57, 79, 80, 125, 126, 157
—— II, King of England, 46, 57, 79, 80, 81, 83, 84, 85, 216

Edward III, King of England, 45, 50, 84, 85, 216
—— VI, King of England, 160, 163, 167
—— Prince of Wales, 10
Eglwyswrw, 24, 27, 49, 50, 51, 91, 101, 104, 106, 119, 175, 183
—— Church of, 96, 118, 173, 174, 175, 178, 179, 180, 181, 182, 183
—— Manor of, 219
—— Vicar of Dom Phillip Lloyd, 91
—— Rectory of, 105, 119
Eifl, Yr, 12
Eisteddfod, 216
Elena Brazon, 52
Elizabeth, Queen of England, 124, 173, 174, 175, 176, 177, 181, 184, 185, 187, 189, 190, 192, 193, 194, 195, 197, 215, 219, 222, 223
—— Princess, 94, 140, 141
Ells, 194
Eltham, 84, 86
Ely, Bishop of, 69, 71, 72, 78
Emlyn, 46
Empress Matilda, 59, 60
English Religious Houses, Dom Gasquet, 158
Erleng, John de, 128
—— John the Younger, de, 128
Esgryn, 17
Ettrick, Mr., 212
Eugenius Pope, 19
Eure et Loir, 22, 30, 32
Eva, wife of Guy de Brian, 56
Exeter, 60
Exchequer, 81
—— Augmentation Office, 97, 145, 146, 155
—— Book of Decrees, 211
—— Chambers, 211
—— T. R. Miscellaneous Books, 79, 80
Eynon ap David, 109, 121
Eynon, son of William, 52

Fan Tracery, 215
Farm of demesne lands, 118, 129, 131
—— of the Mill (Pill), 130, 131
Fenton, 19, 50, 65, 157, 169, 170, 200, 214, 215, 216
Ferentino, 76
Ferns, Bishop of, 160, 162
—— —— Patrick Barret, 162
—— —— Thos. Den of, 160, 161, 162, 163
—— Diocese of, 159, 161, 162, 164, 165
Ferramuige, 160, 161, 163
Ferrers (Ferres), Lord, 96, 111
Fête of St. Bernard, Abbot of Tiron, 37
—— St. Justin, 37
Ffox, Thomas, 130
Ffunhone=ffynon, 101, 103
Field of Slaughter, 24
Fish, Beavers, 221
—— Crabs, 221
—— Dogfish, 222
—— Ells, 221
—— Grampus, 222
—— Gray Mullet, 221
—— Gurnard, 221

Fish, Herrings, 221, 222
—— Lamperies, 222
—— Limpets, 222
—— Lobster, 221
—— —— Its qualities, armour, etc., 222
—— Mackerel, 221, 222
—— Mussels, 222
—— Otters, 221
—— Plaice, 221
—— Porpoise, 222
—— Salmon, 218, 221
—— Seal, 222
—— Sewin, 221
—— Shrimp, 222
—— Silver Bass, 221
—— Soles, 221
—— Turbot, 221
—— Whiting, 221
Fisher, John, Bailiff, 143
Fisher Road, 149
Fisheries, 47, 51, 91, 98, 115, 138, 159, 174, 221
Fishery of St. Dogmaels (Seine fishing), 47, 221
Fishguard (Fyssingard), 24, 26, 49, 50, 51, 82, 91, 95, 105, 106, 119, 183, 187, 188, 189, 190, 191, 192, 193, 194, 195, 196, 198, 209, 219, 222
—— Bay of, 12, 23
—— Church and Rectory of, 96, 104, 106, 175, 180, 182, 187
—— Parish of, 175
—— St. Nicholas, 173, 174, 175, 178, 179, 180, 181, 182, 183
—— Vicar of, Dom John ap Atho, 91
Fitts, John, 159, 160, 161, 162
Fleming, David, 131, 132
Flemings, The, 124, 135
Flood, 54
Flood, The, 218
Florence, 72, 78
Foliot, Reginald, 68, 70, 71, 72, 76
—— Master G., 76
Forest Quarries, 45
Fortesque, John, 182
France, Louis le Gros, King of, 34
Franciscus, 17
Fraystroppe, 145
Free Rents, 129, 130, 134, 152
Frenny fawr, 13
Fulchardus, 1st Abbot St. Dogmaels (1118), 31, 45, 47, 52
Foulques, Count of Anjou, 34, 57
Foundation of St. Dogmaels Abbey by Robert Fitzmartin (1118), 42
—— —— Priory by the Martins (1113),
Fynette (ffyntte), John or Lord John, 160, 161, 163

Gablers' Rents, 129, 130, 134
Gaedeilg, Gaedeilge, 64
Gallia Christiana, 35
Gambold, Hector, 207, 208, 211, 212
—— John, 207, 208, 211, 212
Gamel, 61

Gardais, 34
Garth y Gwenyn, 190, 191, 192, 193, 194, 195
Garve, 162
Gaul Gallia Galatia, 63
Gay, William, 129
Geoffrey de Mandeville, 59
—— son of Paganus, 42
George, John, 209
Geraint, son of Gerald, 58
Gerald de Windsor, 66
Gerald, the Welshman, 66 to 77, 213, 221
German Mercenaries, 36
Germans, 63
Germin, John, 193
Gilbert de Clare, 45, 62
—— Earl of Gloucester and Hertford, 47
Giles, Seneschal of Pembroke, 128
Giraldus Cambrensis, 26, 35, 66 to 77
Gislebert, son of Crispin, 62
Glaneirw, 186
Glanhelig, 185
Glascareg (Glascarge), 165, 167
—— Foundation of, 159, 160, 161, 162
—— Grants to and Charters, 160, 161
—— Priors of, 159, 161, 164
—— Priory, 96, 102, 104, 111, 114, 126, 159,
    160, 161, 162, 164, 165, 166, 167
—— St. Mary of, 163
—— Prior Andrew Occuryn, 164, 165, 167
—— —— Charles McMurgh, 160, 161, 162,
    163, 167
—— —— Dermit, 160, 163, 167
—— —— Henry of Wales, 164, 165, 167
—— —— Ymar Odwynd (O'dowd, etc.), 164,
    167
Glastir in Cemaes, 83
Glastonbury, Abbot of, 60
Glendalough, 160
—— Diocese of, 161, 163
Glentworth, 61
Gloucester Row (Cardigan), 67
Godebert (1131), 124, 126, 135
Godfrid, or Goisfred Conte d'Eu, 62
Godric, 61
Goidhel, Gael, 64
Golden Vase, 34
Golwen, ex-monk of St. Dogmaels, 73, 74, 75
Goodige River, 197, 198
Gor, 61
Gorry, 159, 161
Gostwyche, Edward, 113, 114, 115
Grangistown (Granston), Parish and Manor,
    80, 82, 95, 101, 104, 105, 106, 119, 175,
    178, 180, 182, 183
—— Rectory of, 106, 173, 174, 175, 179, 180,
    181, 182, 183
Grants of Martin of the Towers, 40, 42
—— Nicholas fitz, 50, 51
—— Robert fitz, 46, 60
—— Particulars for, 102, 113
Great Close, 103
Griffin ap David, 110
—— Ieuan (or Jevan) ap Jenkyn, 109, 121
Griffith, Abel, 202, 203
—— David, 207, 208, 211, 212

Griffith, Engherad, 205
—— James, 201, 202, 206
—— of Cardigan, 202
—— John, 156
—— John, 176
—— Matthew, 202
Grige Pende (Crugiau pen du), 101, 103, 115
Grove Common, 97, 98
Gryffydd ap Ieuan ap Rees, 194
—— Rhys, 66
—— Phee (Philippe), 193
Guales, Galles, Gallis, 46, 47, 62, 63, 64, 65
—— land of, 45, 46, 62
—— Prieuré de, or Priory of, 37, 38, 39, 41,
    46, 59, 62, 63, 64
Gudendag, Mr., 9
Guy, David, 152
—— de Brian, 52, 56
—— the younger Count of Rochfort, 34, 59
Gwayne, 26, 49, 50
Gwawl (the radiant one), 11
Gwyddel (Irish), 64
—— Fichti (the painted Irish or Picts), 64
—— =Gwy-el=Gual, 64
Gwynefardd, The Regulus, 20, 25, 216
Gwynne, Mr., 200

Hagetom, 61
Haigh, Dr., 172
Hamlockes, David, 131
Hammersmith, 172
Hampton, John, 216
Hants (Hampshire), 221
Harlech, 12
Harleian MSS. (see MSS.).
Harp, The Silver, 21, 61
Harrow School, 169
Harreyes, Davye, 147
Haver Brokechelley=Hafn brochell y lle (or
    llys), 101, 103, 116
Haverford, 66, 102, 106, 114, 129, 132, 136, 137,
    149, 150, 151, 156, 173, 174, 175, 176,
    178, 179, 181, 183
Haverfordwest, 68, 95, 104, 120, 129, 149, 185
Hay, William, 149
Helen, Helena, The Empress, daughter of
    Coel Godebog, 11, 12
Helmswell, 61
Helyot's Histoire des Ordres Monastiques, 59
Hendre, 19, 20, 21, 220
—— Chapel of, 20, 219
Hengurto, 110
Henllys, 26, 185, 218
Henry, Brazon, 52
—— de Lacy, Earl of Lincoln, 52
—— de Tracy, Baron of Barnstaple (Barn-
    stable), 56
—— Earl of Warwick, 31, 34
—— I, King of England, 29, 31, 34, 37, 39,
    40, 41, 42, 43, 44, 45, 46, 47, 53, 54,
    55, 56, 57, 58, 60, 88, 217
—— II, 53, 58
—— III, 79, 80
—— IV, 48, 88
—— V, 48, 88, 89, 135, 136, 137, 138

Henry VI, 88, 134
—— VII, 90, 91, 92, 214, 215
—— VIII, 88, 94, 95, 97 to 105, 107, 109 to
    116, 118 to 122, 134, 140, 141, 142,
    146 to 158, 160, 161, 163, 165, 166,
    167, 174, 210, 212, 219, 222
—— Philip, Vicar of St. Dogmaels, 217
—— son of Gerald, 128
—— —— Robert, 127
Herbert St. Leger, 51
—— William, 10
Herbiand (Herbrandstown), 124, 127
Hereford, Bishop of, 69
—— Master J., Canon of, 69, 71
—— Precentor of, 69, 71
Heriot, 177, 180, 184
Herle, Mary, 142
Herrings, 221, 222
Hews, William, 103, 116
—— —— John, 193
Heywarde, John, Canon of St. David's, 133
Hill, William, 150
History of Abbeys, etc., 54
Hitchets, Thomas, 142
Hoare, Sir Richard, 170
Hoda, Lucas de, 25, 49, 50, 159
—— —— sons of, 20, 25
Hoell ap Jenkyn ap Owen, 109
—— John, 149
Householders, Number of, in St. Dogmaels,
    220
Howel Lange, Priest, O.S.B., 88
Howell ap Owen ap Powell, 109, 121
—— ap Thomas ap Owen, 108, 120
—— David, 207, 208, 211, 212
—— Dda, 218
—— —— Laws of, 27
Huberstownship (Hubberstone), 125, 127, 142,
    143, 144, 152, 154, 157
—— St. David's of, 128, 143, 144
Hubert de Vaux, 45, 47
Hugh de Fossar, 52, 53
—— Earl of Chester, 60
—— de Montfort, 43
—— the Young, 129, 130, 131
Hughe, John, 198
Hugo (Gualensis), 45, 46
Humphrey de Bohun, Earl of Hereford and
    Essex, 48, 52
—— Duke of Gloucester, 49
—— son of Gosner, 47
Hurtley Coppice, 97, 98
Huscart, Richard de, 126
Hustard (Uscard, Huscard, Huscart), 126,
    143, 144, 154, 155, 156
Hytes, Thomas, 149

Ieuan ap Powell ap Ieuan David, 121
—— William, 194, 195, 196
—— Powell, 103
Ignatius, 17
Inishannon, 165
Inispir (see Ynys Pyr).
Inleyn, Church of, 160
Innocent, Pope (see Popes).

Inquisition (Legal), 188
Ioan, 18
Ion, 17
Ireland, 62, 69, 96, 111, 159, 213, 223
Irish, 49, 63, 64, 187, 213
—— Coast, 12
—— Maqi (son) on Ogham Stones, 14
—— Princess, 213
—— Sea, 69
—— Settlers in Cemaes, 28, 64
Isabella, Countess of Pembroke, 128
Ithel (Ithael), 11, 15

James ap Bowen (or ap Owen), 110, 121
—— ap Owen, 142
—— ap Powell Lloyd, 103, 116
—— I, King of England, 187, 188, 190, 191,
    192, 193, 194, 195, 196
—— Owen, 204, 209
Jenkin ap Ieuan, 103, 116
—— Matthew, 176
—— Philip, 197
—— Rogers, 103, 116
Jenkins, William, 205
Jenkyn ap Griffith, 110, 121
Jermyn, John, 195
Jerusalem, Foulques Conte d'Anjou, King of,
    34, 59
—— St. John's Hospital of, in England, 133
Jevan ap David, 110
—— ap Madoc, 130
—— Powell, 110
—— Jacob, 176
Joan (see Martin).
—— Warlaugh, 84
Jockyn, David, 131
Joel, or Judhell, 60
—— the Chaplain, 58
John, Canon of St. David's, 53
—— Master, Canon of St. David's, 53
—— of Osterlop, Canon of St. David's, 53
—— Barret, The Apostate Monk of St. Dog-
    maels, 78
—— David, 193
—— de Buffelo, 50
—— de Castro, 51
—— de Warrenne, Earl of Surrey, 48
—— Henry, 133
—— Herbord, 86
—— King of England, 68, 77
—— of Castle Martin (? son of Martin of
    the Towers), 50, 51, 52
—— of Chartres, Abbot of Tiron, 30, 35
—— of Eltham, Earl of Cornwall, 48
—— of Sherburn, 52
—— Owen, 192
—— Sampson, 86, 87
—— son of Walter, 126
—— Sprang, the Jester, 67
—— Stevens, 54
—— the Archdeacon, 53
—— the Steward, 53
—— Thomas, 205
—— Thomas, 145

John's township=Johnstown, 127, 143, 145, 150, 154, 155, 156
Jones, Capt. Bryn Teify, 213
—— Capt. Cardigan Bay, 199, 213
—— John ap John, 211
—— Rowland, 187
—— Sir Thomas, 155
—— Thomas, 201, 206, 207, 208
Joram, Chapel of, 160, 161, 163
Jordan de Cantington, son of Lucas de Hoda, 20, 25, 49, 50, 187
Justiciar, Roger de Mortimer, Earl of March, King's, in Wales, 84, 85
Kemes, Tracts (George Owen), 62
Kemeys, Kemes, Kamays, Rammaes (see Cemaes).
Kemeys, Register Book of (George Owen), 216
Kemlas, 162
Keppoghe, 160, 163
Ketyngeston, 142, 151, 152
Kilerat, 160, 163
Kilgwyn Vychan (and Vechan), 63
Killaloe, 164
Killemaght, 165, 166
Killemonde, 163
Killenaule, 165
Killenerlde, 163
Killmalapoke, 160, 163
Kilreny, 160, 163
Kilsy Fawr (Cilfawr), 205
Kiltenen, 160
Killwch and Olwen, 28, 64
King's Supremacy, Act of Acknowledgment, 163
—— —— Pill, 140
—— —— St. Dogmaels, 93, 94, 95
—— Clipton (Chepstow), 52
—— Treasury, 52
Knightley, John, 132
Knight's Fee, Cassia, 83, 84, 85, 86, 216, 219
—— Kefen Chymwyrth, 83, 219
—— Maenclochog, 216
—— Monington, 216
—— Randykaith, 216
—— Whittokesden, 84, 85, 86
Kylinnaghte, 165, 166
Kylmoche Irysshe, 165, 166
Kylpatrick, 165, 167
Kylynghill, 165, 166
Kynaston's, Mr., Garden, 170

Laceria Delturon, Chapel of St. Brigid, 160, 161, 163
—— Church of, 160, 161, 163
Lacryne, 163
Lagen, 160, 161
La Haden (Llawhaden), 52, 108
Lakerly Larcharle, 101, 105
La Manche, Archives of, 57
Lancashire, 100, 185
Lancaster, Duchy of, 154
Landau, 103
Landfrey (Lamfrey), 51
Langley, 52
Langnages, Cymraeg, 64

Languages, Erse, 64
—— Irish, 63
—— Latin, 63, 168
—— Welsh, 63, 64
Lanven, Chapel of, 163
Lateran, The, 75
Latin Inscriptions, 63
Laundre, laundry=Llandre, 101, 103, 109, 114, 115, 116
Laurencetown, 165
Law's Little England beyond Wales, 26, 168
Lead of Windows, 117
Leche, James, 107, 108, 111, 112
Lechmere, Sir Nicholas, 207, 211
Ledameston, 142, 147, 148, 157
Leddin (Liddestone), 125, 127
Leenduly, Dr., 9
Leet Court, 191, 194
Le Forren, Court of, 129
Legend of Irish Princess, 63
Le Gros, Geoffrey, 3rd Abbot of Tiron, 31, 32, 36, 37
Le Hunt, Mr., 157
Leighlin, Diocese of, 160, 161, 163
Leland, 54, 55, 135, 172
Le Monkton, 145, 150
Les Compagnons de Guillaume le Conquerant, Mon. E. Dupont, 61
Lewis ap Bowen, 155
—— ap Ieuan, 109
—— Dŵn, 30
—— George, 205, 207, 208, 209, 210, 211, 212
—— James, 110
—— Jordan, 96
—— Major, of Clynfiew, 20
—— Topographical Dictionary, 185
Leynthole, Roland, Knt., Lord of Haverford, 136, 137
Leytmagh, Church of St. Barburga, 159, 161, 163
Life of St. Bernard, G. le Gros, 31, 32
Lincolnshire, 60, 61
Lincoln Taxation, 172
Lhwyd, Edward, 15
Llamesfelde, Thos., 154
Llanbadenfawr, 62
Llanbloden, 28
—— Manor of, 45, 47
Llancolman, 97, 102, 104, 178
—— Rectory of, 106, 107, 108, 120, 173, 175, 178, 179, 181
Llandaff Dubricius of, 12, 169
Llandilo, 97, 102, 104, 178
—— Rectory of, 106, 107, 108, 120, 173, 175, 178, 179, 181
Llandu, Church of, 76
Llandudoch (Llandodog, Llan Deulydog), 46, 49, 115, 217
—— —— Bishop's House, 217
Llandygwydd, 186
Llanfair Nant y Gof, 219
Llanfyhangel Penbedw (Penbeador), 205
Llangolman Penbeador (Llancolman Penbedw), 205
Llangadocke, 110

Llangathen, 168, 171
Llangele, 48
Llangoedmore, 204, 205
Llanhever (*see* Nevern).
Llanllyr, 186
Llanthony, Foliot, Prior of, 72
—— G., Prior of, 161
Llantood, 45, 91, 97, 101, 104, 105, 113, 218
—— Church of, 118, 173, 174, 178, 179, 183
—— Rectory of, 106, 119, 173, 175, 180, 181, 182
—— Vicar of, Dom Hugo Harris, 91
Llanwnda, 188, 189, 197, 198
—— Dom Griffin Cedres, Vicar of, 91
Llawhaden (Loghaden, La Hadden), 52, 108
Llechryd, 204, 205, 218
Llewelyn ap David, 176
—— ap Jevan Pickton, 110, 121
—— ap Madoc, 83
—— ap William, the Reeve, 126, 129
—— Goch, 52
—— Robert, 188, 189, 190, 191, 192, 194, 195, 196
—— Sir Hugh, Vicar of Llanwnda, 197
Llisprant (Llysvrane), 52, 104, 105, 119, 175, 183
—— Chapel and Church of, 96, 101, 105, 106, 173, 174, 175, 178, 179, 180, 181, 182, 183
Lloyd, Fylip, of Hendre, 20
—— Ieuan, of Hendre, 20
—— John, of Hendre, 20
—— Thomas, of Hendre, 201, 206, 207, 208
—— T., of Hendre, 20
—— William, of Hendre, 20
—— Alban, 188, 192, 196
—— Edward, 153, 156, 157
—— Griffin, 112, 144
—— Mr., 211, 212
—— Morgan, 186
—— Robert, 202, 208, 209
—— Sir Marteine, Bart., of Bronwydd, Lord of Cemaes, Dedication.
Lochtyn, 12
London, 185
—— Dean of, 69, 71
Longton, John (2), 143
Lord Julius, 162
Lords or Barons of Cemaes, 27, 29
Lord Marcher of Cemaes, 56
—— Marchers, 27
Lorome, 160, 163, 165, 166
Louis le Gros, King of France, 34
—— son of King of France, 34
—— XIV, King of France, 36
Lucas de Hoda, 25, 49, 50, 159
—— sons, Jordan and Richard, 20, 25
Ludlow, 101, 105
Ludovic ap Jevan, 121
Lupo, Stephen, 127
Luscombe, Barrudge, 79, 80

Mabinogion, 28, 46, 62, 63, 64, 122
Maenclochog, 79, 82, 83, 104, 178, 181, 183

Maenclochog, Rectory of, 101, 103, 104, 107, 108, 120, 173, 175, 177, 178, 179, 181, 183
Maenochlogddu y thache (Mynachlogddu), 120
Maglia Dubracuna, 168
Magnomia, Church of St. Mary, 160, 161, 163
Magolite Bar Cene, 168, 172
Malcolm III., King of Scotland, 31
Malesant, Walter, 128, 154, 156
Malgwyn ap Rhys, 66
Mallt's (Matilda's) grove=Moylgrove, 45
Manaian (Manegan, Man eigion) fawr, 201, 202, 203, 205, 208, 209, 210, 214
—— Marsh, 218, 219
Mangunel, Richard de, 127
Manisty (or Manesey), John, 97, 98, 102, 107, 120
Manobier, 168, 169
—— Castle, 66
Manordeify (Maneerdivy), 205
Manor of Taunton, 59
MSS., Additional, 159
—— Cotton, Cleopatra, E. IV, 94, 135
—— Dale Castle, 219
—— Harleian, 52, 53, 88, 160, 161, 187
—— Lansdowne, 140, 177
—— St. Sergius and St. Bacchus Angiers, 60
Maqi (son), 14
Mardnawen, 189
Margaret, niece of William de Roche, 126, 129
Margaret of Anjou, Queen of Henry VI, 134
Margot, sister of William de Roche, 126
Marshall, William, 10
Martin, Colinetus (great, great grandson of Martin), 57
—— Geva (=Eva), wife of Martin of the Towers, 28, 40, 45, 54, 59, 60, 168, 169, 170, 172
—— Joan, 57, 83
—— John of Castle (? Martin of the Tower's son), 50, 52, 60
—— Matilda, wife of Robert, Lord of Cemaes, 20, 27, 28, 45, 46, 47, 57, 58
—— Nesta, 25
—— Nicholas (son of Martin), 49, 50, 51, 60
—— Nicholas, Lord of Cemaes (great-grandson of Martin), 49, 57, 79, 80, 83, 125, 128, 135, 158
—— Robert (eldest son of Martin of the Towers), Lord of Cemaes, 23, 27, 28, 29, 31, 34, 37, 39, 40, 41, 42, 43, 45, 46, 47, 49, 50, 52, 54, 56, 57, 58, 59, 60, 62, 88, 95, 168, 170, 172, 214, 219
—— Robert (? grandson of Martin of the Towers), 52, 60
—— of the Towers (called also de Turribus de Tours, Tironensis, Turonensis, and of Wales), 22, 23, 24, 26, 27, 40, 41, 45, 46, 49, 50, 52, 54, 55, 56, 57, 58, 59, 60, 62, 83, 95, 128, 133, 156, 169, 178, 187, 204

Martin, Landing of Martin of the Towers, 26
—— of Wales, 60
—— William I (grandson), 25, 26, 49, 50, 51, 56
—— II (great-great-great-great-grandson), 56, 57, 79, 80, 82, 83, 85
—— III, Sir (great-great-great-great-great-grandson), 57, 83, 84, 85, 86, 216
—— Lands of, 60, 61
—— St., of Tours (4th century), 23, 54, 95, 134, 158, 159
Martine, Anne, 203, 207, 208, 211, 212
Martinvast, 61
Mathias, James, 209
Matilda, the Queen, 53
Maud, daughter of Guy de Brian, 50
Meath, Diocese of, 164
Meleri, or Eleri, daughter of Brychan, wife of Ceredig, 11
Melin Manor Nawon, 190, 195, 196
Meline, 27
Meller, John, 152
—— Philip, 149
Melota, 76
Mendus, John, 195
Meredith, Thomas John, 193
Merlet, Mons. Lucien, 32, 35
Meurig ap Elaeth, 14
Milford, 156, 157
Milford Haven, 156
—— Lord, 170
Mill Broke, 103
Mill, Fishguard (corn), 104, 119, 174, 175, 178, 179, 180, 181, 182, 183, 187, 189, 190, 192, 193, 194, 195, 196, 197, 198
—— Manor nawon (corn), 190, 195, 196
—— Glascareg (corn), 159
—— Pill (corn), 124, 125, 126, 128
—— St. Dogmaels (2 corn), 97, 105, 115, 116, 119, 174, 181, 182, 199, 200
—— —— (1 Fulling), 97
Ministers' Accounts, 129, 134
Moat, 125, 126, 128
Moel Hebog, 12
—— Trigarn, 13
Monachlog yr hên, 12, 14, 15, 17, 24
Monasticon, 44, 54
—— Angl., 172
—— Hibernicon, 167
Monastry of St. James, 60
Monington, 91, 97, 209
Monks' Benedictine, 161
—— Caldey, 169
—— Pill, 125, 126, 133
—— St. Dogmaels, 35, 47, 50, 51, 79, 88, 163, 169, 172, 213, 221
—— of St. Dogmaels, Dom David (16th century), 92
—— —— David Res, 95
—— —— David William, 95
—— —— Hugo Eynon, 93, 95
—— —— John David, 95
—— —— Philipp Laurence, 92
—— —— Phillip Griffith, 95
—— —— Lewis Lawrens, 95

Monk of St. Dogmaels, Robert Thomas, 94, 95
—— —— Thomas Baron, 92
—— —— Thomas Jevan, 92
—— —— William Bonne, 95
—— —— William Griffith, 92
—— St. Maur, 36
—— Tiron, 36, 43, 46, 48, 54, 58, 59, 128, 158, 159
Monkton, 127, 142, 150
Montfort sur Risle, 43
Morgan ap Owen, 176
—— John, of Llangadocke, 110, 111
—— Jones, 122
—— Rd., 176, 177
Morgeney, The Brooke, 218
Morgenau, Morganeu, The Judge, 218
Morice ap David, 103, 116
Moris, David, 129
—— Richard, 129
Morris, John, 204, 207, 210
Moritonium, 43
Mortimer, John, 103, 116
—— Ralph de, 128
Morva, 63
Morvill, 27, 84
Mount, 204
Moylgrove (Moelgrove, etc.), 16, 27, 28, 45, 46, 63, 91, 104, 105, 106, 174, 177, 179, 183, 200, 217
—— Rectory and Church of, 96, 101, 118, 119, 173, 175, 178, 180, 181, 182, 183
Munster, 165, 167
Mynne, John, 160
Mynachlog Ddu, 28, 80, 95, 108, 109, 120, 173, 175, 178, 179, 220
—— Chapel, 101, 104, 106, 110, 122, 173, 175, 178, 179
—— Chaplain, 111
—— Rectory, 111
Mynyth tergh (Mene cregh), 82, 95, 108, 120

Nantgwyn, 27, 104, 175
—— Chapel of, 96, 101, 105, 106, 119, 173, 174, 175, 178, 179, 180, 181, 182
National School, Davies Street, 199, 200
Nennoc, St., 13
Nesta, great-great-great-granddaughter of Rhys ap Gryffydd, 25
—— daughter of Rhys ap Tewdwr, 66
Neugol, 125, 127, 152
Nevern, Carnarvonshire, 12
—— Castell, 25, 26, 56
—— Pembrokeshire, 25, 63, 84, 174, 176, 202
—— River, 218
Nevil, Ralph de, 128
Newcastle, 25, 26, 152, 155, 156, 157
—— Church of, 143
—— Little, 124, 157
—— —— Church of St. David's (now St. Peter's), 124
—— —— Court at, 216
New Moat, 124, 126, 145, 153, 156
—— Church of St. Nicholas, 124, 143
New Parke, 103, 115
Newport, 26, 27, 91, 216

Newport, Church of, 91, 139
Newquay, 12
Newton, Church and Chapel, 96, 101, 104,
    105, 106, 109, 173, 174, 175, 178, 179,
    180, 181, 182, 183
—— Parish of,
Newtown, 175, 183
Nicol, Ralph, 133
Nicolas, Griffin, 188, 189, 190, 191, 192, 194,
    195, 196
Nigra Grangia, 28, 82
Nogent, Castle of, 33
—— -le-Rotrou, 30, 37
Nolton, 143, 144, 154
—— Church of, 144
Nominations of Abbots, Form for, 37, 38
Non, St., 13
Norlias, 156
Normandy, 22, 30, 34, 35, 56, 58, 60
Normans, 45, 54, 57, 64, 216, 217
Noyadd Trefawr, 185
Nutt, Hugh, 149

Oderic, 43
Office of St. Bernard, Prayer from, 37
Ogham Character, 14
—— Inscriptions, 63, 168
—— Stones, 14, 15, 168, 170, 172
Olwen and Killwch, 28
O'Maershayn Eugene, Canon of Killaloe, 164
Order Cistercian, 69
—— of St. Benedict (O. S. B.), 92, 136, 164,
    165
—— St. Dogmaels, 156
—— St. Maur, 36
—— Tiron, 34, 36, 54, 124, 126, 128, 133,
    135, 142, 156, 157, 158, 159, 162, 165,
    167, 214
Orleans, 35
Other, son of a Count, tutor to Prince Wil-
    liam, 42, 43, 44
Owain, 49
Owen Alban, Lord of Cemaes, 185
—— George, Lord of Cemaes, 20, 23, 26, 28,
    46, 47, 62, 64, 65, 83, 168, 169, 170,
    174, 185, 200, 216, 218, 219, 221, 222,
    223
—— William, Lord of Cemaes, 12, 219
—— George, History of Pembrokeshire, 46,
    47, 62, 63, 65, 169, 200, 216, 217, 219,
    222
—— —— Lords of Kemes, 83
—— —— Pembroke and Kemes, 219
—— —— Taylors Cussion, 220
—— —— Note, by Dr. Henry Owen, 219
—— Henry Gerald, the Welshman, 77
—— ap Philip, 103, 116
—— ap Powell, 110, 121
—— James, 186
—— V. Stafford, 188
Owestrop, 61
Owyn, Dame, 152
Oxford, 60

Pantirion, 220

Pantsaeson, 17, 24, 200, 217
Pant-y-Groes, 20
Pant y Grundy, 218
Papal Chamberlain, 74, 75
—— Letter, 164
—— Registers, 78, 88, 132, 217
Parc y Capel, 67
Parc y John Lloyd, 103, 116
Parke Close, 202, 203
Parke glas (green meadow or field), 206
—— le cleg (mass, hard lump), 203
—— Pen y Gragge (Crugiau=top of the
    crags), 204
—— Rolle (Parc-y-rheol), 101, 103, 115
—— y Coed (the wood), 204
—— y ffryer, 206
—— y Hinen (eithinen=gorse), 204
—— y Reese (Rhys=meadow), 204
—— yr Abbot, 204, 205
Park Weir glodd vaier (St. Mary's Meadow),
    206
Parker, Owin, 187
—— Thomas, Collector, 133, 134
Parliament (English), 49, 69, 102, 105, 118
—— (French), 35, 36
Parnel, Thomas, a priest, 134, 144
Paris, 39
Parot, 108
Parry, Ann, 186
—— Bridget, 186
—— David, 185, 186
—— David II, 186, 202, 203, 204, 205, 206,
    209, 211
—— Elizabeth, 186
—— Joan, 186
—— John, Archdeacon of Cardigan, 186,
    201, 206, 207, 208
—— Margaret, 185, 186
—— Stephen, 186
—— Stephen II, 186
—— Susan, 186
—— Thomas (ap Harry), 185, 186
—— William, 204, 207, 208, 211, 212
—— William of Brethyr, 186
Patrologie Migne, 31, 32
Pebidiauk, 88
—— Deanery of, 91
Pembroke, 84, 95, 96, 102, 104, 106, 107, 112,
    114, 120, 155, 173, 178, 179, 181, 183,
    190, 191
—— Co. of, 38, 39, 46, 54, 63, 64, 65, 66, 91,
    98, 102, 108, 109, 115, 116, 118, 124,
    140, 158, 159, 161, 162, 169, 172, 174,
    175, 176, 178, 181, 182, 183, 185, 187,
    188, 189, 191, 192, 193, 194, 195, 196,
    197, 198, 200, 202, 205, 208, 209, 211,
    217, 218, 219, 222
—— Earls of, 84, 125, 126
—— Earldom of, 90
Pemery (Pomery), 161, 162
Pen Cerwyn, 13
—— Crugiau (grige, gragge), 204
Penfoos, 133
Penfro, 62
Penkelly Vychan, 63, 64, 175, 183

Penkelly Vychan, Chapel of and Rectory of, 96, 101, 104, 105, 106, 119, 173, 174, 175, 178, 179, 181, 182, 183
Penrallt, 101, 103, 116
—— Ceibwr, 19
—— Esgob, 17
Penros, John, 132
Pensions, 97, 111, 154
Pentre Ifan, or Evan, 18, 25
—— ithe, 102, 121
Pen y Wern, 220
Perche, 30
—— Contesse de la, daughter of Henry I, 37, 42
Percy, Thomas de, 132
Perquisites of the Court, 122, 130, 134, 154
Pers, Robert, 149
Peter de Champnent, 48
Peverel, John, 216
—— Matilda, 20, 59, 60
—— William, 27, 57
Peverels, The, 59, 60
Philip, a false deacon, 74
—— de Stackpool, 50, 51
—— John, 133
—— Owen, 187 to 194, 195, 197, 198
—— the Clerk, 128
—— Thomas, 110, 121
—— William, 149
Philipe, son of Louis le Gros, King of France, 34
Philips, John, 131
Phillip, grandson of Lucas de Hoda, 25
Phillips, James, 196, 204
—— John, 152, 153, 154, 155, 156
—— Roger, 201, 206, 207, 208
Philpine, Walter, 169
Pickton, Owen, 188, 192, 196
Picton, William, 216
Pill, 125, 127, 128, 129, 133, 134, 141, 156, 158
—— Chapter House of, 139, 141
—— Lands of, 126
—— Manor of, 126, 131, 132, 133
—— Monks of, 125, 133
—— —— John (about 1500), 145, 150
—— —— Dom John Castell, 140
—— —— Dom John Dore, 140
—— —— Heliseas Pecocke, 141
—— —— Dom Mauricius Ieuan, 141
—— —— Dom William Hire (Hyre), 139
—— —— Dom William Watt, 139, 142, 145, 146, 151, 154
—— Priors of, 125, 132, 133, 135, 136, 137, 138, 139, 140, 144, 145, 146, 150, 151, 152
—— Dom David Luce, Prior of, 139, 140, 217
—— Phillip, Prior of, 125, 128, 217
—— William Watt, Prior of, 140, 141, 217
—— Priory or Convent of, 80, 81, 82, 86, 87, 93, 96, 100, 104, 111, 114, 124 to 128, 135 to 137, 139, 140, 142, 144, 147, 149 to 153, 155, 157, 158, 159, 161, 169
—— Rector of, 91
—— Great, 143, 147, 148

Pill Oliver, 125
—— Rhodal, 135
—— Roos, 156
Place Pen Abounte = plas pen-y-bont, 101, 103, 116
Plas Newydd, 185, 186
Plas Pant-y-Rege, 109, 121
Ploughs, Number of, in St. Dogmaels, 220
Plwyf bach (little parish), 211, 220
Plwyf fawr (great parish), 203, 220
Poitevin (St. Bernard's Donkey), 34
Poitou, 61
Polsawe, Thomas, 132
Pontvrayne, 143, 144
Pope Alexander II, 38
—— Boniface IX, 164
—— Clement VI, 133
—— Eugene III, 38
—— Eugenius, 20
—— Innocent I, 71, 72, 73, 75, 76, 78
—— —— VI, 133
—— Leo XIII, 37
—— Nicolas, Taxatio of, 41, 79, 80
—— Urban V, 133
—— The, 69, 140
Poppitt (Potpyt), 101, 103, 115, 219, 222
—— The Sands, 219
Population of St. Dogmaels, 220
Portmadoc, 12
Powell ap Owen, 176
—— Edward, 188, 192, 196
—— Sir John, 207, 211
Powes, Edward, 192
Precelly Top, 13, 27, 28
Preseley (Preceley, Breselech), 45, 47, 68, 97
Presteign (Presthende, Preston), 100, 113, 115, 116, 174
Prior and Hospital of St. John of Jerusalem, 133
Priory de Guales, Galles, Gallis, 13, 31, 62
Products, 222, 223
Pugh, 15
Pwll-cam, 101, 219
Pwll-y-Granant, Mr. Vincent, 220
Pwyll (Mabinogion), 122

Quimperle, 13

Radenor, son of Philip, 128
Radnor, Co. and Shire of, 100, 113, 115, 177, 185
Ralph Nevill, 48
Ranulph, 43
—— Earl of Chester, 60
Raoul, Count of Fougeres, 32
Rastell, John, 176
Rattry, Rattre, Rattreu (? Wadtree), 28, 29, 41, 45, 47, 80, 86, 96 to 102, 104, 106, 107, 112, 120, 122, 173, 178
—— Rectory and Church of St. Mary, 97, 98, 99, 107, 120, 122, 175, 178
Raymond, Abbot of St. Cyprian, 31, 32
Redderch, 125, 127
Registers of Canterbury, Courtney, 86, 87
—— —— Warham, 90, 91, 92

Reginald, Ffolliot, 68, 70, 71, 72, 76
Regner, 135
Rents at Will, Haverfordwest and Pembroke, 120
—— Resolute, 154
Rees, Beauties of England and Wales, 169
—— William, 207, 208, 211, 212
Retford, 125, 127, 152
Rewan, 130
Rhos, Deanery of, 139, 145
—— Wrdan, 50, 67
Rice ap Morgan, 176
Rhydderch ap Rhys fychan, 185
Rhys ap Gryffydd, 26, 66, 67
—— Tewdwr, 24, 66
—— Castle, 117
—— James, of Mynachlogddu, 185
Rhys' Lectures on Welsh Philology, 172
Rhys Vychan, Lord of Towy, 186
Ricart, Risiart, son of Lucas de Hoda, 20, 28
Richard I, King of England, 58, 77
—— II, King of England, 48, 49, 50, 86, 88, 90, 129, 130, 131, 132, 136
—— de Wood, 48, 52
—— Earl of Chester, 58
—— Hutley, 90
—— Margaret, 205
—— son of Gosner, 47
Right of Pasture on Mynachlogddu, 220
Risdon, 23, 28
Robert ap Price ap Powell, 103, 116
—— Arbrisel, 34
—— Crippinges, 51
—— de Baldock, 83
—— de Bikkenor, 84, 85
—— del Val, 53
—— de Tybbot, 52
—— de Vawr (Vaux), 52
—— de Watevill, 84, 85
—— Earl of Leicester, 58
—— Fitzmartin (see Martin).
—— —— Journey to Tiron, 31, 37
—— Marmion, 58
—— of Caen, Count of Gloucester, 34
—— of Languedoc, 45, 46
—— The Clerk, 127
Roch Church, 96, 143
Roche, 125, 127, 129, 130, 133, 134, 143, 152, 153, 156, 157
—— Adam de, 124, 125, 127, 128, 132, 134, 135, 142, 156, 157, 158, 161, 210
—— David de, 79, 82, 83, 124
—— David II (of Ireland), 159, 160, 161, 162
—— Lord de, (of Ireland), 160, 161, 163
—— Gilbert de, 51, 52, 83, 128
—— Henry, 124
—— John de, 124, 125, 127, 135
—— Sir David de la, 131
—— Matilda de, 124, 127
—— Thomas de, 124, 125, 127, 132, 134, 135
—— Thomas de, 125, 131, 132
—— Thomas de la, of Langum, 131
—— William de, 125, 126, 131
—— The Lordship of (Ireland), 161, 163

Roches, The, 124, 125, 132, 159
Roche, The Manor of, 126, 131, 133
—— Tower or Castle, 96, 143
Rock of Golden Grove, 79
Roger, a monk, 75
—— de Mortimer, 51, 52, 85, 135
—— —— (Mortimer's) land, 125, 126, 128
—— of Mathone, 45, 46
Roll of Battle Abbey, 22, 23, 50, 56
Rolls, Augmentation Office, 102, 104
—— Charter, 46, 50, 126, 157
—— Close, 85, 140
—— —— Calendar of, 84
—— Court, 130
—— Dives, 61
—— Duchesne's, 56
—— Hollinsheds, 56
—— Lelands, 56
—— Memoranda, 79, 81, 88, 136
—— of Taxation, 82
—— Originalia, 53
—— Patent, 50, 77, 79, 83, 86, 88, 97, 98, 115, 132, 177, 179, 181, 185
—— Pembroke, 177
—— Pipe, 60
Roman remains, 63
Romans, 64
Rome, 70, 72, 73, 75, 88, 133, 164
Roose, 124, 135, 156
Roosland = Rhosland, 101, 116
Roslyn, Master, 58
Rotherothe ap John, 147
Rotrou, 33
—— Count of Perche, 33, 34
Round, J. H., 41, 44
Rowe, William, 149
Rowland, Alice, 207, 208, 211, 212
—— James, 208
Royal Military School, 36
Ruffo, Henry, 127
Rules of St. Benedict, 140
Rupe, de la (see Roche).
Rushes, 151
Rymer, 53

Saer, Saeran, Sagramni, Sagranus, 14, 15, 185
Sagramore, Sir, 14
Sagranus, son of Cunedda, 14
St. Albans (Herts), 118, 175, 178
St. Andrew's Cross, 201
St. Badock, 142, 147, 148, 149
St. Benedict, 54, 55, 95, 139, 159, 161, 162, 165
St. Bernard, 31, 57, 59, 135, 159
St. Bernard's Well, 68
St. Budoc, 124, 125, 126, 127, 128, 158
St. Cewydd (St. Kewit), 124, 126
St. Cradoc, 125, 127
—— Chapel, 152
St. Cross Hospice, Winchester, 123
St. Cyprian, 31
St. David, 39, 52, 54, 68, 70, 74, 77, 125, 133
—— Bishop of, 44, 45, 53, 55, 68, 71, 77, 78, 156, 217

St. David, Bishopric and See of, 43, 68, 69, 72, 73, 91, 104, 105, 146, 147, 153, 174, 175, 178, 181, 182, 183
—— Canons of, 53, 133
—— Chapter of, 69
—— Diocese of, 38, 59, 62, 81, 87, 88, 94, 104, 112, 133, 136, 140
—— Gerald, Keeper of the Church of, 71
—— Little Newcastle, 124
—— of Newcastle, Church of, 126
St. Edryns, 196
St. Eloi, 36
St. Inleyn, Chapel of, 161
St. Julian's Chapel, 109
St. Leatrina de Nayt, Church of, 160, 161, 163
St. Leyre of Bastoro or Boscum, Chapel of B.V.M., 160, 163
—— —— Church of, 160, 163
St. Lo, 57
St. Madoc's, Nolton, 125, 128
St. Martin, 36
St. Mary of Cathmais, 38, 40, 42, 43, 44, 50, 51, 53, 55, 158
—— —— of Glascareg, 161
—— —— Pill, 126, 127, 128
—— —— Roch, 124
St. Matthew, Church of, 50
St. Meigan's Fair, 215
St. Merleyn, Church of, 163
St. Nicholas, of Fishguard, 101, 104, 105, 118
—— —— Rectory of, 106
—— —— New Moat, 126
St. Patrick, Chapel of, 162
—— —— Church of, 160, 161, 163
St. Paul's, London, 90, 136
St. Peter's of Montacute, Church of, 59, 60
—— Rome, 88, 133, 164
SS. Sergius and Bacchus, Angiers, Abbey of, 60
—— —— MS. at, 60
St. Swithin's Church, London, 133
St. Thomas the Martyr, 125
—— —— Chantry, Chapel of, 131
St. Walburga, 42, 43
Sale of Works, 129, 130
Salisbury, Earl of, 35
Sandre, Simon, 130
Sandy, Walter, 131
Saverinus, Bishop of Bath, 58
Savigny, Abbey of, 32, 57, 58
—— Cartulary of, 57, 58
—— Forest of, 32
Savory, Rd., of Totnes, 97, 98, 99, 100
Sawyer, Sir Robt., Knt., 212
Saxons, 24
Seal, Conventual of Pill Priory, 141
—— —— St. Dogmaels Abbey, 93, 108, 109
Seberius of Quineaco, 58
Seine or Shot fawr, 221
Seisylt Esceif (Longshanks), 68
Seman Scopell, 125, 126, 128
Sewant, 124, 127
Shepey Island, 170
Shingrig, 200

Shrewsbury, 223
Shropshire, 101, 105, 185
Sigelai, Hundred of, 60, 61
Signatures to Act of Supremacy, St. Dogmael, 93, 94, 95
Signia, 71
Sire de Tours, 56
Smyth, John, 107, 114, 120
Smythston, 165, 166
Snowdon, 12
Somerset, 26, 84, 85
Somersetshire Record Society, 60
Speed, 54, 135
Sperrus, 61
Sporier, John, 103, 116
Stags Valley, 13, 28
Stainton, 124, 125, 126, 142, 145, 147, 148, 154, 155, 156, 158
—— Church of, 143, 147
—— Highway, 147
Staneberg, Hundred of, 80
State Papers of Ireland, 165, 167
Stephen, Count of Mortain, 58
—— Dapifer (The King's Steward), 47, 52
—— Edesworth, 52
—— John, 152, 155, 156
—— Philip, 142
—— Thomas, 145
—— William, 176
Stephens, 54, 55
Stevens, 135
Steward or Seneschal of Pembroke, 83, 84
Stockport, 185
Stodach, David, 131
Stodhart (Studdolph), 124, 127, 142, 149, 150
Stolen Horse, The, 74, 75
Stone Altar, 199
—— Coffins, 214
—— free, 200, 217
—— green porphyritic granite, 201, 206
—— Manaian fawr, 201, 214
—— Redd, 199, 217
—— Russet, 218
—— Sagranus, 14, 15
—— Slates and tiling, 217
—— with shaft of Cross, 215
Stopell Mill, 126, 128
Stories, Gerald the Welshman, 67, 68, 76, 77
—— Mr. Vincent, 18, 19
Strathclyde, 64
Strickmeres (Dredgman's) Hill, 125, 127
Strumble Head, 12
Styles of Architecture as shown by remains, Norman Early English, decorated perpendicular, 215
Suthoc (South Hook), 127, 142, 143, 147, 148, 154
Sweyne, 61
Sword of Joel, 60
Symon of Durham, History of the Acts of the Kings of England, 58

Tanfield, Lawrence, Knt., 188
Tangustel, son of Keybour (Ceibwr), 83, 84
Tallage, The, of Wm. Owen, 219

Tankard, 51

Tanner, 55, 157, 172

Taunton, 59

—— Manor of, 59, 60

Taxatio of Pope Nicholas, 41, 71, 80

Taylors Cussion, The, George Owen, 220

Taylour Xerpofer, 144

Teify River, 12, 24, 25, 28, 41, 44, 45, 46, 62, 67, 216, 218, 221

Temple Boyne, Chapel of, 159, 161, 163

Temple Bodigane, 160

Temple Derry, 165, 166

Temple Landecan, Church of, 159, 161, 163

Temple Mallyne, 163

Tenby, 169, 179

Testa de Nevill, 79, 80, 84

Teulydog, Abbot of (St. Dogmaels), 217

Teutonic, 63

Teutons, 64

Tewe, Owen, 155

Thibaut, Conte de Blois, 34

Thiron au Perche, 30

Thironne River, 34

Thomas ap dio Gwilum, 120, 121

—— ap Rice, 176

—— Basset, 58

—— Becket's Bishop, 103

—— Beke, Master, 53, 54

—— David, 207, 208, 211, 212

—— Fitz Henry, 166

—— Howell, 209

—— James, 188, 191, 206

—— Matthew, 176, 186, 203

—— Richard, 131

—— Wake, 48

—— Wallensis, 124

Thorneton, 125, 127, 142, 143, 151

Tilbarg, 130

Tinagh, Church of St. Brigitte, 160, 161, 163

Tirion Uchaf, 220

Tiron (Thiron Gardais), 22, 30, 31, 33, 34, 35, 38, 41, 57, 59, 161, 162, 217

—— Abbey of, 23, 28, 30, 31, 34, 35, 36, 37, 38, 39, 40, 54, 56, 57, 172

—— Abbots (see Abbots)

—— Cartulary of, 31, 37, 41, 42, 44, 46, 58, 62, 63, 167

—— Chapter of, 38

—— Congregation of, 59

—— Convent of, 43, 44, 46

—— Treasury of, 36

—— The Trinity, 36

Tipperary, Co. of, 165

Tithe Dispute, Examination of St. Dogmaels Tithes, 201, 206, 208, 212

Tiverton, Church of, 60

Tivyside Observer, 200

Toads House and the Toads, 67, 68

Tonker, John, 134

Tor Abbey, 41

Torquay, 28

Totnes (Devon), 28, 29, 45, 97, 98

—— Priory Church of, 60

Tours, Bayeux, 56, 61

—— Ille et Loir, 61

Tours, Touraine, 22, 23

Towey, Lord of, 185, 186

Trahir, 159, 160, 161, 162

Trecart, Trereikart, 25, 51

Trecoom (Trecwm), 192

Tredafed, 186

Trefas, 19

Treffgarne, 130

Tregamon (Trecamon), 20, 27

Tregent, Church of, 40, 41

Tregoes (Tregroes), 190, 194, 196

Trellyfant, 67, 68

Trenvan Maurice de, 127

Treprisk, 20

Trewidwal, 220

Trewrdan (and uchaf and issaf), 25, 50

Trewyddel, 46, 63

Triggs, Richard, 131

Troedyrawr, 186

Twrch Trwyth, 28

Ty Hyr, 202, 208, 209, 210

Tyler, Mrs., 185

Vachketerlmechan, 126

Vaghan, John, 112

—— William, 152

Val, Sir Robert de Val, 28

Valence, 38

—— William de, 48

Valor Ecclesiasticus, 95, 96, 142, 169

Varn Parke, 103

Vaughan, Richard, 133

Vengeons, Wenion, Vengions, Venions, 57, 58

Verney, Eleanor, 131, 132

—— Robert, 129, 131, 132

Verwick, 205

Vienna, 164

Vincent, The Rev. H. J., 15, 16, 19, 20, 203, 220

Virgins' Fountain, The, Rome, 75

—— with Christ, 142

Vivien, 14

Vychan, William, 142

Vyndessors (Windsor), 125, 127

Wadtree, Church of, 40, 41, 45

Waffret, 125, 126, 128

Walensium, 63, 64

Wales, Charles Prince of, 10

—— Edward, Prince of, 10

Walisc, Waelisc, Weahl, Wallachia, Walloons, Wälshland, Wallach, Wales, 63, 64

Walker, John David, 196

Walter, Beauchamp, 52

—— The Chaplain, 53

—— Malesant, 51

Wars of the Roses, 90

Warren, the Archdeacon, 129, 131, 132

Watevill, Margaret de, wife of Robert, and widow of William Martin III, 84, 85, 86

—— Robert de, 84, 85, 86

Walters, Edward, 111, 155

Webbe, Philip, 145

Welsh, 46
—— Character, 24
—— Language, 24
Welshery, The, 65
Wenloc, Prior of, 69, 76
Wermyngton, John, 133
Westcote, 23
Westminster, 48, 49, 79, 81, 83, 86, 89, 90, 98, 100, 105, 108, 111, 118, 129, 132, 136, 137, 140, 141, 146, 148, 153, 169, 175, 181, 184, 188, 192, 207, 211
—— Chapter House, 93, 94, 95
Westwood, J. O., 15, 172
Wexford, Co., 159, 165, 167
Whiskey, 28
White Oxen (see Whittokesdene, in Dean Prior, 84
White Ship, The, 44
White, Stephen, 132
Whitland, Abbot of (Cistercian Order), 69
—— Peter of, 70, 71, 76, 77
Whittokesdene (see White Oxen), 79, 80, 84, 85, 86
Wigmore, Monastery of, 114, 117
William I the Conqueror, King of England, 22, 29, 56, 61, 62
—— III and Mary, King and Queen of England, 206, 207, 208, 211
—— Prince, son of Henry I, King of England, 31, 37, 41, 42, 43, 44
—— Albignero, 43
—— ap Rice, 176
—— Count of Nevers, 34
—— de Albineis, a Briton, 42
—— de Baray, 66
—— de Bolevill, 51
—— de Canvill, 51, 52
—— de Cantington (grandson of Lucas de Hoda), 49, 50, 51, 88, 187, 217, 219
—— de Morlegh, 80
—— de Rollo, 43
—— de Valence, 48, 52
—— Duke of Acquitaine, 34, 59

William Marshall, Earl of Pembroke, 125, 128
—— of Falaise, 28, 29, 57
—— of Malmesbury, 31
—— of Stannus, 58
—— of Worcester, 170
—— Peverell, 27, 45
—— Puerello-Cloun, 43
—— son of Ralph, Seneschal of Normandy, 58
—— son of Roger, 46
Williams, Elizabeth, 103, 116
—— Robert, 15
—— William, 189, 190, 194, 195, 196
Willyams, David, 110
Winchester, 123
Windsore, 152
Winstanley, Edmund, 185
Winterscombe Coppice, 97, 98
Wode, Le, 129
Wogan, John, 128, 143, 145, 146, 147, 155
—— Thomas, 144
Woodward, 169
Wool Fair, 223
Woolley, John, 207
Worcester, 70, 117
—— Abbot of, 69, 76
—— Bishop, 60, 72, 78
—— Canon J., of, 69
—— Precentor of, 69
Wrdan Uchaf, 50
Wrexham, 207
Writ, 223
Wroughton (Urchstone), 60, 61
Wyott land, 103, 116

Ymar, Odinyd, Odwynd, O'Dowd, 164
Ynys Pyr (Island of Pyrus), 168, 169, 172
Yound, John, 156
Y Weirglodd dan y goyed grodig (y drym), 190, 192, 194, 195
Y Plwyf Bach, 211, 220
Y Plwyf fawr, 203, 220

16

Ingram Content Group UK Ltd.
Milton Keynes UK
UKHW051831260623
424090UK00009B/389